CATCH A FIRE

CATCH A FIRE

THE AUTOBIOGRAPHY

MELANIE B

headline

First published in 2002
by HEADLINE BOOK PUBLISHING

10 9 8 7 6 5 4 3 2 1

Cataloguing in Publication Data is available from the British Library

Typeset in Zapf Elliptical by Avon Data Ltd, Bidford-on-Avon, Warwickshire

Printed and bound in Great Britain by
Clays Ltd, St Ives plc

Text design by Viv Mullett

HEADLINE BOOK PUBLISHING
A division of Hodder Headline
338 Euston Road, London NW1 3BH

www.headline.co.uk
www.hodderheadline.com

To my inspirational, active friend and daughter Phoenix Chi. Hopefully when you're at a certain age you'll read this and understand what Mummy's been through and not be embarrassed but proud. You've enabled me to write this book and put down all my past experiences, ready to start a new chapter of my life as a devoted mother to you.

CONTENTS

ACKNOWLEDGEMENTS

Mum: what can I say? Through my childhood, adolescence, adulthood and motherhood you've been more than a woman/mother to me. You gave me and my sister the best head start imaginable, constantly reassuring us with love and attention. Throughout my traumas and temperamental outbursts, you've understood everything. I couldn't have written this book without being so close to you. I hope I've made you proud, Mum.

Dad: believe it or not, I am thankful to you for being so bloody strict, because you truly have made me who I am. Obviously I've had to trim the edges a bit, but I'm glad you brought me up the way you did. You know my inner srength comes from you. And guess what? I will always want to be a Daddy's girl, so you can't wash your hands of me yet!

Danielle: the sister I never allowed myself to get to know properly. In the last five years you've been absolutely amazing and I realise what I've been missing. Our friendship and sisterhood is going to grow and grow. Thank you for being so amazing. I'm sorry I tortured you as a child – my excuse is that I was confused!

My mum's family: White Grandma, Auntie Sheila, Auntie June, Auntie Di, Auntie Pamela, Uncle Eric, Uncle Michael, Uncle Big Barry, Uncle Mick – you're all crazy northern folk! I know I was hyperactive but thank you for helping with my upbringing. Even though I don't get to see you often these days, I love you all very much.

To cousins Little Barry, Andrew, Joanna, Michael, Sophie, Nicholas, Alex and Christian – our camping days were top! I still haven't forgiven you for taking the mick out of my stutter when I was younger though.

Sherrel and Bernie: you really have had a massive impact on my life and you've both made the most ordinary situations the most hysterical, belly-aching experiences I've ever had.

Rebecca Cripps: the woman who has seen absolutely everything over the last six years and has become one of the most important people in my life. Thank you for giving me my belief back and motivating me to do this book. You truly are an inspiration to everyone who knows you. Promise me our friendship will grow and grow. You're an intelligent airhead and that's what I love about you!

Rebecca: through school years, teenage and adult years! We may not see each other often now but we both know we've been through so much and our spiritual connection will be there forever. Thank you for being you.

Charlotte: thank you for helping me through my divorce and for being a great friend.

Rose: from the day I got married to the day Jim left, you've been a silent supporter and a great helper. Thank you. Phoenix and I love you.

I also dedicate this book to Lindsay Symons, Juliana Lessa and everyone at Headline, as well as my agent at William Morris, Stephanie Cabot (we've still got to have that drinks night out). Thank you for all your focused hard work.

To Charles Bradbrook, my accountant, and Andrew Thompson, my lawyer: you two have really seen it all! As well as having to shout the c-word at *The Vagina Monologues*, you now know everything about me from this book – you poor bleeders. Thank you for making my life run smoothly.

To Julia Curnock: I've yet to conquer you by taking over your entire life! Thank you for your loyalty, support and honesty over the last four years. I've greatly appreciated you.

Bunton (Emma): my partner in late night snacks! Through all the tears and laughter, we've always connected and been there for each other, sometimes even without words. Thank you for letting me write about you in this book. You know that Phoenix and I see you as a friend for life, you moody cow!

Melanie: this book officially apologises to you. You've always been wonderful and caring to me. You're a born star and I'm glad I've been a part of your life. Thank you.

Vicky: we made it through the tour pregnant together and many other things. Your dry sense of humour is forever uplifting.

Geri: even though we don't see each other these days, I can honestly say that I spent many fantastic times with you and they will be in my memory bank forever. I wish you all the best in life.

Simon Fuller: hope you enjoy reading this. You are still my guru, you know. And without Camilla (my secret friend) I don't think we would have made it on stage in time! Thank you.

Dean Freeman: the guy who's been to hell and back with me and the Spice Girls. I know you've worked ridiculously hard on everything you've ever done with us. Your camera lens really has seen it all! A friend who's always made time for me. Thank you.

The team around the Spice Girls: Karin – you had to make five girls up in such a ridiculously short amount of time. Hopefully your life is much calmer now. Thank you for making me look so good for the movie, the tour and many, many TV, video and magazine shoots. Jennie – from one big-haired girl to another, thank you for making my nutbush stay strong. You're missed. Kenny Ho – what the bleedin' hell did we put you through? (I'm a nice girl now.) I wish you all the best for the future.

To Jamie, Jo, Sarah, Ying and Nancy: the Spice Office crew. You all individually gave me strong support and helped me on my merry way. Thank you.

My press agents Sandra Casali & Co: thank you for making me cool! Thank God!

Alan Edwards: those beautiful blue eyes! Thank you for all the hysterical, neurotic, ridiculous stories that you kept out of the press for me. You truly are one of a kind. You still haven't called me about you-know-what.

Nicole, Sinead, Joanna and Gareth: thank you for helping me to get off to a good-looking start with my solo project. You're great, you guys.

Michelle: thanks for kicking my arse into shape. Rip it up, rip it up! And Rob Hunt: the crazy guy who helped me start the book!

Sandie Shaw: you taught me a lot about myself and my career. Thank you for being honest.

Mandy and Eddie Duick: from the day we met at Phoenix's birth, thank you for being great friends and helping me through personal and public disasters!

To Dave: I'm your biggest fan. Thank you for driving me everywhere. Hope I didn't drive you round the bend. The ultimate professional always. Thank you!

To the fans that have been with me through the Spice Girls and have supported me through my divorce: thank you so much. You really have been consistent and always there for me. I really do know that you care, believe me. Now stop sending mail to my house and send it to the PO Box instead!

1

WALKING ON
BROKEN GLASS

T*hud.*

I froze. Every muscle in my body tensed up.

A vase went flying. Just like in a bad movie, I watched it arc across the room in slow motion.

Crash.

It shattered on the floor of the hotel suite. Jagged pieces of glass span out across the polished wooden surface.

I couldn't believe this was happening.

'F*** you Melanie!'

It was 4 a.m. The rest of the hotel was asleep and silent, accentuating the deafening bursts of sound coming from our room.

'Don't shout,' I whispered. 'Please!'

But the situation had taken on a life of its own. The shouting got louder, the cursing more aggressive. I felt helpless, trapped in an angry, uncontrollable nightmare.

'Stop it,' I begged. 'Stop this now!'

Huge tears welled up in my eyes, blurring my vision. They spilled down my cheeks and coated my face and lips.

'Please go home Jim, just leave!' I sobbed. 'I need a break. I can't work under this kind of pressure.'

'Why should I?' roared Jim. 'I have a right to stay. I'm your husband and I'm not going anywhere.'

As I bowed my head in despair, my mind flashed back to our wedding day less than a year before. On that day I'd been so sure of what I was doing, so happy, so in love. I'd had no doubts that Jim was the one, the man I wanted to spend the rest of my life with, twenty-four hours a day, seven days a week. Now I couldn't bear to be with him for another second. All he seemed to do was criticise me, day in, day out. Nothing I did was right and our constant bickering inevitably erupted into full-blown arguments because I just couldn't help lashing back at his criticisms. And now I felt like I'd reached breaking point. I couldn't cope any more. I needed some time away from Jim before I totally lost it. But he wasn't having any of it.

'I'm not leaving!' he shouted again.

I looked up and into Jim's eyes, which were blazing with – what was it? Fury? Hatred? Suddenly I found it hard to breathe, I began gasping for air, panic coursed through my body, the room felt tiny, I needed to get out of there, away from him. Now.

I edged towards the door. *Get away from the shouting. Get out of here.*

Jim beat me to it, blocking the way, muscles tensed.

'Let me out,' I pleaded in a low voice.

'Don't even think about it!' he yelled.

In my distressed state it seemed as if his face was contorted, dark with anger; a nerve was throbbing at his temple. I began to feel really freaked out. I hardly recognised this man. Come to think of it, had I ever really known him?

'Please don't shout,' I repeated softly, like a mantra. The more I said it, the more it wound him up. 'Please don't shout, please don't shout, please don't . . .'

But it just went on. My brain felt hazy and unconnected. Far away in the background I thought I could hear a phone ringing. Instinctively I stumbled towards the noise.

'Don't answer that,' ordered Jim.

I grabbed for the handset.

'Hello?' I croaked, my chest heaving. The line crackled. Long distance.

'Happy birthday Melanie! You're up late. Are you having a good time?'

'Mum, I'll have to phone you back.'

'What is it? What's wrong?'

'I said I'll phone you back, Mum.'

I replaced the receiver. With my head drooping, I sat on the floor, trying to clear my mind and make some kind of sense of the situation. Happy birthday, I thought. Yeah right.

May the twenty-ninth, 1999, my twenty-fourth birthday. We were in Minneapolis where I was working on my solo album with Jimmy Jam and Terry Lewis, the production team most famous for their work with Janet Jackson. Jim hadn't wanted me to go without him. The evening before I was due to leave there had been such a scene that I ended up sobbing all night in one of the other bedrooms.

He'd assumed that I wouldn't go until we'd sorted things out, but I couldn't cancel. You just can't mess people like Jam and Lewis around.

I didn't want Jim in America with me because I knew he'd bring me down. We hadn't been getting on for a long time and I was drained by all the arguments and tension. I needed a break. I also had to be on top form for recording. On the other hand I knew that I'd be miserable if I went away without sorting things out between us. I hadn't been separated from him for a single night since the day we were married and I was going to miss him, despite everything. At last, though, I decided to stick to my plans.

The next day I flew out of Heathrow with my PA Julie Cooke. Poor Jules. She soon became caught up in a domestic hell, with nowhere to run apart from the safety of her hotel suite.

From the moment we took off it felt weird – really horrible, in fact – to be apart from Jim. The pain of separation was definitely physical as well as emotional. I wasn't sure how long I'd be able to stand it.

Four days later I caved in. I was desperate to face our problems and make things all right again, plus I couldn't bear the thought of being alone on my birthday. So I booked Jim on a flight to join me.

Up until that point things had been going smoothly on the work front. After three productive days in R&B producer Teddy Riley's Virginia studios, I flew up to Minneapolis where Jam and Lewis were based. They were great to work with. Jimmy Jam, a stocky guy with glasses and a rat's tail, was friendly and seemed very wise. Terry Lewis was slightly more old school – a clean-cut smooth type with smart suits and a cute face.

They're both approachable but Jimmy's far chattier. He'll talk to anyone.

I threw myself into my work, hoping it would take my mind off what was going on at home. Obviously I wasn't going to open up about my private life to people I hardly knew and in a funny way it was quite a relief to be hiding my feelings beneath a professional persona. I worked mainly with Jimmy Jam in the studio and on occasion he left me alone to get on with the writing. We recorded two tracks together, 'Feels So Good', which went on to be my second single off the album, and 'Feel Me Now', the final song.

When I got into the studio, my first question was, 'So, do you change your mics regularly?'

'No, we just use the same one all the time,' drawled Jimmy.

Gulp. 'Does that mean that Janet Jackson has used this mic?'

'Yeah. And sometimes we dim the lights and put out some candles and she stands or sits or lies in whatever position she feels most comfortable in.'

'Okay,' I said. 'Can you light some candles now, because I want to lie down like Janet!' I ended up sitting in Janet Jackson's massage chair every afternoon, just to chill and focus.

The next day we drank some wine and spent a few hours chatting before I recorded the vocals for 'Feel Me Now', which is a bit of a sexy track. We'd laid the chorus and the bridge down, which were sung, but I still hadn't got on to the verses. They were to be spoken.

'Whatever comes into your head, let it out,' said Jimmy Jam. 'We can't see what you're doing in there Melanie, so whatever it takes to get you to talk in that way, do it,' he added.

'Do you mean, play with myself?' I asked.

He didn't reply, just laughed.

Jim arrived three days before my birthday. It had seemed like a good idea for him to fly over, but sadly it didn't work out that way. The moment I clapped eyes on him I wanted him to leave. We were bickering within minutes. I realised I had actually been happier when he wasn't around. Instantly I knew it had been a mistake to have him come, birthday or no birthday. I always find birthdays not exactly depressing, but there's too much pressure on you to wake up and be happy. And you're not always. Well I'm not. I certainly wasn't happy this birthday.

The fight in the Minneapolis hotel room was one of the worst yet. The next day I was being filmed for a documentary for Flava Productions (to be shown on Channel 4). As I chatted light-heartedly on camera about my life and career I wondered if any of the crew could tell what was really going on in my head. The horror of the day before was on repeat in my mind, along with a barrage of questions that I just couldn't answer. How did I get here? How did this happen? Can I go on pretending? I need a shoulder to cry on but I'm too scared to open up – what will my friends and family think?

When I was a teenager I used to discuss with my friends what I'd do if I found myself in an unhappy relationship. 'I wouldn't stand for it!' I always said. Then all of a sudden you're madly in love with a guy in a bad marriage thinking, What the hell is going on?

During the five days that Jim was with me my schedule was totally disrupted. I had to cancel a whole day's filming and was constantly rearranging my time in the studio. Things were so bad between us that my work was beginning to suffer big time.

It took me ages to persuade him to go. I'd book a flight, we'd have an argument, then he'd ring up the travel agent and cancel. I'd book another flight; we'd argue; he'd cancel again. I was on tenterhooks for hours on end, wondering if this time he really would leave. As long as Jim was around I couldn't focus on my work. The constant friction between us was exhausting.

A couple of days after my birthday he finally packed his bags, thank God. Without telling him, I flew my mum out to Minneapolis on the day that he left. Jules was worried that he'd bump into her at the airport, but luckily he didn't.

It was such a relief to see him go. Now I could relax.

My next stop was Los Angeles, to shoot a second video for my single 'Word Up' (featured on the soundtrack of the cult Austin Powers film *The Spy Who Shagged Me*). I'd given Jim the job of directing the original video. The end result was an amazing piece of animation but a bit too wacky for the Americans, so I was advised to make something more mainstream for the US market. The second video was directed by Matthew Williamson and featured Mini Me, the comically evil dwarf character from the film.

Matthew Williamson insisted that I had a facial the day before the shoot. Well, I did have really bad acne at the time, a definite sign of stress. (Whenever I get run down or stressed it shows on my skin. It's one of the ways my body tells me that things are not right.) I had pus-filled boils under the entire surface of my face and I could feel every single one of them whenever I spoke or smiled.

So I went to see a famous beauty therapist whose clients included Halle Berry and Vanessa Williams. She gave me sixteen injections in my face to bring the swelling down. That pretty much tells you what kind of a state my skin – and my mind – was in.

I was very vulnerable at that time. Someone could have said something trivial to me like 'Oh my God, look at your shoes!' and I would have taken it completely to heart, even though it would have been totally out of character for me to do so. Being in a bad relationship can do that to you. It can take away your confidence, eat away at your self-esteem and make you feel utterly unworthy.

I still had a bit of a pregnant belly and was feeling insecure about my body. The stylist on the video had done the TLC video for 'Unpretty' (the song that's played at the end of *The Vagina Monologues*, the play I appeared in during March 2002) so I was really pleased to be working with her. However, I was very self-conscious about my figure and insisted on wearing a corset underneath my outfit.

When she came to measure me for the tight-fitting silver catsuit that I was planning to wear, she tried to reassure me.

'What's wrong with you? You look fantastic! You don't need a corset.'

I didn't believe her. I felt ugly and misshapen.

It was the first time I'd ever felt like this. Normally I don't dwell on my appearance too much. I just get on with it and wear whatever. I'm usually a wash-and-go kind of girl, but right then I just didn't have any confidence – mainly, I think, because Jim could be so critical of me. He would make little comments about what I wore, how I spoke, and what I said and did, in a subtly undermining way that proved to be far more damaging than straightforward criticism.

I was a bit embarrassed because when you work with someone and you admire the other people they've worked with, the last thing you want is for them to go away saying, 'That Melanie B is very self-conscious about her body!' Still, I had to have the corset. No one could change my mind about that.

It was very disorientating to find myself thinking in this way. What had happened to Melanie Brown, the feisty girl from Leeds who didn't care what anyone thought of her? I tried not to think about it. I couldn't admit that I'd changed so much, become an insecure wreck with no self-belief or confidence. I couldn't face up to the reality of the situation, so I just put my head down and got on with it, as I always had.

A couple of days later Melanie C and I went to the premiere of *The Spy Who Shagged Me*. She was in LA finishing off her album and it was really great to see her. We had our make-up done at the flat she was renting and we both decided to wear miniskirts and big boots. I also wore a totally see-through beige top saying LIFE IS PAIN on it.

I hadn't seen Mel for a few months and we hadn't spoken for ages so we both felt a little bit strange at first. After five years of living in each other's pockets we weren't used to spending time apart. Suddenly I found myself in her LA flat getting ready to go to a premiere with her as 'two of the Spice Girls', not just a couple of friends hooking up for the evening. In a way I wish we'd just stayed in and watched a video.

The premiere was quite a big deal and there were salsa dancers, ladyboys and carnival acts before the screening. We had to walk up a long thick red carpet lined with photographers and fans, posing for photos and signing autographs. The pictures of Melanie and me made the front page in more than one country.

Mel had been on the LA scene for a while and she knew a lot of people at the premiere. I didn't and I just wanted to be with my mate. She obviously didn't realise this because just before the film started she said casually, 'I'm going to go and sit down there, okay? I'll see you in a bit,' and went to join some people she knew a few rows away. Before I knew it I was sitting with an empty seat beside me, feeling very alone and sorry for myself. Ridiculously oversensitive, I know.

Later that evening at the Four Seasons hotel, I lay on my bed and sobbed. Why am I so easily upset about everything? Why do I feel so worthless? It seemed incredible that someone who had spent so many years championing Girl Power could find herself in such a powerless situation. I'd shouted it all around the world: Stand up for yourself! Don't take any shit! Never let him tell you what to do! Yet I didn't seem able to practise what I preached. I lay awake trying to work it all out, going through everything that had happened with Jim.

I was used to lying in bed at night worrying about what had gone wrong in my relationship. Usually I tried to find ways to blame myself. At least if it was my fault then maybe I could do something about it.

I was unbelievably depressed. Things had got so bad that I was beginning to lose hope of finding a solution to our problems. I racked my brain for answers. I tossed and turned, crying continually, praying for guidance. The pillow was soaked with tears. My eyes became swollen and I sensed that my eye infection was on the brink of starting up again.

Then as ten thousand tortured thoughts whirred around my mind, in the half light of my hotel suite I began to ask questions that I'd never asked before. *Wait a minute.* For so long I'd been trying to mould myself into the person I thought Jim wanted me to be that maybe I'd lost sight of the bigger picture. A glimmer of insight flickered inside my head. *What if . . . ?* Slowly it brightened into a glow. *What if it isn't me . . . ?*

Then suddenly it exploded in a flash of inspiration. *Wait a minute! This isn't my problem at all.*

My mind started racing. You can only blame so much on yourself before you think, Well actually, it's *not* me! When you feel like you're being criticised day in, day out, you take it up to a point until you think, Well actually, what you're saying about me *isn't* true!

The moment I had that realisation, things started to change. I sat bolt upright in bed and began to think it through afresh. My mind took on a clarity that I hadn't experienced for months, years even. I wasn't going mad, thank God. (It had often crossed my mind.) The truth was far simpler. I was married to someone who didn't appear to love me or even like me. No wonder I was unhappy. My core senses of identity and morality began to fight back and from that moment I started to build myself up again, very gradually.

For ages I had been too scared to face up to what was happening in my marriage and I shut down my inner self. I was so low that there wasn't any further to go down, apart from trying to top myself, and I wasn't going to do that because I had a baby to live for. That night in the Four Seasons I began to rebuild my true self and my confidence. It was time to stand up for myself and what I believed in, just as I'd been telling other people to do for years.

Looking back now I realise that being with Jim taught me a lot and in a way I have to thank him for that. I allowed myself to get to the point where I had to rediscover myself, especially my bad and weak qualities, which brought out a positive strength in me and made me stronger than I'd ever been before.

I flew home in mid-June. My heart sank as I walked into the house, even though I had to laugh at the new doormat my mum had sent me as a present. In big bold black letters it spelt out SHIT HAPPENS. It's still there today, just outside my front door.

As usual, Jim was in the TV room. I felt weighed down as I sensed his presence in the house. I didn't want to see him, didn't want to look him in the eye. I walked softly into the kitchen and turned on the kettle. Just as it was about to boil I heard footsteps behind me.

'Melanie,' said Jim.

'Hiya.'

'What's wrong?' he asked.

I took a deep breath.

'I want a divorce,' I said bluntly.

Admittedly it wasn't the first time I'd said it. The difference was, this time I meant it.

They say that when a relationship breaks down, it takes two to build it back up again. But in this case one and one didn't add up. There was no 'two' with Jim and me. We lived separate lives. We didn't connect. It was over.

Arguments, coldness, insecurity, sadness. How had it ever come to this?

2

THERE WAS A LITTLE GIRL, WHO HAD A LITTLE CURL

I was brought up to believe that one of the best ways to deal with your problems is to laugh at them. Sense of humour was always a big thing in my family, especially on my mother's side. My mum and her four sisters inherited theirs from Grandad, who was hilarious, although he definitely had a cruel streak as well.

White Grandma (I always called her that) was usually exhausted by the end of the day. She took in sewing at home and worked seven days a week. Grandad was an engineer and when he got back from work she'd be knackered, flat out on the sofa, with all the kids (five girls and two boys) jumping up and down around her. One evening Grandad, being the joker, gathered the children together, rolled up a piece of paper, put it in sleeping Grandma's mouth and lit it. She only woke up as the flames neared her lips. 'Oh you're bloody stupid!' she shouted. 'You're gonna turn these kids bloody barmy!'

My mum was around ten when she and the others begged Grandad to let them have a pet rabbit. 'All right,' he said to them, 'You can have one if you promise to look after it. It's up to you to feed it and clean it.' They all said they would, but of course they didn't.

So one evening after dinner – stew and potatoes – he asked, 'Did you enjoy your dinner?' And they all said, 'Yes, Dad, it was lovely!' And he said, 'Good, because you've just eaten your rabbit.'

A few days beforehand my mum and her best friend had made several rounds of sandwiches with rabbit poo in them. They laid them out on a plate and carefully positioned a few jam sandwiches on top of the pile.

'We've made you something to eat!' she told one of her sisters, who was in the next room with a group of her friends. Grabbing a couple of the top jam sandwiches for herself, she handed the rest around the room. I can imagine her cheeky smile as she watched them all chomping their way through bunny droppings. It was just the kind of trick Grandad would play.

Surprise snacks are a favourite with my mum's family. Auntie Sheila once fed her husband dog food and my mum's done garlic sandwiches for my dad's packed lunch in the past. Why food? My guess is that there's a dark, deep reason for it buried in the distant past, but perhaps they were all just incredibly childish. Blame it on Grandad. Everyone else does.

My mum and her sisters grew up to be strong, individual characters with a brilliant shared sense of humour. Auntie Di, Auntie June, Auntie Sheila, Auntie Pamela and my mum Andrea are all incredibly funny. They were happy, smiley children who grew into lively, laughing adults. They're the heart and soul of the family.

Their childhood stories get told time and again, just like nursery rhymes or fairy tales. One of my favourites is the one about the day all the kids were playing darts in the front room. Grandad's holding the dartboard in front of his face and Auntie Sheila is umming and ahhing, taking forever over her turn. Finally Grandad lifts the board up and says, 'Are you ready yet?' and of course, at that very moment, a dart lands straight in his neck.

'Bloody 'ell, Sheila,' he rasped, 'you've nearly killed me!'

I definitely inherited the family sense of humour. For example, on holiday with a boyfriend once I genuinely had something in my eye. 'Can I wipe my eye on your shorts?' I asked him. As I leant down I had a brainwave and whipped his shorts right down to his ankles. I laugh thinking about it now. The best bit was that it was in front of a whole beach full of people. He wasn't best pleased, to say the least, but he laughed in the end. He had to.

My aunties would have giggled if they'd been there. When they get together they do nothing but take the piss out of each other. My mum and

Auntie June slag everyone off, Auntie Di sits there and takes it all, Auntie Sheila just shuts up and Auntie Pamela gets snobby. This is my quick sum-up of them: Di's the dizzy lizzy; Sheila's the sensitive one; Pamela's the posh one; my mum Andrea's the nutter; and June's the one everyone calls Akela. She's the controller, the fire fighter and the one they all call in a crisis.

They're still like kids, especially my mum. She is a complete child, constantly snitching on the others and winding them up. They rarely confront each other but they'll say all sorts of things behind each other's backs. There is always something going on between them and they gossip like you would not believe. It's worse than being in the school playground.

Quite a few years ago, Auntie June started going to French classes. The college organised a trip to France and she stupidly invited my mum and her best friend Bernie, as well as Auntie Pamela and Auntie Di. True to form my mum and Bernie got really drunk and it wasn't long before they were on the tour guide's microphone on the bus shouting, 'Comment t'appelles-tu?' repeatedly. The next minute they pulled up their shirts and squashed their boobs against the windows. Auntie June was disgusted, even though she was only really going on the trip to stock up on booze and fags. She's never been able to go back to her French lessons since.

Every year, from when I was tiny up until I joined the Spices, we'd go camping in Abersoch, Wales. Those were wicked holidays, absolutely fantastic. Sometimes we'd go for the full two weeks, or just join the rest of the family there for a week or a long weekend. Auntie June organised it – she had the caravan and the portaloo, we had the tents. There were so many of us – all my mum's family and their kids – that we'd more or less hire out half the campsite.

I used to want to travel there with Auntie Sheila and Uncle Mick. They were amazingly organised, with delicious packed lunches for the four-hour drive. Everything was precise and perfect, whereas our car was just a mess. My mum would be late and my dad's habit of waiting for everyone to be ready and then saying, 'Right, I'll be five minutes!' was intensely irritating. Fifteen minutes later you're still waiting.

Uncle Mick let me drive home with them once, but unfortunately I projectile-vomited all down the back of his neck.

Auntie June set up camp and organised everyone because she was the experienced camper – and the posh one with a caravan. Every morning someone went for the papers and the bread and someone else went to the farm for eggs. Then we'd sit at a long plastic table and tuck in to the kind of breakfast that you'd never eat at home – fried eggs, toast, beans, mushrooms, tomatoes, sausages, bacon, the lot. It was a full-on hearty English breakfast, cooked to perfection.

We always seemed to have hot weather and a lot of the time it was just like being abroad. The beaches were lovely and jellyfish-free. Uncle Barry used to bury all twelve cousins up to the neck in the sand and leave us there. It would take him forever. 'I wanna be next! I wanna be next!' We'd lie incarcerated for hours laughing away, loving the fact that we couldn't move, nodding frantically at each other. 'Hiya, how are you?'

In the evenings without fail we'd play rounders, then gather for a singalong around a fire on the beach. All the grown-ups would get drunk and end up in the sea and us kids loved being up late enough to watch them do it. As a treat we were allowed one day a week at Butlins, which the adults hated but the kids loved.

Uncle Barry worked as a driver for heavy goods and he usually brought along plenty of tyre inner tubes, which we blew up and used as floats. Unfortunately they were always being blown out to sea. We'd start the holiday off with at least six of them and by the end they'd all be lost. And every time another one blew away the aunties would panic and chase after it without remembering to refasten their bikini straps.

There were more serious mishaps as well, of course. One of my earliest memories is of lying on the sofa in Auntie June's caravan with the blinds down, suffering from a horrific eye infection. It was hell listening to everyone playing outside while I lay there in the dark with antibiotic cream in my eyes, waiting for the blisters and swelling to go down. My vision was completely blurred by that cream. It was hideous. I had a horrible pair of big blue plastic sunglasses that I had to wear whenever I went outside.

The doctors took ages to diagnose that it was a rare form of conjunctivitis. It flared up once or twice a year like a cold sore and lasted a week, sometimes even longer. My mum would say, 'Has that spider weed got in your eye again?' I hated it and my mum and dad loathed having to put the cream in my eyes while I screamed my head off. I still get the same infection now when I'm really stressed. It's one of those things that has plagued me throughout my life.

When I was a bit older it was my job to take the rubbish to the dump. One year I was running down there with a full bin liner in my arms when the top of a baked bean can fell out. I stepped on it and it sliced through my foot, nearly taking my toe off. I had to hobble all the way back up the hill to the tents, screaming blue murder, blood gushing everywhere. My cousin Barry wrapped my foot up in a towel and took me to hospital, where I involuntarily slapped a nurse on the face when she tried to stitch it up. She did a good job, considering. My scar's quite neat. Little did she know that she had my future career in her hands. If I'd lost my toe I probably wouldn't have become a dancer or, subsequently, got into the Spice Girls.

I had to be supervised whenever I went near my sister Danielle after the time I took her crabbing. When the tide goes out in Abersoch it leaves deep ridges – Danielle fell down one and I just left her there. 'Ha ha, get out of that, then!' She was five years younger than me, tiny and gorgeous, but I was really cruel to her. (I wonder how many brothers and sisters actually manage to kill their younger siblings?)

It was Auntie June's idea to have a change of scene. 'I've been to another campsite and it's fantastic.' So the next year we changed campsite. It was a totally different experience. To get to the beach you had to go up an enormous hill and scramble down a landslide of rocks. By the time you got there you were knackered, then you'd sit there in a gale force wind, unable to go in the sea because it was so rough. Fantastic! Not.

One day my mum and Bernie went to see the owner of the campsite. Those two were just mental together and they loved winding him up. 'Oh Dave, your house is just so nice!' Bernie would coo, wearing one of his sofa arm covers on her head.

Dave asked my mum how she liked the shower. (Strange question – there was only one shower. You put in 10p and got about thirty seconds of water.)

'It's great Dave,' said my mum, 'but it seems to have brought me out in these big brown lumps!' And with that she pulled up her T-shirt and flashed her boobs. (She totally denies it now of course!)

He was such an old man that he probably hadn't seen breasts for a while. 'Mmm, lovely!' he said appreciatively and gave them both free Carling Black Label lagers.

Those camping trips were always full of fun and stories. They were like a series of *Carry On* films. One night my mum was up feeding Danielle, who was only six weeks old, when she heard this heavy pumping sound coming from Auntie Sheila and Uncle Mick's tent, which they were sharing with Grandma.

Auntie Sheila was saying, 'That's it. It's hard enough.'

'No, just a bit longer, just a bit more,' panted Uncle Mick.

'Do it faster, then you can finish sooner,' she whispered.

'I'm going as fast as I can!' he croaked.

'Get on with it then, I'm really sleepy now,' she purred.

'It's still a bit soft, just give me five minutes . . .' he pleaded.

Oh my God, thought my mum, they're doing it and our mother's in the same tent! The noises went on for ages.

'Aren't you satisfied yet?' sighed Auntie Sheila finally. 'I want to go to sleep.'

'I don't know why you're complaining. You're just lying there while I do all the work,' gasped Uncle Mick between short breaths.

The next morning my mum got up early and ran to Auntie June's tent to tell her.

'I bet you're tired,' she said when she saw Auntie Sheila at breakfast.

'No, why?' Auntie Sheila looked surprised.

'Well *I* heard all that noise. You nearly woke up the whole bloody campsite!' Mum's face was a picture of disgust.

'Oh yes!' said Auntie Sheila as the penny dropped. 'That bloody airbed went down in the middle of the night and we spent ages trying to inflate it again!'

It was in Abersoch, round the campfire one night, that my mum first told me about how she'd met my dad. I sat there listening intently, absolutely fascinated.

Andrea Dixon was seventeen when she met nineteen-year-old Martin Brown on Christmas Eve 1972 in Chapeltown, which was and still is a ghetto area in Leeds. Her parents would have gone mad if they'd known she was out in Chapeltown, but they didn't know she was out at all, although Grandad probably suspected. He used to nail down the windows so that she couldn't get back in again after she'd sneaked out, or if she wasn't back by a certain time.

There weren't any black people in Seacroft, where her family lived, so it was a real shock when she took my funky black dude dad home. Her parents just couldn't get their heads round it. Strange, I know, but in those days a mixed race couple was just one of those things you very rarely saw – and if you did, you gasped and stared.

My mum's parents were against racially integrated relationships. They'd had no experience of black people and when my mum and dad first went over for dinner, they talked very slowly and loudly to my dad, as if he couldn't understand English. 'HELLO . . . Martin . . . HOW . . . are . . . YOU?'

Why are they talking like that? wondered my dad.

'I'm all right thanks,' he replied, shaking Grandad's hand.

'Bloody 'ell, you're a Yorkshire man!' Grandad bellowed, finding it hard to believe that my dad had the same accent as he did. Nevertheless, White Grandma went on to painstakingly explain everything on my dad's plate, as though he was from outer space.

My mum's sisters thought nothing of her being with my dad, but her parents were disgusted with her. She soon realised that if she was going to go on seeing my dad she'd have to leave home, so she moved in with him three months later, just to get a bit of freedom more than anything. Her mum and dad pushed her away, although they accepted the relationship later.

She got into big trouble for not going home on Christmas Day that year. My dad had nowhere to go so Mum decided to have Christmas dinner at his bedsit in Headingley, opposite the cricket ground (where I was later conceived). They ate scrambled eggs and baked beans and stayed in bed all day. Cool or what?

My dad was used to family hoo-has, even though he wasn't nearly as close to his parents and sisters as my mum was to hers. That's partly because in 1955, when he was two, his parents left him and his sister Kathleen behind in Nevis (a small island in the Caribbean) with their grandmother, and came to England to earn a living. Like many West Indians of their generation, they had looked into the future and realised that they could have a better standard of living if they left Nevis.

First they went to stay with Grandma's brother in Ipswich. After six months they moved to Leeds, where they had more chance of finding work – Grandma was an accomplished tailor and Leeds was the heartland of the tailoring industry.

My dad says that even to this day his mum still bears the scars of what happened to her when she first came to Leeds. She never forgot the way white people crossed the road to avoid her and my grandad as they walked down the street. It took them ages to find somewhere to live. Everywhere they went there were signs in the windows saying 'Vacancies, No Irish, No Blacks'. Grandma never got over it.

It took them seven years to get steady jobs and buy a house. Only then could they start saving for my dad and his sister's boat fare. They sent for the kids when my dad was nine and his sister was twelve, but by then it was like coming to live with strangers. My dad didn't want to leave his grandmother and screamed all the way to Chapeltown. I think it was hard to build a relationship with his mum and dad once he was here. His mum, especially, was very strict and he's never had the courage to stand up to her. It's common for West Indian kids to be brought up strictly, but Black Grandma was even stricter than the rest, according to my dad.

I've often asked him about his childhood and background, but it is still painful for him to talk about it, so the details are sketchy. I know that it was a terrible wrench to leave the only life he'd ever known and move to a strange country, although he quickly adapted, as kids do. In Nevis he'd lived with his grandmother on a small farm. She was strict, but he had a lot of freedom as well. He fed the pigs, goats, hens and chickens and helped with the household chores before and after school, but the rest of the time he was free to roam the island with his mates. They played cricket on the beach and wandered up into the lush forests and mountains, feasting on fruit along the way.

It was an almost perfect life for a young boy so it's no surprise that he didn't want to leave it behind. On the day he was due to say goodbye, he disappeared into the forest and hid, desperately hoping that he'd miss the boat. But his grandmother knew all his hiding places and he was dragged kicking and yelling into a small boat, which took him to a bigger boat, which took him to England. He really missed his grandma. Although he often wrote to her, he didn't see her again for a full thirty years, when he went back to Nevis for his aunt's funeral.

It took a month to reach England. Stepping off the boat at Southampton Docks on a freezing February day, my dad saw snow for the first time in his life. The ground was thick with it. It was a complete shock; he'd never even heard of snow before. It appeared so pretty and fluffy that he was amazed to find that it was ice-cold as he reached down to touch it. And when he looked back at his snowy footprints he freaked out, convinced that he was being chased by a ghost.

At the docks his mother rushed over to him and his sister and swept them into her arms. Luckily they recognised her from all the photos that she'd sent them over the years.

My dad was used to strictness – his grandmother wasn't a soft touch at all – but he found his mother quite formidable. She had an exceptionally strong presence and was very closed off emotionally. My dad doesn't talk much about this period in his life, but I know that he rebelled. In his teens he used to wear black eyeliner and draw on a thin moustache, because that was the thing to do back then. Later it was all big afros and platforms.

When he left school he did a two-year engineering course. The firm he trained with was going to take him to Canada, but then he had a row with his parents, left home and resigned from his job. His mum and dad found it hard to forgive him for that. I think that's partly why they didn't speak to him for years. Whatever the reason (he won't discuss it) they had a huge falling out.

My dad went to live with an auntie for a year, then shared a flat with five young guys. He was living alone and working as a tailoring cutter when he met my mum. Two years later he became an engineer's assistant at Yorkshire Imperial Metals, where he has worked shifts for the last twenty-five years. One thing I can say about Dad is that he's the hardest-working man I know. He rarely has sick days off and never complains about work. He often did double shifts (sixteen hours) all week when I was a child and my mum sometimes did three jobs in one day. From an early age they instilled in me that the only way to get what you want is to work hard for it.

My mum left school at fifteen and did general office work for a while, but it was so badly paid that she got a job in a biscuit factory instead. After that she did loads of different things, including two nights a week at the front desk in a nightclub at the Bellevue Centre, where my dad played championship table tennis.

My parents got married on 2 August 1975. I love their wedding photo. My mum's in a tight pale blue dress with massive platform boots and my dad's got these enormous lapels, huge bushy hair and massively wide flares. They look like a proper rock and roll couple.

People on both sides of the family said, 'Mixed marriages don't work. It's not fair on the kids.' But my mum was sure about what she was doing. She just thought that none of them understood.

I really admire both my parents for standing up to all that family pressure and going ahead with their lives. Mixed relationships were rare at that time and nobody really agreed with them. It must have been hard to have everyone against them but they didn't let it stop them doing what they wanted.

As for me, I wasn't planned. Finally free from her mum and dad's curfews, my mum was out partying most nights and kept forgetting to take her pill. That's when I happened. Once she was pregnant, my mum was determined to get Dad to contact his parents. They hadn't seen or spoken to each other for years, and Mum felt that falling out with your family was one of the worst things that could happen in life. So on Christmas Day 1974 she made a suggestion.

'Why don't you ring your mum and tell her that you're going to have a baby?'

Although my dad had actually wanted to make the call for a long time, it was very difficult for him to pick up the phone. His heart was pounding as he dialled his parents' number. He swallowed hard as he heard his mother's voice.

'Hello Mum. Are you okay? How's my dad?'

Grandma was shocked to hear from him and the conversation was understandably awkward. She hadn't spoken to her son for several years and now he was ringing up out of the blue on Christmas Day to tell her that his girlfriend was pregnant. There were lots of embarrassed pauses. My dad still finds it hard to talk to his mum. He sees her as a very introvert, private person who keeps her emotions to herself, (just like my dad does, in fact). She's the complete opposite of his father, who is a real extrovert. Black Grandma and Grandad are like chalk and cheese.

My dad arranged to see his parents soon after the phone call. The second time he visited them my mum went too. It wasn't a very happy experience for her. She was surprised that his family disagreed with their relationship as much as her family did. Black Grandma kept saying to my mum that life would be hard because she and my dad were brought up so differently. 'It won't work and the baby won't fit in,' she insisted. My mum found this very upsetting and kept looking to my dad for support, but he was too scared to open his mouth. Respect for his mother was so deeply ingrained that he didn't dare contradict her. My mum and dad argued all the way home. 'How could you just sit there while they said all that?' my mum asked him over and over again.

After sixteen hours of labour, at 5.59 p.m. on 29 May 1975 I was scooped out of my nineteen-year-old mother with a pair of forceps. 'This is the bonniest baby that's been born here all week,' declared one of the nurses. I had lots of thick black loose-curled hair and perfect little features, according to my mum.

My birth definitely drew the family closer. Black Grandad, who was far less disapproving than Grandma, was one of the first people to come and see me. Unfortunately my mum was wearing a backless hospital gown and as she leant over to pick me up, her boobs fell out in front of him. (Judging by how I later turned out I think I must have been aware of this early lesson in how to make a man blush!)

My colour was a huge debating point. One of my dad's relatives said, 'She's neither black nor white. She doesn't belong anywhere and that's going to be hard.'

In a way she was right, kind of, but it was the last thing my mum wanted to hear about her newborn baby. She was deeply upset. It was an incredibly insensitive thing to say to a new mother, especially since there was a massive National Front scene in Leeds at the time. There were loads of racists around and it was so bad that my mum used to hand me to my dad when they got on the bus, because she knew that if he was holding a young baby then he wouldn't get beaten up. They often felt threatened when they went out at night and always had to avoid Leeds City Centre after football matches. Luckily, though, my dad didn't get involved in the batterings or any of the mad counter-attacks against white people.

There were skinheads all over Leeds during the 1970s. (If you were white and shaved your head back then, the chances were that you were also wearing army boots and a Swastika badge.) Some areas were very dangerous if you were black. Even when I was a child I was aware of the tension when I went into predominantly white areas like Seacroft. There were massive National Front and anti-Nazi marches going on in town and I found it really frightening when my mum explained it all to me as I grew older. I couldn't believe it was going on, plus, half of my family still lived in Seacroft.

It was unheard of for White Grandad to visit any of his daughters after they'd given birth. I was his eighth grandchild and he hadn't been to see any of the others in hospital, but for some reason he came to check me out. Mixed race babies often start out very pale skinned so when Grandad saw me he breathed a sigh of relief. 'Oh, she's white, just like us!' A month later when I'd gone quite a bit darker he couldn't help asking my mum, 'Bloody 'ell! Are you washing her?'

Ironically, I became his favourite, his special little granddaughter, God bless his soul. The moment he saw me he fell in love with me and there was a strong bond between us until the day he died. Seeing how tenderly my doting father held me in his arms changed his attitude towards my dad too, so I guess my arrival made quite a difference, all told.

For the first week I opened only one eye, so my mum and dad called me 'One Eye' until they'd decided what to name me. My dad wanted Caroline but my mum was insistent it was Melanie, thank God. Years later Emma's mum Pauline gave me a coaster printed with an explanation of the meaning of Melanie: 'Dark skinned, caring, affectionate and romantic, builds relationships day by day, able to brighten a day with her smile, accept others for who they are and make the impossible possible.' Thank you Mum for sticking to your guns.

Mum stayed in hospital for seven days, mainly because the landlord at the Headingley bedsit didn't allow babies. The council had promised a house after I was born but in the meantime my mum and dad had no alternative but to stay at my mum's parents' house, which was awkward to say the least.

Still, it wasn't long after my mum left hospital with me that the housing department handed over the keys to 1 Harold Grove, a back-to-back house in Hyde Park. Luckily it was a racially mixed area.

Money was tight and so my mum went out to work when I was about a month old. Without a babysitter or childminder she could only work when my dad came home, so again she did all sorts of things, including serving fish and chips in a chip shop. That only lasted a night, though. She realised that she wasn't cut out for it when she sprayed her feet with boiling chip fat and almost burnt her fingers off while moving a load of fish from one fryer to another.

During the day she'd take me to the park or to her mum's. She didn't visit my dad's parents very much because it was two long bus rides to their house in Chapeltown.

At the end of our street was a corner shop where my mum was always popping in for milk or teabags. 'Ah, little Sherrel!' the owners would coo when they saw me. 'Noooooo,' my mum would correct them, 'It's Melanie.'

It turned out that little Sherrel's mum Bernie, who lived nearby on the same estate, was experiencing a similar case of mistaken identity. 'Ah, little Melanie!' they'd say to her. 'Who the hell is Melanie?' she'd ask. 'This is Sherrel.'

Inevitably the two mums finally bumped into each other and laid down the beginnings of what was to become a friendship for life. The similarities between Sherrel and me were amazing in a time when mixed race babies were so much less common. Not only did we look like sisters, but there was only a month between us. Bernie and my mum hit it off from the start, both being slightly crazy. It was great because they began to share the babysitting of Sherrel and me and soon we were permanent fixtures in each other's lives.

We lived in Harold Grove for five years. In the early evening when everybody was coming home from work I'd sit on the doorstep and wait for people to stop and talk to me. We lived in a student area and the students loved me, but my favourite passer-by was the woman I called My Lady, who gave me a sweet every day. She was a really eccentric old woman decked out in beads and old-fashioned earrings and elegant shoes. When I saw her coming I'd shout, 'My Lady's here!' During the day I often wandered over to chat to the neighbours. Hyde Park was a buzzing place to be a child and seemed very safe to me.

I had lots of energy to expend. I've been hyperactive all my life, so much so that Bernie used to call me 'the draught' because of the air currents I created while rushing here there and everywhere. She'd ring my mum and say, 'Bring her over, it's a hot day!'

My mum would have to beg Auntie Sheila to babysit me. She'd say, 'Please, please, *please* babysit her,' and Sheila would reply, 'Oh, I'll have to ask Mick.' Uncle Mick would say, 'Bloody 'ell, she never lets up! Jibber,

jibber, jibber, jibber, jibber, jibber, jibber.' I was passed round the family like a hot potato. No one could handle me for long, apart from Auntie June. Everyone said that keeping up with me was like trying to catch a fire.

I wasn't that naughty, just a live wire who wanted and needed attention. You couldn't just hand me a book to read, you had to read it with me. You couldn't just give me toys to play with, because I wouldn't play on my own. I made my mum and dad sit in my Wendy house for hours on end while I fed them sandwiches and taught them games. It must have driven them up the wall, but I don't remember them once complaining.

From the moment I could talk I needed to know everything about everything. I was a nightmare! I couldn't just ask a question. I always had to know more. 'But why is that?' No matter what answer they gave me back, I'd ask, 'No, but why *is* that?' I needed to know the tiniest details, about why birds have feathers, how their eyes move, why they don't have eyebrows, how long they live – everything. Obviously my parents didn't have all the answers.

The only hiccup in my rocket-powered life was that I tended to stutter when I got too excited. Sitting at the kitchen table trying to ask my cousin Andrew f-f-for the t-t-t-t-tomato sauce wasn't f-fun.

I was always on the go. My cousins loved it, because I was so mad. I used to jump on their beds for an hour, shouting, 'Yeah, yeah, I'm at Joanna's, yeah, yeah!' I idolised my cousin Joanna. She was the perfect one with blonde hair. I wanted to look like her and I couldn't understand why I didn't.

When I was four, in the bath with my mum, I said, 'Mummy I love you because you're white.' My mum found this very disturbing but my dad told her not to make a big thing of it. He'd thought the same way about some of his teachers when he was a child. Back then you didn't see black people in adverts or on the front of magazines. They were virtually invisible in the media. Blonde hair and blue eyes were the pinnacle of beauty, almost exclusively. I grew to hate black and white films when I was older. I hated the fact that they all seemed to have black slaves and servants in them. It upset me to see the way black people were being portrayed, even though that's the way it was in those days. Those films made my heart bleed and I can't bear to watch them to this day.

When I was nearly five my mum explained that I was going to get a brother or a sister. 'Will it be white with blonde hair? That's how I want it,' I pleaded.

'You'd better ask your dad if you want it to be white!' she laughed, adding, 'No, it's going to be just like you.'

When I went with my dad up to the hospital to see the new baby, I took one look at Danielle and cried tears of disappointment.

'Take her back,' I insisted. 'She's not white and her hair's black.' I was used to being surrounded by my mum's family who were all white with blonde hair and that's the kind of child I expected my mum to have.

Danielle went through a similar thing. She used to say, 'I know I'm called Danielle Brown because at the moment I'm brown, but when I'm older I'll be white.'

My mum had to explain, 'You're never going to change the colour you are. You've got a bit of your dad and a bit of me and you're coffee coloured. You're mixed race. You have the best of both worlds.'

Danielle was a year old when my mum started work again, this time in a clothes shop. She enjoyed it up to a point. On her first day there she didn't mention to her workmates that she was married to a black man. Why should she? No one came to her and said, 'Oh by the way, my husband's Scottish or Irish.'

Unfortunately the other sales assistants told a lot of racist jokes. My mum kept quiet for a few months, mainly to spare their embarrassment, but after a while she felt that things were getting out of hand. There were so many racist comments going round the staff room that she decided she was going to have to say something. Bear in mind that my mum is the kind of person, unlike me, that can hold her tongue. It takes quite a lot for her to speak her mind, but when she does, you know about it.

So she showed them all some photos of Danielle and me and said, 'These are my kids.'

'Oh, you know, it's not *black* people we don't like, it's *Asians*,' said one of her colleagues in a pathetic attempt to justify herself. My mum said she felt really embarrassed for the lot of them.

Me and Sherrel were in the same class at nursery and primary school. Story time was the best part of life at Westfield Grove Primary School, when you had to sit cross-legged and keep quiet. It was then, and only then, that you allowed a boy to put his arm round you when the teachers weren't looking.

My best friend at Westfield was a girl called Julie. She was really beautiful, with long dark hair, and I wanted to be like her so much. She had dirt under her nails and I used to scrape my fingers on the ground to achieve a similar effect. I often laugh to myself about it when I'm having a manicure. These days I spend hours and hours (and an absolute fortune) on creating the total opposite of the 'Julie look'.

I had really good reports at primary school. 'What a polite child. A pleasure to teach!' The teachers all liked me. I was energetic, but not naughty.

When I got home from school I'd change out of my school clothes into my scruffy 'playing out' clothes, put on my coat and shoes and wait. The coat and shoes were particularly important because when my mum said, 'Right, I'm off to Bernie's!' I'd be able to say, 'I'm ready!' If I didn't have my coat and shoes on she'd say, 'No you're not. I'm off!' and disappear out the door. She was very impatient and I hated being left behind. To me, she had a really exciting life – always popping over to someone or other's house.

Sundays were great. The aunties and husbands and kids would go round to Grandma's for dinner and I'd help out with the Yorkshire pudding mix. We were a really tight family. Grandad was always there with a bag of mints for me. He usually got drunk and swayed around, smoking his pipe, telling jokes and being funny. I used to go out into the garden and pick raspberries with him. We had a very special relationship. Thinking of him makes me smile.

When I was five we moved to 74 Westfield Road, also in Hyde Park. All that concerned me on the day that we packed up and left was, 'How will Father Christmas know where we've gone?'

The new house was on quite a big council estate. The place had a real community spirit and everybody's door was open in the summer. There was always something going on – somebody getting caught having an affair or owing drug money or wheeling and dealing, or there'd be sugar daddies knocking on the neighbours' doors. There were drug dealers and prostitutes and lots of this, that and the other going on. I loved it.

I spent most of my free time in 'the den' hanging out with all the rest of the kids. We set up the den between two parallel walls across the road from our row of houses. Thick with undergrowth and debris, closed off from the world, it was the perfect place to build a hideout with odd pieces of wood, then lay out blankets on the floor.

The house in Westfield Road was bigger than the one in Harold Grove. My bedroom was wicked, with a pink carpet, pink walls and bunk beds. I even had cowboy-style saloon doors on my bedroom wardrobe. I loved those doors and used to dress up and burst through them, singing and dancing. They provided an excellent way to make an entrance. 'Da-da!' *Swing.* 'Here I am!'

My best toy was my Barbie House, which was almost as tall as I was. I also had a fake Cabbage Patch doll called Luby Lou that I became very attached to, and a Tiny Tears that weed. Like all the other kids in my area I didn't have much but what I had I treasured and shared. I didn't really notice my mum and dad scrimping and saving. I don't think kids ever do. They said the odd thing like, 'Well you just can't have it,' but they didn't go into explanations and I didn't feel deprived.

When Sherrel stayed over, which was quite often, I'd beg her to tell me the Snotbag story. There was nothing to it really – 'Snotbag got out of bed, went to the shops and bumped into Bogeybag and Poobag . . .' – but I found the words snot, bogey and poo hysterical. Sherrel would have me in fits on the top bunk. She always had and still has a wicked sense of humour. It takes her a while to warm up with people but once she lets you in you can't stop her.

Rude words were funny; sex wasn't. One night I heard my mum and dad having sex and I was appalled. Obviously I didn't realise what they were doing and I rushed into their bedroom shouting at my dad, 'Get off her now!' Then I raced downstairs into the kitchen.

My mum found it hard to stop giggling. 'You go down and tell her it's all right,' she told my dad.

So my dad came downstairs and tried to explain. 'Me and your mum are just loving each other.'

'No! I heard her screaming! You're hurting her.' I was furious with him but he just wanted to laugh. It was a dilemma. He didn't want to explain sex, because I was too young, but he didn't want me to think he was hurting my mum. He managed to calm me down in the end.

My mum hated sleeping alone when my dad was on night shifts, so she'd usually make me or Danielle share the bed with her. She'd say, 'One of you has got to sleep with me, which one is it going to be?'

We'd both say, 'Not me!' because you had to lie really still in Mum's bed and suffer the sharpness of her razor-stubbled legs as they brushed against you in the night.

For a while Aunty Di and Uncle Steve moved in. Nine months previously they'd been saving up to get married and buy a house, but decided to spend the money on travelling instead. So they toured India and became, like, 'really multicultural and experienced'. By the time they got back they were full-on hippies and their clothes were covered in little mirrors. They arrived at our house on Christmas Eve 1981 and stayed two years. Auntie Di went back to working as a secretary and Uncle Steve moved into car sales.

I'll never forget having to do my homework in the kitchen. I was really bad at maths, so Auntie Di would try to teach me to divide and take away. After a while she'd say, 'Right, my time's up.' Next Uncle Steve would come in and give it a go and still I wouldn't get it. Then my dad would come and go and, finally, my mum would arrive. She'd last two minutes, because she's got no patience. After I'd gone through everyone, I'd have to sit there and try to finish it alone. The tacky old smoky frosted glass that ran from the kitchen to the front room meant that you could kind of see into the front room, but not really. I'd sit with my books thinking, Oh God, I've got to get this right before I can watch TV or go out to play.

I never got it done properly, that maths.

When I was six White Grandad started getting really bad chest infections. After a few months he slept in a bed downstairs in the front room of the house because he was too ill to go upstairs. I had no idea he was so bad until the day he died, when I was seven, and even then I was a bit too young to understand. I really missed him when he was gone and I still do, although I know he's watching over me somewhere.

A few days after he died my mum asked Auntie Sheila to babysit me. Without telling Mum she took me to the funeral chapel to pay our last respects to Grandad in his open coffin. Lying there wrapped in a cloth with his eyes shut, his snow-white skin was tinged with garish blusher. I touched him, cuddled him and chatted away to him as normal, a bit confused because everyone around me was crying and I didn't understand why. 'What's wrong with you all?' Needless to say my mum went absolutely ballistic when she found out where I'd been. She was really worried that I'd have nightmares about it. I didn't, but I do have a very strong memory of him lying there, as if it was only yesterday.

After Grandad died, Grandma moved out of the family house into a little flat. All the sisters helped her out with the decorating, especially Auntie Pamela. Grandad's spirit lived on in my mum. When we went to visit Grandma she'd say things like, 'So then Mum, are you having sex?' I used to cringe.

'You're bloody disgusting talking like that in front of Melanie and Danielle,' Grandma would reply. 'Come into the kitchen Melanie, and help me with the Yorkshire pudding mix!' My mum used to laugh her head off.

When I was very young Christmas was spent at various different aunties' houses. Sheila, Di, June and my mum all had two kids each, so it was madness. It was really special when we went to Auntie June's house because she lived in Manchester and we'd drive down there in convoy. Her spread was definitely the best.

We played fantastic games on Christmas Day. Uncle Barry would make massive Brucie-style playing cards and we'd gather round for *Play Your Cards Right*. 'Higher! Lower! Higher!' Everyone would let their hair down and the kids were allowed to stay up really late and be a part of it. We were never told, 'Right, off to bed now.' It was great and, of course, I was one of the loudest. Us girls used to play 'rudies' with cousins Barry, Andrew, Michael and Nicholas. It was like doctors and nurses without the science bits.

Auntie June's house was posh. You knew it because she had a window seat with cushions. (Later my mum tried to copy it but didn't get it quite right.) June's bathroom was full of tiny frog statues – she had a thing about them and you weren't allowed to touch them. You'd be dying to, but you just couldn't.

After Grandad died we stopped going to the aunties for Christmas and everyone took it in turns to have Grandma to stay. At that point Bernie and Sherrel started coming round to ours on Christmas Day. Sherrel usually brought some of her presents round unopened. 'Sherrel, what have you got?' I'd ask, eyes gleaming. Before she knew it I'd have unwrapped the lot and be sitting there in her new dress and shoes.

'I've got Sherrel's Christmas presents on!' I'd yell triumphantly.

'Yeah, you have,' she'd say calmly, completely unflustered. She was so laid back that I could get away with murder. I even opened her presents on her birthday because she didn't get to them quickly enough for my liking.

Despite being high-maintenance, I had a strong sense of justice from a very early age. When I was eight, the news came through that they were delivering a new computer to the school and the head teacher decided that it would be shared by the top two classes. The other class got it for three days and we got it for two.

All week I kept going home saying, 'But it's not fair! Do you think it's fair?'

My dad could see how distressed I was. 'If you don't think it's fair, it's up to you to say so to your teacher and explain why,' he said.

So I did.

'It's not my decision,' shrugged my teacher. 'It's up to the Head Teacher. I'm afraid that's just the way it is.'

I still wasn't having it. I went on complaining at home. It was really bugging me.

At the end of the week when my mum came to pick me up from school, I told her, 'I've got to go and see the Head Teacher now.'

'Oh my God, what have you done?' she asked, flushing with panic.

'I just know that I've got to see him now!'

I made her wait outside the office. When I emerged I had a very smug look on my face, apparently. 'I've sorted it out,' I announced. 'The computer is going to be shared out equally between the classes. Two and a half days each. It's fair now.'

I needn't have bothered, because not long afterwards my mum decided that she wanted to move, which meant that I'd be changing schools too.

She could tell that I'd started noticing that he's beating her up down the road and there are men going in and out all the time. So although she and my dad loved it in Hyde Park, she told him, 'Look, I'm not seeing my kids grow up in this area and going the same way everybody else's kids are going. I want to move to a different area and give my kids a chance, even if it means taking out a loan.'

My dad didn't really want to move because he had a lot of friends on the estate. What's more, he could play his music loud without any complaints. He had hundreds of tapes, ranging from pop and reggae to folk and country music. He was into everything, even Dire Straits, although he did play a lot of reggae.

The lifestyle on the estate suited my mum as well but she knew that she could find a better place to bring up children and that was the priority.

They found a house in Kirkstall, a very old-baggish area. There were hardly any black people – just two couples in the next street, which felt like miles away. Our next-door neighbour was a mad woman who'd wander round the streets in her dressing gown. She was really old and my mum used to force me to go round and make tea for her, which I hated.

The new house was a right mess at first. My bedroom had a filthy wooden floor with odd bits of carpet strewn across it. There were mice in the kitchen and you had to clap loudly before you went in there. One morning my mum put her hand in a cornflakes box and pulled out a wriggling rodent. I was terrified to go into the kitchen after that.

The house was a three-bedroom semi with a little bit of front lawn that always looked terrible, all lumps and bumps, as if it had been through the war. My dad got a bit posh with the back garden though, and decided he was going to slab it all with his own bare hands. It took him about three years to do but he got there in the end! My mum and dad still have that house today. That was the house that turned our family around.

My mum did up the inside of the house, although it was always going to be 'an ongoing process'. She artexed all the walls and ceilings herself, mixed up gallons of white paste and spent hours on end up a stepladder reaching into inaccessible corners. She painted the walls in country greens and reds and polished and varnished the wood floors. It was really stylish, my mum's great with stuff like that, but it was very small. Upstairs were three small bedrooms, all very close together, a tiny little landing and a toilet. Downstairs consisted of a small kitchen with a table and a fireplace, and the front room.

To a great extent, my mum and dad had reversed gender roles. He did the cooking and shopping, she did the DIY and decorating. My dad had lived on his own for ages and was used to cooking and shopping, whereas my mum lived at home until she moved in with him and didn't have a clue, so it made sense for him to take care of that side of things.

They once tried to decorate together when I was a baby, but it ended in a blazing row. My dad was up the ladder trying to paste on some wallpaper but it kept falling down on his head. 'That's it!' he announced in frustration, ripping the strip of wallpaper off the wall and throwing it over my mum. 'I'm never decorating with you again.' The next day my mum rang Bernie and asked if she would help instead. She always did the decorating after that.

I didn't miss our old home too much because Bernie and Sherrel often came to see us. Now when Bernie and my mum get together for a drink they are completely outrageous and always have been. Like most of the adults I grew up around, they worked so hard at juggling jobs and family that they needed at least one night a week to let off steam – so that's what they did, big time. Friday nights round at our house were always hysterical, involving lots of jokes, laughter, screaming and messing around. They used to put me and Sherrel up to all sorts as well.

For example, the community centre next door wouldn't let us be members. Well, they accepted our application and then reversed their decision, even though we'd been proposed and seconded by other members.

So Sherrel and I dressed up as robbers, in head-to-toe black with fake guns and balaclavas, and when any of the club members walked past we'd scream, 'BANG!' and leap up from behind the front wall. It made the old biddies jump out of their skins; meanwhile my mum and Bernie watched from inside the house, pissing themselves laughing.

There were people popping in and out the whole time; it was always a full house. That's probably because my mum came from a big family and was used to having loads of people around. She doesn't really like to be at home alone, whereas my dad likes to have the house to himself. He's a bit of a loner, really, like his mum. Black Grandma can spend weeks without going out or seeing anyone and it doesn't bother her at all.

My mum's the kind of person who lives life to the full, makes a beautiful home and has everyone round. She created a really nice secure family environment, but that didn't slow down my endless attention seeking. I was quite needy, I suppose, along with being hyperactive and a bit of a show-off.

By now, my mum was almost at breaking point with me. She'd run out of ideas for how to tire me out. Brownies didn't do it, swimming didn't, nothing did. She was tearing her hair out.

Then, just before we moved to Kirkstall, something happened to turn my life around. Sharon, the pretty dark-haired girl with a big smile who lived next door, completely reshaped my destiny with one simple question. She asked my mum if I could go to a dancing class with her.

Maybe dancing was the answer.

3

DANCING ON THE CEILING

Yes, miracles do happen. Not only did dancing wear me out, but I loved it. At the Jean Pearce School of Dance (a cold run-down basement in a house with no heating) I began a blissful journey into tap, ballet, jazz and modern.

From the start Mrs Wood, who taught and played the piano, would shout, 'That girl. Talking. That girl!' (Yes, me!) She was the type of older woman who wears flowery frocks and glasses – she dressed for a vicar's tea party, but was a fantastic choreographer. Her stage name was Jean Pearce and in her day she'd been quite a big teacher. She was known for choreographing all the *Junior Showtime* TV Shows, where the Nolan sisters made their name.

We were scared of her. She was like a mad woman, really driven. She worked non-stop.

She'd show the class a step and say, 'If you can't pick it up, you go to the back.' She had an uncanny way of sensing who was going wrong behind her while she was playing the piano. That made you learn quickly.

In actual fact she was preparing us for auditions, although we didn't realise it at the time. At dance auditions you'll be shown a routine two or three times and if you don't pick it up then, you're out, no matter how good you look or dance. There would be no point in hiring you if you weren't a quick learner.

In my view it was something that Mrs Wood had over all the other dance schools, like Mullen's and Doreen Bird (where Mel C went). She would teach you to pick up a routine within a few minutes. She forced your mind to work overtime, which was a fantastic challenge. Her classes weren't massively packed but they were so interesting that no one ever stopped going. You never did the same thing twice. And Mrs Wood's dancers always passed their ballet exams because she was really good at teaching technique.

She inspired respect. Even though she bullied you to the point of being on the verge of tears and hating her, you'd still want to come back and prove to her that you could do it. You'd never be rude or want to tell her to f*** off because she'd make you feel really, really good when you got something right. When a competition was coming up she gave private lessons upstairs in her attic with the electric fire on. Sometimes her assistant Jennifer took the classes. Jennifer was a wonderfully expressive teacher with loads of energy and great peach lipstick.

Mrs Wood was an excellent motivator and surprisingly unconventional in that she'd let us bring in our own music and then play along to it on the piano. All our routines were a bit quirky. They weren't your usual ballet routines because they all had a bit of jazz to them. Within no time I was going to Jean Pearce three times a week, including a two-and-a-half-hour class on Saturday mornings. It was all funded by Mum's extra jobs. As she worked I played – that's what mums do for their kids.

Most of the other kids had private lessons every week, but my mum could only afford the main classes with occasional private lessons. 'If you want to be as good as the others,' she said, 'you'll have to give yourself private lessons in your bedroom in front of the mirror.' So I practised non-stop at home. I worked hard, like my parents had shown me to, but even they were shocked by my determination to improve.

I didn't leave Jean Pearce until I went to dance college. I met my three childhood best friends there – Charlotte, Rebecca and Carly. Charlotte and Rebecca are still my best friends to this day.

Charlotte is pretty much the same today as she was then – petite, outgoing and bubbly. She's not your stereotypical blonde at all, she's a very good judge of character and she's got balls. No one could ever tell her what to do when she was a child.

Charlotte had an older sister called Lisa, who was one of the 'big' girls at Jean Pearce. I idolised Lisa and her friend Jodie. When they brought back little tin boxes of sweets from Japan for Carly and me after a cruise job, we felt so special. It meant that we were their favourites. Lisa was blonde and lovely. I wanted to be like her, a great dancer with long legs and blonde hair, even though I knew I'd never have blonde hair, obviously. (Well, not until I went straight and blonde for my first *This Is My Moment*. Yes! I got there in the end.)

To me, Carly was Miss Perfect. We clicked from the moment we met. Later her parents used to take me out to Sunday dinner, on days out, even on holiday with them. They more or less adopted me for a while. They had a massive detached house that was just heaven because I could do ten cartwheels down their hallway. My mum had soap, deodorant and a bottle of perfume, but Carly's mum's dressing table was heaving with products. I think it was around this time that I started to develop my obsession with toiletries.

I was horrible to my mum because I'd ask, 'Why haven't we got a house like they have? I don't want to live here any more, I want to live in Carly's house.' On the other hand, Carly couldn't wait to spend time at my house, because it was so slapdash. There would be food flying everywhere and bedtime was very chaotic and the house seemed tiny, with everyone coming and going.

Carly's house was so much bigger. We'd sit down to dinner in a massive front room. There was a downstairs toilet and Carly had her own private dressing room, her own big wardrobe and a huge peach and grey bathroom. She even had a dance studio where we'd practice all our dance routines. We were very similar in physique and used to perform a lot of duets together.

To me Carly's house was pure *Dynasty* and I was so lucky to have experienced it, because otherwise I wouldn't have known that a life like that existed, apart from on TV. I also loved going to her friend's house down the street because they had electric doors in the sitting room. I was like one of the family, but Carly went to private school so I tended to drop into her life and then drop out of it again.

Every season there would be dance competitions for all levels from novice up, mainly held in school halls. I found it incredibly nerve-racking to dance on stage in front of a panel of judges, not to mention fellow dancers and everybody's mums, dads and relatives. I used to get anxious to the point of feeling sick, sweating and shaking backstage. I think that's why I don't get pre-performance nerves now. I used them all up dancing in those early competitions.

Your number was called out before you went on. 'And now we have Number Eight, Melanie Brown'. You walked out from the wings, took your position and waited for the music to start. At that moment your stage fright became heart-stoppingly intense.

The feeling of relief and delight when you came off stage, having remembered all your steps, was amazing. It was a huge buzz to be entertaining an audience, more than a buzz, in fact. This was it. At the age of nine I had discovered what I wanted to do with the rest of my life.

At the end of each competition everyone lined up on stage holding their numbers. Sometimes it was a ten-minute wait before the judges decided the results and Charlotte and I used to drop our numbers, pick them up and drop them again, just to have something to do. When the winner was announced, we'd sigh dramatically, acting out a hugely exaggerated scene of disappointment and despair to keep ourselves amused. If on the other hand we won, we gasped and looked at each other in a really over-shocked way. We messed about a lot.

Getting ready was great. The preparation room usually had oak floors, mirrors around the walls and loads of mums putting make-up on their daughters. Each dance school had a slightly different way of applying make-up. At the Mullen School of Dance they put blue and white on their eyelids and a red dot in the corners of their eyes to make them look bigger. Blusher and bright red lipstick were universal, of course. You were marked on your presentation, so your hair and make-up had to be perfect.

Your mum made your costumes. At first my mum wasn't great but she improved beyond belief over the years. If I needed a hat, she would find a large yoghurt or margarine carton, stick material and frills around it, fasten elastic to it and – hey presto! – a hat. Luckily costumes and song and dance routines were passed down from the older girls. Once, I ended up doing one of Charlotte's old routines to 'These Boots Are Made For Walking', wearing a blue bolero jacket from World of Dance in Leeds over a red leotard, with my hair scraped back in a high, deliberately messy ponytail.

At the end of each competition you'd get a piece of paper with the judges' comments. You were given a certificate and a medal if you came first, second or third. Collecting medals was a major obsession with everyone. I've still got all of mine.

Mrs Wood organised trips to see West End shows like *Cats* and *Miss Saigon* on tour and if one of the 'big' girls was in something we'd get a coach load together to support her. Lisa was brilliant in *Singin' in the Rain* in Manchester. Everyone at my dance school had ambitions to be in a West End show – and nearly every single one of them actually went on to be in a West End show, as it happened.

Three times my mum and dad, Danielle and me went to Skegness for a week long dance festival over the May bank holiday. Dancers from all the different schools met up there, along with everyone's mum and dad. Mostly the dads went off and got drunk while the mums got their kids ready for the competitions. But it wasn't just dancing; we had a really good time on the beach and the fairground rides as well.

The Jean Pearce mothers would get a list of boarding houses in advance and try to book everyone into the same one. In Skegness you stuck with the people from your school. 'Oh, she's from Mullen's!' 'She's from Doreen Bird.' There would always be a little bit of tension there but you didn't really see it as competitive, it was more of a jokey rivalry. The whole experience was a confidence booster for me.

Danielle was three the first time we went. She'd already started dancing and was chosen as among the best of the festival at the end of the week. She did a little solo piece at the final show, in front of the Mayoress of Skegness. I was asked to do a duet with a girl called Joanne Long – 'The Lady is a Tramp'.

We'd done the routine a few times before and I was sick of it. I hated the hideous dress I had to wear and considered it incredibly babyish. It was white, with a tight-fitting basque covered in red bows, and a frilly fru-fru skirt. I started moaning about it as we were changing and putting on our make-up and by the time we were ready I'd decided that I wasn't going on, not in that dress.

Joanne began to cry her eyes out so my mother stepped in and did a bit of wheedling. If I danced the routine one last time I'd never have to do it again, she said. I finally came round when I heard her telling Joanne's mother that they'd have to find another 'Lady is a Tramp' partner in future. Like Charlotte, I wasn't one of those kids that could be made to do things just like that.

The Miss Dance championships were at the pinnacle of the competition circuit (and I never got there!). It was a massive event, which you were eligible to enter when you reached eighteen. I was mesmerised by the salsa display that was staged while the judges were out, entranced when the new Miss Dance was presented with a crown and a sash. One girl from each school took part and you'd set off on the coach at 5 a.m. to cheer yours on, taking a good luck card along with you. We were like a large extended family. Miss Dance was a really big deal and you respected and supported whoever your girl was.

I couldn't get enough of dancing, so when my mum heard that there were night classes being held just down the road at the Sacred Heart school hall, I begged her to let me go. The woman who ran them was called Nadine, a very serious but caring teacher. She now heads the Northern School of Contemporary Dance in Chapeltown.

Nadine started off charging 20p or 30p a class. She was planning to start a kids' class but no one turned up for it, so I was allowed in with the older students even though I was only nine at the start. I was Nadine's favourite for a long time. 'I'd like Melanie to come to my dance college when I set it up,' she'd tell my mum. I went to Sacred Heart twice a week for years. It was brilliant because we used to dance to the rhythm of live bongos. Since it was contemporary dance, we were encouraged to be as expressive and creative as we wanted.

I also loved acting, but the lessons were very expensive. When we were ten, Sherrel and me had private classes at a drama school in Headingley for about a year (after which my mum said that she couldn't afford them any more). Instead, I used to do role playing in front of the mirror. I'd make myself cry, then comfort myself. 'Stop crying,' I'd say in a gentle voice before I went into another role – happy, angry, shocked, scared, basking in adulation. I'd sit there for what seemed like hours, talking away to myself, loving every minute.

During the Easter holidays we entered a competition together. I did a solo turn – Coco the Clown – then me and Sherrel acted out a scene in which we had a big argument. In the course of the argument one of us threw down a cup that was supposed to smash on the ground. Ingeniously Mum cut up a plastic cup and stuck it loosely together with

Sellotape, so that when you threw it, it appeared to break.

Bernie and my mum giggled hysterically throughout our scene, not because they found it funny, but because they were so nervous for us. Now Bernie used to get a bit panicky and flustered and by the end of our performance she was in the middle of a full-on freak out and had to leave the room. Something always had to happen when those two got together. Sometimes I'd take friends home and my mum and Bernie would be dressed up, embarrassingly, in my dancing competition outfits, things like my Hungarian beaded dress. How painful for me to see that! Life was never dull.

As my love of dance and drama increased, my interest in school began to go a bit downhill. When I was nine there was a crisis in the teaching profession and a long string of NUT strikes disrupted my school life no end. I've got a lot of sympathy for teachers and I believe that the value of teaching is frighteningly underrated, but the strikes meant that I never seemed to have a full week at Kirkstall Road Primary, which didn't do my education a lot of good.

My dad used to take me training to prepare me for sports day. We'd get dressed up in sports gear, drive down to the common next to West Yorkshire Television and play running games and football. He really pushed me; it was like a scene out of junior *Chariots of Fire* or something. 'Come on Melanie, you can do it, you can make it! Go!' As a result I used to win everything on sports day. It was brilliant.

But around this time my dad's attitude to me began to change. He had always been quite strict but almost overnight he switched off the emotional/affectionate side that I took for granted and turned into a grim disciplinarian. Suddenly rules replaced cuddles. I can only speculate as to why this was because my dad's never given me a logical explanation for the sudden change. I think I was probably at an age when I started thinking for myself, questioning my parents' decisions and answering back to them, so maybe my dad had a sense of control slipping away from him – and he likes to be in control. My mum has suggested that, as Danielle and I began to grow up, he became scared of losing us.

He partly blames his West Indian upbringing. Having total respect for your parents is a big part of his culture and it was instilled in him from an early age, so of course he tried to pass it down to us. He was also very fearful that unless he was strict with us, we'd go off the rails and end up hanging around on street corners, snogging boys and smoking fags. What's more, he thought that Mum was too soft with us and tried to compensate by being overly controlling. He began to lay down all kinds of rules and regulations. Don't come downstairs unless you're fully dressed. No eating in the front room. Bed by a certain time, to the minute. Friends have to call at the gate and are not allowed in the house. And on and on.

You even had to wash up a certain way: knives and forks first, then little plates followed by big plates and finally you had to soak the pans.

It was like being in the army 'You HAVE to have your breakfast before you go to school!' It didn't feel like I had to have my breakfast to give me energy or strength. It was just, 'You have to have your breakfast!' as though we'd signed some kind of breakfast contract.

There was no flexibility in his world. If I were watching a film that finished at 9.05 p.m., I wouldn't be allowed to stay up for the extra five minutes beyond my bedtime at 9 p.m. My mum often had to watch the end of *Dallas* and *Dynasty* and update me in the morning because I couldn't be the only person in my class who didn't know what the final cliffhanging moment of the episode had been.

If I did something wrong in front of my mum, she would explode and often smack me there and then. With my dad there was never a spontaneous reaction, it would be next Wednesday after school at 6 p.m. 'Remember what you've just done because you're going to get punished for it next week!' he'd threaten.

The anticipation was worse than the punishment. I hated the days leading up to it. I knew exactly what was coming. I'd walk into a silent room, bend over, get smacked (by his hand or a belt), then stand up and walk out of the room without saying a word. Sometimes he used to count the smacks out loud because if I was naughty twice in a week I'd get a double dose. It was so cruel, yet strangely matter-of-fact.

Amid the frantic whirlwind of life and work I still sometimes wake up in a sweat, thinking, What am I supposed to be doing today? It's that same feeling of anxiety that I experienced in the lead-up to getting smacked. I used to open my eyes with a sinking heart, thinking, I've got four/three/two more days to go. I dreaded it. Sometimes, though, I think I was naughty on purpose, just to get my dad's full attention for a few minutes.

All a little girl wants is for her father to say to her, 'You're fantastic and wonderful!' I wanted mine to be proud of whatever I was good at and I was constantly seeking his approval, but I didn't get it until years later. (Even to this day I'll look to my mum for reassurance and get it, but I won't ask my dad for his opinion because I want it to come from him first. When he does praise me, it brings me close to tears.) Unfortunately as I grew older, he became very critical and rarely praised me for anything. He was only interested in education. In fact he was obsessed with education – again, the product of a traditional West Indian background, I think.

'You have to get As, Bs and Cs in everything,' he insisted. 'You have to. If you don't, I'm going to stop your dancing classes.' I was constantly on the edge, thinking, Sh**, I don't really care about my education. I just want to dance. I was above average at school, but not brilliant, and I sensed his disappointment at that. Now he says, 'I wish I'd been more behind you in your dancing because that's what's made you.'

My parents were rarely in agreement about me. My mum would tell me one thing and my dad would tell me another. I'd say, 'Well, no, my mum said . . .' and he'd say, 'Well, whatever your dad says goes.' My mum would make a face behind his back, as if to say, 'It's not my fault, it's him.'

In contrast my mum was a pushover. My dad's strictness was a nightmare for all of us and when he wasn't around – out on the night shift – there were no rules, although she never let us take things too far.

She had her foibles too. We had to suck, not crunch, our crisps while we were watching TV. 'It's irritating when you've got two kids munching crisps on either side of you while you're trying to concentrate!' she'd complain. But she was still a million times more relaxed than my dad was. We went to bed when we were tired, not at a set time. We'd act out plays and sing and dance and generally have a bloody good laugh. Mum enjoyed being with her children.

She thinks my dad's problems stemmed from his difficult childhood; he also had no idea how to deal with his daughters as they were growing up. Putting tight controls on us seemed the most sensible option at the time but it was totally counterproductive.

Back then there were a lot of Asians and black people living in Leeds, but hardly anyone was mixed race. So a lot of people didn't know whether to call me and Danielle 'nigger' or 'paki'. It was like, 'Well, what are you, then? You're light-skinned, your eyes are different, you've got a European nose, your lips aren't the typically stereotyped full lips, your hair's different, so what are you?'

'Well, I'm a bit of both. I've got the best of both worlds,' I'd say hesitantly, remembering my mother's explanation.

My mum says that Danielle had it the worst, because she didn't have any mixed race friends, whereas I had Sherrel. Sherrel and me looked almost like twins, so at least I had someone I could identify with, but I still got chased home from Kirkstall Middle School aged eleven and twelve. Literally chased home, and it was a good fifteen-minute walk. The other kids wanted to batter me because of the colour I was, but I didn't fully understand that at the time.

'Why can't you go down to the school and complain?' I'd ask my mum and dad.

Whenever I got home, totally exhausted and out of breath, my dad would say, 'No, you fight your own battles,' and mum would say, 'No, you fight your own battles.' I suppose it taught me how to stand up for myself. Everybody else's parents used to go and complain if their Tom got a flicked eyelash at school while there I was running home shouting, 'Quick! Shut the door now!' thinking, Why won't anyone stick up for me? Eventually I realised I had to do it for myself and since then I always have.

But I think that if I were a parent in a similar situation, I would confront the issue head-on with the teacher or head-teacher. Bullying shouldn't ever be tolerated. To be fair, though, like anorexia, it's a much hotter topic these days than it was when I was at school.

I was lucky that my parents were so cool about race when I was growing up. They respected each other's cultures and mixed them and were happy about it, which was rare. They taught me always to respect both black and white people. I've since noticed that mixed race kids can get really confused if their parents sway one way or the other and are prejudiced against white or black, because they become alienated from one side or the other.

It's difficult, because you've got your black communities and you've got your white communities. There are black churches, white churches, Jewish, Buddhist, Muslim and other places of worship, but you don't get anything officially for mixed race people.

I'm not saying that being mixed race is a defined culture and has a history – well, it has got a history but it's been taboo for a long time, because society has always been so divided. For centuries, mixed race children were mainly associated with being products of rape, the result of forced encounters between masters and slaves on plantations. They were ignored, their existence was brushed under the carpet and they were part of a forgotten history. Things have changed now. We're starting to mix more and you get people who are a quarter this, a half that and a quarter something else, which is great. The only problem is that there are a lot of kids growing up who don't feel they belong anywhere. Their identity isn't black or white.

I had problems knowing where I fitted in sometimes. I had black friends and I also had white friends and some of my black friends would be completely on the black side dissing the whites, while some of my white friends were completely on the white side and didn't really know anything about the history of black culture. They had no idea about all the suffering that had gone on.

I was different to the other mixed race kids at school because I never chose one side over the other. I got on with everyone, and as a result I was called 'Bounty' – black on the outside, white on the inside. I remember thinking, Why are they calling me that? My parents had black friends and white friends and I spent time with my mum's family and my dad's family, so my life was properly mixed, even down to the music I heard at home – from Aswad to the Eurythmics.

Whenever I went round to Black Grandma's house I'd clean all the posh china and glass in her cabinet before going up to the attic to try on her old clothes. I was her first grandchild and felt privileged to be allowed to go through her stuff and my dad's old things. That attic was a room full of memories that Grandma could not let go. She's a hoarder like me. I've got everything from way back in my attic as well.

Black Grandma and Grandad lived in a huge five-storey terraced house in Chapeltown. They had some strange lodgers there over the years. One of them was always coming downstairs for a nip of brandy.

They had a bedroom on the ground floor equipped with a tin pot to wee in. Their reasoning was that you couldn't go upstairs every time you wanted a wee at night. You'd just do it in the pan and chuck it away in the morning. They didn't think there was anything strange about this at all. Their front room, which looked out onto the street, had all the fancy furniture in it. With plastic covers on, of course.

Grandma was very into religion and praying. If you swore or said something untoward about someone she'd say a prayer for you there and then. 'Oh my God, bless your heart, praise the Lord!'

I have very happy memories of sitting in their kitchen, watching TV on the knackered television while Grandad popped in and out and Grandma prepared the meals. They had very traditional gender roles. In West Indian culture the man's job is to bring home the money. The moment he hands it over to his wife his job is done – she does everything else, from paying the rent to cooking, cleaning and looking after the children.

Grandad was a taxi driver and always had a twinkle in his eye. He's a looker, often complimented on his young appearance. To this day he's so chic, almost too chic and trendy. His hair is always perfect. He was a bit of a partygoer, a hardcore liver of life who worked hard and played hard. He enjoyed his dominoes at the Mandela Centre and drank his whisky, brandy and rum straight. He's a great talker. I was always enchanted by his stories.

Grandma was the sensible one who ran the household and kept everything together. My dad found her intimidating but I remember her laughing a lot. One morning I rushed into her bedroom and jumped up and down on the bed while she and Grandad were just waking up. Mid-bounce I noticed Grandma chuckling to herself. 'So crazy!' she was whispering. 'You're so crazy!'

Chapeltown is a close-knit community. I was never Melanie, I was 'the granddaughter of Iris and Jim, the daughter of Wingrove.' (Without fail Grandma called my dad by his middle name, her mother's surname.)

I loved going to Grandma's because I could snitch on my dad and watch him get into trouble. He seemed terrified of his mum. Usually he was silent on the bus to her house, almost as if he was preparing himself. All the while I'd be thinking, I'm going to get him into trouble today!

'Do you know what my dad's done?' I'd start off. Then I'd half make something up or exaggerate on the truth. It would usually be something petty like, 'He went to my open night and one of the teachers complained about me and he didn't stick up for me even though he knew I'd got an A in that subject.'

'I say Wingrove!' she'd call. 'Come into d'kitchen and wash up.'

Behind the kitchen door she'd go into one, not just about me but harping back to her favourite subjects – his life and education and how she's brought him up not to be like that with his children and how she expects him to lead the way. She'd be cursing and speaking really fast while my dad stood in front of her with his head bowed. I didn't understand a word she said, I just thought it was funny, although I now realise that it must have caused Dad a lot of pain. It was the only chink in his armour though, the one way I could pay him back for the way he treated me. Ironically it probably just made him worse.

In a way it's strange that he went on to be such a disciplinarian. After having such a difficult time with his own mother and rebelling against all her rules and regulations, you'd have thought he'd have learned a lesson from it and tried to be a bit more relaxed when he came to be a parent himself. Instead, he was as strict and unemotional as she had been. I hated it.

4

YOU DON'T KNOW ME

If you talked to my teachers, they'd say I was a rebel at school without mentioning that I could do two things at once. I could be sitting there having a good gossip in class while listening in to the lesson at the same time. If the teacher asked, 'Melanie, what have I just said?' I'd be able to tell him exactly. 'Right then, er, stop talking!' he'd mutter, going back to the lesson.

Intake High School, where I started when I was thirteen, was in the middle of an estate in quite a rough area. I went there because it offered a Dance Drama Music strand to about thirty pupils in each year and that's all I was really interested in. I'd done well at Kirkstall Middle School but my grades went down in most subjects at Intake High. I did well in art, music, dance and drama though.

I loved English. I had a great imagination and was good at writing stories. As for everything else . . . I enjoyed reading, but I was never into maths. History fascinated me. Science did too, mostly when we did experiments and I blew up test tubes and set things on fire. Apart from that lessons were boring.

I spent a lot of my free time in the music room playing the drums. You had to book the drum kit in advance and stick to your allotted time. Once I turned up for a session to find a girl in there, practising a complex drum roll. I waited for her to finish, but she kept right on playing. She was eating into my time! Well I wanted to get on the drums so badly that I tapped her on the head with my drumstick. 'Get off the drums now, it's my turn!' Of course she couldn't resist tapping me back and within seconds we were in a full-on drumstick fight in the corridor. By the time it was over I'd missed my slot altogether.

On my first day at Intake High I bumped into Rebecca Callard, who I knew vaguely from Jean Pearce. We clicked immediately and became best friends forever more. (Sherrel and I got into separate crowds but we were still really good friends, almost like sisters.) Rebecca and I are definitely soulmates. From the start we seemed instinctively to know what the other one was thinking and our lives have followed a very similar pattern. We don't have the kind of friendship where we call each other up every day, but we are always there for each other when there's a crisis. We're totally on the same level and always have been. It's almost as if we know each other from a past life – or several past lives. There's a very strong connection between us.

Rebecca was small and gorgeous like a little doll, with lovely brown curly hair. The first thing we noticed about each other was that we both had our hair down with a clip on one side. It was a sign! After that we'd call each other in the morning and decide how we were going to wear our hair that day. We were both Gemini. Coincidence! Before long we were joined at the hip.

How you were going to look each day was a big deal. Our uniform was a burgundy V-necked jumper and a matching stripey tie, white shirt and black skirt or trousers. I wore trousers mostly, although I went through a short skirt phase for a while. Because it was a performing arts school, you were allowed to express yourself a little bit. I remember wearing bright orange lipstick with black eyeliner around my lips and a bright orange denim jacket over my red school jumper. That was nothing compared with some of the others. There was a girl in my class who looked like Tina Turner, she must have used a can of hairspray every morning. Her hair was really punky and I'm surprised that she didn't get picked on more than she was. Then again, she looked hard and she was hard.

A lot of the hard girls didn't like me or Rebecca and they targeted us all the time. Some of them took against Rebecca because she'd been on telly and in films like *Scab* and *Will You Still Love Me Tomorrow?* When her mother got a part in *Coronation Street* the jealousy intensified. We hung out with Sherrel and her gang a bit – Susan, Deslyn, Nicola, Sarah and Samantha – but there was a lot of 'I'm not talking to her' bollocks that went on within the group. My dance partner (and best friend when Rebecca and me fell out) was called Kerry; she had ginger hair and massive boobs. She was tall and freckly and wore lots and lots of sovereign rings. All the guys really fancied her.

At Christmas me and Rebecca bought each other exactly the same presents because we always wanted the same things. One year it was an eye shadow kit full of greens and pinks and purples, another year it was Benetton perfume. We went through a phase when we didn't wear any make-up, apart from lip gloss, so no prizes for guessing what we bought each other that Christmas. We were like two peas in a pod and went everywhere together.

When Rebecca started smoking she told me I should try it. I resisted for ages but curiosity got the better of me in the end. We used to hide our fag butts under the pot-pourri basket at her mum's house and when her mum found out we got a right telling off. To be honest I didn't enjoy it much and soon gave up. Unfortunately I took it up again later and although I don't smoke much, it's definitely a habit I could do without.

I liked Mr Connell's contemporary classes. He was a 'Feeeeel the movement through your arms,' kind of a teacher. From time to time he let me take the class to give me a chance at choreography. It was great. I got to try out something new and boss everybody around at the same time.

When I dislocated the patella in my knee in Mr Connell's class and an ambulance arrived to take me away, I was at that age when all I was worried about was looking cool. That wasn't easy as I screamed at the paramedics, 'Just put it back in! Now!' or when I later hobbled through the playground in my little skirt, with a plaster cast on my leg (we call them 'pots' in the North). I could still do the splits though. Coincidentally Rebecca dislocated her patella a couple of weeks after I'd hurt mine. (Another sign!)

Rebecca's mum and my mum had similar values and we weren't allowed to go out much when we were fourteen – never during the week and only occasionally to parties. We can only remember going to one party back then. I think we were allowed to go because we both had pots on – and you can't get up to much with a virtually wooden leg, or so our mums thought.

We turned up to the party wearing matching outfits (planned days in advance of course). As a tribute to Neneh Cherry I wore a black rugby shirt with stripes – Rebecca's was lime green – and jogging bottoms. On my feet were blue Travel Fox trainers; Rebecca was wearing green Filas with orange laces. Cool, man. We both had our hair up in pineapples, with carefully arranged curly strands dangling down.

You've probably guessed that it was around that time that Neneh Cherry's 'Buffalo Stance' video was out! Rebecca was also a mad Bros fan and wore a hideous leather jacket and Grolsch bottle tops fixed between the shoelaces on her shoes. I was more of a Neneh Cherry/Tracy Chapman fan, and later Bobby Brown. I loved Whitney Houston too. In my bedroom at night I wrote down and learned every single word of the songs on Whitney's first album.

We were going out with identical twins at the time – Andy Wilkinson (me) and Tony (Rebecca). Since we weren't allowed out much, we mainly went over to their house on Sunday afternoons. It was all very innocent – holding hands and stuff – we weren't the kind of girls you'd find snogging behind the bike sheds.

Back to the party – I don't know where Andy and Tony were but we were in the kitchen being blabbed at by an irritating guy called Mark. He was so annoying that after a while Rebecca picked up an egg, held it above his head and threatened, 'If you say that again I am going to smash this egg over your head.'

Well the outcome was inevitable from that moment. Mark said it again. Rebecca smashed the egg on his head. Mark went berserk.

Me and Rebecca clonked up the stairs, gagging with laughter but desperate to get away from Mark, while he chased us furiously, swearing and shouting like a maniac, with yolk dripping from his nose. When he caught up (it didn't take long) he pulled both of us downstairs by the hair. That put us off parties for a while.

After the cast came off I was prescribed a course of physiotherapy. I looked forward to the physio sessions every Saturday at the local hospital in Leeds because they were full of footballers in tiny shorts. (Of course I made sure that I wore the shortest shorts of all.) A couple of weeks later my dad started going with me because he had really bad knees from playing football. That put paid to most of my flirting opportunities unfortunately.

Intake High was really well known for its musicals but me and Rebecca were never given good parts. We were both in the chorus of *Godspell* with two lines each to sing. Mine were 'You are the salt of the earth, you are the salt of the earth' and I'd usually try to get a muffled 'Ragamuffin!' in there somewhere. Rebecca's lines were, 'You are the city of God, you are the city of God.' Although we didn't do much, we had to stand on stage throughout the whole show. You can see us in the official school video, chatting happily away at the back for the full ninety minutes.

Most of my teachers didn't seem to know the meaning of the word support. One teacher was from Birmingham. He told me I'd never go anywhere because my mouth was too loud. 'You'll amount to nothing Melanie Brown!' another teacher said. I needed to be encouraged, not put down, if I was going to do well. It's a real pity that I wasn't. My mum was the only person who said, 'Go and make something of yourself. You can do it.' She always believed in me.

I was convinced that one particular teacher was picking on me so my mum confronted him when she went to open night. As soon as she sat down and he saw her name badge, he slumped in his chair and sighed, 'Oh, Melanie Brown!'

'Melanie thinks you pick on her,' said my mum. 'You always shout at her whether or not it's her who's causing trouble. She says that every time you go into the classroom you tell her off and send her out.'

He thought about it for a couple of minutes, then said, 'I can't help it. As a teacher you automatically shout at the loudest child, the one you can hear from the corridor. Sending the loudest one out shuts the rest of them up. Unfortunately Melanie is always the loudest. In that respect it might seem like I'm picking on her . . .'

It was a fair point but it was still unfair on me.

I didn't find my teenage years very easy. As I matured, I began to feel more and more detached. I suppose it was the usual teenage thing – feeling totally alone, misunderstood and isolated, with no one to answer my questions or help me through the massive changes that propel you into adulthood. Your parents don't really communicate with you, apart from saying 'Eat your dinner!' and 'Do the washing up!' Life seemed increasingly boring and meaningless.

I felt disconnected. I couldn't accept that being alone with your thoughts is a fact of life. Now I understand that you can share your thoughts and feelings with somebody, you can explain yourself until you're blue in the face, but at the end of the day even when somebody's on your wavelength you are actually alone with what you think and what you feel.

I was still asking endless questions. 'Where would we be if we weren't all here?' 'What if we wanted to go and live on the moon?' 'How do I get to a star?' 'Is there a different world somewhere?' 'What would happen if we died and where would we go?'

The universal answer was, 'Shut up!'

The older and more complicated I became, the less attention I got, partly because I had a younger sister. Danielle and I had that kind of love-hate relationship going on, that sisterly tension. She used to do my head in. She was always hanging around my door saying, 'I'm going to get you told off, Melanie.'

I wasn't very nice to her, either. I used to strangle her and give her Chinese burns and tie her to chairs. My mum had to get a babysitter in even when I was old enough to look after Danielle myself. The babysitter was more of a bodyguard than a childminder. I was in trouble a lot of the time and I'd have to bribe Danielle not to tell Dad. You couldn't tell Dad anything for fear of being punished.

By now I was often getting grounded, which meant that I couldn't have friends round, couldn't watch TV in my room, couldn't answer the phone and had to go straight to my room after tea and stay there. Alone in my room I'd write and write and write – really heavy, intense stuff. When you read it back, it's quite intelligent, but it's a bit like you're on a trip. I've got all my old diaries, from when I was about twelve up until the present, and I still write about how I'm feeling when I'm in the mood. It's a good way to express your innermost thoughts, sort out your head and begin to understand yourself.

I spent a hell of a lot of time in that bedroom. As I grew up I slowly but surely began to be excluded from the adult goings on. I'd be sent up to bed when friends came round to see my mum and dad at night, which was annoying because when I was younger I'd been allowed to join in. Now, because I understood so much more, I wasn't wanted. I didn't like it. I'm an adult, I thought, but they're treating me like a kid. It just added to my sense of isolation.

I know my dad loved me but at the time he just didn't show it. He didn't express his emotions at all, as far as I could see. It was just, 'Don't do this, don't do that, you're grounded!' The rules multiplied; he became stricter by the minute. I often found myself chanting I hate you, I hate you, under my breath. But I had very mixed feelings about him because as much as I hated him I obviously loved him too. He was my dad.

Sometimes I felt incredibly sorry for him. I'd cry my eyes out as I watched from the window as he put on his cagoule and rode his bike to the welding factory in the pouring rain or snow. 'My dad's got to cycle forty minutes to work,' I'd sob, racked with pity.

Like my dad, my mum was working really hard. She held onto the same job at C&A for eighteen years, and also took on extra work to pay for mine and Danielle's dancing classes, cleaning loos in an old people's home. She said that it was worth it because dancing wore us out and kept us out of trouble, but it meant that she wasn't around as much as I would have liked. When she was there, she was knackered a lot of the time.

To make things worse, I fell out with Rebecca in my second year at Intake High. It was that girls ganging-up thing that set it off. Someone goaded me into saying something bitchy to her in the toilets – neither of us can remember exactly what it was – and it really annoyed her.

'How can you say that Melanie?' she shouted, pushing me hard against a wall.

I was shocked. We'd argued before but it had never got physical.

'That's it! I'm not talking to you,' I shouted back and stormed off. We didn't say a word to each other for seven months after that. It was awful and depressing, but we were both too proud to back down.

A couple of weeks later I got into really big trouble at school. I feel ashamed of what I did to this day. Some other girls and I composed a filthily obscene poison pen letter and addressed it to this weird boy we used to see around. He was special needs and found it hard fitting in, so it was particularly nasty of us to pick on him. I guess we spotted his vulnerability and took advantage of it. Kids can be so cruel. Some of the worst things a person will ever do take place at school. It's there that we learn right from wrong and test out our moral boundaries, I suppose, but I still feel guilty about the things we put in that letter.

Well, a teacher found it and confiscated it and we were sent home. It was so bad that the head was even thinking about expelling us. I was totally panic-stricken. What was my dad going to say? Later in the day my mum and dad were summoned to the school. My dad had to change shifts at the last minute and my mum took the afternoon off work. It couldn't have been much worse.

My dad was so, so angry when he got back home. 'Can you imagine us reading that filth in front of your teachers?' he asked me repeatedly. He went on and on about it, wiping the floor with me. I hung my head in shame. I had nothing to say in my defence. I was grounded for a month.

I'd never been in trouble like this before and I dreaded facing everyone at school. Stuck at home, I felt incredibly sorry for myself and started on a downward spiral of depression. Soon I found myself at such a low point that I couldn't see the point of carrying on.

I don't know where the idea of taking an overdose came from. I just know that I planned it for two or three weeks in advance. My dad would do the shopping on a Friday – when he got his pay cheque and the fridge was empty – and he always bought Anadin or paracetamol. This Friday he bought Anadin Plus, which was the strong version. (I didn't know it at the time, but later I found out that headache pills are the worst things you could possibly try and kill yourself with. They make your insides bleed and it's a horribly slow, painful death.)

I had to plan it because it would look strange if I took all the Anadin out of the cupboard at once. I nicked a few at a time and then that Friday I nicked the whole packet, to add to the bits I'd saved from the weeks before.

I was fourteen when it happened. I felt misunderstood. I wanted to escape from my bedroom, that house, that family, world and life. I didn't dislike myself, I just thought, This place would be so much better off without me because all I seem to do is cause aggravation, upset and chaos. I thought that it would give everyone a break if I wasn't around. I wanted to be free. I felt like an alien. I didn't think my parents would be sad when I'd gone. Well, maybe deep, deep down I thought they would, but I didn't acknowledge that until recently. I blocked the whole thing out for years.

What I remember most about the overdose is looking at myself in the mirror, taking the pills one by one, tears trickling down my cheeks, swallowing my sobs. Freaky or what? I gazed at myself as I took each pill, but this wasn't another role play, it was real. I'd already written my note.

Just two weeks old with White
Grandad. We had an incredible
bond until the day he died.

August 1977. Back in the days when
I was a good little girl.

What a lovely 'fro.

Some things never change!

Trying to suffocate my sister
with love on our tasteful
1970s sofa.

Although we lived in quite a
rough part of Leeds, there was
such a sense of community spirit that we always felt safe playing out in the street.

What a poser! My trendy glasses had a purpose too – to cover one of
my many eye infections.

Carry On Camping: one of our annual holidays to Wales.
Always eventful, sometimes disastrous!

Three of my aunties –
identical bodies, identical hats,
but individually insane.

Big Uncle Barry's
burying game.

Say hello to my aunties!

Mum and her best friend being normal for once.

Me, Sherrell and two identical cheesy grins.

The Hair Bear Bunch pose for a once-in-a-lifetime photo opportunity at The Bonnie Langford Show studios.

Can you spot me? Clue: I'm the one without the horrific make-up.

Me, Danielle and Carly: luckily we were all winners that day.

1988, Skegness – one of those memorable trips away with my dancing class.
My friend Charlotte is in the back row, second from right.

I couldn't get enough of dancing. By the time I was nine
I was going to five classes a week. Here I am halfway through
a balletic fish dive, wondering if I'm about to be dropped!

I don't really remember what it said, but my dad says it wasn't self-pitying or blaming. It was just, 'I don't like school. I don't like my friends. I hate my dad and he doesn't understand me. It's best if I get rid of myself.'

I climbed onto the top bunk, where I always slept, and lay there thinking, That's it, all over. Any moment now I am going to die. That's great, I'll just close my eyes. And I gradually drifted into unconsciousness . . .

Only that night my mum happened to have a frigging headache – thank God she did. She went to look in the cabinet for the headache tablets and they were all gone, so she came straight into my room and said, 'Melanie, are you all right?'

'No, mum,' I said, 'I feel sick. I've taken some tablets.'

The next thing I remember was literally being pulled off the top bunk bed by the neck of my pyjamas, half-unconscious, dragged down the stairs by my screaming panic-stricken mum and into an ambulance, while my dad shouted, 'Get her out of this house! She's insane! Don't let her come back until she's normal.' I vomited all the way to the hospital and when I got there, I remember having this thin tube rammed down my throat, *rammed*, and them forcing me to be sick again. I spewed up pill after pill after pill. I don't think my dad was there, but my mum was at the end of the bed saying, 'Why have you done it? How could you?' I half-remember hitting one of the nurses too. What is it with me and nurses?

Later on, I woke up to see all my schoolteachers around my bed – and that freaked me out. I thought, 'What the f*** . . .?' then turned over and went back to sleep in the hopes that they'd disappear.

The weirdest thing was that when I went back to school after a couple of weeks off, it wasn't spoken about. All the teachers were like, 'We know what's happened to you Melanie, but shhh!' It was really strange. Nobody talked about it and I couldn't understand why. I went to counselling a couple of times on my own. It didn't help because I was at the age where I gave short sullen answers like, 'Well, I just hated myself and I wanted to do it.' Nobody bothered to look into it. I think that my parents were just too scared to explore it. The incident was locked away, by everyone, and inevitably I did the same. I've only just recently started talking about it and addressing it. Interestingly, the first time I actually went into it in depth, my eye infection instantly started up again. It's hard to say why, it may not even have been connected, but I think it could have been because I'd bottled it up for so long that letting it out caused a physical reaction.

Let me get this straight. There wasn't a deep and underlying reason for taking an overdose. I wasn't abused or beaten or treated badly. I just wanted to get away. It was pure teenage angst, the kind that everybody experiences. Nobody understood me, I was pissed off with it, nobody was on my wavelength, I had all these questions and nobody was answering any of them, the world was boring – nothing was happening. 'Shut up!' or 'Stop talking stupid,' were the only answers I got to my questions.

My dad really did think I was going insane. I don't think he could comprehend why his daughter would do something like that to herself. Instead of trying to understand it, he just wrote it off as the action of someone who was mentally ill. In his mind, there couldn't be any other reason. 'You can't be unhappy, you're just insane.'

My mum was devastated. She asked to see a doctor and couldn't stop crying. To some extent he put her mind at rest. 'Do you realise how many teenagers do this? So many! I can assure you that she will not do it again,' he told her. He was right.

I know that my mum and dad still carry the blame and burden of my overdose. Now that I'm older I don't blame them for it at all. I just regret that they didn't try to talk to me about it afterwards. Everyone blanked it out like it never happened, and so I did too. Life carried on. I didn't even think along those lines again. I was a positive person basically. It wasn't like I was a clinically depressed kid or had bad psychological problems. It was just a phase I went through.

The whole thing has stuck with my mum and dad far more than it's stuck with me. I want to say to them, 'It's not your fault. It was obviously something to do with you, but you're not the reason why I did it. I was unhappy within me. Yes, you could've helped, but at the end of the day I would still have done what I did.' But they just feel pure blame and guilt. It's understandable, really.

The advice I'd give to someone who feels like I did at fourteen would be to acknowledge your feelings, then try to put them to one side and carry on. Try and remember back to how you felt before you got depressed and keep hold of that feeling. Don't home in on your unhappiness, keep yourself occupied and try to stay as sane as possible. It won't last forever. Even if it feels like your whole world is falling down and you'll never rebuild it, you've got to believe that things will work out in the end. They always do.

Taking an overdose was a real turning point for me because once you've been through something like that and come out the other side, you never let yourself get like that again, no matter what happens. I learnt self-worth from it, just by stripping everything away and being left with nothing. So even though it was a bad thing, something good came out of it. In one respect I think I was incredibly stupid, but then again I wouldn't be the person I am today if I hadn't tried it, because everything that's happened to me in my life is character-building. Still, some people never return from overdoses and I was lucky. I could easily have died and that's a very frightening thought.

I know now that nothing is so serious that it's worth risking your life for, but I was so low then that I couldn't imagine what was ahead of me, didn't know that there was so much to see and so much to do. If I'd known what my life was going to be like I'd never have taken such a risk. I didn't realise that the way I felt was just a passing phase, a state of mind that you can snap yourself out of, instead of wallowing in it. I had tunnel vision and was very self-absorbed. It's only now that I think, God, I could have died and I would have missed all this.

5

FEEL ME NOW

By my early teens I was walking through the Welsh holiday town of Abersoch wearing nothing but a really sexy black bikini and little Kickers shoes.

It was a totally sleepy place. At night my cousin Joanna, Sherrel and me sometimes walked into the centre of town and hung out near the chip shop, just watching the world (what little there was of it) go by. We weren't into drinking so it was Cokes and Fantas, chips, scraps and baps. I didn't hang out on street corners in Leeds so it was a bit of a thrill to do it in Abersoch, however dull the action was.

One night we clocked a group of three boys. They were quite tasty, we agreed, so we smiled at them as they walked past. Five minutes later they walked past again.

'Hiya!' I ventured. Muffled giggles.

'What you doing?' Trying to be cocky.

'Eating chips, what does it look like?' Titters all round.

'What you doing after that?' Definitely not giving up.

'Going back to our campsite. Wanna come?' Hold your breath.

'All right then, why not.' Trying hard to be cool.

Yes! We've pulled.

Mine was a bit Chinese-looking and I fancied him immediately. Soon we were holding hands. The vibe between us was an electric teenage shockwave and the walk back to the site was beautiful. Hundreds of glow worms lit up the hedges along the way, which was very romantic.

Halfway there I told Sherrel, Joanna and their boys to walk on ahead. He started kissing me. The attraction was very physical. Within a couple of minutes we were lying in the middle of the road, cuddling and rubbing against each other madly. I don't think either of us really knew what we were doing, it just felt nice to be doing it. A lovely taste of things to come. After about half an hour rolling around on the ground we got up and went to join the others at the campsite.

Boys weren't a big thing for me then. My mum used to say, 'Have loads of boyfriends! As long as you don't have sex with them you can have ten boyfriends if you like and I'll cover your back for you.' So I did.

'Don't let them tell you what to do,' she'd say. She was so open, not about sex, but about the opposite sex, that I became almost a snob. I was like, 'Don't try and flirt with me or fancy me – I'll decide if I want to flirt with you.' It was a power thing, a Girl Power thing in fact.

Then came that teenage nightmare, oh yes, THE PERIOD! And guess where it happened? Just before I went on stage to perform in a dancing competition. I was too embarrassed to tell anyone about it, so I went through my mum's bag and nicked one of her Tampax. What a disaster. I tried to stuff it up in the loos but didn't really know how to do it. Unbeknown to me I walked out of there with half of it protruding, although I did wonder why it was so uncomfortable.

I was doing a song and dance – lots of kicks and turns – in a tight red leotard with red and white frills. It must have looked like I had very large labia! Afterwards my mum said to me, 'Have you got something to tell me?'

'No,' I answered, blushing bright red.

She knew.

Periods and family are a strange combination when you're a pubescent girl. I remember watching *Blue Lagoon* with my dad and feeling highly embarrassed during the scene where Brooke Shields gets her period in the sea, but Dad was very down to earth about things like that.

'Right, let's get your Lillets!' he'd say in the supermarket. I'd freeze with shame.

'Mum, can't you come shopping with us?'

'You know I don't do the shopping with your dad.'

Luckily I met quite a lot of older teenagers at the dancing classes at Sacred Heart. I made one really good friend there – Jason Pennycook – and we used to hang out together a lot. Sherrel and I called him Compass Head because he had a really round head. When his mother died my mum and dad took him under their wing and he practically came to live with us. He's a close family friend to this day.

My mum trusted Jason because he was a bit older than I was and she let me go to Teen Scene with him, a wicked under-eighteens club held at the massive Miriam Hall Centre. She allowed me out because she sensed that I'd be leaving home at sixteen and she wanted me to have a taste of freedom before I left. Otherwise, she thought, I'd go absolutely wild at the first possible chance. Charlotte and Sherrel also came to Teen Scene; my mum took us and picked us up. We had such a brilliant time there, dancing all night to tunes like Bobby Brown's 'My Prerogative'. Getting ready was one of the best bits. Charlotte, Sherrel and me would spend hours trying on clothes. It's funny, because I was always borrowing Charlotte's clothes back then, but nowadays it's the other way around.

I didn't have much money to spend on what I wore so my mum helped me make the best of what I had, by adding all kinds of special touches. When basques and hot pants were in she sewed little sequins down the side seams of my hot pants and made me a fully-sequinned basque. The basque was amazing and I wore it constantly. She also bought me a catsuit and attached lace behind the zip, so that it didn't just show my breasts when I unzipped it.

I've always loved outrageous clothes. I think that's why I don't get too affected by people staring at me now that I'm famous, because it's been like that since I was young. The way I laughed, what I wore or how I spoke, however loud or quiet it was, just seemed to attract attention. So when I go out today and my sister or a friend says, 'Do you realise that everyone is looking at you?' I'll go, 'Are they?' I've never been very aware of it. It hasn't fed my ego, I've never thought, 'Oh my God!' I don't react because in a way I'm used to it. People have always stared at me, either laughing at me or looking at my clothes – or it would just be, 'Oh it's that Melanie again.'

When I was fourteen I started wanting to go into town on Saturdays to hang around with my friends. My mum suspected that some of them were into 'pinching' so she said no. 'Instead, get a job in town. Then your friends can come to see you,' she suggested.

I lied about my age and got a Saturday job in a trendy jeans shop on the high street. (I said I was fifteen.) It was a very cool place with a DJ who played songs like 'Poison' and 'Humpty Hump' at top volume. I usually wore tiny frayed shorts, a tight top and my hair up in a ponytail with strands strategically hanging down.

When the manager was asked to put on a fashion show in a club for the late night TV show *Hitman and Her*, a leery beery live ladsfest that started at midnight, he in turn asked me to be one of the models. My heart leapt. Then it sank right back down to my red Wallabies. I knew Dad wouldn't allow it. It was past my bedtime, it was in a nightclub and I was underage. I couldn't do it on the sly because he regularly watched *Hitman and Her*. If he missed it, he taped it.

My mum said no straight away, even though she would probably have liked me to do it. There was no getting around her. I tried pleading but she wouldn't change her mind.

'Mum, I've been asked specially!'

'Melanie, you can't do it,' she argued. 'You're going to have to make up some excuse. There's no way your dad's seeing you on that programme.'

One major dilemma I had was that if I did say that I couldn't do it then I'd have to say why. I didn't want the people in the shop to know that I'd lied about my age. I couldn't say that I didn't want to be in the show because nobody would believe me.

'Sorry, my mum won't let me,' I admitted, highly embarrassed.

The manager rang my mum.

'Please reconsider. She'd look brilliant in the clothes.'

'I'm sorry but she can't,' said my mum abruptly. She felt sorry for me but there was nothing she could do.

On Thursdays and Saturdays, (but only when my dad was on night shift) me and Charlotte went to Warehouse, a funky R&B club in Leeds City Centre. My mum drove us and picked us up but obviously my dad had no idea that we were out. Just in case he came home unexpectedly I put my fake Cabbage Patch doll under the covers to make it look as though I was asleep in bed. Luby Lou had an oversized head and a nutbush, which made her the perfect double. She was my saviour and I actually began impersonating her. When my dad came in to say goodnight, I'd lie as still as a doll, in exactly the same position that Luby-Lou would be in when I was out.

When a boy came round my mum insisted that I kept my bedroom door open. Sometimes she'd warn him as he arrived, 'She's still a child and I want her to come downstairs tonight as a child.' How embarrassing is that?

I wasn't told sex was good or bad – I wasn't given any guidelines on the subject at all. Neither of my parents talked to me about when to do it, how to do it or who to do it with. All they implied was that if you're going to do it, respect it.

Well, I lost my virginity to a smooth-talking mixed race guy from Huddersfield, on a beanbag in my bedroom. 'You're not a virgin,' he challenged when I told him that I'd never had sex.

'I am!' I replied. 'I'll prove it to you if you want. Have sex with me and then you'll see it's true.'

One of my friends had described the first time she had sex as a hugely symbolic moment. 'I lay there and watched my virginity fly out the window.' In my own little fantasy I lay there and imagined a similar scenario. Apart from that I felt nothing, absolutely nothing.

Afterwards I said, 'See, I am a virgin, aren't I?'

But by then I obviously wasn't.

Oh how I wish I could turn back time and make the man who was going to take my virginity woo me with roses and run me hot lavender baths! (Obviously we would have been dating for months, maybe even years, before the momentous event.) But it didn't happen like that. Instead I was with a guy who had been lying to me about virtually everything. Not only did he already have a kid but he'd also got someone else pregnant while seeing me.

My next boyfriend was an older guy. He was really cool and had his own flat. Perhaps because he was older, he had more of a responsible attitude towards sex. He used to say to me, 'What do you say when someone wants to have sex with you without a condom?'

I'd reply, 'You say NO!'

Safe sex (i.e. condoms) was an important early lesson for me. From my work with the AIDS charity Blackliners I know that around a third of the people with HIV don't know that they've got it. Taking someone's word for it just isn't enough.

In those days I had a theory that everybody has an internal box of lights and numbers. Every so often you meet someone whose numbers 4, 5, 7, 28 and 29 go bzzzzzz at the same time as your numbers 4, 5, 7, 28 and 29 – and you connect. That was my explanation of why you get on a vibe with some people and not others. I hadn't heard about the possibility of having met someone in a past life, so I concluded that we're all programmed.

One night at Warehouse I was introduced to a tall fit lean guy with mesmerising eyes and a bald head, a better-looking version of Carl Lewis, the runner. I had that number-buzzing feeling as soon as he smiled and instantly knew that I was going to be with him. It was love at first sight, not with violins playing in the background, but with hot fiery passionate salsa beats.

Stephen was a reserve for Leeds United and took it all very seriously. He was fanatical about football. He was also a fantastic boyfriend – very caring and loving and up for a laugh. We had a lot of fun together and used to dare each other to do the stupidest things.

One day I dared him to put on one of my mum's outfits – a dress and jewellery and high heels – and walk down the street to the corner shop. He did it, for a laugh. He even let my mum and me slap make-up all over his face. When he came back from the shop, he calmly changed back into his clothes and joined in with the laughter. He was just great.

This was my first love and it was true love. Our relationship was absolute heaven. Stephen understood me, I understood him. We were on the same wavelength. Soon we were inseparable. Locked in each other's gaze and embrace we went everywhere together, did everything together. We got on well with each other's friends and shared a really good social life, mostly clubbing at The Gallery and Warehouse.

We had a great sex life and had sex all over the place, from the back of the late night bus to a market stall at midnight, with a little old tramp watching us. We'd drive to Rounday Park in Stephen's little car, have sex in the back, then drive home. Once we did it on the kitchen table while my mum was in the front room. There was only a partition wall between the two rooms and in a couple of steps she could have walked right in on us.

We were rampant. I remember one time in Stephen's bedroom when we were on the floor and I was on top of him. His mother stomped upstairs and tried to get into the room so I slammed my hands against the door and held it shut. We carried on as before. We didn't care.

'What you doing in there?'

'Go away, Mum!'

It wasn't all laughs though. Stephen was black and a lot of black people, particularly girls, would spit at him for going out with me. He got loads of stick from black and white people for going out with a mixed race girl. Back then, if you were a black man you'd either go out with a black woman or a white girl. Some of black girls hated mixed race girls and I got nasty comments all the time. I was called half-breed, half-caste and redskin, which were terms I really hated.

My mum and dad obviously knew I was having a full sexual relationship with Stephen, although they never said anything about it to me. It was a small house, however, and I couldn't help overhearing their conversations from time to time. Just before my mum took me to the doctor's to get the contraceptive pill I listened in on my mum and my dad in the kitchen.

'You're giving her a licence to have sex!' my dad was saying furiously.

'But she's with Stephen, we know his family, we know him, he's a nice guy, he's got a good job,' my mum replied soothingly.

I went to Stephen's house for dinner a lot, partly because of his mum. She was loving and caring and cuddly; she taught me how to wind and grind to reggae; but most of all she was the best cook that I've ever known. I didn't have much to compare her to, because my mum's cooking was terrible, but Stephen's mum's meals were always outstanding. Her macaroni cheese was the best I've ever had and as often as possible I went round on a Sunday for her West Indian chicken, rice and peas. She had a habit of sucking the bones of her curried goat at the end of a meal and loved the odd nip of brandy. We got on well and I still see her. The last time I went round there was in 1999. 'I know why you married that man. He resembles my Stephen!' she chuckled.

My mum rarely cooked. My dad made his own packed lunch and prepared a meal for the rest of us if he was going to be out on a shift at dinnertime. He often made what me and Danielle called 'army slop'. Oxtail soup with a tin of beans, bits of lamb or beef and a few potatoes or carrots would be called 'Beef Stroganoff' or beef stew. Our Sunday dinners came with oxtail soup gravy.

'I've done the gravy!'

'What, is it oxtail soup, Dad?'

'No, it's special gravy.'

At which point me and Danielle would sniff the air and say in unison, 'Aaaaah, oxtail soup!'

My mum would occasionally do something. She always cooked Christmas dinner and you could guarantee that she'd cry over it. At least one pan would be thrown out onto the lawn because it was burnt. The timing would all be wrong and the turkey would be ready long after the vegetables, until Danielle and I started helping that is. Then I'd do the starter – traditional prawn cocktail with thousand-island dressing and a lettuce garnish, perfectly presented – and the roast potatoes (one of my specialities).

Danielle was supposed to help me set the table, but I wouldn't let her. 'F*** off Danielle, I'm doing it!' It had to be exact and beautiful, even though I didn't know much about knives and forks and just piled loads on.

My mum made sure that Danielle and I were close to all of her family, especially at Christmas. She expected my dad to do the same with his but they've always been a little more distant. His oldest sister Kathleen emigrated to America when I was two so we didn't get to see much of her.

I felt very protective over my mum and I had the feeling that dad's younger sister Beverley, who had been born a couple of years after Dad came over from Nevis, didn't really like her. It seemed to me that she didn't think my mum was good enough for her brother. Now the Brown family rarely seem to say what they really feel or think, whereas I'm completely the opposite. So when Beverley came to one Christmas dinner and brought everybody a card apart from my mum, I wanted to know why.

I wasn't having it. It was all unspoken. Why didn't Beverley tell my mum why she hadn't brought her a card? Dad kept quiet. After two Babychams (all I was allowed) I questioned her and we got into a big argument. In the end I threw the money back that she'd given me in my Christmas card and stomped off.

I do blame my dad that I'm not close to his family. My mum made such an effort to get us camping with her side of the family and invited my dad's side of the family too. But you rarely get a team of black people camping. It's almost unheard of! I suppose that my dad wasn't close to his family in the way that my mum was close to hers, but he could have made a bit more effort to pull them in if you ask me.

By now my dad's rules were still getting me down so much that I spent as much time at Stephen's as possible to escape them. My mum often said to him, 'If you're not careful you're going to drive these kids out of the house and far away.'

You'd have thought he would have loosened up with his second child, but he just got worse. Danielle was grounded for almost all of her teens. I used to stick up for her when I was at home, but it didn't do a lot of good. One particular incident sticks in my mind. (Sorry Dad, but it's too funny to miss out!) Every September we had a new winter coat, which usually cost about £30. One year Danielle fell in love with a £50 coat from Top Shop.

'Please can I have it Dad?' she begged. 'please, please, please, please, please!'

After thinking about it my dad said, 'Well you can only have it if you wear it two years running.' Danielle wanted it so badly that she promised to wear it for two whole years.

A year later, as the nights drew in and it started getting cold, she realised that she'd gone off the coat from Top Shop. So she did a paper round, saved up some money and bought herself another winter coat. My dad wouldn't budge though. He insisted that she wear last year's coat to school, as agreed, from September through to March.

He seemed to take pleasure in catching her out. One day he actually cycled to her school to spy on her and find out what she was wearing. As expected, it wasn't the old coat. 'I'll see you when you get home,' he called from across the road before cycling off.

Danielle had to be home on the dot. My dad timed her. He knew that it took fifteen minutes to walk from the school bus to our house and if she was late, she'd be grounded again. She always had to come straight home even if she went straight out again.

My mum used to hide the old coat in the boot of her clapped-out car so that my dad wouldn't find it in the house when Danielle wasn't wearing it. On her way home from school one day my poor sister couldn't see my mum's car in our road. In a panic she rang Mum on her mobile from a phone box.

'Where are you?'

'Why, what's up?'

'I can't go home. You've got the coat in the boot!'

My mum had driven round to a friend's and forgotten all about the coat palaver.

On a Saturday afternoon around this time Mum and Dad went to buy some cement from Homebase. The shop assistant carried the two leaky bags of cement dust out to the car park for them.

'Can you open the boot of your car?' he asked my mum politely. As she went to unlock it she suddenly remembered that the coat was in there. If my dad saw it he'd go mad.

'Why don't you put them on the back seat?' she suggested.

'Are you sure about that, love?' asked the assistant, looking perplexed. 'They're very heavy and tend to make a bit of a mess.'

'I am sure about it, thank you. I want them in the back please.'

My dad thought it was really odd. 'Why don't you put them in the boot Andy?' he asked. 'They're going to mess up the back seats.'

'Oh I just think they'll be easier to get out of the back,' she trilled.

'Andy, are you thick? Just put them in the boot!' he snapped.

'I DO NOT WANT THEM IN THE BOOT. PUT THEM ON THE BACK SEAT!' she yelled.

The assistant shoved them hurriedly into the car and scurried off back to the shop. 'You're strange,' said my dad as the car pulled off. 'Even the bloke in the shop thinks you're strange.'

6

EVERYTHING HAPPENS
FOR A REASON

If at first you don't succeed, try, try, try again. For years I lived by my favourite proverb. Auditions were part and parcel of life and I spent a huge chunk of my teens to-ing and fro-ing to them. I'd turn up to try-outs for school plays, dance competitions (tap, ballet, character and duet), advert castings, auditions for shows and I even did a screen test for *Coronation Street*. (It was between four of us, including me and Angela Griffin, who was in the year below me at school. I'd heard that one of the reasons *Coronation Street* was looking for somebody of colour was because they'd had complaints from the public that the show was too 'white'. When I didn't get the part I decided that it was because I was darker than Angela, i.e. a bit too black! That argument went out of the window when I finally saw her on the show. She was – and is – a truly fantastic actress.)

I quickly developed a tough skin and most of the time I didn't mind whether I got a job or not. I just loved the whole experience of auditions. The frenzy generated by a whole load of girls fussing around, high on anticipation, was incredibly exciting. You'd have no idea of the routine you were about to learn, which group you'd be put into or what would happen next.

It was real panic stations for some people. You'd see them getting dry throats and mouths because they couldn't pick up or remember the steps. Sometimes they'd just make it up on the spot and you'd be watching them out of the corner of your eye, thinking, *What* are you doing? It was a buzz.

When it came to auditions it didn't matter whether I thought I was in with a chance or not, I just wanted to go, whatever my mum said. Once she tried to discourage me from going to an audition for *The Sound of Music* at the Leeds Grand Theatre, but I wouldn't have it.

'Melanie, there's no point.'

'Why?'

'You're not going to get it.'

'Why?

'You're the wrong colour.'

'No I'm not!'

I didn't have a clue what she was talking about. I could dance, I could sing. Where did colour come into it? 'I want to go to the audition!' I insisted.

'Okay,' agreed my mum, weakly.

She drove me there. I lined up. I did my routine and felt quite pleased with my performance. The judges weren't. When it was over I went to find my mum again.

'Mum, I haven't got it.'

'Well I told you that you wouldn't. They're all white with blonde hair! Never mind.'

The judges must have had a giggle that day. A mixed race Liesl Von Trapp? (Well we might see a multicultural *Sound of Music* one day, who knows!)

It was quickly forgotten about and a couple of months later Mrs Wood told the class about some auditions for a show in Blackpool over the summer. Lots of the girls she trained did the summer seasons and it was on my list of ambitions. I had a vision of myself on stage in Blackpool, dressed to the nines in a sensational outfit, all glitz and glamour and gorgeousness, wowing the crowd with my stunning moves. Right then it was my ultimate dream.

First of all, however, I had to get round my mum. There were just a few obstacles – the audition was on a school day, the dates of the job meant I'd have to miss the end of term, the rehearsals in Blackpool clashed with some of my GCSEs and at fifteen I was too young to sign an Equity contract. It was a long shot, in fact a miles-away-in-the-distance-practically-out-of-sight shot, but hey, why not give it a go?

I went to work on my mum.

'Melanie, you can't miss school with your exams coming up. Your dad would go mad.'

'Please Mum!'

'No, you're too young.'

'Please Mum!'

'You won't get it, you know.'

'You always say that. Please Mum!'

I wouldn't give up. Finally I convinced her that it would be really good experience for other professional auditions, if nothing else. The only reason she said yes in the end was to shut me up. Plus, I think she was convinced that I wouldn't get the job.

'Don't tell your dad,' were her final words.

Two weeks later Joanne, Mrs Wood's daughter, gave me a lift to Blackpool. Luckily my dad was on an early shift – hurrah! – so he didn't have a clue what I was up to.

Joanne parked the car in the Pleasure Beach car park directly opposite the Horseshoe Bar, where the audition was being held. From the outside it looked like a dingy little dive of a club, but you could see the Pleasure Beach rides round the back so it was quite exciting to be there. Upstairs, in a wide studio room with a wooden floor and mirrors lining the walls, there were about fifty girls. Some were changing and putting on make-up, others were warming up at the bar and a few were sitting around chatting. There was an unwritten rule about how you wore your make-up – thick eyeliner, lots of mascara and blusher and darkened eyelid sockets.

I felt privileged to be at the audition. I was the lucky one who'd been brought there by the dance teacher's daughter (Joanne knew the owner of the bar). I was also quite embarrassed and shy because everyone else was a lot older than I was.

We gathered on the T-shaped stage of the Horseshoe Bar. Just below the stage was a woman with long blonde hair, chunky thighs and an authoritative-looking face.

'Hi everyone, I'm Amanda. I'm overseeing the auditions today.'

We divided into groups and were shown some steps by the

choreographer. It was easy stuff and I picked the routine up really quickly. After about an hour Amanda called me over, unable to contain her excitement. 'She's great! She's great!' she said to the choreographer, almost as if I wasn't there. 'She's got pzazzz! She's got a tiny bum and her waist is the right size. We must employ her.'

I didn't know what to think. Did that mean I'd got the job or was she just being nice? I smiled, said nothing and waited. Ten minutes later Joanne sauntered up and whispered in my ear.

'You've got it!'

Wow.

My mum went into shock when she heard. She literally went white. It was the last thing she'd expected to happen and it totally threw her.

'You can't do it Melanie! You can't miss your exams. And what about starting college? You'll be missing the start of term.'

Oh yes, there was that added complication. Nadine had fulfilled her dream of setting up a dance college – the Northern School of Contemporary Dance in Chapeltown – and I'd been given a place there. Classes started in September, a full month before the summer season ended.

'But Mum, who cares? I'll be dancing in Blackpool!'

As it turned out, Amanda wanted me badly enough to fit around my schedule. She employed another dancer to stand in for the weeks before I left school and somebody else to take over in September, when I went off to college. She also overlooked the fact that I was still too young to sign a contract. All in all she bent over backwards to get me into her show. I was incredibly excited. This was the next best thing to getting a part in the West End and I was still only fifteen.

All I could think about was going to Blackpool, dancing every night and being independent. My GCSEs came second and although I worked hard and tried my best, my heart wasn't in it. I did well in Dance, Drama, Music and Art, but I missed a few of the other subjects because my mum was driving me to and from Blackpool for rehearsals. I wasn't really bothered about my results, however much my dad tried to put pressure on me. (I'm still not sure how many missed exams he actually knew about. It was a bit of a secret between my mum and me.) All I was bothered about was moving onto the next stage in my life to become a professional summer season dancer. It was a major break for me.

I left home on a clear sunny day in the first week of June. As I walked out of the house my dad sweetly said, 'If ever you want to come home, your bedroom is always here for you.' My mum and I packed up the car, Dad waved to me from the gate and off we went.

I wasn't leaving home permanently because at the end of the contract I'd be back home, but it felt like a major step all the same. It was the first time I'd be gone for any real length of time and escaping from my dad's rules would give me the chance to start living life my way, even if it was only for a few months.

My poor mum was upset though. To this day she blames Dad for driving me away from home so young. It was my choice to leave, but she thinks that if my dad hadn't been so strict I might not have been so desperate to go. She still confuses my ambition with the emotional crap that went on at home and doesn't understand that I would have wanted to leave anyway. This was the beginning of my career. My entire life so far had been leading up to this point and Mum's blue Polo couldn't get me to Blackpool fast enough.

One of the girls I met at the rehearsals had found me digs near the Pleasure Beach. Originally we were going to live together, but she'd had to drop out because she didn't lose enough weight before the start of the season. They were very strict about weight gain. You were weighed every week and had your wages docked if you put on even a couple of pounds. Luckily I never had that problem and didn't have to focus on it. I ate what I wanted and stayed the same size, so they didn't bother to weigh me after a while. Still, a lot of the dancers I knew were constantly on diets. I used to see them upset after they'd been weighed, then hardly eating the next day. Not surprisingly, anorexia is very common within the dance world. There's no getting around the fact that to be a dancer you cannot be overweight.

My mum approved of where I was living because it was very close to work and she was worried about me getting home at night. But I found it really depressing. The flat was dull and dingy, in a modern block of holiday flats, with one tiny grey bedroom and a tiny kitchen within a tiny sitting room.

Before my first week was out I was in trouble with the porter. Wandering back from the corner shop one morning I found him waiting impatiently at the entrance to the block, a look of suppressed fury on his face.

'What the hell do you think you're doing, young lady?' he spluttered, unable to contain his anger any longer.

'Why? What've I done?' I asked innocently.

'You've nearly set the whole place up in flames, that's what!' he shouted, his face swelling up like a red balloon.

Oops. The bacon! I'd forgotten to turn the grill off. Perhaps subconsciously I wanted the flat to burn down so that I could live somewhere else.

My mum came back at the weekend to see how I was settling in and walked in carrying a big plastic bag full of food. She needn't have bothered. 'I've already been shopping,' I told her.

She opened the kitchen cupboard and let out a long sigh. 'Oh Melanie!'

The cupboard was stuffed with my favourite foods – sweets, crisps and biscuits. What's wrong with that? I thought. Surely it was one of the advantages of leaving home – you could eat what you wanted. In any case we were given food vouchers along with coupons for free rides at the Pleasure Beach, so she didn't have to worry. Sometimes I cooked – mainly corned beef and rice – but I ate out a lot. You could get really wicked hamburgers and hot dogs on the beachfront.

Mum was appalled though, especially when she noticed that I'd bought the wrong kind of tea by mistake, tea leaves instead of bags. Well how was I to know? My dad had always done the food shopping at home.

Mum came to see me religiously at weekends even though I was often quite horrible to her. Sometimes she'd travel all that way and I wouldn't even offer her a cup of tea when she arrived. In those days I could be a moody, grumpy little cow. Although I wanted her there and I'd ring her sobbing saying that I needed to see her, by the time she got to me I wouldn't want her around any more. I suppose I was torn between the safety net of mother love and my determination to be independent, but looking back, I was downright rude and horrific and I don't know how she put up with it.

Although I didn't let it show too much, I was feeling really homesick in Blackpool. I spent a lot of time in my bedroom feeling miserable, listening to tapes of my dad's music to remind me of home – Annie Lennox, Dire Straits, Fleetwood Mac, Tracy Chapman and Maxi Priest (a strange combination, I know). I didn't like my flat, I didn't have any of my friends around me and I was missing Stephen like mad. I was alone and felt isolated. It didn't help that I appeared to be the only mixed race person in the whole city. I was even a bit scared about going out at night because the streets were full of holidaymakers from places like Scotland and I'd overheard quite a few racist comments already.

So when my mum said she had to be getting back home, I was tempted to leave with her. But I didn't. I couldn't. It was time to get ready for my first show of the day.

A few weeks later I moved into a shared house with some of the other dancers and life became a bit happier. It was a big improvement on my lonely flat even if I did have to queue up for the bathroom.

I danced in two productions that summer – the *Jump and Jive Show* in the open air theatre in the middle of the Pleasure Beach and an evening pre-show before *Mystique*, the main attraction at the Horseshoe Bar nearby, which was owned by the same people.

At the *Jump and Jive* it was all soft rock and roll numbers in little skirts, really cheesy stuff like 'Great Balls of Fire', 'Let's Twist Again' and 'Surfing USA'. Six of us – four girls and two boys – bounced around, miming to songs with lots of *da doo ron ron*s and *oo-aah*s in them. The pre-show at the Horseshoe also involved miming to songs but it was a bit classier and the costumes were nicer. It was a proper sit-down club and we performed the warm-up cabaret.

Getting ready at the Horseshoe Bar was really exciting. In the dressing room upstairs you were given your own little space to lay out your make-up and sort out your costume. All the dancers and entertainers got ready in the same area, apart from the star comedian and singer, who had their own dressing rooms. It was always very sociable, with people coming and going and chatting and gossiping. After the half-hour call bell rang there'd be a real sense of anticipation in the air as the countdown to curtain-up began.

After the show I'd either go home or make my way downstairs to watch *Mystique* and have a drink. As the weeks went by I made friends with Anthony Windmill, one of the *Mystique* dancers, and we began to go out together, mainly to gay clubs. Anthony was a really nice mixed race guy from Birmingham. He was very funny, an amazing dancer, really tall, very supple and so much fun. You'd be doing your make-up and suddenly he'd be tearing down the corridor half-naked and screaming, just for a laugh. He soon became my best Blackpool mate.

I'll never forget the night my mum and dad came to see me perform at the Horseshoe. They sat right at the front, inches from the stage. All of a sudden there I was, in a see-through catsuit with my bits covered by a few sequins and just a G-string underneath. They could see absolutely everything.

My dad tried to put on a proud face but he must have been totally horrified at the sight of all those feathers and glitter and G-strings. After the show I rushed over to find out what they thought.

'Isn't it great Dad? Aren't I fantastic?' I asked, brimming with pride.

'Yes, it's really good Melanie,' he replied, not quite looking me in the eye.

I could see what he was really thinking. My daughter hasn't done her exams and this is what she's doing instead!

But I loved it and he could see that. When I was up on stage I forgot about feeling lonely and homesick. I stopped missing Stephen and Charlotte and Rebecca and all my other friends in Leeds. The thrill of performing made up for everything else. It was such a brilliant feeling and I'd be high for hours afterwards.

Danielle had packed in dancing two years before. I think she started to regret it when she saw me up there on stage, because she turned to my mum and said, 'Why didn't you *make* me carry on with my dance classes?' She was well impressed.

After a few weeks though, I began to get a bit bored with doing the same old naff routines, day after day. Not wanting to feel like a robot I began to add a bit of my own style. This didn't go down well with the other dancers, who understandably felt that if I didn't do exactly what they were doing it would make them look bad. In actual fact it probably made me look bad, because it must have seemed like I couldn't stay in step with them. However that wasn't how they saw it.

Because I did things slightly differently I was always getting corrections in rehearsals, so I started doing it the 'right' way when we were practising then kept adding my own little twists during the shows. It drove everybody mad. There were also complaints about me being too loud. It was a repeat scenario of school and dancing classes. 'Shut up! Stop talking back there!' For Christ's sake, is a dancer not allowed to have a brain or personality?

By now I knew the routines inside out and couldn't see any point in rehearsing them over and over again. I could pick up any changes within seconds and once they were in my head my concentration tended to wander, which infuriated the director. To make things worse, I began to get offers from other shows to come and work for them. I was Blackpool's fresh new dancing girl and quite a few people tried to poach me from the Horseshoe. All that attention, along with my refusal to conform on stage, caused friction within the dance group. Being the youngest I was an easy target for bitchy comments. My sense of isolation grew and although I liked the freedom of being by myself and not under my mum and dad's roof, I actually started looking forward to going home.

The final straw came towards the end of the season when I clashed with one of my bosses. Apparently she had her eye on a singer in the *Mystique* show and thought that I fancied him too. He was a very talented guy, really hot property, but I wasn't interested and hardly went near him. Maybe he liked me, I don't know, but I do know that I wasn't into him at all. That didn't stop my boss spreading really childish rumours about me. She obviously couldn't forgive me and vowed never to work with me again.

Although I really liked my first professional job in many ways, it was nice to get back home to a bit of normality. Cooked meals at last! It felt good to be looked after instead of doing everything for myself, even though my dad's rules were as bad as ever.

I started college two days after I got back. I had to catch two buses to get there, one into the centre of town and another from there to Chapeltown. The Northern School of Contemporary Dance (NSCD) was a predominantly black college where they gave people who had talent but no technique the chance to train to be dancers. A lot of the students didn't know the first thing about dance, but had the buzz to do it, whether it be street or club dancing. There were quite a lot of Eastern European students there too, studying for teaching diplomas. From the moment Nadine set up NSCD, I wanted to be a part of it. In my mind every dancer had to go to dance college and this was the best place in Leeds. I didn't want to go to London – yet.

I felt really comfortable walking into the college on my first day because I already knew quite a few of the teachers. The building was absolutely beautiful, shaped like a mosque with a big domed roof that echoed with students' voices. That same day I met Julia, who later on became my best mate. Julia was from quite a well-to-do family in Barnsley – as in, they lived in a detached bungalow – and had a really strong Barnsley accent. She had beautiful blonde hair and constantly wore brown lip liner, which was really in at the time. I continued to wear black lip liner.

Julia was always up for a laugh and we had some brilliant times together. We hung out a lot with my old friend Jason Pennycook and soon Julia and Jason's relationship began to flourish (although I didn't find out about it for ages).

My year was full of really nice girls and guys. It was funny seeing a whole load of black guys in the college uniform – tight Lycra pants, belt and vest. After class they'd change back into their big baggy trousers, hats and bandannas. Hardly any of them were gay, believe it or not.

I enjoyed being at college, but it was a bit of a farce in many ways because there were lots of people of all ages there who had never danced before. It was a brilliant idea in theory because it gave them the chance to get a qualification in dance and then go on to teach, but for someone like me who had already trained for years it was all a bit too easy. Going back to basics meant that I often got bored. I just wasn't getting what I wanted out of it.

When you were in a class with somebody who couldn't even point their toes, you began to wonder whether you were wasting your time. Their feet would be like solid bricks and they'd be straining to make them move, which was almost painful to watch. In some cases you sensed it would take them years to work out how to get beyond that first stage.

Some of the classes were accidents waiting to happen and had me and Julia in fits. I loved pointe lessons, where the girls danced on pointe ballet shoes and the boys were supposed to support, lift and throw them. Most of the time you could guarantee that you'd be partnered with a boy who wouldn't be able to lift you properly. Because Julia and I were really well trained, we found it the most hysterical class of all time. We'd wet ourselves as we tried to get our partners to hold us correctly as they carried us. Pointe spins were even worse. Imagine twirling around at top speed waiting for your partner to stop you and hold you. Then he stumbles, fumbles or simply misses you altogether and you spin out of control across the room. We thought it was hilarious.

I lived on the money I'd saved up in Blackpool for a while, but it wasn't long before I was broke. Most of the other NSCD students were on grants, but I didn't get any help because I lived locally. I wasn't entitled to draw the dole either. I had no living expenses because I was back at home, but I still had to find my own lunch money and bus fare, which became harder and harder. Sometimes I couldn't make it into college because I just didn't have the bus fare, even though Stephen helped me out quite a lot. He often caught three buses to come and meet me at the end of the day. Occasionally I walked to college from the centre of town, but it wasn't a very pleasant experience. To attract your attention a lot of the boys in Chapeltown would 'pssssst!' at you as you walked past, which infuriated me.

I needed an income and a job that didn't interfere with my course work. But what? I was too young to serve drinks, so that was out, and I didn't want to work in another shop. But I was broke; I had to find some way to earn some pocket money. In Blackpool I'd earned about £250 a week and it was hard to get used to having zero spending power again.

My friend Levi came up with the solution. More or less a younger version of my dad in appearance, he mentioned that he was now running aerobics classes at the local leisure centre. 'Why don't you come down there and teach a class?' he suggested. 'You'd be good at it. All you have to do is boss people around and get them to sweat a lot.'

Perfect!

So I became an aerobics teacher at the Mandela Centre in the heart of Chapeltown. First I made up some wicked compilation tapes at home and worked out a series of routines. Then Jason helped me design a small poster which I photocopied and put up on notice boards throughout the area.

The day of my first class, I went down to the Mandela Centre an hour early. I was feeling quite nervous – would anyone turn up? I changed into the skimpiest of outfits, set up my tape player and sat down to wait. About ten minutes before the class was due to start, in walked five big black mamas.

'Is dis de aerobics class?' one of them asked, puffing slightly.

Gulp. Would these formidable women be willing to take orders from a sixteen-year-old in a tiny leotard?

'Yes, this is it. Come on in!'

Five minutes later a couple of boys turned up and the class began.

I loved teaching from the start. At first I taught mainly women (and a lot of them were really massive) and I used to be quite horrible to them, because once I get on one I can be really mean. I'd say things like, 'Get your legs up you fat cow, come on!'

They didn't seem to mind. They were there to get fit so they needed someone to be strict with them. More and more people started coming to the class and within a few weeks it was packed out.

As the classes grew I started to collect my own little fan club of people who looked in through the window as I taught. There would often be ten or fifteen boys hanging around outside after their basketball and football training, staring away, so I started to put sheets of paper up so that they couldn't see what was going on.

After a while I couldn't be bothered with that any more so I told them, 'Right, well if you're so desperate to watch me, you're going to have to do the class and pay!' Within weeks I had around sixty people at every class.

At the beginning of class, the boys would form a line at the front so that they could get the best view. No such luck. I'd wait until everyone was in place, then go to the back and start teaching at the other end of the room. Ha! I charged £1 a class, gave half my earnings to the Mandela Centre for the room rental and had £30 left for bus fare, meals, clothes and going out. It was mainly my pocket money to get to college, although it wasn't long before I began missing lessons because I felt that there was nothing new to learn. Julia and I used to skive off and go round the shops. Around this time Rebecca started to get a lot of job offers down in London, so she moved south and we lost contact for a while.

After a couple of terms, college began to lose its appeal big time. I'd always been Nadine's favourite at Sacred Heart but the older I became, the louder I became and when I finally got into NSCD and she got to know me better, she began to dislike me. I often got into trouble because of my laugh. Apparently it echoed throughout the college. She could never tell me off for not listening in class though. Even though I'd be having a conversation with one of the other dancers, I'd be able to pick up everything because I'd been trained so well.

I began to have tutorials with Nadine because none of the other teachers felt they could get through to me. She decided to sit me down for a weekly chat to try and instil some discipline. 'But don't think you're special because you're having tutorials with the Head,' she warned.

Here was where I was supposed to discuss what I'd learned and gained through my classes. 'I haven't learnt anything,' I'd say. 'All I've done is go through the same routine ten times because the others don't get it.'

Nadine reacted angrily. 'Melanie, there are lots of girls here who can kick their legs far higher than you can,' she retorted.

So what? I just didn't get it. She'd always been so supportive of me in the past and she'd begged my mum to let me come to the college, but now it just wasn't working out.

To be honest I had a lot of distractions, from Stephen and my social life to auditions and learning to drive. My mum gave me an intensive course of driving lessons for my seventeenth birthday in May – two hours a day for a week – but somehow I failed my test on practically every point. I cried afterwards, saying that the examiner was just racist, but the truth was that I wasn't a good driver. End of.

I had to wait a month before I was allowed to take my test again. This time my mum couldn't afford to pay for more driving lessons so she taught me herself. It didn't go very well, to say the least. After hundreds of laps in the private car park on the Kirkstall Road she let me start driving to college. We had some explosive arguments on those journeys. With her fingers clasped permanently around the handbrake she'd scream 'I don't enjoy doing this at all!' in the middle of a blazing row as we were driving through town.

Just before we set out on our daily assault course on wheels one morning, I saw a letter on the doormat addressed to me. I very rarely received post so I instantly ripped it open. It took me a while to make any sense of the contents.

Dear Melanie, Well done! You've been selected as one of the final fifteen in the Miss *Leeds Weekly News* 1992 beauty pageant!

'Mum, what's all this about?'

'Oh I entered you into a competition,' she said matter-of-factly. 'I sent off your picture to the *Leeds Weekly News*.' *Without asking me first.*

'You what? I'm not doing it. How dare you send my photo off without telling me about it?' I spluttered.

'Come on Melanie, it'll be a good laugh for you!' she countered.

'Why will it? I don't know anything about it! I refuse to wear a swimming costume and I haven't got any high heels.'

My mum could be very persuasive and I gave in on the condition that nobody came to watch me apart from her. The next day I sorted out my swimming costume and went on the hunt for some shoes. Mum didn't have anything I liked, but May, an older Irish woman who lived two doors up, had the perfect pair of stilettos that she kindly lent me.

As agreed, my mum was the only person with me downstairs at the old Digby's Club on the day of the competition. She must have wet herself when she saw me parading on stage looking like something from *Miss World* twenty years ago. I found it very hard not to giggle as I tottered along in May's stilettos, but I kept myself together and got on well with the compère during my onstage chat.

Afterwards I was standing at the back having a nice free glass of wine when my name was called out.

'Melanie Brown!'

I hardly heard it. The competition was over and in my head I'd already moved on.

'Melanie! Melanie Brown!'

'That's you isn't it?' said the girl standing next to me.

'Yes . . .' I replied. 'What?'

'Well I think it means you've won,' she said.

'You've won!' agreed another girl. 'They're calling you.'

'Oh shut up, you're all having a laugh,' I said. But they weren't.

I think it took about ten minutes to register that I was now Miss *Leeds Weekly News*. I just hadn't been expecting it. It only began to feel real when one of the judges led me back on stage and sat me down on a makeshift throne. He helped me on with my Miss *Leeds Weekly News* satin sash and plonked a crown on my head. I was a beauty queen.

It took ages for it to sink in. As I was crowned it felt like I was watching myself through a tiny hole in a TV screen, wearing a muslin veil over my eyes. Is it? Really me? Is that me there – here – now? It was amazing and I was thrilled.

My prize was the use of a car for a year, a brand new imported Renault Clio. How ironic! I hadn't passed my test so I couldn't drive it, even though I was itching to. For months it sat in this frigging shop window staring at me, with Miss *Leeds Weekly News* in letters down the side.

My driving tests were some of the worst experiences I've ever been through. I just couldn't take the pressure. It took me three attempts to get my licence and before each test I'd sit there in the waiting room, sweating and shaking and rushing to the toilet with diarrhoea. Every time I got into the examiner's car I'd think, In an hour, I could be driving around in my very own Renault Clio. In fact it took five months.

Not long after I passed my test I drove to Manchester for a Kinky Delinky club night at the Haçienda with some gay friends from college. It was brilliant there and I loved it. Women walked around topless or with gaffa tape stuck across their nipples, no one gave a damn. I really fancied one of the guys in my group. He was very odd-looking actually – really thin and white, almost albino – but he was right on my wavelength and I was convinced he was going to fall in love with me. We used to sleep in the same bed sometimes, before I finally accepted that he wasn't interested.

My mum had no idea I was at the Haçienda. I knew she'd disapprove and so I made up some story about going to a friend's house instead. Unfortunately I was photographed in my see-through fishnet catsuit that night and the photo ended up in the club magazine. Someone my mum knew had a subscription. 'Isn't that you at a gay night at the Haçienda?' she asked. Busted!

'Please don't tell my mum! Please!'

Along with the car I won a trip to Disneyland in Paris. Stephen came with me. It was a proper package deal and so of course there was construction work going on in our hotel. All you heard all day was crashing and banging.

Over breakfast on the second morning a woman sitting at our table looked up and remarked, 'I can just about put up with it in the day, but did you hear that dreadful banging all night?'

Stephen and I exchanged a look.

'More orange juice anyone?' I offered, picking up the nearest jug.

Another of the prizes was 'a day of etiquette', when I was taught how to do my hair and nails, how to get in and out of a car and the correct use of knives and forks at the dinner table. I was contractually obliged to attend four events during the year that I held the title. One of them was handing out awards at a ceremony honouring disabled people, another at an awards ceremony for the elderly. I liked the socialising and mixing, but I didn't enjoy being kissed and cuddled by the recipients of the awards, who seemed to think it was their automatic right to get physical.

College was becoming really dull. Then, when I heard that Julia and Jason had gone to an audition at the Studio Centre in Leeds without telling me, I lost interest altogether. I felt really upset and excluded. There seemed little point in making the effort at college after that – I wasn't learning anything and I'd fallen out with my best friends there. Although I kept on going to classes, I stopped concentrating on what I was doing. I guess it was only a matter of time before I was chucked out.

But I was still teaching aerobics and loving it. After class one evening, one of my friends from the old Sacred Heart days – Malcolm, also known as 'Mr Freeze' – popped in to see me.

'Would you be interested in teaching dance to kids in Austria for a month in the summer?' he asked.

He described it as a bit of a summer camp vibe, where a bunch of underprivileged kids from Newcastle were given the chance to rehearse and stage a show. I'd be running daily dance workshops. It sounded like a fantastic opportunity. I'd hardly been abroad and was desperate to see a bit more of the world. Perhaps it would also lead onto something else, something more interesting than watching people trying to point their toes. I instantly said yes.

My mum was pleased to hear that I was going to be working in a quiet village where there wasn't any nightlife. Little did she know that I only had to teach for an hour a day and had the rest of my time off. Within a couple of days I'd found a great club on the other side of Austria and the fun started.

Often I'd stroll into class at eight in the morning having been out all night. The kids could always tell.

'Miss, Miss, you're wearing the same clothes as yesterday!'

'Don't you dare tell anyone!'

I was really grateful that I had that teaching job ahead of me, especially when, towards the end of the first college year, the inevitable happened. Nadine asked my mum and dad to come and see her in her office, while I waited outside. 'I don't want Melanie to come back next year,' she said.

I wasn't that disappointed. I was more worried about my mum saying, 'Well there you go. Another one saying that you're too loud.' (Which, of course, she did.)

7

WILD THING

I really didn't have a clue what I was going to do next. The rest of my life just stretched blankly before me. Instinctively I was sure that something would come along, but I was getting quite a lot of hassle at home.

'Get a job!' my mum kept saying. 'Will you get out of bed and look for a job!'

'It's time you started earning your own money,' said my dad.

Okay I will, I thought, so I started looking through the Situations Vacant pages in the local paper. I went for a few interviews for office work but on more than one occasion I had the feeling that I was the wrong colour for the job, although obviously no one ever said so. You could just see it in the condescending eyes of the receptionist as she told you where to wait, or in the bemused expression of the interviewer as he strode down the corridor to meet you. Some of them treated me like an idiot; others were downright rude. I hated it.

Finally one of my mum's friends helped me to get a job selling advertising space on the phone for a car magazine called *Motor Mart*, in the *Yorkshire Evening Post* building. She worked there in quite a high up position and was able to pull a couple of strings. At first I rather liked the whole idea of doing a nine-to-five and going into an office wearing a smart suit and carrying a briefcase. I was particularly proud of the suit and briefcase. I'd park my car and totter off to the office – it was a whole big role-play for me, even though I wasn't aware of it at the time.

I wasn't bad at the job and it was nice to be earning a salary (although it wasn't very much), but I'm the kind of person who gets bored very easily. It wasn't long – a couple of months – before the endless repetition of each day got me down. Then my boss kept telling me off for getting into work late, being loud (what a surprise!) and wearing short skirts. So I left in search of something more interesting.

I did all kinds of things to earn money in the months that followed, including (fully clothed) podium dancing at the Yell Bar in the centre of town on Thursday, Friday and Saturday nights. That was a fun, easy job. I got cash-in-hand for dancing on a high stage to songs like 'Rhythm Nation' by Janet Jackson and 'Got To Show Me Love' by Robin S, plus free non-alcoholic drinks all evening. I'd arrive when the club was already packed and do twenty-minute slots with a ten-minute break between them. At the end of the night when everyone else had been kicked out, I'd sit back and soak in the atmosphere of the club after hours, which I loved.

I started auditioning again and came really close to getting parts in *Cats* and *Miss Saigon*. My mum was convinced I would get *Miss Saigon*. She bought me all the tapes and we learnt every song – I used to make Stephen sing the men's parts. I also signed up with a local agent, but all he got me was lots of extra work on the set of things like *A Touch of Frost* and *Coronation Street*. Still, I was happy to do it for a bit of cash – around £40 or £50 a day.

On *A Touch of Frost* I was cast as a policewoman and spent the day pretending to look busy in the background of a police station. During my lunch break I wandered off to a nearby petrol station to get some crisps and a drink with one of the other extras, completely forgetting that I still was in costume. As a result I couldn't work out why the people in the garage were behaving so differently towards me – extra polite and ultra efficient – until suddenly I realised. They think I'm a cop! It was a weird feeling.

I got a few jobs through Mrs Wood, too. Charlotte and I were employed as dancers on *Keith and Orville's Quack Chat Show*, which was filmed in Manchester and turned out to be good fun. I also appeared on *The Bonnie Langford Show*, which was less memorable.

At one audition I was asked to sing. Oh dear. Time to get some lessons. I couldn't afford to have one-on-one training, so my mum came up with the idea of joining an operatic society in Doncaster. It was a great way to get free singing lessons and I loved it. They were all old biddies and I was the youngest there by miles, but it didn't matter. I turned up to every rehearsal until I was offered a job that clashed with the dates of their next show. It was unfortunate because they'd been training me up for months and I was looking forward to performing with them, but what could I do? I certainly couldn't turn down paid work.

At the beginning of 1993 I auditioned for *Starlight Express* and got through to a second and then a third audition. The next stage was learning how to dance on roller skates, so I signed up for weekly classes on the three-month *Starlight* training course. The way it worked was that you had to complete the *Starlight* training and then re-audition for the show at the end of it.

Around the same time I auditioned for another summer season in Blackpool, this time dancing in a variety show at the Grand Theatre. The auditions were held in the skating rink in Blackpool and I got the job. I was so excited. Despite the homesickness I'd experienced there two years before, I knew that I wanted to do this. I was older now and more confident. Blackpool was going to be a blast.

A few days before I left Leeds to start rehearsals at the Grand I went over to Stephen's house to have a talk with him. I found it incredibly difficult to say what I had to say to him.

We'd been happy together for so many years and there was no real reason to end it. I could have stayed with Stephen when I moved to Blackpool, but I selfishly wanted a clean break so that I could concentrate on my own mission.

I'd thought it over again and again. As far as I saw it I had a choice – either stay in Leeds, get married and have a baby with Stephen, or split up, and go off to pursue my career. I'm not surprised I made the decision I did. I thrive off change. But that didn't make it any easier at the time. Stephen was absolutely gutted and, in my own way, so was I. Still, I think he understood. He was a professional footballer so he knew how important a career was. (Just think, I could have been a footballer's wife!)

'If it's meant to be, then we'll be together again in a couple of years,' we promised each other. 'If you love someone, set them free.'

Rehearsals for the show lasted for three weeks. It was a busy time for me because I was also going to London for my *Starlight* training once a week. Luckily two other girls in Blackpool with me were also doing the course and we shared the driving to London.

It felt good to be away from home and living independently that summer. The only downside was being apart from Stephen. In the early part of the season I'd wake up crying because I missed him so much. I'd be in the supermarket and our song would come on – 'Get Here' by Oleta Adams – and I'd rush straight to the phone to call him and sob out the words 'I miss you' repeatedly. Later in the day I'd be on stage performing and loving every minute of it, but I'd still have that pain – that eurgh! – in the core of me.

Strangely, the fact that I was able to cope with the sadness of our separation helped me believe in myself – and what I was doing – more than ever. I was sure that my life was going in a fantastic direction.

Once you got to Blackpool you had to team up with a couple of other people and find somewhere to live. I arranged to move into a house with Selina Joscelin, who I knew from my Horseshoe Bar days, and Becky Muskett, who was also in our dance group. Selina was very tall and slim, with short hair. She always slapped on lots of make-up and mainly wore light blue drainpipe jeans and white Reebok trainers. Becky was loud and bubbly and articulate. She had a very distinctive look – spiky blonde hair, flawless skin and a great body. We moved into the house on a temporary basis and had a month to find somewhere more permanent.

There were a couple of other lodgers there when we arrived. On our first day we were introduced to Julian, who was living upstairs in the attic room. Short, stocky and fit, he had blonde hair that hung like curtains on either side of his head and twinkly blue eyes. As soon as I saw him I thought, Cor.

Julian seemed to be perfectly normal at first, but during that first week we began to notice that whenever he left the house he'd be wearing a completely different outfit. One morning he'd be off to catch a plane dressed as a businessman, the next he'd be off to the station looking like a student, or wearing a boiler suit. He always seemed to be in a different character role. I thought it was a bit weird, but also quite exciting.

We'd say hello in the mornings but rarely saw him in the evenings because we were at The Grand. Then, one night after the show, I went up to the attic in my negligee to visit 'The Man Upstairs' as he became known, just because I wanted to. After that I started seeing him on and off. It didn't stop me missing Stephen, but it helped.

Julian was about ten years older than I was and he intrigued me. I often asked him what he did but he wouldn't say. Then one day he brought home a small suitcase. He threw it on the bed and as it landed it sprang open and loads of cash came spilling out. There in front of me was the most money I'd ever seen in my life, at least fifteen grand. I sat on the bed and looked at it in amazement. One last time I asked, 'Well what do you do?'

'It's best if I don't tell you,' he replied.

We just left it at that. I guessed it was something dodgy, but it didn't occur to me that it could be anything illegal. Totally thick, I was.

From 8 July to 30 October 1993 I was a dancer in *The Billy Pearce Laughter Show*, starring Claire Cattini, Joe Pasquale and, of course, Billy Pearce (who was Mrs Wood's son coincidentally). It was the same year that Barbara Windsor was appearing at the end of the pier and Jim Davidson was starring in one of the big shows too.

Billy Pearce was an old-style comedian – lots of slapstick and obvious gags. Joe was best known for his high voice and for singing 'I know a song that will get on your nerves, get on your nerves, get on your nerves, I know a song that will get on your nerves ...' (and God was he right!) Claire Cattini was a song-and-dance entertainer and as far as I was concerned, a big star.

According to the programme notes I wasn't doing too badly myself:

Melanie has appeared in quite a variety of things since leaving Leeds Theatre Arts. Savages *at the Leeds Playhouse,* Old Time Music Hall *at the City Varieties, the* Billy Pearce Show, *the summer season in Blackpool and cabarets all over Yorkshire. On television she has appeared with the likes of Keith Harris and Bonnie Langford. Melanie likes tennis, dancing and performing on the Grand stage.*

Haven't you heard of artistic licence? It's another way of saying tennis!

There were eight dancers in the show – two boys and six girls – and three knockabout entertainers who called themselves The Acromaniacs. I suppose you could describe them as gymnastic comedians. Their act was very physical and they were a bit like clowns.

The show opened with a big samba dance to the Gloria Estefan song 'Rhythm is Gonna Get You'. The dancers wore very loud outfits – purple corset dresses lined with fuschia pink satin, with beiged out elastic shoulder straps; wide-rimmed deep purple hats, worn on a slant, held on with beige elastic that sliced your cheeks and chin; and bright pink open-toe high-heeled shoes.

When the curtain went up Claire was lifted on high by two male dancers and carried halfway down a staircase. Then she started into her dance routine and the dancers came on stage. One night she lost her footing and fell down the stairs. Well the rest of us just couldn't help pissing ourselves. Believe me, it's very hard to dance well when your body is heaving with laughter.

I was Claire's understudy, although it never occurred to me that I might have to go on in her place. Strangely I can't really remember it, but Becky recently reminded me that late one afternoon, a few hours before curtain up, the director summoned me and told me that Claire was ill. I had to take her place in the opening number – was I up to it? I don't recall being nervous or anything. I just went on and did what I had to do. It was all a bit of a laugh to me.

Our costumes for the second set were ridiculous. The song had a gladiator theme and we wore all-in-one Lycra tunics with blue and pink lightning flashes down them – very embarrassing. While the Acromaniacs knocked each other over with gigantic cotton wool bud 'weapons' and did back flips, we jumped up and down in the background, being gladiator people.

We also did a *Starlight Express*-style number on roller skates, when someone would invariably veer off to the left into the wings and have to be pushed back on stage again. Luckily I didn't have that problem because of my *Starlight* training.

The audience was generally made up of older people, a family crowd, parents and kids (no teenagers), lots of Scottish, plus of course the odd few blokes who turned up to watch the dancing girls. It was packed every night and the response from the crowd was always enthusiastic. The show started at 8 p.m., finished about 10.45 p.m., and then I often went out on the town. Me, Becky and one of the other dancers, Jo Warrington, were the hardcore clubbers and we went on club crawls to some really naff places. We usually got in free and then we'd take over the club and steal the stage, dancing wildly and yelling our heads off. Becky used to flash her tits a lot (and I bet she still does). It was a scream.

It sometimes felt like I was the only black person in Blackpool, though. I used to wear a long black straight wig so that people wouldn't recognise me half as much. I'd go out in a denim A-line skirt, a knotted top, high heels and the wig, so I looked a bit Asian, I think.

There was a late-night drinking club called The Leopold where all the artists from the different shows in Blackpool would end up, partly because it had an extended licence. It was Blackpool's equivalent of Soho House, but thankfully without Soho House prices. Sometimes we'd go to the casino and play a bit of blackjack – very sophisticated, darling!

I earned about £300 a week, plus the money I got for playing an extra in Curly Watts' Better Buys Supermarket on the set of *Coronation Street*, which I did most Sundays. Manchester is only half an hour from Blackpool, so it was easy to get there and back. I had to pay my rent and buy a bit of food, but apart from that I could go completely mad with the rest of my wages. And I did, although I never touched drugs, just drank gallons of alcohol. Being a dancer I was incredibly fit, so however much I partied I never had trouble getting up in the morning.

A few weeks into the season me, Selina and Becky moved into a house on the posh side of Blackpool. That house was a mad wild party house. The Grumbleweeds turned up to one of our parties and the one with the glasses hypnotised me and took me into regression. (Apparently in my previous life I was a mother of three who worked in a factory.) Then he hypnotised me into keeping my arm straight. I just couldn't bend it, no matter how hard I tried, so I wandered around the party for the rest of the night with a wooden limb stretched out in front of me.

A famous topless model was in Blackpool that season and she came to one of our house parties. She was wearing a lilac mini-dress and all I remember is seeing her clamber up the stairs on all fours with no knickers on, followed by a man. Oh my God, what kind of party has this turned into? I thought.

I was no angel, though. After years of being with Stephen I was finally single and I made the most of it. If I was to tell you how many people I've slept with, you'd probably say, 'Oh my God, that is disgusting, you tart.' But every relationship I've had, whether it's lasted one night or four years, has taught me a lot about myself. I've taken each lesson with me into the next relationship and I get to learn more with every encounter, however fleeting or passionate or stressful.

I've still got boyfriends from years ago phoning me up. I think that's because I've never been a bitch or treated a man badly, even though I've always been the one to end it and move on. I'd see my friends get cornered by men but it wasn't ever like that for me, except for that short space of time that was my marriage, which was unlike anything I'd ever experienced before. It's not that I've always been the dominant one, but I've usually chosen a relationship that I've had a certain amount of control over.

I look back on that summer in Blackpool as a time of experimentation and self-exploration. One particular incident stands out in my mind. During the show at the Grand one night I noticed a man in the audience who wouldn't stop staring at me. He didn't seem to notice anything or anyone else, his eyes were fixed on me and they never wandered. It got to the point that when I went off between numbers I couldn't wait to get back on stage to see if he was still staring. He was. He didn't take his eyes off me once throughout the whole show. It was a buzz.

That was that, I thought. You don't get to meet people in the audience unless you jump off the stage and say hi, which is unheard of – although at the end of the show, Nicky Hooper the choreographer would normally bring people backstage to say hello to Billy and Joe. Sometimes she'd bring them up to our dressing room too.

Nicky was pretty and small with fiery red hair. She somehow reminded me of Toyah Wilcox. That night I heard her down the corridor introducing people to the Acromaniacs, so I popped my head round for a look. There in the corridor was the staring man.

'Oh my God, that's him!' I was shocked to see him. Did this mean he knew Nicky Hooper?

He was an older man with short, brown curly hair and green eyes, wearing a cream suit. He had a high-powered air about him.

Nicky introduced us and we started chatting. 'Would you like to go for a drink?' he asked after a few minutes.

'Yes of course I would. I'll just take my stage make-up off.'

Getting all that make-up off was horrific, especially the thick catty eyeliner that we wore to make our eyes look bigger to all the biddies with thick lenses on at the back of the auditorium. Not to mention the white eyeliner that was applied inside the eye.

He drove me to a bar on the South Shore and we had a drink and a chat. Then in the middle of a perfectly normal conversation I said matter-of-factly, 'I've never had sex with somebody over forty.' (I presumed he was over forty. Well I think he was. I hoped he was!) 'I'd like to try it because I've heard that the older the man, the better the sex is.'

Back then the big theory was that you don't sleep with younger boys or boys your own age because it's over too quickly and they don't know what to do. So you sleep with an older man because he's got experience. He knows where everything is on your body and can satisfy you. I don't know who told me this but it had been on my mind for a while and I just blurted it out. I think he was a bit shocked because we were just having a casual social drink, nothing sexual or overly flirty.

'Really?' he said, trying hard to mask his surprise.

'Yeah.'

'Right then,' he gulped. 'So when would you like to do that?'

'Well, why not tonight?' I replied, feeling spontaneous.

So we went back to mine. I had a glass of wine in the front room and then we moved into the bedroom. I was feeling quite up for it and very excited because this was a new experience for me. I had a man in front of me who was guaranteed to be amazing in bed because you hear so many stories about 'the older man'.

We got down to it (obviously safe sex) and it wasn't long before he started saying, 'Come on baby, come on baby!' That's strange, I thought, but I just let it carry on. He kept on repeating it until he'd said it about fifty times. Needless to say I never saw him again. I think I chose the wrong older man. I should have asked for references first!

I was totally open about my attitude to sex. 'Yeah, I've had a one-night stand. What's the big deal?' It was only when people were obviously shocked and horrified by what I told them that I thought to question it. 'How could you sleep with a stranger?' they'd ask.

'I picked him out at a club, I went back and I had sex with him, then I got up and left.'

'But didn't you *feel* anything?'

Did I feel anything? To be honest, enjoyment was the driving factor and my emotions didn't even remotely come into it. I was gung ho back then.

Emotions weren't going to stand in the way of my passionate sexual drive, which people often suppress because they're worried about what other people will think. I didn't care, I was just like, Vrooom! When I think back I have to laugh to myself. I was enjoying myself so much and there was no doubt or negativity in my mind. I didn't once question myself.

I was still sort of seeing Julian and I was very excited when he invited me to Marbella during the mid-season break. A couple of days before we left I phoned my mum to tell her.

'I'm not coming home, I'm going on holiday with Julian to Marbella.'

'But I don't know anything about him!' she protested.

In my mind Julian was manly, grown-up, organised and reliable. He had proper friends that went down the pub and really respected him. We'd drive to Liverpool and all these older people with families and kids would say, 'Julian's so great!' Little did I know that they were his personal mafia gang, because he protected me, never told me anything. I was his 'special girl' back then and we're still friends to this day.

Julian was a bit of a father figure. He let me drive his car and always made sure there was food in my fridge. I really, really fancied him too. He found me intriguing, I think. He couldn't believe I fancied him, couldn't understand why I tended to choose guys that weren't fantasy figures.

Sometimes he'd drive me home in his flash Audi convertible and drop me off without coming in, then pick me up later and take me back to Blackpool. 'Who is this man who drives you home?' my mum would ask. 'We don't like it Melanie. Don't bring him into the house.' Looking back I can understand why she was so nervous about Julian. He could have been anyone. I'd had a sheltered upbringing and she often worried about how I would handle the big bad world. However, I thought I was handling it fine, just by having fun.

Our house in Blackpool was above a café near a venue called The Castle, where a massive annual snooker tournament was being held. One morning I went downstairs to get a bacon sandwich and there was a whole load of foreign snooker players in the café, having their mid-morning break.

I instantly looked over, because I love a bit of foreign. As I was waiting for my order, one of the gang came over and started chatting. Then he introduced me to his friend.

Blonde, tall and very muscular, the friend told me that his name was Fjöljnir Porgeirsson – Fjöl for short, (pronounced Fee-oll) – and that he came from Iceland. Back in those days I didn't have much of a clue about Iceland and I was fascinated to hear more about it. I'd always been curious about other countries, their culture and customs. Fjöl had a picture of his mum and dad's house in his wallet and, with its clean lines, large windows and sea view, it reminded me of the house in the film *Sleeping with the Enemy*. After listening to Fjöl's descriptions, Iceland became a bit of a fairy tale in my mind. Later it lived up to all my expectations. It's a beautiful country.

Fjöl asked me out for a drink and we started seeing each other almost daily. Things began in a very innocent and childlike way between us. It was as if we were courting in the old-school mode. We didn't do anything intimate or sexual with each other for quite a while – we kissed and held hands but didn't go beyond that. We were friends on the same vibe, aware that we were only going to know each other for a few weeks.

I was intrigued by the way Fjöl spoke English and he was curious to learn more about how to pronounce things and describe them. I got him tickets to the show at the Grand. He taught me how to play snooker and invited me to his tournaments.

His competitions were all very serious because there was a lot at stake. You could win scholarships, championships, crowns – it was quite full-on and the players had been training for years to get this far. I often went to watch Fjöl play. It was hysterical because I was meant to sit there and stay absolutely silent, but I never quite managed it.

Mostly it was Fjöl's fault. Before one particular tournament he said, 'When I wiggle my bum as I go to pot a ball, you know that's a sign to you.'

Well I burst out laughing at the first sign of a wiggle, of course I did. The next minute I was banned from ever going near the place again and a security guard marched me out of the building. Striding along in my skimpy top and little shorts, I tried but failed to stifle my giggles.

I totally fell for Fjöl. He was a proper gentleman, the kind that would open doors for you and walk on the outside of the pavement to protect you from the traffic. He was a proper, spiritual and romantic guy. His brother had died a few years before, a tragedy that taught him to value life and relationships and people very highly.

You could tell that he was just so proud to have me on his arm. He'd never slept with a black woman before, because there are hardly any black people in Iceland and even though he'd travelled a bit it just hadn't happened. He was fascinated with my background, my hair and the colour of my skin because he was so used to seeing beautiful blonde *Miss World* Icelandic girls everywhere. We had a very exciting time together.

On his last night in Blackpool I cut off a lock of my hair and gave it to him. 'We will be together someday, I know it,' I said, tears rolling down my cheeks. I believed it, too.

Fjöl's plane was due to leave the next morning. We went back to my room, lit loads of candles and fell into each other's arms. We chatted and hugged and laughed together semi-naked, then made love on the floor as dawn was breaking. It was amazing. By the end we were crying and holding on to each other, not wanting to let go.

Fjöl promised to come back soon, but a couple of weeks later he had a motorbike accident in Iceland and was hospitalised for months. It was awful. I missed him a lot. I couldn't afford to go and visit him and he couldn't come back here, so although I wrote him loads of letters that was it for us. Or so I thought at the time.

When he left I threw myself back into work to take my mind off missing him. By this point there were tensions beginning to appear among the dancers. I suppose we'd just been together too long and were starting to get on each other's nerves.

Before the show you had to lay out your costumes for the quick changes. It was your responsibility to make sure everything was in place so that nothing held you up in the rush to get back on stage again. If you were late or bust something on your costume you had your wages docked. One night I went to do a quick change and couldn't find my gladiator costume anywhere. I rummaged all over the dressing room and finally found it slung in a cupboard, but the extra minutes of searching meant I was late on stage and had my wages docked. To this day I'm convinced that someone had hidden it, just to be spiteful. Another time I found a slash in the arm of one of my outfits, for which I was penalised as well. After that I began to feel a bit uncomfortable within the group.

As the season drew to a close and I began to look around for another job, the choreographer Nicky Hooper mentioned that she might have some dancing work for me. A couple of weeks after I'd gone back to Leeds she phoned and asked if I was still interested.

'What's the job?' I asked.

'You're not going to believe this, but it's entertaining the troops!' she replied with a chuckle.

It was quite good fun actually. There were eight of us in the troupe and we rehearsed for a week with Mrs Wood's assistant Jennifer before being flown to the Falkland Islands to dance in front of hundreds of rows of men in uniform. We also went to Bosnia and Northern Ireland, where we had to have bodyguards even when we went to the shops. It was a paranoid environment and there were moments when I worried that, being the only black girl, I'd be easier to pick out and shoot. But most of the time it made us feel special to have security guards watching over us and we stayed in very nice hotels.

The routines we did were fairly straightforward. They were old festival routines, passed down from the 'big girls' in Mrs Wood's classes. It was a bit of a strange programme that included anything from the Can-Can to 'Amadeus' and Prince songs, but we didn't get any complaints. The outfits were ridiculous. For 'Amadeus' we wore huge hooped dresses with knickerbockers underneath, which were a real tease for the men. I loved it, especially since the soldiers in the audience were banned from clapping or reacting in any way whatsoever. Half of them hadn't seen women for God knows how long but they were under orders to sit and watch the show without moving a muscle, which I found very amusing, although it seemed a bit unfair.

After the show we had to socialise with the officers, which I hated. I wanted to be with all the young guys but that wasn't allowed. We had to hang out with the officers because they were the ones who had booked us, to give the younger soldiers a bit of a treat. They were always polite and well spoken, and we had a laugh getting drunk with them, but sometimes I wondered whether the job was just a bit too close to prostitution for my liking.

It was through the same company that I got my next big job – in a pantomime in Lewisham. *Jack and the Beanstalk*, starring Saracen from *Gladiators*, was set to keep me in work for most of December and January. It was another exciting opportunity, because this time I had an acting part as well as being one of the dancers. Okay, I only had one line to say, but it was a start.

I moved into a room in a little house in Lewisham owned by a nice, funny Polish woman. I lived there with a girl called Amanda and I had the front bedroom that looked onto the street. It was quite a cold bedroom, but it was sweet. In a way it was like living with a family because we all used to have dinner together downstairs.

I found that area of London quite rough and didn't really enjoy living there. When I walked home at night I'd see people bottle-fighting in the streets, which was frightening. It was a lonely period in my life, even though I was still seeing Julian and he'd come and visit me from time to time, which made it a bit easier.

To be honest, I didn't take the job seriously and perpetually got the giggles when it came to saying my one line. Just before my cue came the guys in control of the scenery would whisper down from the rafters, 'Go on Melanie, say it!' They were trying to encourage me but it just made things worse. I'd look up, crease up and somebody else would have to say my line into the lead guy's turban, where his microphone was hidden.

I was often late to rehearsals and a couple of times when Julian came to see me, I pretended I was ill and I missed them altogether. One day someone from the crew saw me out and grassed me up to the director. So I got the sack. Even worse, I was told that I would never work again as a dancer.

My mum couldn't believe it. 'Oh no! Not again!' This time, she insisted, it was time to get a proper job. 'You're not going to work as a dancer again, not after you've been sacked,' she warned. My heart sank because I suspected that she was right. The jobs at the Grand, entertaining the troops and the pantomime had all come through the same company. As far as I knew, it was unlikely that they'd consider employing me again.

So it was back to scanning the Situations Vacant in the back of the *Yorkshire Evening Post*. I'd come full circle. After a few unsuccessful interviews I came home one day to find my mum on the phone. She hung up and said, 'I've got you a job. I rang up pretending to be you and they're expecting you in on Monday morning.'

It was telesales again, this time for *Auto Trader Magazine*, in the same building as *Motor Mart*. I came home after my first day saying, 'Mum, you forgot to tell me you'd said I could work a computer!' Still, I managed to blag it. I think I lasted about three months this time. I had some wicked suits and a briefcase, but inevitably got bored. The job was completely soulless and draining and I got nothing out of it. It was awful calling people up and getting a rude response, then trying to persuade them into buying advertising space. It was time to move on, but where? What the hell was I going to do next?

8

POWER TO THE PEOPLE

'**M**um, can you lend me a fiver?'

Once again I started madly auditioning for summer seasons and West End shows, going to London about three times a week. I used up the last of the money I'd saved from doing telesales and then relied on my mum to help me out with my coach fares. The journey took about four hours each way and I usually slept right through it. Mum would drop me off at the National Express coach station in Leeds at 6 a.m. and then pick me up again at midnight. They were long days, but I didn't care. I wanted a job really badly, something that didn't involve going into an office and sitting at a desk from nine to five. I got *The Stage* paper every week and read it religiously. I had to find something in the end.

'Melanie! Breakfast!'

I ran downstairs. The latest *Stage* was lying on the kitchen table. Great. I noticed my mum had circled a couple of ads as usual. She used to mark the jobs she wanted me to go for and leave the paper open at that page. She knew what I was like, she couldn't say, 'Go for those jobs!' So she'd wait for me to say, 'That looks good. Oh, and you've circled it mum!'

One of the ads was for a girl band.

WANTED

RU 18–23 with the ability to sing/dance?
RU streetwise, outgoing, ambitious, dedicated?
Heart Management Ltd are a widely successful
Music Industry Management Consortium currently
forming a choreographed, singing/dancing
all female Pop Act for a Record Recording Deal.
Auditions on 27 March 1994 at Dance Works
opposite Selfridges 11–4

The other ad she'd marked was for a cruise audition. It was being held upstairs from the band audition on the same day. National Express bus, here I come.

It was the usual scene. Four hundred girls in a huge studio room, probably not much chance of getting it, but c'mon, give it a go. It was just another audition, after all. One of the main things Mrs Wood had taught me was to go to auditions without an attitude and do your best. If you don't get it, you don't get it and it's on to the next audition.

I looked around me. Everyone was in full make-up, their hair done perfectly, wearing co-ordinated outfits, legwarmers and jazz shoes, clocking everybody else as they waited for the routines to start. Some people were struggling to get a place at the front and the wimps were lining up at the back. I wasn't bothered about where I stood. In every audition I've been to, the person demonstrating the routines stands at the front for a while then goes to the back and says, 'Right! Now turn and face this way!' So everybody at the back ends up at the front anyway, just like in my aerobics classes.

We were auditioning for a group called Touch, they told us, 'they' being a father and son team called Bob and Chris Herbert and Chris's girlfriend Shelley, although I didn't know their names at the time. I wasn't really interested in who they were. I just wanted them to be interested in me. How was I going to make them notice? I wasn't wearing anything particularly distinctive – black shiny shorts and a black striped crop top. But my hair was all out and not many black or mixed race girls wore it like that back then. There weren't many black or ethnic girls there anyway – just a handful. I was constantly aware of the lack of trained non-white dancers.

'Can everybody get into groups of ten please?'

We divided up and did a routine to 'Stay' by Eternal, some of it choreographed and some freestyle. It was really exciting. After a couple of hours there were only fifty of us left. It wasn't at all like the auditions you see on TV. You didn't see anyone wailing and crying, 'Oh no, I haven't got through!' like on *Pop Idol* and programmes like that. It was just, 'I didn't get it. Where's the next audition? I'm off.' Everyone had a tough skin. You had to.

To me *Pop Idol* didn't seem very realistic. It was forced and false because the cameras were there. In real life, the people auditioning don't behave like that and the panel judges don't act like that. The programme is completely hammed up and gives the public the wrong impression. In fact it's probably put a lot of people off the idea of going to an audition.

Those of us still left were asked to do a song. I sang 'The Greatest Love Of All', one of my favourite Whitney Houston tunes (I didn't know at the time that Dolly Parton wrote the original). All I said before I launched into it was, 'Hi! Hope you like it.' You didn't have time to sell yourself. You sang your song and that was it.

Afterwards I missed the cruise audition upstairs because I was too busy chatting to everyone downstairs. I was going to auditions so regularly by then that I'd got to know a lot of the other people on the circuit. It's a bit like a little community. You've all got something in common and you don't want to miss out on the latest gossip that's going around, because it just might get you a job.

I didn't hear anything from Bob and Chris, so it was back to scanning the ads pages and catching the bus to auditions. Around this time Black Grandma and Grandad went back to live in Nevis. Like many West Indians, they had always intended to return home when they'd earned enough for their retirement.

The day we waved them off at the bus station on the Kirkstall Road was a very sad one for me. Tears poured down my cheeks as I watched their coach pull away. Black Grandma and Grandad had been slightly distant figures during my childhood, but as I'd grown older and got to know them better I'd been spending far more time with them. When I was younger I'd always had the feeling that I should be scared of Grandma. I picked up on my dad's fear of her, I suppose. Later, when my own identity took shape, I started to be more forward with her and I often popped into the house when I was in Chapeltown. I always felt completely welcome there. Now I didn't know when I was going to see them again. I just couldn't imagine saving up enough money to pay my plane fare to the Caribbean.

Two days later there was a call for me.

'Hello Melanie. Would you be able to come to another audition?' It was Chris Herbert.

Yes. Something told me this was the one. I was going to get it. I just knew it. I've always had a sixth sense about things. In this case everything suddenly felt right.

There and then I decided to stop auditioning for other jobs. My mum thought I was mad. She'd seen it all before when I assumed I'd got a part in *Cats* after four auditions, but didn't make it at the last stage. 'Go on auditioning!' she urged. I wouldn't, even when the panto company rang and offered me another job. Too late, mate.

So it was back to the National Express station for the 6 a.m. coach to Victoria Station followed by two tube stops on the blue line and seven stops on the red line. After a quick search for 3H, 73 in the A-Z, it was a short walk from Shepherds Bush station to Nomis Studios, Sinclair Road, W12.

Even though I'd been to London many times I always had a butterfly flutter in my stomach when I arrived. I'd wake up in my seat with a jolt and think, You're here! Find out where you're going! In Leeds, London seemed like the big bad world, with drugs and muggings and people looking at you in a funny way but never talking to you. So when I got there I always felt a bit of a naughty thrill run through me. Hee hee, I'm in London by myself! Where do I go? On the tube you could generally clock who else was going to your audition. Sometimes I'd put away my A-Z and just follow the person in front who looked like a dancer. You could tell by their posture and turned-out feet that you were both heading for the same place. Plus the fact that they were splattering make-up all over themselves on the tube at ten in the morning.

I wasn't wearing a lot of make-up on the day of the second audition but I'd planned my outfit quite carefully. I wore brown knee socks, a little beige skirt, a brown polo neck top and a black Kangol hat reversed. Bob and Chris, the team that made up Heart Management, were waiting at the studios. Bob – God rest his soul – was golden-haired with leathery skin. He had a permanent *Miami Vice* tan and wore loafers and cream suits with V-necked jumpers or shirts. Chris was like a posh little gangly public school boy with long blondish-brown hair. He was quite funky and wore jeans and nice tops. Shelley was there too. She was introduced as the stylist.

There were twelve of us. First we were called in for a quick conversation about our CVs and previous work experience. It was the usual getting-to-know-you chit-chat.

'How do you think you would handle being in a girl group?'

'Yeah, whatever, I can handle girls! I worked for months on end with the same group of girls in Blackpool . . .'

Next we were divided into three groups and told to put together a routine to 'Just A Step From Heaven' by Eternal. My group all mucked in to choreograph the routine and it soon began to come together. We weren't particularly well matched as a group but it didn't matter because each one of us was trying to stand out from the crowd.

I really remember meeting Victoria Adams. She had big brown eyes and long legs and I thought her hair was really lovely, dark brown and glossy. Victoria's style was very jazz, a bit Hot Gossip. Michelle Stephenson was quite pretty too. Dark blonde curly hair, quite tanned and freckly, size ten, operatic-sounding voice.

We performed our routine to Bob, Chris and Shelley. Halfway through the set, someone walked into the room. When we'd finished dancing, I noticed a girl standing by the door.

'Come on over, Geri,' said Chris with a wave of his arm. 'We'd like you to join this group now.'

She looked like a mad eccentric nutter from another planet. She was absolutely tiny, with reddish hair, massive blue staring eyes, a funny nose, perfect skin and full lips. She was wearing a big fluffy pink jumper over a tight black and white stripy top, tiny hot pants and massive platform shoes. She had two small pigtails sticking out at angles at the front of her head. I looked at her and thought, My God, you look like a freak. Immediately she went into this whole big drama.

'Oh, I'm so sorry! I got sunburnt while I was skiing and I couldn't make it to the last audition. I was so upset and I'm really sorry if I've messed things up for you and it was so unfortunate that I got sunburnt but I really couldn't go out until I was better and . . .'

She went on and on about it, speaking in a posh London accent. Her voice was really penetrating. I thought my voice was loud but when I heard hers I thought, Oh my God!

Geri was the worst dancer I've ever seen in my entire life. I think my mum could have danced better than Geri could – she had no rhythm at all. She's come a long way since then, though. She's incredibly fit from doing yoga and you can see from her solo videos that her dancing has improved beyond belief.

I clicked with Geri immediately because she was fun and exciting and full of ideas – a real liver. 'I'll drop you off at the station if you like,' she said at the end of the audition. I got into her little green Fiat Uno and we began chatting away. It was weird, we instantly felt like old friends. There was a real connection right from the start and we laughed and giggled all the way to the station.

Victoria, Geri, Michelle and me were given tapes of Stevie Wonder's 'Signed, Sealed, Delivered' to take home and learn. When I got back to Leeds, I put it on the tape machine, wrote down all the words and sang along endlessly. I sang it to my mum, to Sherrel and to anyone else who would listen. I sang it so much that I started to annoy myself, let alone anybody else.

My mum kept telling me to slow it down, but I wanted to sing it faster and funkier than the Stevie Wonder version. I couldn't help adding a bit of my own style, as usual. It probably wasn't a very sensible move because we all had to sing the song together a week later back at Nomis Studios. I think the others must have had the same idea about coming up with a distinctive version, because it sounded terrible when we were given our harmonies. Can you imagine five totally different renditions squashed into one cats chorus? Oh dear.

This was the first time I met Melanie Chisholm, who had missed the second audition because of tonsillitis. Melanie had a really good voice and was one of those perfect dancers. Every move was exactly right. She seemed very nice and easy to get on with and had a strangely calming effect on everyone. She gave the impression that she was someone who could approach any situation with a smile. You would have thought that she didn't have a bad-tempered bone in her body.

(Little did I know that we'd get into a fistfight a couple of years later when she tried to break up an argument between me and Geri.)

Bob introduced us to Chic Murphy, a cigar-smoking old guy with white hair. ' 'Ello girls, nice ta meet ya.' Chic was the money man and looked like something out of an East End gangster film, although you could imagine he'd been really good-looking when he was younger. He was immaculately dressed and completely clean-shaven. Like Bob, he was a bit *Miami Vice*, but without the tan. Unlike Bob, who was a real Medallion Man, Chic didn't wear much jewellery but I did notice he had crosses tattooed on his ear lobes.

Chic was a gambler and decided we were worth a bet. So a few days later Chris phoned and said he wanted the five of us to spend a week together to see if we got on and gelled. He and Bob had booked us into a guesthouse in Surrey, with a studio nearby to rehearse in. By this stage I was popping with excitement. I vividly remember packing my bags and leaving to get on the coach. As I was getting ready, my dad sighed and said, 'Oh God, what is it *this* time?' I didn't bother answering. Nothing could affect my excitement. I was on a mission, having an adventure, buzzing.

As the coach drew into London, I wondered how long it would be before I finally left Leeds. I loved the city, most of my friends and family were there, but I'd known for a long time that I'd have to leave if I wanted to pursue my career. My best friend Rebecca had already made the move and she often said to me, 'You have to come to London!' Although the thought was frightening, I knew I'd have to do it one day.

I took the train to Windsor and Chris picked me up at the station. The guesthouse was a really nice homely place. It had a big hall, a huge dining room and a small cosy front room with really comfortable chairs and sofas. The bedrooms were cosy too. I dumped my bag in my room and ran back downstairs. The other four were already in the front room. I couldn't stop smiling and neither could they.

'Hiya!'

'I'm so excited!'

'So am I!'

'Eeek!'

'What happens next?'

'How about we record a No.1 single, perform on *Top of the Pops* and take the world by storm?' That was Melanie.

'Can we have some food first?' That was me.

Now we knew we were all in the group, instead of competing with each other we could just get on with it and enjoy ourselves. It was a brilliant week. We never stopped laughing. Every morning we'd go off to Trinity Studios in Woking and spend the day working on dance routines and songs. We did the routines ourselves and a woman called Pepi Lemer helped us with our harmonies. We all gave Pepi a hard time and took the piss, especially me. She was small and immaculately turned out, with a full mouth and a head of ruffled dark blonde streaked hair. You could tell she was from money.

It was the first time we'd done harmonies before – except Melanie – and Pepi made us work on them individually. We each had private singing lessons and mine usually ended in an argument. Pepi made me do the same thing over and over again until I refused to go on. 'I can't do it,' I'd say, and stop.

'You *must* do it Melanie. You *have* to do it. You won't get anywhere if you don't learn how to blend and harmonise,' she insisted. The high notes were the worst.

The point about Pepi was that she got us going. She was good for us because she motivated us and somehow helped to give our vocal harmonies a beautiful distinctive ring to them. There was never a lead singer in the group. That went without saying for us – it seemed fairer to take it in turns. Bob and Chris weren't very happy about it, though. They'd have preferred to have someone fronting the group, but we said, 'Well, we've done it like this.' No argument. We weren't going to be made to do something we didn't want to, even then. Bob and Chris had no choice but to agree. That was the first time we realised that we could get what we wanted as long as we stuck together. After all, who wants to pick a fight with five mouthy girls?

I'd like to think I was chosen to be in the group on the strength of my personality, rather than as the token black girl. I still don't know to this day. When I looked around at the others it was obvious that we'd been picked because we were all so different. We covered the spectrum – red haired girl, blonde girl, two dark haired girls and a mixed race girl. Right across the board.

In the evenings we'd have something to eat back at the hotel, then phone home, mess around, watch telly, gossip and dream out loud about the future of the group. We got on from the start, probably because subconsciously we knew that we were all in this together and needed it to work, but also because we had a lot in common. We were around the same age, liked a lot of the same music and were all trained dancers, apart from Geri.

One night we decided to go to the pictures. I wasn't feeling great because I was on antibiotics for my eye infection and they were making me queasy, but I didn't say anything. I wasn't going to miss out. On the way there I developed a really weak bladder and we had to keep stopping the car. Then I was sick on someone's lawn. As I vomited my guts up I could hear the other girls laughing and taking the piss out of me.

'Got much more in there have you Melanie?'

'That's nice, leave the birds a treat for the morning! Very thoughtful.'

Suddenly I realised something. They weren't disgusted or embarrassed that I was spilling my insides. They thought it was funny. They were taking the piss, like mates do. We were becoming friends.

On our last day in Surrey we did a little performance of the song we'd been working on all week, 'Take Me Away'. It wasn't our song, we didn't write it, but Bob and Chris seemed happy with the way we performed it. Chic was smiling in between puffs on his cigar. Did this mean we had a future? 'We'll call you,' said Chris.

9

WE'RE JAMMING

I was never allowed to use the phone much when I was younger. Maybe that's why I'm such a phone-aholic now. When I was living at home I'd rush to pick it up as soon as I heard it ring. That was partly because if my dad answered it he'd say sternly, 'WHO IS THIS?' when he heard a male voice at the end of the line. I had to grab the receiver away from him as quick as I could before he said anything else to embarrass me.

In the weeks that followed our trip to Surrey I spoke to Melanie, Geri, Victoria and Michelle quite a few times. The idea of being together in a girl group was so exciting for us all that we didn't bother with the kind of preliminaries that characterise most new friendships. We just jumped straight in, feet first. Melanie phoned the most. One of the first times she rang she said, 'It's a bit confusing that we've got the same name, isn't it?'

I agreed. It was going to do everyone's head in. She'd have to be Melanie C and I'd be Melanie B.

Then Chris called to say that he and Bob had found us a house in Maidenhead from July onwards. The idea was that we'd live together, be self-sufficient and spend our days rehearsing at Trinity Studios again. We'd have to be self-disciplined, he said, because there were no set times for doing anything. It was up to us when we got up in the morning and went to the studio, how long we rehearsed and how much work we put in. There would be nobody wagging the finger. This was a test to see if we really were motivated.

I didn't have to think twice. I was definitely up for it. We all were. I took a few changes of clothes, enough to tide me over for a few weeks, and got on the bus wearing the red bomber jacket that Claire Cattini had given me in Blackpool over a denim jacket and tight high-waisted jeans, with multicoloured imitation Kicker boots. I met up with Melanie at Waterloo Station and we took the train to Maidenhead together.

The house we were going to be living in for the next nine months (although we had no idea it would be that long at the time) was one of Chic's houses, a small grey semi on a typical sixties estate. I was really impressed to see it had a downstairs loo. I'd always wanted one at home. Upstairs there were two bedrooms, a bathroom and a tiny box room that was more of a cupboard than anything.

I shared a double bed with Mel C and slept on the right nearest the door. Melanie snored very loudly because she had something wrong with her sinuses. Our room was really cool. It had light pink chipwood walls and red bedding. I put a red lightbulb in the main socket, which made the room look like a brothel from the outside.

Everyone gathered in our room because our bed was the biggest and we could all fit on it and chat. Michelle and Vicky shared a room with twin beds and Geri was put in the little cubby hole because no one could stand to sleep in the same room as her. Her mind was just too hyperactive and eccentric. She was so specific about everything. She seemed like a bit of a loon.

In the early days, Victoria hardly spoke, Mel C was too timid to say much and Michelle was fairly quiet. Geri was definitely the most confident and had more of a mature outlook on things. She was on it, a workaholic, and her mind would race nineteen to the dozen. She was a go-getter and she wasn't going to let this fail. She had too much counting on it. If it went wrong for the rest of us, we'd just go off and do more auditions, get a cruise, go into acting or do a West End show. Michelle even had a place at university if she wanted it. We four had a back up, but for Geri this was her one chance. She'd already spent quite a while trying to break into show business, without much success, and she wasn't a trained dancer or singer. If she didn't succeed at this, she'd be f***ed. You really got that feeling from her.

Victoria was very organised, ladylike and quite fussy. I could never understand why she wore one particular outfit so much. A white shirt with big collars and cuffs and a black tank top over it, with a little black skirt and boots. She ate nothing but breadsticks and dips. I can picture her now, sitting in a chair on the right side of the front room, with a bowl of dips in front of her, all night. She'd watch TV sucking her thumb while clutching a furry rabbit toy. Strange.

I'd never known a Victoria before and I find the name Victoria a bit pretentious, to be honest. So I called her Vicky from the start, even though she didn't like it. I couldn't see what the problem was. Melanie was the same about 'Mel'. She preferred to be called Melanie. As far as I'm concerned, people can call me what they like, as long as it's not the c-word.

I found Vicky fascinating. It was amazing to see her planning in advance exactly what she was going to wear, from her eye make-up down to her toenails. She corrected her hair every five minutes. There was something very sexual about her, although she probably didn't realise it herself. It wasn't just that her legs were so long and cellulite-free. It was the way she sat, the way she talked, everything. Her clothes were just fantastic, mainly because she looked after them. I was the opposite. I might save up for ages to buy one little top from the designer shop in Leeds, but it would be ruined within a month because I couldn't be arsed to look after it properly.

To me Vicky was inspirational. I don't care what anybody says, she has got a touch of 'royalty' about her. It's hard to imagine her in her pyjamas, farting and burping. She's incredibly elegant. 'I can't wear flat shoes because they hurt my feet,' she told me soon after we first met. I couldn't understand it.

If Bob and Chris hadn't brought us together I don't think I would ever have made friends with someone like Victoria. She's the type that I would see in a club or a bar and literally turn my back on, not because I didn't like the look of her but because I could tell that we had nothing in common.

As it turned out we did have something in common – our sense of humour. We were always the ones that laughed at the stupidest, most ridiculous jokes about pooing yourself or someone leaving a stench in the toilet. As I later found out, humour is as important to the Adams family as it is to mine. Her mother Jackie and father Tony are hilarious. Vicky was a little bit more cautious than I was, though. She was never really rowdy.

Melanie seemed quiet and shy and easygoing at first and it was only later that she came out of herself. We bonded instantly – partly because we were both Northerners living with a bunch of Southerners who just didn't get it a lot of the time, but mainly because we were really compatible as friends and flatmates.

We were very different too. I still had a major thing about toiletries and I filled the whole shelf on my side of the bedroom with bottles and beauty products. I was so obsessed that I'd write lists of all the products I had: *exfoliator gloves, hair mousse, shampoo, conditioner etc*. Mel's shelf on her side of the room had about three things on it. One day we were having a half-jokey argument and she said, 'Watch this!' Suddenly she whacked her arm along the whole length of my shelf, sending the bottles and tubes flying. It just killed me, although I didn't show it.

Michelle was sweet, very upper class and very well turned out. I got on with her but I used to shout at her a lot because every time we took even a minute's break in the studio it seemed she'd be outside worshipping the sun. 'Michelle! Get back in here now, you lazy cow!'

She didn't seem that bothered. She wasn't a worker like the rest of us. While we were dancing our arses off in the studio, all she could think about was topping up her bleedin' tan. Or that's how it seemed at the time. I don't think Michelle had ever struggled for anything in her life.

I did quite a bit of snooping around the bedrooms. One day I was looking under a bed when I saw a massive pair of knickers with skid marks all over them. Eurgh! I found a pencil and used it to pick them up, then called to the others. Three of them came in to find me swinging this pair of knickers around shouting, 'Woohooh!' They all screamed at once. 'Oh my God! Skiddy knickers!' It was ridiculous really. We were like eight-year-olds.

Whose were they? Most of us wore G-strings, apart from Geri, but Geri's room was two doors down. They couldn't have been hers. I had a good idea who they belonged to, but it's not the kind of thing you can bring up very easily. 'Um, about those skiddy knickers under your bed . . .'

We tended to work hard during the week and flop at the weekend. The house was a Do Not Disturb zone on Saturday and Sunday mornings. Michelle had a Saturday job at Harrods and her mum used to pick her up and drive her there. Normally she was up and ready to go, but one morning, after a late night, she was still asleep when her mum arrived and started pressing the front door bell frantically.

'Are you there Michelle?' she shouted through the letterbox. No answer. She knocked and buzzed and shouted again.

A few minutes later this piercingly shrill mega-decibel screeching voice answered, 'I'm coming! I'm coming Mummy!' It woke the whole house up. To this day we can make each other cry with laughter by mimicking that call.

She wasn't a great dancer. Not as bad as Geri, but . . . I gave Geri a really hard time about her dancing. I often reminded her quite nastily that she wasn't trained like the rest of us. 'Durr! Haven't you got it yet?' It was unfair of me. After all, she hadn't spent the previous ten years going to five dance classes a week like I had. But I was impatient (like my mum!) and she was always standing at the back saying, 'What?'

We'd spend ages learning a routine and then have to go over it a million times waiting for Geri to pick it up. After a while we'd agree to move onto the next routine and she'd practice in her room for hours when we got home. I did feel a bit sorry for her but I didn't show any sympathy at the time. It didn't matter anyway because Geri was a good speaker, extremely articulate. Everyone had key roles in the group and hers was more verbal than anything. She was also good at coming up with ideas for strategies and outfits. There was no question of her importance to the group.

In our eyes, though, Michelle just didn't seem to be making the effort. By this point the group had really taken shape. We were very independent and began behaving as though we were running a company. Business-minded and self-sufficient to the extreme, we never let up with each other. One night the rest of us had a talk and decided that Michelle wasn't right for the group. When we discussed it with Bob and Chris, they agreed. She had to go. Maybe if she'd looked into a crystal ball and seen how successful we were going to be she'd have put more into it. Who knows?

It was Pepi who suggested Emma Bunton as Michelle's replacement. Emma was blonde, pretty and a good singer according to Pepi. She'd spent six years at Sylvia Young's stage school and done *Grange Hill* and *EastEnders*. She sounded perfect, but would we like her?

We went to pick her up at Maidenhead station in Geri's battered old green Fiat Uno. As the train pulled up, we began to get excited. 'What's she going to look like? What's she going to *be* like?' Geri instantly moved into mature, motherly mode. 'Everyone stay calm, okay? We'll see her in a minute.' Geri could be really annoying at times.

The train pulled away and we watched a pretty young girl walk across the station forecourt, her mother by her side. She was wearing a short white dress, a fluffy white top and a beige reversed hat. Her hair was in pigtail plaits and she had a really cute face with wide open big blue eyes, a button nose and pink lips. She and her mum looked very alike. We said hi and she said hi. We were all conscious of being extra polite, what with it being our first meeting.

What a really nice girl! I thought to myself. Not my kind of girl, but nice and sweet. We got in the car. Geri and me always sat in the front and I could see that Geri's staring eyes were fixed on the wing mirror, checking out the new girl. She couldn't stop watching Emma's every move and hardly looked at the road as she drove us back, which was typical of Geri anyway.

Geri had minor crashes quite regularly. She hit the kerb on the way to Trinity Studios once. The car skidded off the road and swerved into a muddy ditch. 'Oh my God!' the rest of us shouted. But Geri just revved up, drove back onto the road and we went on our way again. It was like *Wacky Races*.

Back at the house we showed Emma where her room was and explained that she'd be sharing with Vicky. Then we showed her round the rest of the house and went off to bed. As I was taking off my clothes I thought, Why am I going to bed so early? I'm really hungry. So off I went downstairs again. Emma must have heard me because she followed me down.

'What are you doing?' she whispered.

'I'm just cooking some scrambled eggs.'

She let out a huge sigh of relief and laughed. 'Thank God somebody else eats round here!' (Vicky picked at breadsticks and dips; Melanie's meals were usually made up of mushed vegetables; and I hardly ever saw Geri eat.)

We sat down, ate scrambled eggs together and had a really good chat. She told me all about her Greek boyfriend, who didn't sound ideal.

'Why are you with him?' I asked.

'I really like him,' she said.

'He has to go,' I said later. Not long afterwards she realised he wasn't right and dumped him.

That night Emma and I realised that we were night birds of a feather. This was the first of many late night talks and they continue today.

I didn't really like Mark, Vicky's boyfriend. Although he seemed like a nice guy, good-looking with long legs and jet-black hair, I just didn't connect with him. Mark was an alarm fitter and Vicky had met him when he came to do some work in her parents' house. I used to tease her and say, 'Yeah you shagged him on your mum's bed when he came to fit your alarm.'

She'd be outraged. 'No I did not, Melanie!'

Teasing was a way of life for us and we wound each other up all day and night. We'd be shouting things into each other's rooms long after we'd gone to bed. It was constant – a bit like being with my aunties, in fact. Humour, work and even things like watching TV and cooking together brought us closer by the day.

As the weeks passed we told each other everything and became completely involved in each other's lives. It must have been terrible for our boyfriends. None of us made a move without asking the others and we really did have a big impact on the outcome. It's no surprise we became so close. We were living in each other's pockets. We even linked arms as we walked to the corner shop together.

'He said this and that to me. What shall I do?'

'Say this, do that and go for it. Now!'

We'd all be waiting to find out the latest on someone's relationship or friendship. It was like being in a school gang. We should have walked around with a sign saying, 'Watch out, Girl Power's about!' as a warning of the chaos we were about to create. We didn't invent Girl Power but we definitely lived it.

Although we developed a good understanding of one another once we settled into the house, after a couple of months I began to miss my friends in Leeds. I wasn't homesick when we were working and everything was lively and spontaneous, but there were only a certain amount of times I could sit down and watch TV before I started thinking, I could be doing this at home.

Maidenhead was totally dead and there were hardly any black people living there. No one popped in to see me, like Charlotte and Sherrel did in Leeds. I didn't have my mum to talk to, I wasn't in familiar surroundings and I felt like I was missing out on the Leeds scene. I used to phone Charlotte and my mum in tears. 'Come on, just stick it out a little bit longer,' they'd say. In my heart I knew that I would be able to stick it out, I just phoned them to have a good old cry and feel sorry for myself.

It didn't help that we were without a contract. My mum and dad went on and on at me to hassle Bob and Chris, but they just wouldn't budge. The moment we asked they'd give us a slightly patronising look and say, 'Let's see how it goes,' or 'You're not ready yet.' To be honest, this just made us wonder what they were up to. We were working really hard but began to feel unappreciated and insecure about our future with Heart Management. Strangely though, instead of making us feel sorry for ourselves, Bob and Chris's lack of enthusiasm just strengthened our self-belief. We reassured each other a lot and constantly reaffirmed that we were 'in this for us' and nobody else was going to take control.

At first I went back to Leeds every weekend. Then I gradually brought my belongings back on the bus with me and the house in Maidenhead began to feel more like home. Sometimes Chic invited us over to his house, which had a lovely pool with his daughter's initials painted onto the tiles at the bottom. Our mouths dropped open the first time we went there. It was so posh. Vicky was the only one who wasn't totally amazed. I guess she was quite used to that sort of thing, because she came from a really nice background and a beautiful home. I, on the other hand, was running round like a headless chicken.

I took Chic's kids to one side and said, 'Show me around the house, everywhere!' They took me upstairs to one of the bathrooms, which was done out in peach, all mirrors and marble. There was a low basin with taps beside the toilet. I stepped into it, turned the taps on and watched water gush over my feet. Chic's kids looked at me as if to say, 'Are you crazy or something?' Well I'd never seen a bidet before.

I couldn't quite work out what Chic was about. I was also fascinated by Chic's wife's life. Did she work? What did she do? She always looked amazing and well groomed and their house had a lovely vibe. We'd go there and play with the two kids while Chic was having meetings with his strange cockney rhyming friends.

One afternoon we were all in the pool and Chic started telling Melanie and Vicky that they should lose weight. 'You could f***ing lose a few f***ing pounds, couldn't ya? What's wrong wiv ya?' He spoke like a real East End cat. 'You'd better f***ing start watching what you're f***ing eatin'.' You just didn't know whether to sit there and take it or say 'F*** off' back to him. More often than not we'd just sit there in shock. Nobody had ever spoken to us like that before, especially not a man.

He was always saying things like, 'I'll tell you what you need to do. You need to do a bit of this.' Then he'd go into some old Temptations dance routine, clicking his fingers in a showy display of 'rhythm'. We'd look at him blankly. 'What?' He just wasn't speaking our language.

We also went round to Bob's quite a lot. We'd get drunk at his big Sunday barbecues and spend evenings in front of his widescreen TV watching films. He had a great tacky Benidorm-style bar where we poured ourselves cocktails and pretended to be posh ladies. We were like kids in a sweet shop at Bob's house and he really made us feel welcome.

One week Melanie had tonsillitis and went to stay at Bob's house. Bob's wife was a lady of leisure and went on these courses where she learnt all about colour co-ordination, based around the colour of your eyes. 'Your irises are brown with a hint of yellow, Melanie. Well, that means yellow is your colour for this season.' She'd go on for hours on end about it.

Bob and Chris's favourite subject was Bros. They were perpetually showing us scrapbooks with Bros cuttings in them. As they told it, they'd *made* Bros and Bros had let them down and run off. That seemed like a good moment to ask for a contract. 'All in good time, all in good time,' Bob would say with that look in his eyes again. Oh, right. That means you don't think we're good enough yet, we'd think.

Geri and I started spending most of our weekends at the house together. Vicky and Emma went home and Melanie went to mad parties in Sidcup. A lot of Mel's friends were in Sidcup, including her best friend, because that's where she went to dance college. They're a full-on, crazy, lovely bunch of people. I went down there a few times because I fancied one of her mates.

Vicky used to take as many clothes home with her as possible but she couldn't take everything. So Geri and me raided her wardrobe. We spent ages putting everything back neatly, hoping that she wouldn't realise. (But when I read Vicky's book I found out that she did realise. Damn!)

Sometimes Geri and I went to bed on Saturday afternoon, woke up around 2 a.m., got dressed up and went to the all-nighter at Ministry of Sound. We used to drive down the motorway with our boobs out for a laugh. It was hysterical until we noticed a weird looking guy driving alongside us with a manic grin on his face.

'Oh my God, Geri, he looks like he's wanking!'

Suddenly we were scared. It was really frightening. For all we knew he was a complete nutter with an axe. Geri swerved into another lane and eventually we lost him. We were really shaken.

Did it stop us flashing our boobs? No!

Geri became my best, best friend. I'd found my friend for life, or so I thought. Instinctively I knew her down to a T and she knew me just as well and we had a very similar sense of humour. We even started going out in matching outfits. One Saturday we went to Marks and Spencer in our pyjamas. Why? For a laugh, of course. As we were wandering around the racks of bras and pants Geri suddenly came to a standstill. She looked down at herself, raised her eyebrows to their highest point and exclaimed dramatically, 'Oh my God I'm still in my pyjamas!' As though she'd only just realised it.

'Oh my God, so you are!' My expression was pure shock. Then I looked down at myself and screeched. 'So am I!'

And on it went. We acted out a mad scene and everyone turned to look at these strange girls in their bedclothes. It made us giggle for days afterwards.

We were like boyfriend and girlfriend in that we could have horrific arguments always knowing that we'd make it up afterwards, even though everyone around us at the time would be saying, 'Christ, they are never going to speak to each other again!'

We had infuriating rows, got irritated over the slightest things and swore like fishwives at each other. Our arguments went off with a bang from the moment they started. They were really dramatic and at times you'd have thought that she'd cheated with my boyfriend or something. I remember being in her little Fiat Uno shouting, 'You f***ing little sh**. Why don't you f***ing shut up!' The other three sat silently in the back. Then five minutes later everything was fine again. It never took long for one of us to laugh or say, 'All right, I'm SORRY!' and that would be that.

If I had something I wanted to say to Geri I wouldn't be able to concentrate on anything else until I'd got it out. It would eat me up. Sometimes it was personal, like I wouldn't like the way she was behaving towards me, the way she looked at me in a meeting, or spoke over me when I was saying something. At other times it would be about the strategy of the group. Our disagreements didn't stop us being inseparable though. I got on really well with the others, but Geri was the one.

We were so close that when her eating disorder spiralled out of control, I was the one she confided in. Until then she'd been very secretive about it, but after she opened up she was able to say things like, 'I'm having a bad week. Do you mind if I don't come food shopping with you?' I knew nothing about eating disorders really, never having had that problem myself. No one close to me had suffered from anorexia or bulimia before so I wasn't aware of the warning signs. Geri never explained what she was going through in depth and I didn't dig. It seemed like she was keeping it under control so I didn't worry about her too much. I didn't know her when she was overly thin, as she had been a couple of years before she joined the group, and I never saw her as fat later on, because to me the bigger she got the better she looked.

Deciding that she needed professional help, Geri found out about a hospital that specialised in eating disorders and booked herself in for a week. I dropped her off. She told the other girls that she had to go home to sort out a family crisis. No one thought to question it and obviously I said nothing. I desperately hoped that Geri would find the kind of help that she was looking for, because it was awful to see her unhappy. She did seem better when she came back, but unfortunately eating disorders are very difficult to get rid of permanently. She managed to cope, though. I really admired her for the way she kept fighting back.

There was one (that's right, one!) disco in Maidenhead. Called The Avenue, it was as suburban as its name. Emma and I used to go there on a Wednesday night, when they played jungle music and charged £1 a pint. One night I went with Geri. I was wearing a bright orange hot pants suit and she was in a bright blue hot pants suit, with long socks and trainers to match. 'Yes! It's the two lippy girls,' smirked the bouncer as he walked up. He was referring to our Camden Market hot pants, which were so tight that we both had VWs. 'Oh he's disgusting!' we exclaimed,

Sporting a bouffant, having just won a Renault Clio
in a beauty contest in Leeds.

My first love Stephen and I were totally on the same wavelength. I once dared
him to dress up in one of my mum's outfits and walk down the street to the
local shop and he actually did it!

Stylishly posing in our Blackpool show outfits, giving it the big 'un.

My first ever photo shoot, on the beach in sunny Blackpool.

Wearing my Asian wig: I needed a disguise for my nights out as I was the only black person in Blackpool.

Cuddling up with Fjöl, my hunky Viking. He was the perfect boyfriend – romantic, loving and funny.

Me and Richie having a moment together in Mum and Dad's back garden. Richie was very grounding for me and helped me to stay sane when it all kicked off with the Spice Girls.

In the back of a limo on a night out with 'da manager'.

In my mum and dad's kitchen proving to the family that we're a group and we're going to make it happen! Check out what's in my hand…

Just landed at the start of our first holiday together: with no security looking over our shoulders, we were five girls let loose in Hawaii.

Sunning it up in Hawaii.

Slumming it in a cheap hotel on our last night away, having got the departure date wrong. It actually turned out to be the best night of the holiday.

The making of the infamous 'Wannabe' video. We filmed it at St Pancras Station on a freezing cold April night and the video was later banned in Asia because of my erect nipples!

Having a laugh on one of our crazy promotional tours. We were on a constant high back then. Wherever we were, whenever we were together, it was us five against the world.

20 July, 1996, Japan. Getting into the drunken spirit of success, having just received a call from Simon to tell us that we were number one.

On our private jet and tour bus. Things could get pretty rowdy on our bus bu
our band's was far worse. We went on it just the once and vowed never
to repeat the experience.

dismissing him with a flick of the wrist as we walked in. Once inside, Geri went behind the DJ's decks and announced, 'Hey everybody, Touch is in the house!' She really made me laugh. The only other night spot we visited was the little pub at the bottom of our road. When we weren't totally broke we'd wander down there for a pint and a game of snooker.

The five of us got on well because we didn't pretend to be anything we weren't. We were totally open with each other. For instance none of us shut the bathroom door, even when we were on the toilet. We got a reputation for going to the loos together in clubs. Whether we were having a wee or a poo we'd leave the cubicle doors open so that we could look at each other in the mirror and chat. One by one we admitted, 'I'd never do this back home. The door would be well locked.' It was something we had a good giggle about. Our other friendships were different. None of us had ever been to the toilet in front of our mates before.

I think the others used to dread it when I had a bath because I'd always put on the same Mary J Blige song full blast and sing along to it. I played it so loud that everyone in the house, wherever they were, would be singing along too. There was a really high note that I could never reach, however hard I tried, and I know that they were all thinking, Oh God, here comes the high bit. Is she going to get it? I'd take a deep breath, let out a massive screech, then get out of the bath.

In the mornings, the others went to the gym while me and Emma stayed in bed until it was time to get up for *Home and Away* at 12.30 p.m. Then we'd jump in Geri's car and zoom off to the studio to practise songs and work on our dance routines. Sometimes Bob and Chris would come down to watch us, but mostly they left us to it.

On the way to the studio we stocked up on bread and doughnuts at Cullens. We were high on bread and ate toast non-stop. In the evenings I often cooked corned beef and rice for everyone, then Geri would help me write letters to Julian in prison. (Yes, 'the man upstairs' became 'the man inside' for a couple of years!) Meanwhile Melanie sat in the front room and watched Take That in concert over and over again, so much so that we all ended up watching and copying their routines. We were fascinated by their freestyling, particularly Jason's.

There was one particular routine they did with microphone stands. We perfected it, especially the bit when Mark wiggled around, gyrating with the mic between his legs. I liked the drum solo, when a boy with very pale skin, coiffed hair and a drum around his neck led a march across the stage. Little did I know at the time that it was Max Beesley, one of my future boyfriends. On the video he looks like a little gay boy with his white vest and baggy jeans. I later found out that Jason Orange is one of Max's best friends.

In moments of madness me and Melanie played this intense game where we'd come head to head, with our faces practically touching, and sing Neneh Cherry songs at each other, including the raps. *So you say you wanted money but you know it's never funny when your shoe's worn through and there's a rumble in your tummy, but you had to have style, get a gold tooth smile, put a girl on a corner so you can make a pile. Committed a crime and went inside. It was coming your way but you had to survive. When you lost your babe, you lost the race. Now you're looking at me to take her place.* We'd go on and on, getting faster and faster and more intense until one of us tripped up or got a line wrong. 'Ha! I won!' At that point the veins would be practically popping out of your neck because you were concentrating so hard on getting it right. It was great, totally mesmerising, like a musical duel.

Melanie is the kind of person who will not be defeated. I remember asking her to open a bottle of beer for me when I couldn't find the bottle opener. After a couple of tries, I told her not to bother and started searching for the opener again. 'No!' she said. 'Just give me a minute. I *will* open it!' She won't allow herself to fail at anything. She also does the best imitation of Kate Bush singing 'Wuthering Heights' that I've ever seen. If she performed it on *Stars In Their Eyes* she would win hands down.

We had a lot of time on our hands and sometimes we sat in and got a bit drunk together. (Or, I should say, *I* would get drunk with myself.) We opened our hearts up about things like ex-boyfriends, dance auditions and how your mum does your head in. I used to get battered but Melanie didn't really drink much until she got into lager (and I really encouraged her!). Geri never got drunk but was always there with her own brand of analysis. 'It's really good that you told that story. Now we can all understand you from a different point of view. What do the others think about that?' She was like our therapist mediator.

We did our weekly shop together – tuna and pasta and corned beef and rice, not forgetting Vicky's breadsticks and dips of course. In some ways we lived a very carefree life. We didn't bother with a TV licence and were always dodging the housing benefit inspector. We were extremely serious about taking control of our careers, though. Our goals and dreams meant everything to us.

We had a rota stuck up on the fridge alongside a cut-out of some hunky guy's face. Everyone had a different job around the house, although of course it never quite worked out that way. Laundry was the job I dreaded being lumbered with. I knew how to cook and clean and do general domestic things, but my mum had always done my laundry for me. I had no idea how to work a washing machine. Luckily Melanie told me that everything had to be colour segregated. 'Can't I just put everything in together?' Vicky would have killed me!

Our kitchen had a wet patch on the carpet. You could tell when someone had forgotten about the patch because they'd be walking round with one sock on and one sock off. 'Ha ha, you've stepped in the wet patch!' There came a point when you knew the house so well that you could walk around the kitchen half asleep and avoid it. But if you weren't thinking you'd step in it. It was so annoying.

As time went by we became quite friendly with our neighbours. One of them entertained us with his wicked record collection when we went over to watch him playing his decks. Another was a city boy with long hair and I quite fancied him, but never did anything about it. I was going out with a guy from Manchester at the time – 'Mucky Manchester Man' as Vicky called him (let's call him Triple M for short). I'd met him a few months before I went to Maidenhead. After an audition Charlotte and I had pulled into a garage in Manchester – and by chance there were loads of gorgeous guys there. One of them was tall and mixed race. He was a bit rough-looking but his eyes were beautiful. I got talking to him, we went out, had a drink, played snooker and I ended up staying with him for about three weeks, at his mum's house in Moss Side. I heard a lot of gunshots in those weeks.

I didn't know what Triple M did but it wasn't an issue. As long as he was nice to me it didn't matter. Once when he came to visit me in Maidenhead we got locked out of the house. Geri and I were always losing our keys and knocking up the nice old couple next door to borrow their ladder. This time, before we could think, Triple M whipped out his credit card, slipped it between the lock and the frame and the front door swung open. We were amazed. How did he do that? Another time he proudly showed me an array of what looked like rough crystals, laid out on a board. They glinted in the sun. 'Oh what lovely diamonds,' I said admiringly. 'Are they yours?' He laughed. I was so naïve.

After a few months I began to lose interest in Triple M. One Saturday night Geri let him in, even though I'd told her not to. 'We've got to think of an excuse why he can't stay,' I whispered in her ear. So she went to her room, wriggled into a flamboyant dress and came down looking really smart, with her hair up.

'Me and Melanie are going to the opera,' she announced. What? Couldn't she have thought of a better excuse? She went into a long explanation about how much we loved theatre and opera. 'Culture, it's so inspiring, so good for the soul!' It was some typically mad story and I didn't know what to do apart from go along with it.

Triple M left looking pissed off. If we were going to get away with it, we realised, we would have to follow through with the story and pretend to go out. He was still parked outside when we left the house. Obviously he suspected that we were lying and was trying to catch us out.

'Oh God, what are we going to do?'

'Let's drive around the block and see if he's gone.'

'Oh no, he's still there!'

'Quick, grab those skirts off the back seat. One each, put it over your head. Then he won't recognise us.'

As if. We drove round and round like idiots, with skirts over our heads, giggling manically. I didn't see Triple M again. He sold a story when the Spice Girls became known but I didn't read it. All my stories were about sex and how great I apparently was. I suppose it was good for my man-eating profile, but boring for me to read. Mel shags five times a night! Big deal.

As the weeks in Maidenhead turned into months, the group got better and better. Our routines were slick and we were excellent at harmonising, although the material wasn't great. We now had three new songs written by other people, to go with 'Take Me Away'. They were fairly similar, bland and boring. We put as much pzazz into them as we could, but the lyrics were a nothingness, so Geri and Melanie began to rewrite them. We wanted to sing lines that we could relate to, about real situations, instead of cheesy meaningless rubbish about falling in love.

One night we were lolling about in the front room, feeling a bit restless and bored.

'Let's write a song,' suggested Geri.

'Yeah! What shall we write about?'

'Mmmmm . . .'

'I know,' she said, 'Let's write about how we're feeling right now.'

It was called 'Just One Of Those Days', a song about feeling restless and bored and wondering what to do next. It wasn't a masterpiece and didn't really have much of a tune, but it was a start. Melanie and Emma were brilliant at harmonies, which always made everything sound fantastic. Right there and then was the moment that we got the buzz for writing our own material. We didn't want to be robots any more, we wanted to do our own thing.

But we still weren't getting anywhere with Bob and Chris. We went on hassling them about a contract but it was like talking to a brick wall. It was so frustrating. The idea of being in a girl group had seemed so great when I first went to Maidenhead, but we still weren't earning any money. They weren't paying us and there was no sign of a contract. My mum started saying, 'Well we still haven't heard of you. Why don't you just leave and get a job?' She wasn't bothered what I did. It didn't matter if I was in a pop group or an office, she just wanted me to be independent with a job and a wage.

Bob and Chris obviously didn't have much faith in us, but we persuaded them to let us do a mini showcase at Trinity Studios. Chris invited a few people and we did three or four numbers, including 'Take Me Away' and 'We're Going To Make It Happen'. We wore baby doll dresses and long socks. Mine were pop socks with stripes on them and I had my hair in nodules at the front and back. Geri wore a red baby doll dress with a polo neck underneath. Emma was in pink with her hair in bunches, Melanie had a blue theme and Vicky wore black with her hair down. We looked good, even though baby dolls weren't really our style, except for Emma. Afterwards we got our first feedback.

'They thought you were great, but you need more work,' said Chris. Fine, we thought. We work our arses off anyway and we enjoy it. So we went on driving to the studios armed with bags full of Cullens bread. We practised and practised. We sang scales with Pepi until we were blue in the face – and we changed our name from Touch to Spice.

If we couldn't have a contract, then we wanted another showcase. Maybe Bob and Chris didn't believe in us, but someone out there would. We were determined to be heard and give the industry a taste of what we were about.

The big day was planned for November, back at Nomis Studios in Shepherds Bush. Shelley, Chris's girlfriend, styled us. Round and pretty, with clear skin, bright eyes and really slick black shiny hair, she was a buyer for Sock Shop, which we all thought was amazing. We'd been impressed by her from the beginning and really took on board what she had to say.

Shelley brought round a big black bin liner and tipped it upside down on the lounge floor. Out tumbled a pile of second-hand Adidas tops in different colours that she'd bought at Camden Market. We all chose one and that was that. Jeans and tops, plain and simple. We dressed alike, except for my Kangol hat, because I had a thing about my Kangol hat and wore it all the time. Of course Geri wore a beret, because she loved her beret, and Melanie wore tracksuit bottoms instead of jeans. With a red and white pirate scarf on her head. We couldn't help adding those personal touches. Our different personalities were bursting to come out. But Bob and Chris wanted us in uniform, so we did our best. Sort of.

The showcase at Nomis Studios confirmed what we already knew. We had something. We did our set several times during the day and a constant stream of people came over to tell us how great it was. Chris had invited a range of people from the music industry, from producers to A&R, and they all seemed to like us. It was a bit shocking how much they liked us in fact. It put us on a huge high.

It got us thinking, Why should it take a whole bunch of people to tell us that we're good? We know we're good. If Chris and Bob aren't aware of that now, they can piss off. As it happened Bob and Chris were seriously impressed by the industry response to us. Within days we had our contracts, long boring documents with clauses and sub-clauses. The ball was in our court now. They wanted to sign us. But did we want them after all? It was our turn to hesitate. Finally we had a bit of real power.

10

FINALLY

I've never been single for more than a couple of weeks. It's not that I'm needy-needy, I just like male companionship. With triple M out of the picture, I went out with a guy who owned a tea house/restaurant in Marlow. It didn't last long. The two most memorable things about that relationship were: one, we shagged on the table in his restaurant; and two, during the summer he took Geri and me to the Henley Regatta. We dressed up posh and play-acted all day. 'I say, do look at that punt over there!' It was hysterical.

One night while he was away on holiday, Geri and me went to the cinema with her lawyer friend James and his brother Richie. They both had terribly posh accents. After the film I said to Richie, 'I quite fancy you,' and he said, 'Yeah, I fancy you too.' So when Marlow Man (Double M!) got back from his holiday I told him I'd met someone else.

When I started going out with Richie, James asked, 'How did you manage to get her then?'

'I don't know, she's just hounding me,' Richie said.

As it turned out, Richie was very grounding for me. A jewellery engraver, he came from a solid, loving family, was a nine-to-fiver and liked cooking dinner. (Somewhere in the back of my mind I'd set myself the goal of being with someone who wore a suit to work. I was fascinated by the idea, because in Leeds I rarely saw people in suits apart from the odd teacher.)

He was a fantastic boyfriend and really helped to keep me centred when everything kicked off for the Spice Girls a bit later down the line. Most of all he gave me a loving, understanding relationship. His parents were lovely and very welcoming. His father made me laugh because he was always going on about his teeth and how he was convinced that one of them was going to fall out. His mum was Australian and I used to have very interesting conversations with her. She was a brilliant, powerful, family woman.

Richie lived in St Albans and sometimes came to stay at the house in Maidenhead. He got on well with the other girls, especially Melanie, who cooked us some fantastic dinners. By this point the group was seriously considering leaving Bob, Chris and Chic. Our ideas about which direction we should go in just didn't match theirs. They wanted to dictate what we wore and the material we sang. We wanted to write our own songs and wear what we liked. Incompatible isn't the word.

The showcase had been a turning point in more ways than one. It had made us realise how good we were, but it also brought us together with several songwriter/producers. The first writer we worked with was an American called Alan Glass, who had a small studio in his house just outside London. It was our first taste of co-writing and together we came up with some good R&B numbers, pretty much copying the style of Eternal, our favourite girl group of the moment, although the vocal arrangements were different. From the start we shared out the singing between us – one person sang the first verse, someone else sang the bridge and we all came together for the chorus – which set the pattern for the future. Our month with Alan also gave us our first experience of recording and we loved every minute of it, even though he didn't give us much control over the musical side of things.

After Alan came a writer named Roger, a tall black guy who had a studio in his flat on a little housing estate in London. The studio equipment was in his front room and you sang on the landing, in an improvised 'vocal booth'. Things didn't work out with Roger. When the demos came back they sounded terrible because he'd added his voice to all the harmonies!

The two most significant people we met at the showcase were Matt Rowe and Richard 'Biff' Stannard, a song writing team that went on to have a massive influence on the Spice Girls sound. We got on with Matt and Biff from the very start. Instinctively they seemed to understand what we were about and soon set about incorporating the spirit of five loud girls into great pop music. They weren't in the least bit patronising or superior, although they had every right to be. They were experienced writers and producers who had done a lot of work with East 17, whereas we were absolute beginners.

We may have been naïve but we weren't short on ideas and the great thing about Matt and Biff was that they listened. How, I don't know, because quite often all five of us would be shouting at once, but between the lot of us we created some fantastic songs in The Strong Room, their studio in Curtain Road, EC2. Although we didn't have much experience of writing, we were always listening to music. We had music coming out of our cars and rooms constantly and were into all the newest clubs, tunes and pirate stations.

'Let's write a ballad today!'

'Yeah!'

'What about?'

'Is there anyone you want to slag off?'

'I've got one! This boy really pissed me off once . . .'

The one rule was that we wouldn't write a love song. Our mission was to tell men what we wanted from them instead.

I thought Matt was a complete freak when I first met him but I instantly gelled with him. We had a special relationship. He's a highly intelligent guy – almost too intelligent for his own good, in each and every area – but with a nervous energy that takes a while to get used to. He's got a bit of a stutter and sometimes seems as though he's just been told that World War Three is about to break out at any minute. We got into a lot of debates and I really enjoyed talking to him. When he and Geri started making eyes at each other I knew what was going on, even though they denied it. I knew them both too well for it to be a secret from me.

Matt was the main music guy and Biff worked on the lyrics, but they used to swap and change and mix it all up. Biff (please Biff, do not be offended) is exactly what you would think a Biff would look like. His name is so perfect – and I mean that in a good way. He's a big, cuddly man with that newborn baby look. There's no one else like him. He's incredibly open and you can learn a lot from him. You always felt like you could say anything to Biff. Sometimes he seemed just like one of the girls, other times he was quite fatherly, passing on advice and warnings about the way the music industry works. There was never a ruck between the five of us when Biff was around. He could spot trouble a mile off and knew how to keep things smooth.

The fact that things were working out so well with Matt and Biff made it harder to make a decision about the contract. Would they still work with us if we left Bob and Chris? It was a risk we were going to have to take, although we delayed for as long as we could. Inevitably, though, there came that point when we knew it all had to end. Chris and Bob and Chic were hassling us to sign and we ran out of excuses. It was time to leg it.

We did a midnight flit from the house. Well it was more of a 9 p.m. flit but that doesn't sound quite as dramatic. Vicky and Emma both went off home and Melanie headed back to Sidcup. Geri and me were the last to leave. We really played up the drama of the situation and acted like B-movie criminals.

'Quick, get in the car! Is anybody looking? Let's get out of here!'

Just then I half-expected the *Starsky & Hutch* theme tune to start playing out of a music system in the sky. Off we went to stay at Richie's house in St Albans, where Geri had to sleep on a bed frame that had no mattress. I didn't feel guilty about leaving Bob and Chris. We were just going in different directions.

We phoned Matt and Biff. 'We've left Bob and Chris. Will you still work with us?'

'No problem,' said Biff. 'Of course we will.'

Thanks Biff. We needed that. Now we knew for sure that we'd done the right thing. It was a crucial confidence booster.

A couple of days later we were due to be working with a writer called Elliot Kennedy at his studio up in Sheffield. Elliot had worked with Take That and obviously we didn't want to miss the chance to write with him too, but the session had been organised by Bob and Chris and none of us had a clue how to get hold of Elliot. Or whether he would agree to work with us now.

So Geri and I decided to drive up to Sheffield and find him. After talking it over, Melanie, Vicky and Emma agreed to catch the train up the next day. Melanie had just come into some money – a family inheritance of about £300 or £400 – and she offered to pay for the petrol and fares to Sheffield as well as a week's rent in a cheap bedsit. It was typically generous of her – she's always been very giving – but I think it's fair to say that any one of us would have done the same if we'd had the money. We were in this together, all for one and one for all. (Sorry Mel, I think that to this day we've never paid you back.)

Halfway to Sheffield we were bombing down the motorway, swerving all over the place, when we saw a phone box on a slip road. Screeeech! We looked through the yellow pages and found nine Kennedys in the area. The third number we called was Elliot's.

'Hi!It'sMelandGerifromSpiceandweneedtotalktoyouwe'reonour wayuptoSheffieldcanyoumeetustonight?'

This was urgent, man. The words came out so fast that they almost had a heart attack. Elliot was 'the guy', Mr Big. For the whole journey up from London we had been consumed by one thought: Will he or won't he work with us?

'Hello MelandGeri,' said Elliot warmly. 'Look, I've got to go and see a violinist about some recording work. Meet me there.'

Geri wrote down the address and at around midnight we found ourselves driving along a bumpy winding country road in what seemed like the middle of nowhere. Up ahead loomed the shadowy silhouette of a huge country mansion, all leaded windows and turrets. Two massive Alsatians met us at the gate, barking ferociously. We looked up at the house. There weren't any lights on and not a noise could be heard. Was anybody in? I caught Geri's eye. I could tell we were both thinking the same thing. This is really fishy. We knew virtually nothing about Elliot, after all. I think we both felt a bit frightened deep down.

The house was in almost complete darkness. On the first floor we saw a light under a door, so we knocked and went in. We walked into the room to find a tall chunky guy with dark reddish hair and glasses, sitting on a sofa with a girl with long hair. She looked young and fresh and gooey-eyed.

'Uh, hi, Elliot?'

'Ah. You must be MelandGeri! Come in.'

Elliot seemed pleased to see us so we told him our story there and then. 'Look, we've split with Bob and Chris. We've got the money together to pay for the studio. The others are coming up tomorrow. Will you still work with us this weekend?'

'Yeah, fine,' he said with a friendly shrug.

'Oh my God!' we gasped, our knees practically buckling beneath us. We were on a high for weeks after that.

The first song we wrote with Elliot was 'Love Thing', which is one of the tracks on 'Spice', the first Spice Girls album. A far cry from the stuff that Bob and Chris wanted us to sing, it set a precedent for the Spice sound (and message) with its punchy melody and assertive lyrics. Elliot had already set down a beat for the song and sketched a melody; the rest came together in a kind of jam. Geri and I made up the rap on our second day. *God help the mister, yeah god help the mister/That comes between me and my sisters.* At that point in our lives boys and love were second to what we had as girls together and most of our early songs reflect that. Girl Power was partly about getting what *you* wanted out of a relationship or a friendship with a boy, and not pandering to the male ego.

> *There's no room for lovin' stop that push and shovin' yeah,*
> *Don't wanna know about that love thing,*
> *Give me what I'm needing you know what I'm dreaming of*

Being without a manager seemed to energise us. It didn't matter that we were broke and practically homeless, we were on a fast track to . . . somewhere! As we sat in Elliot's vocal booth recording our first proper song, it was truly amazing to think that Take That had been in the very same studio a couple of months before us. We were so impressed.

Elliot very kindly let us stay at his house, which was a little semi that used to belong to his mum and dad. Most nights I dragged Emma back to Leeds with me and we'd go off to Charlotte's house or Maya's. Maya was – and is – another very good Leeds friend. I drove my mum's little Polo between Sheffield and Leeds, constantly paranoid that I'd get caught because I wasn't insured. The others stayed at Elliot's, in his mum's old bed. In the evenings they'd change into their nighties and pyjamas, go downstairs and watch TV with him. He was mad on *Star Trek*, a proper anorak.

Whenever I stayed at my mum's she'd moan, 'What is this bloody group anyway? You've got no money, no work, no manager.'

I'd been 'borrowing' money off her for months now and it infuriated her that I'd turned down work to concentrate on the group. It just so happened that I'd auditioned for a film about a year previously and suddenly they wanted me to fly out to America for the shoot. Then a German record company executive rang up and asked if I would be interested in discussing a deal. A few offers came and went – for all of us – but we stayed firm. We were in the group and that was that.

'We're going to make it no matter what,' I told my mum.

'But what's the next move? How long is it going to be before you start earning some money?' she complained.

My mum's car would never have got her to London, so while we were in Sheffield I said, 'Right, I'm going to bring the others down this weekend and show you.' So I took them all home. We did a mini perform-ance in the kitchen, told my mum and dad about our plans and recited quotes from all the people at the showcase who'd told us that we'd got what it takes. My mum and dad were amazed at our performance. 'Oh my God!' Suddenly they understood. That night all my aunties came round and we had a slap-up dinner, watched TV and got completely smashed. Welcome to the mad Brown family, girls!

I think we'd all have liked to continue working with Elliot, but with 'Love Thing' finished it was time to go down South again. Back in The Strong Room with Matt and Biff we wrote another new song. It only took about twenty minutes to write in a sudden creative frenzy, but we in-stantly had a feeling that it was something special. Matt and Biff were incredibly excited. Matt stayed up all night working on the track and Biff found him snuggled in a sleeping bag on the vocal booth floor the next morning. There was a post-it note stuck to the decks saying, PRESS PLAY. Biff cranked up the volume and Matt woke up to the sound of the opening bars of what was to become the first ever Spice Girls single, 'Wannabe'. (Me and Geri shouting!)

Now we had two fantastic songs it was time to find a new manager. We were in a strong position to conquer the world – we knew that. All we needed was someone to help us come up with the master plan.

We thought about the artists we admired and why we admired them, then it was Geri's job to find out who looked after them. She made loads of phone calls and soon had a long list of potential managers. She also enlisted the help of Mark Fox, a music publisher at BMG Publishing who'd been at the showcase. We became very friendly with Mark, who'd been the drummer in eighties band Haircut 100 and looked a bit like Morten Harket from Aha (another eighties band). He took us to dinner at places like Julie's in Holland Park and was very well connected, helping us with names and numbers and arranging interviews with record companies and managers. Sometimes he'd be our spokesperson when we went to meetings, other times we went alone.

Geri's car was our think tank and her Filofax our computer. We bombed our way around London, exploding into the offices of agents, managers and record companies – well, the ones that let us in, anyway. A tape of 'Wannabe' would be shoved hurriedly into the music system, then I'd shout 'C'mon!' and jump up on the table while Mel did a back flip, Victoria flashed her legs and Emma jumped up and down. We all bounced around like maniacs for a couple of minutes, singing and dancing, then Geri would introduce us and explain why we were there. It was great. They didn't know what had hit them. I think it's safe to say that no one we have ever 'Spiced' has forgotten the experience.

The others became used to seeing me write in my diary. Wherever we went, one of my little notebooks always came too. *The group as a whole is a magical joining of forces*, I wrote at the time. *It's so powerful that on a good day it blows your mind away.*

One of the managers on Geri's list asked us round for dinner. We were so skint that we decided not to eat all day and then stuff ourselves when we got to his house. In the car on the way we started fantasising about the meal to come.

'I hope it's chicken!'

'Or a stir fry!'

'Lots of salad!'

'Chocolate cake!'

The first thing he did when we arrived was pull out a big plate of doughnuts, which he handed to me first. 'Oh no thanks,' I said. 'I don't want to ruin my appetite. I'll wait till dinner.'

'This is dinner!' he said.

Oh no.

We might have considered him after some chicken fried rice, but a lardy plate of doughnuts just wasn't doing it.

We met up with another potential manager in his basement office in central London. 'Hi! We're the Spice Girls,' we announced as we piled in and introduced ourselves in our typical all-singing, all-dancing, over-the-top way. Well, you could tell he was impressed. If he'd been a cartoon character we'd have seen the pound signs ring up in his eyes as his mouth dropped open and gold coins came pouring out. He was frothing with glee and rubbing his hands together like Scrooge in front of a treasure chest.

It was his turn to talk and he turned it on big time. Uh-oh. As I sat there listening to him doing this big old 'I can take you girls to the top of the charts, bosh-bosh' spiel, I thought, Oh my God. Please no.

We came back out onto the street and looked at one another. 'Actually he was talking a load of bullshit, wasn't he?' I ventured.

'Total crap,' said Vicky.

Phew! All together now in a Dalek voice: 'Eliminate!'

It was Geri's job to tell people when we weren't interested. To our amusement, some of them went ballistic and really took it to heart. The rest of us would listen in as she broke the news. 'Sorry, we're going to look elsewhere. You don't quite fit what we're looking for in a manager at the moment.'

One guy took it so personally that she had to hold the receiver away from her ear as he ranted on at her. It was hilarious; we laughed our heads off. These were grown men who'd been in the business for years and years and they were behaving like two-year-olds. It felt good to be telling them where to get off. It made us feel like proper power chicks. But as the weeks passed and we still didn't have a manager, we started to get a bit anxious. All our potential candidates had been crossed off the list.

At least we knew what we didn't want – no controlling, pleased-with-himself, greedy, tightwad manager was coming anywhere near us. We needed someone with brilliance and integrity. Now who was it to be?

Meanwhile Mark Fox had introduced us to Paul Wilson and Andy Watkins – known as Absolute – another team of writers/producers. Paul was thin, tall, quite young-looking and almost Harry Potter-ish with his round glasses. Andy was cooler, a bit more London, with a street edge and very short hair-baggy jeans vibe. They made a good match – sensible and kind of not sensible – and we started working with them around April 1995. Their studios were miles away in Twickenham. We'd have to park the car, cross the river by bridge and walk for ages until we came to a massive cul-de-sac containing a scrap yard, some lawyers offices, the Absolute studios and a café. The café did fantastic toasted egg-mayo-bacon-ketchup sarnies.

Paul and Andy were more old-school soul than Matt and Biff. They were into the funk vibe – more Angie Stone than Bananarama. We wrote 'Something Kinda Funny' with them and they also went on to produce the two songs we did with Elliot, 'Love Thing' and 'Say You'll Be There'.

When Paul and Andy mentioned that their manager was in partnership with Simon Fuller, Annie Lennox's manager, Geri wrote his name down in her filofax. Before she had a chance to call him he phoned and asked to meet us. He'd listened to 'Something Kinda Funny' and he was curious. Well, so were we.

Simon Fuller had been a publishing scout for Chrysalis Records in the mid-eighties, then left to set up a company of his own. He called it 19 Management because 19 was most definitely his lucky number. His first big break came when a young producer he was managing – Paul Hardcastle – put out a best selling single in 1985. An anti-Vietnam War song called, you've guessed it, '19', it sold bucket loads and was number one for weeks.

Next he discovered Cathy Dennis. I particularly remembered Cathy because of the red catsuit she'd worn in one of her videos. She was a pretty singer/songwriter who we all admired. As well as having had a successful career as a solo artist, Cathy is a respected writer, responsible for tracks like Kylie's 2001 hit, 'Can't Get You Out Of My Head'. Simon also managed Annie Lennox. Well, I had a special connection with Annie Lennox because my dad used to play her music all the time when I was living at home.

The offices of 19 Management were in Ransome's Dock, Battersea. We were all quite giddy as we went up in the lift – as we always were – wondering what this guy was going to be like. Stepping out into a large, light-filled open-plan office, we instantly clocked that it wasn't a stressed working environment. Everyone seemed chilled. I don't remember seeing any men working there, it was all women, and quite classy women too.

I'd become accustomed to seeing into this kind of environment and I did regularly notice that black and mixed race people and people of colour were nowhere to be seen. This didn't bother me outwardly but became more and more of an issue deep inside, even though I didn't express it at the time.

Simon Fuller's office was in the corner of the room. It had smoked-glass walls so that you could see out but not in, and blinds. In my fantasy world I'd dreamed of a beach house with those kinds of smoked-glass walls.

We waited for what seemed like ages, although it was probably only a few minutes, our gazes flicking over the many gold discs hanging on the inner walls of the office. Could Simon Fuller be the one? We'd interviewed so many managers and been disappointed so many times. We generally made up our minds about people on impulse, within the first ten or fifteen minutes of meeting them, so we'd soon know if Simon was right. I had my fingers crossed, desperately hoping he would be.

When Simon finally walked in we collectively held our breath and waited. It wouldn't be long now.

It only took a few sentences.

'What do you girls want?' he asked. 'I'm here to listen to your story. I know your music already, so tell me what you envisage for the future.'

If you're stuck for conversation, always ask a question! It breaks the ice every time, because who doesn't like to talk about themselves and their experiences?

My first impression of Simon was of a small but stocky man with black hair and a tan, who had the presence of a knowledgeable teacher. He seemed very in tune with our vision as we played him our songs and told him all the things we wanted to do.

'We want to be an international band. We want to take over the world. We want to make a film!'

'We want to be a household name, bigger than Persil Automatic!' said Vicky.

'Most importantly we want to be ourselves,' we said. 'Kids can see through bullsh**.'

Simon seemed to take every word we said seriously. Instead of immediately imposing his own ideas he said, 'Well yes, we could do that in this way or in that way,' or 'What I suggest is this . . .' He was very understanding and very calm – not too calm to appear blasé, but interested, relaxed and gentle. He used his hands in an incredibly expressive way

and spoke in the softest of voices. He instantly inspired our confidence.
This was the manager we'd been looking for.

11

FLY WITH ME TO THE SUN

I woke up on my twentieth birthday to find Mel C sitting at the end of my bed holding two steaming mugs of tea and a bunch of flowers.

'Happy Birthday Melanie!' she said handing me a mug. 'How are you feeling today?'

Oh God, my birthday. Despite the good news about Simon I'd been depressed for the few days leading up to it. 'Oh it could be worse I suppose,' I replied, 'but don't expect me to be happy all day. I never am on my birthday.' To be honest, I wasn't too thrilled about leaving my teens behind.

'At least it's twenty and not thirty!' said Mel, looking on the bright side. Knowing how I felt, she'd put five sugars in my tea to sweeten me up (I usually took three). 'Anyway, guess what?' she continued as she handed over the flowers. 'We've organised a magical mystery tour for you! Dress cool and bring a jumper. That's all I'm saying. We're leaving in half an hour.'

Of course halfway down the motorway one of them let slip that we were going to a massive reggae festival in Brighton, but it didn't matter. I was touched that they were making so much effort for my birthday. As we drew up we saw hundreds of people milling around outside the venue. There was a lot of red, gold and green to be seen and we could hear – and feel – a heavy reggae bass vibrating from behind the barriers. Geri went off to pick up the tickets.

Fifteen minutes later she came back looking flustered. 'Something's happened to our passes!' she said, a horrified expression on her face. 'They're saying they never received the booking. It's bullshit.'

'Well what are we waiting for?' I asked, looking around at the others. 'Let's blag it!' So we climbed over a wall and bunked in.

A few hours later we ended up on Brighton beach picking fish and chips and scraps out of a plastic container with a wooden fork. Suddenly I heard a pop. I looked up from my chips to see Melanie holding a foaming bottle of champagne. There were no cups so we passed it around and swigged it. Half an hour later, feeling tipsy, I was overwhelmed by a huge sense of love for these four caring, wonderful, ballsy friends of mine, especially Melanie and Geri, who had organised the entire day. I forgot about feeling depressed. When we toasted 'The future!' I realised that I had everything to look forward to. A new decade and a new way of life were beginning.

The next week we were assigned a personal assistant, Camilla Howarth. Camilla was a very well spoken, loyal, tough but understanding person. She was extremely professional and hard working, and was also someone who loved to enjoy herself. She made sure we were all right from day one. She did everything, from booking cars and buying Tampax to overseeing interviews and checking and planning the schedules. She was very much on the case, almost like a policewoman in charge of a force. She didn't order us around, though. She never said, 'You can't do this,' or 'You'd better do that.' She was a silent leader, subtly showing the way.

She also had her party side and sometimes she'd be up all night drinking. You'd knock on her door and she'd yell, 'Come in!' and you'd have a complete laugh with her. Then the following day she'd be the first up, arranging wake-up calls, organising us again. She was amazing. It was a huge relief to hand all life's details over to someone else. Now we could concentrate on the important things, like recording the album and finding a record company to release it.

Simon recognised that we were all very strong personalities with completely different (but complementary) ways of doing things and he sensibly saw that as an asset rather than an obstacle to our success. After more than a year of being together, we'd developed a dynamic between us that worked. Things couldn't have been any other way. We just had to be ourselves. If anyone tried to meddle with that they were dead meat.

He encouraged us to play up our differences. A highly intuitive marketing man, he could immediately see the widespread branding appeal of five distinct styles within a whole. There was something for everyone in the Spice Girls. Whoever you were, you could relate to at least one of us in a basic way.

Not long after we signed with Simon we chose Virgin Records as our record company. I was attracted to Virgin because their artists included Neneh Cherry (gasp!), Isaac Hayes, Massive Attack and Lenny Kravitz, all big favourites of mine. Even better, we were very different from Virgin's other acts. They didn't have a strong British pop band on their books, so they'd have to concentrate on us if they wanted to make it in that area, which of course they did, because pop is where the money is. We met and liked Ashley Newton, the head of A&R at Virgin, and Ray Cooper, his partner. The atmosphere in the Virgin offices in West London was upbeat. It felt right.

The day we signed with Virgin is a little hazy in my mind, probably because we spent most of the day boozing it up at a London Records party. In a final bid to persuade us to sign with them, Tracy Bennet at London had hired out a boat on the river, piled it high with food and drink and DJs and inveigled us all on board.

It was a great idea and we had a wicked time giggling our way down the Thames, but we'd already made our minds up to go with Virgin. We were totally honest about this with Tracy before we went along and he was really nice about it. 'Why don't you come to the party anyway?' he offered. Okay, we will!

While we were on the boat, we started thinking about the big contract signing later in the day. 'Let's give Virgin a shock! Let's send blow-up dolls to the meeting in our place!' Camilla was duly despatched to Ann Summers in Soho to buy five life-sized rubber dollies, which she customised to look like us by spraying on different coloured hair.

We sent the dolls ahead of us in a chauffeur-driven car with instructions to the driver to announce that the Spice Girls had arrived. I wish I'd seen the faces at Virgin when they saw them. Later on I think we chucked the dolls into the canal at the back of the Virgin offices. Well I remember seeing them floating around, anyway. But I don't remember much else.

After drinking loads more bubbly at Virgin, we trashed a taxi on the way to a restaurant, removing Vicky's knickers in the process. The floor of the cab was awash with fag ends and spilled champagne. What's more we'd had a vicious flower fight with the bouquets given to us at Virgin and there were scrunched up petals and leaves all over the place. Luckily Simon was waiting for us as we pulled up. When the taxi driver complained about the mess, he was given £50 to help clear it up. Thanks, Mr Fixit!

Simon had booked us a table at Kensington Place, a posh restaurant off Kensington High Street, which was probably a bit of a mistake. Geri had to half-carry Vicky to the loo to put some make-up on her and Vicky came out of there with lipstick up to her nose. It had been a long, alcoholic day and we just weren't used to drinking like that. No one's face actually fell in their plate, but it wouldn't have surprised me if it had. We were bolloxed.

Simon had a very good way of introducing us to things slowly. For instance, he'd take us to a posh restaurant once in a while and we'd be totally impressed, then after we'd calmed down about it he'd take us to another one. We were still living on very little money. Emma and Victoria were based at home. Me, Mel and Geri were lodging in a chaotic house in Cyprus Road, North London that Pauline, Emma's mum, had found for us.

Our first real brush with the high life was when we went to meet Virgin America in Los Angeles. It was an unbelievable trip. We were so impressed with First Class. It was the first time any of us had experienced it. We were all gadgeted up. 'How do you work this?' 'Check this out!' It was amazing. You could order your dinner whenever you wanted and I think I ate everything on the menu. But it was still a very long flight and none of us slept properly.

We must have looked about fourteen when we got off the plane, completely unused to flying, with no make-up on. We were *so* excited as we walked into the airport and saw a limo pull up. 'Oh my God, look at that!' we gasped.

'It's for you girls,' said Simon with a grin on his face.

We started screaming and jumping up and down, then bundled in and pressed our faces against the windows. 'Look! Yellow cabs!'

We arrived at the Four Seasons which, well, you only see hotels like that in films like *Pretty Woman*. It's funny because when I go back there now the staff always say how they remember us from that first trip. We couldn't contain our excitement. We ripped our bags out of the car, dumped them outside the hotel and ran into the foyer. Soon we were racing around the bar and outdoor areas like revved-up nutters, before we'd even checked in. It was very, very funny.

We were in each other's rooms all the time because it was lonely just sitting there in a posh suite with no one to talk about it to. When we were together high-energy screeches reverberated everywhere. Our voices were permanently raised two pitches.

Whenever we went back there it was always the same. We'd see somebody famous, like Stephen Dorff, and exclaim, 'Oh my God, look how small he is!' We'd bump into Elton John or Eric Clapton in the lift and explode with amazed laughter, our hands tightly pressed against our mouths. We couldn't contain our excitement and stood there giggling our heads off. They probably thought we were all crazy. The hotel was full of besuited staff opening doors for you and greeting you and bringing room service. It was a huge shock to us all. That's their job, they're used to it, but we'd never seen anything like it before.

From LA the five of us flew to Hawaii for a two-week holiday at the Kea Lani Hotel on the island of Maui – Simon's treat. The idea was to give us time out to enjoy being together, away from daily pressures. It was a fantastic resort set in acres of lush, tropical gardens, with three pools, a private beach and a gym. Paradise as far as I was concerned. I'd never been anywhere like it in my life.

The suite that we stayed in was unbelievable. There was a massive front room with big white corner sofas that went all the way round the walls, a marbled floor, artexed walls and a huge balcony that overlooked the sea. The décor was all whites and lemons and beiges and the beds were enormous. Even if I went back there today I'd be impressed. It was better than the Four Seasons and that's saying something. It was just amazing.

On our first afternoon the hotel manager came across us lounging by one of the pools and politely asked us to leave the hotel premises. The place was so posh that they didn't believe we were staying there. Loudmouthed girls with regional accents in tiny bikinis and skimpy sarongs weren't among their usual clientele, apparently.

The hotel was full of rich kids on holiday with their parents, bored shitless and dying for something or someone to spice up their holiday.

One day we gathered all the strayers together, hired a van and drove around the hot spots of Maui. Needless to say, their parents weren't too pleased when they rolled in at 4 a.m., reeking of alcohol (or in some cases, vomit).

'You're not seeing those . . . those "girls" again, Sebastian!'

There was a lot of sneaking around in the middle of the night after that. We couldn't actually go out and party much because some of us were under twenty-one, the legal age limit for drinking in Maui.

Our suite was like a penthouse. While Geri, Melanie and Vicki were in the gym, Emma and me would put some music on – something tacky like Sinitta – and jump and dance around this massive room for an hour. We were manic. One night we had a big party and invited all the rich kids. It was all paid for by 19, so let's go mad!

There were three nearby beaches: the hotel beach where the waves were small and safe; a longer stretch where the waves were ridiculously high; and a nudist beach. Emma hated the unsafe beach and she was always having panic attacks thinking that one of us would drown. As I ran into the sea she'd scream, 'Please don't go in there!' A few minutes later me and Melanie would come out battered and gasping for breath, bikinis half-off, semi-drowned, having been swept right under the waves and dragged along the seabed. But we kept going back. It was a top surfing spot with loads of gorgeous surfer dudes wandering around.

I often went off alone for long walks down the beach. One afternoon I wrote in my diary:

Being out here with the sound of the ocean and that burning sensation from the sun makes life feel so wonderful. Here I've found things in myself that for once I like and love. You could say that I've grown onto the next level in my head and heart. I now can honestly say that I like my own company. I feel as though I'm a wide open, half blank, half full book waiting and yearning for knowledge about all kinds of things and forms of life.

Some days Emma stayed by the pool while Geri and I went to the nudist beach. I'd go completely nude on the nudist beach (that's the point isn't it?). Geri didn't, but came along because there were plenty of odd things to stare at.

Walking down there one morning, I stopped to watch a guy climb nimbly up a palm tree, pick some coconuts and shimmy down again. When he landed he turned round, noticed me and came over to say hello. Very lean with long black rough matted hair, he looked a bit Mexican-Indian. His green eyes startled me. They were hypnotic. Ding dong! It was that feeling again.

His name was Nalu, which means 'wave' and he lived a very simple life, close to nature, selling coconuts on the beach. He was a bit eccentric, a non-conformist who slept in his car rather than going back to his family home. To me he seemed very spiritual, calm and accepting. And I really, really fancied him.

Vicky wasn't impressed though. 'I saw him pooing on the beach and washing himself in the sea afterwards,' she told me with a look of complete outrage on her face. 'Doesn't he know what a toilet is? It's disgusting!'

I ended up going off with Nalu for nights on end, sleeping rough on the beach under the stars or in his little car. It was a proper holiday romance. But as with all holiday romances, it had to come to an end.

We packed our bags and off we went to the airport. At the check-in desk the man took one look at our tickets and frowned.

'Erm, I think you've got your dates wrong, ladies!'

Dur! We were a day early. We had one more night in Maui and two problems. 1. We'd checked out of the hotel so we had nowhere to stay. 2. We had hardly any money.

We ended up in a tiny shack with horrible beds and dirty sheets. Emma and I were sharing a room and couldn't face the lumps and stains so we stayed up all night on the beach with Nalu, eating ice creams and watching crabs scuttle across the sand. That was our best night of the holiday in my opinion. It was fantastic.

Inevitably England was a bit of a bump down to earth after all that excitement. Back in the house in Cyprus Road, with its dirty green carpet, dusty old fireplace and horrible dining table, we muddled along waiting to put our big plans into action, impatient to get on and rule the universe. It was October 1995, nearly a year before we would release our first single. We had the rest of the album to record before 'Wannabe' came out, but that certainly didn't fill all our waking hours. At one point I resorted to decorating. I did up the boy's toilet with loads of porn and nailed

Madonna's sex book to the wall. In contrast I made sure that the main bathroom was very pretty and feminine.

One day in the Strong Room we started talking about how desperate we were to perform again. Within no time we were planning a showcase for our families and friends, who still didn't really have a clue what we were up to. We booked a small banqueting suite at the Holiday Inn in Borehamwood and rehearsed our set at Cyprus Road. My mum and dad and Danielle drove down from Leeds and met me at the hotel. It was the first time any of our families had met and we'd organised drinks and a sit down dinner to help smooth the introductions.

The whole night went fantastically. Our songs and performance impressed everyone and the mums and dads got on really well. I think it made a big difference to my mum and dad, who were still very worried about my future. It put their minds at rest to talk to the other parents – who all had similar worries – and see for themselves how professional the group had become. It was obvious that we'd been working hard, which meant a lot to them. They were also relieved that I hadn't gone off the rails. One of my dad's greatest fears was of me or Danielle 'going wild' or 'getting into bad company'. He'd seen it happen a lot among his friends' and colleagues' kids. For years he'd been expecting the worst – teenage pregnancy, crime or drugs – and was pleasantly surprised that none of it had happened.

A couple of days after the Holiday Inn showcase I got a letter from my dad. I was amazed to see his writing on the front of the envelope and hesitated before opening it. He'd never written to me before. What did he have to say to me that couldn't be said in person, or on the phone? Nervously I lit a cigarette and started reading.

Hi Melanie,

How are you? I bet you are surprised that I'm writing to you. Well, there are certain things I want to say to you that are more easily expressed in a letter.

I just want to say that I appreciate all you did for me and your mum and Danielle last weekend. I know it must have taken a lot of organising, time and money. We all had a fantastic time, me more than anybody. I can't begin to tell you how proud I felt of you in that room with all of the parents.

I feel proud that you have turned out so level headed, self sufficient, generous and a lovely girl. I hope in times to come you don't change. I don't know what the future holds for you and your group, but I think you will make it big time and I am keeping my fingers crossed. Whatever happens, take in all the experience, all the travel, the people etc, and just enjoy it to the full.

You will make mistakes along the way, everybody does. The way to gain experience is to learn from your mistakes. Always take your camera with you and take lots of photos. When you are an old and married woman not only will you have your memories but also photos to show your kids.

When you make it big and have lots and lots of money, do not ever forget your background or where you were born and brought up. Your family and friends are the ones who have always been there for you and always will.

I know you didn't have a happy teenage life and that was mainly due to my strictness. That was my way of showing how much I love and care for you. I wanted to protect you from the dangers of life. Also, I pushed you too hard with your schooling. I thought education was the most important thing for you to achieve.

Although I have never told her this, your mum is the rock of the family. Without her, both you and Danielle would not be where you are now. Ever since you were five, she's been fetching and carrying you two to dancing school, comps, shows, theatres etc – it must add up to thousands of miles. The main thing I am eternally grateful to her for is for moving us from Hyde Park to here. Also, I thank her for keeping you two occupied. Every night you had somewhere to go and things to do. When I pass Hyde Park or go to Chapeltown and see kids hanging around on street corners, I know the best thing we ever did was move to Kirkstall.

Anyway, I will stop rambling on. I just want to say that I've been meaning to say all of this to you for quite a while. I love you very much and I am very proud of you. And no matter what happens in the future I will always be here for you.

Love

Martin

P.S. Eat your vegetables and STOP SMOKING!

STOP SMOKING
I feel a song coming on . . .
Old Man River, he just keeps rolling along.

I was shocked. It was hard to take in at first. My dad had never been so open with me in my entire life. A huge lump formed in my throat. I slumped into a chair and re-read what he'd written, tears rolling down my cheeks. The letter moved me more than I can say. At long last I had won my dad's approval and acceptance, after so many years of trying to prove myself to him.

Not long after that I moved into a pretty house in Watford with Melanie. It had belonged to Geri's aunt and we rented it from her mother, who lived just over the road. I was determined to make it into a proper home so I bought loads of furniture and made a real effort to decorate. I painted the bathroom deep blue and stencilled fish on the walls. I stuck luminous stars on the ceiling and around the bath and the door. (Believe me, when you came in drunk at night and couldn't find the light in the hallway, those stars were a godsend.)

Each wall in the front room was a different colour – red, blue, green and white. I made the curtains from some multicoloured muslin that I bought from an Indian shop on the corner and ordered a bright green sofa bed from Argos. Next I turned the kitchen/dining room into a leopard skin lounge. I did it all within about forty-eight hours too.

Mine and Melanie's ritual was to watch *Blind Date* together. Then she'd either go off to Sidcup or stay at home with me. There wasn't a lot to do in Watford but one evening we put on our roller skates and skated up a steep hill to the nearest pub. After a couple of lagers we started wondering how on earth we were going to get back down again. At the top of the hill we looked at each other. 'Come on, let's just go for it!' Wheeee! As we gathered speed I began to panic. I grabbed onto a traffic light stand and clung to it for dear life as I watched Melanie zooming towards me. Her face was a picture of fear and giggles as she whizzed along, totally out of control.

Melanie and I had an underlying understanding of each other. At the time I was going through a lot of emotional crap, especially with Richie, and Melanie was always covering for me. For some reason, though, I couldn't open up to her. I think I was unable to accept that somebody could be so nice to me without having an ulterior motive. I couldn't figure her out, even though – or perhaps because – she was really quite straightforward and normal. She was very affectionate and loving and it freaked me out. She'd give me a hug and I'd be like, 'Get off me! What are you doing?'

'What's wrong with *you*?' she'd ask, genuinely concerned.

It became a pattern of behaviour – I was horrible to her, she was nice to me. She'd buy me flowers and I'd respond by saying, 'What have you got me those for? I don't want them!' I was used to my friends saying, 'Sort yourself out!' or my mum saying, 'Forget about it. Tough it out and it will all be all right.' I couldn't understand someone wanting to be intimate and real with me. I think it scared me. Deep down I knew I wasn't all that nice.

I was so yeah-yeah! in public that the last thing I wanted to do was show anyone my deepest emotions. I wanted it to appear as though I was handling things, but because we were in such close proximity Melanie inevitably saw me crying or depressed or spending all weekend in bed in a slump.

'Why are you being like this?' she asked me once. 'You're so lovely, you've got so much get up and go. Come on, get out of bed!'

'I'm fine,' I said defensively. 'I'm just doing the student thing.'

I was an emotional infant. I couldn't understand it when someone wanted to know 'how I felt'. I found it imposing and rude and my first instinct was to react aggressively. Melanie was very sensitive, the kind of person who would get more upset than you were if you were down. I found that unusual. I now thank her for being the way she was with me. She showed me that it was okay to reveal your weaknesses and that a real friend would always be compassionate if you did.

Funnily enough, she was the one that I wanted to get closer to. I didn't show it, but I actually wanted her to understand me and help me. I almost wanted to be like her. When we got drunk together we'd hug each other tightly, but it wouldn't be spoken of the next day. We'd go back to me being horrible and her being nice.

To this day I always say to Melanie when I get drunk, 'I'm really sorry about how I was.'

'It's all right,' she always says.

'No it's not. I really hurt you.'

'I know,' she says.

And I say, 'You see! I did hurt you! I'm so sorry.'

I'm like a stuck record, poor cow, but looking back I must say that I'm quite disgusted by the way I treated her. She was such a wonderful, amazing person and she didn't deserve it.

That Christmas Melanie went home and I went on holiday with Geri to Gran Canaria for two weeks. It was one of those cheap last-minute package deals, the type you pay for knowing that you're going to Grand Canaria but not where you're actually going to stay.

Our rooms were shite but the hotel was amazing. We nicknamed it Frankenstein's Castle. Built into a rock, it was a maze of dark, rocky, hollowed out corridors and open walkways. Geri had a long white dressing gown that she enjoyed floating around in. I remember seeing her from the bedroom window as she dreamily drifted down the stairs in it, out to the car park to get something from the car, and back to the room. She looked like something out of an old French film. 'Let's do that together!' I suggested. Only differently, of course. We floated down to the reception, flashed the front desk, then rushed back up to our room and giggled for hours.

We were two girls on a mission. We seemed totally in synch with one another and there was never a moment when one person wanted to go to the beach and the other wanted to stay by the pool. We hired a hideous purple bubble car with a roof that peeled off (I think it might have been a Citroen 2CV) and drove around the island looking for adventure. We laughed from afar at the big men with 'Gran Canaria bellies' who sun-bathed with their feet in the sea. We giggled at the crap podium dancers in the local 'happening' night club. 'We can dance better than them!' we insisted.

Normally when you go on holiday you take a certain amount of money with you and work out a daily or weekly budget. Not me and Geri though! We spent our money on anything and everything until suddenly it was all gone. We had about five pesetas left. 'What are we going to do?'

There was only one answer. We drove back to the local club and got ourselves jobs as podium dancers. We were paid about £10 a night, enough to keep us in food, petrol and drinks. I wore hipster bell bottoms and a crop top, Geri wore hot pants and a bra. We worked from 11 p.m. until 4 a.m., dancing for a full hour followed by a twenty-minute break. It was a tough workout. By the end of the evening you'd be dripping in sweat, muscles aching, longing for bed, with echoes of Eurotrash rave music throbbing in your ears. It was a laugh, though.

One afternoon I was food shopping on the main street when a man shoved a leaflet in my hand. As I looked up at his face he cheekily stuck his tongue out at me. There, right in the middle of his long, thick, pink tongue was an enormous shining gleaming gold stud. I was mesmerised by it. It was the most beautiful, incredible thing I'd ever seen (or so I thought at the time). Wow, I want one of those, I thought.

'Watch,' I told him, because I was completely confident that he'd be seeing more of me in the future, 'I'm going to get my tongue pierced too.' I thought of how much my mum and dad would disapprove. 'Shomebody shtop me!' I muttered to myself. (*The Mask* was my favourite film at the time.)

Geri and I had another great holiday together the next year, in Sri Lanka, with Richie. So what if I had a boyfriend? She was my best mate and we didn't go anywhere without each other. (Admittedly, I think some of the other people in the hotel thought we were a swinging threesome!)

Geri's and my relationship was unique. We could walk into a room and take the whole place over. She'd take one side of the room, I'd take the other and occasionally we'd glance at each other as we worked our way along. With a look we'd know exactly what was going on, whether one of us wanted to leave, or was bored, or it was time to be outrageous. It was great. Neither of us would ever say, 'Oh no, I don't think we should do that.'

It was always, 'Yes! C'mon!'

So when Nancy Berry, who was then the international president of Virgin, organised a big party at Virgin after a Rolling Stones concert the next spring, it was a bit of a waste of time telling us to behave ourselves. We sneaked into the VIP area by climbing over the fence and managed to stay in there for quite a while, stuffing our faces. We were chucked out in the end though – 'escorted out by security'.

There was quite a buzz within the music industry about the Spice Girls, but people had only heard about us, they'd never seen us perform. Our publicity campaign hadn't kicked in yet because we wanted to have our album finished before we released our first single. So basically nobody had a clue who we were at this point, apart from the people who'd read in *Music Week* that a new girl group had been signed.

You wouldn't know it to watch us, though. At our very first Brit Awards in early 1996, guests of Virgin Records, sitting at a table with Lenny Kravitz, Vanessa Paradis, and Ken and Nancy Berry, we were convinced that people were looking at us, even though they quite obviously weren't.

Nicky Chapman, our PR lady (who went on to become one of the judges on *Pop Idol*) was sitting at a table with Take That. 'They're looking at us!' we kept saying, flicking glances over to their table every millisecond. When Nicky introduced us as we walked past their table we nearly wet ourselves.

We were terribly image-conscious that night, so much so that when Melanie let down her hair in the foyer, the rest of us screamed, 'Oh my God! What are you doing? Put your hair back up in a ponytail again. That's what you're known for!' (It was a huge over-reaction, considering that virtually no one in the whole place knew anything about us.)

'Get lost!' Melanie retorted and we proceeded to have a huge argument in the foyer.

Of course we had no idea that we'd be making headlines at the Brits the next year, even though we behaved as if we did. 'We'll be there!' we'd say to each other with casual bravado. We knew exactly where we were going. 'Shomebody shtop us!'

12

HOT IN HERE

We shot the 'Wannabe' video at St Pancras Station (next to King's Cross) on a cold night in April. Two days previously, when we'd gone to check it out, it was a run-down dump that you'd imagine squatters or tramps living in. By the time the production team had finished with it, it was a palace, even though it was still freezing cold. (The video was later banned in Asia because of my erect nipples!)

It basically features the five of us rampaging through an eccentric bohemian party, running, jumping, singing, dancing and generally having a laugh. Because we were hoping to shoot it in one take, we had to rehearse the routine all the way through without a break, over and over again. Poor Emma kept falling over in her big shoes. I wore a lime green Calvin Klein bed vest with thin straps and a pair of Jean Paul Gaultier loose-fitted hipster trousers. We began shooting at around 9 p.m., endlessly repeating the routine while a guy strapped up to a SteadyCam ran around after us. He looked like Robocop. Filming finished in the early hours; we were cold and exhausted, but ecstatic. Our first video was in the can.

Within a month, 'Wannabe' was 'the most requested video' on MTV's *The Box*. They were playing it seventy times a week, which was ironic because when the people at Virgin first saw it, they'd wanted us to shelve it and shoot it again. The lighting was too dark, apparently, it was too rough around the edges. Well, tough. We loved it and we weren't going to change it for anyone. As planned, it captured the cheekily anarchical essence of Spice, the fun and madness of Spice Girls.

Unfortunately I didn't take much of it in when I watched the final edit in a post-production studio in Soho. Me and Adrian (Matt and Biff's engineer) were quite an item back then. He was a chilled-out pub-going kind of guy, so I decided, Right, we'll go to the pub all day and then I'll go to the screening. It wasn't my aim to get drunk, but I turned up completely battered. I was late too. I got a right bollocking from Simon and the girls weren't happy with me either. 'God, you stink of alcohol! How can you do this? It's the first screening of our first-ever video!'

'I'm sorry everyone,' I slurred.

Adrian was waiting for me outside. I flung myself into his arms and sobbed, 'They all hate me, just because I've turned up drunk. Can't they see I'm having a laugh?'

He didn't know what to say, poor guy.

A month after the video went out, the single was getting intensive airplay on all the main radio stations. We started on the promo trail, appearing mainly on kids TV programmes like *Live and Kicking* and doing shoots and interviews for all the teen mags.

We still had the odd day off. I was on my way to Kensington High Street with Geri one free afternoon when a guy gave me a leaflet advertising a tongue piercing service.

'It's a sign!' I told Geri. 'I have to get it done.' She had just had her belly button pierced. 'Oh my God, I'll do it now,' I decided aloud.

We found our way to a piercing parlour in Kensington Market. It looked clean and proper – the walls were painted white and there was a massage bed in the corner – but when I looked at the guy in charge, with his long hair hanging loose and no apron or surgical gloves, I knew better.

My tongue was inspected. There was a problem because the main vein stretched almost to the tip. If anything happened to that vein, my tongue would be paralysed.

'Just do it!' I insisted.

After lots of umming and aahing and messing around with a permanent marker pen, he daggered my tongue at an angle that narrowly avoided the crucial vein.

'Wannabe' was released a couple of days later and we did a performance on *This Morning with Richard and Judy*. It felt odd miming with a swollen tongue. I also had severe piles and couldn't cough or laugh. Later in the day we performed at our first Radio One road show, in Birmingham. It was 7 July 1996 – my mum's birthday – and she and my dad had driven down to see the show.

Gleefully I took her to one side and said, 'Mum, I've got something to show you.' I stuck out my tongue. 'Look!'

'Melanie!' she spluttered, her eyes popping out at the sight of my new piercing. 'That's disgusting! Why didn't you tell me about it before?'

'Because I knew you'd go mad,' I laughed. (And that's probably partly why I did it in the first place, if I'm honest!)

That day I was wearing a bright red waterproof jumpsuit that I'd copied from the Bobby Brown video for 'Two Can Play That Game'. It was £20 from Kensington Market. I wore it with a pair of mid-calf-length boots I'd bought in Camden Market. They were like coal miner's boots, with *Mad Max* style steel clasps, but funky. They were the kind of thing that a far-out, shaven-headed feminist-type might wear with a dress.

This was our first big performance. We were scared shitless. The audience was a huge rowdy mass. We ran on stage and hundreds of people started cheering. Buzzzzzzzzzzz! Cue the backing track.

Even when we were miming I'd still yell 'Yo, I'll tell you what I want, what I really, really want . . .' and I really went for it this time. However, within seconds I realised that something was different. I heard my voice coming out of the speakers, LIVE. Uh-oh, wrong backing track. The others instantly clocked what had happened. It was a complete and utter shock for us all but we managed to keep it together and carry on singing. We'd never sung live before. And there I was with piles, in pain when I laughed, trying to sing with a swollen tongue and getting palpitations from seeing the entire front three rows singing along with us.

'They know our song! Can you believe it?'

People were actually singing the words to 'Wannabe'. It was incredible, totally mind-blowing. When we came off stage the audience screamed for an encore. There were crowds blocking the way as we tried to push our way back to our Previa van. People were shouting our names and rushing us. It was madness.

We bundled into the van, breathless with excitement. In seconds we were surrounded. Fans (yes, our very own fans!) were pressing their faces up to the windows and frenziedly banging their fists on the doors. The more they crushed around us, the louder they screamed. I loved it. Then the situation began to get a bit frightening. The noise reached a worrying crescendo and the Previa began to sway from side to side. The rocking motion was quite gentle at first, but the momentum quickly increased. At this rate we'd be over on our side within a couple of minutes. The driver looked worried; beads of sweat began to break out on his forehead. He had no idea what to do. 'Start the engine!' we shouted. 'Get us out of here before they knock this thing over!'

Cautiously he inched us out of there. We sat in shocked silence, trying to take it all in. What a reaction! And this was only the beginning.

Soon we were travelling all over the place and there was never a second to think. Every day was completely different to the day before. We met new people constantly and you could chat your arse off. By now Geri and I were pros. We used to work a room together in five minutes and have everyone eating out of our hands.

'Wannabe' was released on 8 July 1996 and went straight to No. 3. Oh my God! Geri and I were in her sister Karen's garden listening to the chart rundown after a barbecue. We screamed and shouted our heads off when the DJ said our names. I wrote:

I'm overly excited; in fact it's cringe making. But I'm gonna take it in my stride and not let it affect me in my outward actions. Of course it's great but I'm trying to be calm and cool, although that doesn't mean I don't appreciate and thank God for my career.

Two days later we flew to Japan. Other acts usually left the Far East until last in their promotional campaign, after Europe and America, but Simon suggested that we target the Asian market first. He sold us the idea by emphasising how different from the rest we'd be to do it this way. We liked to be different. We were planning to break all the rules in the pop book.

Japan was quite strange at first. Our hotel rooms, all dark wood and green carpets, were depressing. They were beautifully kitted out Japanese style, but you did feel a million miles from home. You had to adjust to the time differences and couldn't call England without working out the maths. It didn't matter, but it felt odd. Once again I turned to my diary for self-affirmation.

I am mentally free. I love myself. I appreciate my position. I'm going to the gym as often as possible. I'll always look after myself.

(I had to remind myself of these things! Otherwise I would have gone mad.)

I found the Japanese very serious. I only ever saw the schoolgirls laughing. They were very cool, with their white slouched-down socks and bunches, but I remember thinking, Does nobody smile here apart from the kids? During the day Tokyo is like an over-busy London where everyone just rushes around looking very fit and healthy. Come 10 p.m., it's like a bigger version of Soho and they're all out drinking in bars.

Most evenings we hung out in each other's rooms. 'What shall we do tonight?'

'Let's watch a video and get some Lambrusco in!'

'Oh they don't do Lambrusco. Let's just get some cheap wine.'

'And chip butties!'

We always order chip butties. Even after the MTV Europe Awards in November 2000, our last major performance together (to date), we gathered round the TV and ate chip butties together as usual. Munching away, we caught each other's eyes. 'We always do this!' We always have done.

We were sitting in the lounge of our Tokyo hotel when the first major news came through. I looked up to see Camilla, our personal assistant, hurrying across the lobby with a massive grin on her face. 'Girls!' she burst out. 'Wannabe' is No. 1!' What? We were totally overwhelmed. We screamed the place down. We kissed and hugged and jumped around wildly. We ordered lots of champagne, gulped it down and rushed up to our rooms to phone our families. 'Mum! We're No.1! Eeeeeeeeeeeeeeek!' Then we went out to a Chinese restaurant, stuffed our faces and smoked cigars in the bar until the early hours.

I was so excited that I could hardly sleep that night. From council estate to No. 1, I kept thinking – and here I was lying between Egyptian cotton sheets in a five-star hotel in Tokyo with cigars and champagne on my breath. Somebody tell me what's going on!

'Wannabe' stayed at No. 1 for seven weeks in the UK and went on to sell 4.5 million copies, reaching No. 1 in thirty-one countries. Life was very different when we got back to England. Suddenly we were being recognised, pointed at, followed and photographed. People were asking for our autographs and opinions. The press started running stories about us – and not just the tabloids. We did shoots and interviews and endless questionnaires.

We were famous.

Funnily enough, I wasn't one of those people who always wanted to be famous. I didn't know what I wanted to be. I knew I wanted to be *heard*, I knew I wanted to be *respected*, but I didn't actually know that I wanted to be famous.

At first I refused to read the papers. I'd say to the others, 'You're all a bunch of press junkies and you're fuelled by it!' Really, they were just excited to see themselves in the paper, whereas I was in complete, off-on-one denial. 'I don't care what the papers say about me. I'm not reading them.'

I've still got that mentality but now I know why I've got it – because I genuinely don't care what people say. These days I will browse over an article and look at the pictures, but I won't let it affect me. I'll be able to close the paper and forget about it instantly.

Back in the early days of fame I'd say, 'I'm not reading it because I'll want to kill someone,' when in actual fact I did want to read it and I was proud of what we'd done. I was just so frightened that my ego would be fed by it and I'd fall prey to 'being famous' that I just didn't allow myself to look. My diary at the time is full of extracts like this:

There is more to Mel B than just work and Spice Girls. I love myself and I don't really claim to be anything else apart from me, myself and I. I've got my own pride and morals, my family, Richie and my fish. I'm happy. I have everything I've always wanted and never even realised it was right there in front of me.

Then a lot of ex-boyfriends sold stories about me (*all* my stories were about sex with ex-boyfriends) and the press started going into my family life. Finally I read some of the things they'd written about me and I began to feel very sorry for myself. I couldn't understand why the press were doing it and I took it personally. By this time the other girls were used to it. They'd got over it, whereas I was in bits. 'What's come over you?' they asked. 'Stop being stupid. You were the one that told us not to read the papers. We're not reading them any more, we're just looking at the pictures.' I should have taken my own advice. I felt really vulnerable for a while. I think a part of me was embarrassed about being famous. I was worried that people would think, Look at her, really loving herself! The last thing I wanted was for anyone to catch me smiling at myself in the mirror.

It didn't bother me when all the stuff came out about the nude modelling Geri had done before she joined the band. Simon made a big deal out of it though, so that by the time we got together to talk about it everyone was fired up. But if it hadn't been for him nobody would have given a toss. Geri was very upset about it in some ways, but in other ways it was just, 'Well that's what I did. So what?'

A couple of weeks later one of the tabloids published a photo of me sunbathing topless. I was the first to be photographed topless and I've been caught out quite a few times since. (There's no way I'm going to start covering up, I don't like bikini marks.) Now there wasn't much difference between those old shots of Geri and the pap photos of me, apart from the fact that she was posing and got paid and I wasn't. It was still just a pair of tits. (What *really* got me about that picture was that my nipples looked like bullets and my dad's got the cutting because he collects everything. Very embarrassing.)

The first kiss-and-tell about any of us came out on the day we did our second roadshow in Birmingham – some three-in-a-bed bollocks about me. My mum and dad had driven down to see the roadshow and my mum said, 'Well, at least they're saying you're good in bed, not crap!' I was relieved by her reaction. You start to think, Who's going to believe this? With Simon and our press lawyer (known as The Grim Reaper) making such a big deal about the papers, you lived in fear of a story coming out about you.

As much as Simon said, 'You've all got to be honest with me', we weren't all that honest with him. Why should we be? We had pasts, just like everyone else. At one point it came out that Vicky had played a roller skating sperm in something, but she hadn't told us, or anybody else. With Simon making such a big deal of stories like that when they inevitably came out, it was even harder for the next person to tell him something, or even tell the rest of us. I suppose he was just being protective, but it ended up making us feel paranoid.

The spotlight was blinding as every day we became more famous than the day before. The whole thing escalated beyond our wildest imaginings. 'Spice Fever' swept through the UK. 'Spice this; Spice that. Who's your favourite Spice Girl?' People started using the words 'phenomenon' and 'Spice Girls' in the same sentence. (Phenomenon? The only time I'd heard the word was in the dance track by LL Cool J.) Then Peter Lorraine, the editor of *Top of the Pops Magazine*, took things one stage further and gave us nicknames: Ginger, Baby, Sporty, Posh and Scary.

I was called Scary because I was loud and forthright and brash. I spoke my mind and stuck my tongue out to the cameras. But in my mind I had balls because I was a mixed race person who in the past had gone for job interviews where they'd taken one look at the colour of me and not given me the job. I'd had teachers who'd told me I 'would never amount to anything', domineering employers who'd picked on me unnecessarily and I'd also been brought up by an overly strict father. As a result of all this I'd developed a real dislike of authority figures. So I had lots of issues that I wanted to express to people in power – including journalists – and my way of doing that was to take the piss out of them. Loudly.

Being perceived as rich and famous created a licence for us all to behave how we wanted. I was more extreme than the others, though. Later on down the line I'd be in board meetings with a whole load of lawyers and money men and in the middle of some dull and serious discussion about fund options I'd get up on the table and sing. Once I stamped all over their papers and notes, not giving a f***, shouting, 'Ha, ha, ha, ha, you're powerful, but you can't do F-all.'

They all had fixed smiles on their determinedly upbeat faces, pretending everything was fine. 'Okay, Melanie! We appreciate your point of view!' they said brightly. Not one of them suggested that I get down off the table.

There's no excuse for behaving how I did. I felt very guilty afterwards but at the time I was thinking, I just don't understand why these people are so superficial and treat me in such a false way.

Some bigwig would come down to a TV studio to watch us work and I'd turn on him. 'Why are you looking at my tits? Why?' I'd ask aggressively.

'Oh my God, I'm so sorry, man,' he'd reply.

I'd say, 'That's all right.' Then I'd yell, 'Everybody! He's just looked at my tits, but he's apologised!'

I was horrible, awful. It was my payback to everyone in my past and at times it was quite funny, but it was appalling behaviour, no doubt about it. It was partly my way of coping with the position I'd found myself in. I resented the fact that suddenly people were falling over themselves to be nice to me, when in the past they wouldn't have given me a second look.

Today I'm still an anti-authority person, but I approach situations with more integrity. Over the years you learn to be tactful, not because you have to be, but because you don't want to be that aggressive, ignorant person who enjoys watching people's jaws drop in a room and the dislike show on their faces. Back then I didn't know where my anger was coming from, why I was acting like that or even who I was. I would tear myself apart and put myself through torture afterwards, agonising about why I'd been so nasty. I wrote:

I'm my own worst enemy at times, but that's me. What can I say? I know I'm a bit of a nightmare with my thoughts and feelings and being stressed. I need to sort that out and I will, I know I will.

I was brought up having to scream and shout to get attention so I had it all confused. I spent a lot of time fighting against myself inwardly. I would appear carefree – I'd go out and get a bit drunk – but then I'd be loud and rude to someone and that night I wouldn't be able to sleep.

I spent hours beating myself up, thinking, Shit, what I said must have really offended that person. Rather than going back to them and saying sorry (too much pride), I turned to my diary and worked it through by writing about it. It would have been far better and easier just to say, 'Hands up, I'm sorry I said that.' I just didn't know how. I used to feel let down all the time, but how was anyone supposed to know what I was feeling when I kept everything to myself? I kept telling people how important it was to be open when, in fact, I totally hid my vulnerable side.

The way I thought and the way I wanted to express myself didn't correspond to the way the words actually came out. These days it's a bit better because I usually think before I speak, but back then I'd say or do something spontaneously and then giggle nervously to myself, I can't believe I've said that! I can't believe I've done that! Often I'd have a delayed reaction and it could be as long as three days before it would occur to me, Oh my God! What *was* I doing?

I was driven by every kind of high adrenaline state that you can naturally reach. I still am, but I've got a bit more of a balance now and at least fifty per cent more understanding. I've realised that you can't live like that forever. Eventually you run out of energy and then it's time to deal with the consequences and reflect and chill out.

After 'Wannabe' our lives went crazy. Everyone in the country became Something Spice – Old Spice, Young Spice, Bald Spice, Hairy Spice, Make-a-cup-of-tea Spice. Everywhere people had their own versions of the same joke. We were in the public consciousness, big time. Our nicknames stuck and none of us minded because to be honest, they suited us. They also made it easier for people to tell us apart and we wanted to be known individually, by name, like the Beatles were. Being Ginger, Baby, Sporty, Posh and Scary helped distinguish us in the most basic way. We'd never wanted to be clumped together as a gaggle of young girls singing and dancing – that's why we left Bob and Chris. We belonged together, but each of us had different qualities and personalities and we wanted the world to know it.

The party invites flooded in but we weren't even aware of them. Now was the time to work our butts off in our world-conquering mission. Simon wanted us to capitalise on the success of 'Wannabe' while promoting our next single 'Say You'll Be There'. So the inside of a plane became our second home. Flying was no longer a thrill, it was just something that you did. I started recognising the customs people at Heathrow. Fans gathered to wave us off. Film crews met us when we landed. Bulbs flashed in our faces. 'Mel! Scary! Over here!' People I'd never met were calling me by name. It was mad.

Thank God I had an escape. By this time me and Richie had moved into a beautiful two-bedroom flat in Hornsey Lane, North London, in a big converted church hall with a huge red door. I'd filled it with all my own furniture, plus a fantastic dining table that Simon had lent me. Things had obviously become far more serious with Richie by now.

9.30 a.m., 22 June 1996
I, Melanie Brown, decided today that I am going to engage Richard Meyer. He doesn't know it yet – he is out – and he won't know until I get the rings.

I have told two people – my mum and Vicky. I love him and I want to be with him forever. This will show him how much I love him and I just can't wait to see his face. He is the one and only man I need in my life. We are so right for each other. It's like a fairy tale and it's all coming true. I am so overwhelmed with love and excitement that I don't know what to do with myself.

I began to go away more often but it didn't seem to matter. Richie was a very solid guy who didn't make a fuss about this sudden fame thing. He just used to chuckle. We never had conversations about it unless I brought it up and it didn't seem to affect him at all. At the end of a day he was just glad to have me back in the flat, cooking dinner and watching TV or videos. For me it was reassuring to get back to him after a mad promo trip, although often he'd be asleep by the time I got in.

Richie and I rarely went out or socialised, apart from going round to his friend Ian's house. He never came to any of the industry events I went to. My life started to develop into a 'superstar life' yet I still had the grounding of being with Richie. Here's how I described him in my diary:

Richie is the one who always understands everything about me exactly. He is the only person I can relate to or be myself with in any way shape or form. He has five important roles – he is father, friend, lover, soul mate and stable emotional backbone.

He has such a talent for calming my headless chicken side and making me feel whole. Without him the side of me that wants to learn would be lost and frustrated. Not only does he have the same sense of humour but he gets on a vibe with me that is so refreshing and stimulating that life would be dull without it. That combination of an everyday nine-to-five person with a flair for living and being alive is very rare. He's got earthiness and pazazz and that extra something.

Richie used to teach me a new word every day, including unusual words like facetious or lackadaisical. It was great. Throughout the day I'd try to fit today's word into as many sentences as possible. I was so happy to be learning. It was such a basic, innocent thing but I loved it. I was desperate to learn more. There comes a point when you start to reflect back and think, F***, why didn't I take those French lessons? Now I'm eager to learn another language.

I've always had a thing about proving to people that I'm not stupid. Coming from Leeds to London – the northern accent, the straight talking and not having much of a vocabulary – made me feel inferior or vulnerable for a while. I felt I sounded thick, even though deep down I knew I wasn't.

My mum bought me a thesaurus while I was at school and I was fascinated by it, but I was also worried that if I suddenly started coming out with long words people would say, 'Oh look at you, trying to be posh!' That was my experience of Leeds. Rebecca was the exception to the rule. She was very articulate and when she used words like 'procrastinating' I'd get incredibly excited. 'Tell me how you fitted it into the sentence!' I'd demand. I love learning new words and phrases to this day.

Richie and I didn't go out much. Most evenings he cooked me a delicious dinner and we went to bed early. (Funnily enough I've always gone out with men who can cook.)

One night we'd been asleep for hours when I woke up at 3 a.m. coughing. The room smelled of smoke. 'Richie!'

'Umph?'

'Richie! Get up!'

I heard a crackling sound. 'The flat's on fire!'

We leapt out of bed. Richie opened the bedroom door. The hallway was filled with fumes. Oh God. Panic.

The smoke intensified. The spare bedroom, the kitchen and the bathroom at the back of the flat were already in flames. Any moment now the whole place was going to explode into a fireball.

I slung on my dressing gown and started trying to rescue my clothes. 'Just leave everything!' shouted Richie. 'Get out! Get out NOW!' Seconds later we crawled towards the front door, which thankfully was right next to our bedroom, and bolted. We ran downstairs and crashed outside into the early morning air, gasping with shock. I looked up at the flat. What was happening in there? What was going on?

The people next door woke up and came out for a nosy so we borrowed their mobile phone and Richie called 999. Right then all I could think about were my clothes and, Oh f***, what about Simon's table? It wasn't until later that it sunk in how close we'd been to dying.

The firemen arrived. 'Quick!' I screamed. 'Our flat's on fire!'

'Hold on a minute,' one of them said. 'You're that Mel B from the Spice Girls aren't you? Can I have your autograph first?'

He was actually being serious. ARRRRGGGGHHHH!

Later he brought a Spice single out of the debris. Laughing, he said, 'Look, I've saved this for you!'

'So?' I was well pissed off.

Richie's dad came and picked us up and took us to his mum's house in Highgate, not far away, where we stayed the night. The firemen told us that the fire might have been started by a burning cigarette end, or maybe the ancient gas fire had trick-started.

It was horrible not knowing what had been saved and what had gone. Everything just stank. You can't save much after a fire because it all smells horrific, no matter how much you wash or dry clean it. I've got an antique jacket that I managed to rescue but it still reeks of smoke. A lot of my stuff simply went up in flames. It felt like I'd lost everything. But I hadn't. Apparently, another fifteen minutes and I would have been dead.

13

FAST CAR

There wasn't much time to dwell on the fire and what could have happened. I had a schedule and I just had to carry on, so I went into work the next afternoon. I was worried that Simon was going to ask me about his table, but although he didn't offer me a place to stay, he didn't mention the table either. Richie and I moved to a suite in a hideous business hotel in Watford because there was nowhere else for us to go. We didn't want to impose on his mum and dad because his mum had recently become very ill.

Now the word 'suite' implies something glamorous or luxurious. Well it wasn't. It was an extended bedroom with a toilet. By now I was used to staying in plush hotels and this was back to basics. Mainly it was businessmen who stayed there. For some reason I had a thing about the bed covers. 'Who else has slept under these covers? Yeuch!' It all went through my head. When you've been through a near-death experience, you pick up on the strangest, slightest things.

I wanted twenty-four-hour room service. When I felt lonely or displaced or sad about losing my home, I needed a chip butty and I didn't want to have to wait until after six to get it. Basically I either wanted to go home and be looked after – which I couldn't, because my home had gone up in flames – or I wanted that plush life that compensates for not being at home. This hotel was neither and I hated it.

At this time 'Say You'll Be There' was my favourite single because there were some excellent mixes made of it, especially the disco mix. There had been talk of putting out 'Love Thing' as our second single, but in the end we stuck with 'Say You'll Be There'. We filmed the video in the Mojave desert just outside Los Angeles. As we squeezed into our skin-tight catsuits in the blinding heat we couldn't help remembering how we'd recorded the song in our trackies and socks in Elliot's studio in Sheffield, constantly getting caught out by the damp patch on the floor of his toilet. It was a world away.

It was a fun shoot even though it was incredibly hot. We had a fantastic hair guy who put mad colours in my hair – it was the first time I'd ever dyed it. The set was in the middle of nowhere and we all had our own Winnebagos, which was hysterical. Every take was just such a laugh, for me at any rate. We stayed at a hotel in the middle of the desert that felt like something out of *Thelma and Louise*. The first night everyone stayed up late for a drink but I went to bed. A bit later on Geri came to my room. 'I'm bored,' she announced.

That's what I loved about Geri. We'd wake up in the middle of the night and one of us would say, 'Do you want to go out?'

'Yeah!'

'Come on let's go!'

'Quickly, get dressed!'

'Five minutes!'

'Come on!'

Neither of us ever said, 'Oh no, better not do that.' We'd get in the car, speed up the motorway, whoo-whoo! There would be no stopping us, nobody in the back of our heads saying, 'Wait. You've got a photo shoot on Monday. You want to look fresh don't you?' We just went.

You can't live like that all the time, but I was so glad that I experienced it with someone. Geri never had to persuade me to do anything and I never had to persuade her to do anything. It would just take one look between us and we knew we had to do it, whatever it was. Not because of the other person, but something inside both of us said, 'I've got to do it!' That night we went back into reception, where we bumped into Vaughan, the video director, and one of the cameramen. 'We're going to drive off into the desert,' Vaughan announced. So off we went with them.

We parked in the middle of nowhere and stared in silence at the stars through the car sunroof. They were right there above us, big and clear and glimmering, so close that you felt you could reach out and touch them. All around us was pitch black; the car was the only source of artificial light for miles and miles.

I opened the door and got out. The air felt warm but fresh. Without thinking, I moved away from the headlights and took off my clothes. Out of sight, I began running around in the dark, staring up at the stars and feeling the night air against my skin. It was exhilarating and liberating – the whoosh of air, the sense of space, the endless darkness, the dry earth, the bright sky, the feeling of being nowhere and everywhere. It made me feel so alive, all my senses alert. I called over to the car.

'Come on Geri, try this! It's so freeing!'

Silence.

'Come on! Strip off! You'll love it.'

Silence.

I went on running.

'Come on Geri!'

Finally the car door opened. I knew she wouldn't be able to resist! Off we sprinted across the sand together, totally naked, heading straight into the infinite black of night. It was such a laugh, a very special moment, an ecstatic, giddy buzz like no other.

After a while we decided to get back. 'We're going to get into trouble if we get caught. We'd better not tell the others.' You could see the headlines. Spice Girls In Saucy Strip Scandal!

Presales on 'Say You'll Be There' were huge and it went straight to No.1. Then it was back to the Far East for another long round of promo. It seemed unfair that we couldn't stay in England to enjoy our success there, but in another way it was good to get away from all the madness. One thing was for sure, wherever we were, whenever we were together, it was us five against the world. No one could touch us when we had the others there. I loved those early promotional tours. We were so excited about life that we'd stay up half the night messing around in each other's rooms. Before we became terminally exhausted by our endless, packed schedule, we were on a constant high. When you watch the interviews we did back then, it's obvious how happy we were.

If you were a nervous interviewer, you might have been relieved to interview us in those days. You only had to ask one question and we'd be off in our own world, all talking over each other, dobbing each other in it.

'What about when *you* did so-and-so Vicky?' Then Vicky would have to tell that story. 'And I think you had a similar experience, didn't you Melanie?' We were expert dobbers.

Next we'd get on the Girl Power mission. We were always being asked if we were feminists. Well, feminist is the wrong word for it. (I didn't really understand what it meant until Geri explained the history of the suffragettes.) Girl Power was about girls on top, aware of their sexuality, their power and importance. It was more emotional and less intellectual than feminism as I understand it.

Some fans (mostly in America) would say, 'We're the same as you. We hate men! Women rule. We don't want men in our lives.'

'No,' we'd argue, 'We like to go out with men but we refuse to be bossed around by them.'

Interviewers usually couldn't control or even contribute to what we were saying. Once we got started, that was it. Now and again, if the interviewer was a sexy man (or even just a man), we might listen to one of his questions or say, 'Okay then. Ask us summat!' Of course then he'd start stuttering and rustling his notes. So I'd nick his pad or piece of paper with his list of questions on and from that moment he'd be truly bolloxed. If we were really bored one of us would just get up and sit on his knee or ruffle his hair. He didn't have a chance, poor thing.

It was easier for the women journalists. They just had to sit back with their tape recorder running. Melanie dealt with most of the annoying questions because she could be very diplomatic. We soon discovered that if she gave the answers, we didn't get into trouble. She was the sensible one. 'You know, some groups do that but we don't,' she'd say patiently. At one point we tried to work out a structure for who answered which kinds of questions, but it soon fell by the way.

People sometimes ask whether we were given any advice as to how to handle fame generally, but it came so mad and fast that we didn't have time for any of that. I think the best preparation we could possibly have had was to live together and get to know each other well. We were so much stronger that way. We learnt as we went along and most of the time we were left to our own devices, which was brilliant. We decided between us what to reveal in interviews – and no one else had a say in it.

We were like a fireball of energy that drifted in and out of places on a never-ending blazing roller coaster ride. Once started we didn't stop unless something mind-blowing occurred to halt us in our tracks. We were incredibly rowdy. As soon as we arrived somewhere we ran screaming down the corridor, laughing, shouting and messing about. It was a real mission to get us from A to B, unless we just happened to be in the mood to rush and get something over and done with. At the end of the day, we just wanted to do our job and have a laugh. We couldn't understand why everything was always so serious and formal. Sometimes we'd do as many as forty interviews in a row and be very professional about getting through them all, while behaving like naughty school kids throughout.

I would never have been able to get through all that work on my own. I don't think anybody could. But together it was easy. When one of us couldn't be arsed to answer a question, another person could. Where one person just wanted to go home, there would be another who was well up for staying. The energy vroomed around the group and you'd always catch it from someone else if you were feeling tired or bored. It never stopped. There was never one point where we were all ecstatic or all drained. While one person was falling off the wheel another one would be pulling them back on again. It was a constant checking and re-addressing. That's why it was never boring.

What made us laugh was our growing entourage. We took the piss out of it. 'Yes, we are now arriving with ten thousand people behind us carrying luggage, make-up and clothes!' we'd announce. Sometimes we'd whisper to each other, 'Why do we need all of that? What's wrong?' but obviously we liked it. Still, it was a joke sometimes, especially when all the record company reps and press and promo people started coming along too.

Every time we went to Germany we met up with the same lovely flame-haired Virgin rep, Britta. Over time we became very friendly with her and one day she took us to a Biergarten where they drank yards of ale. (In Leeds we all drank half a lager and lime, or half a lager – draft, Carlsberg – even though you'd be running off to the toilet every five minutes because the beer went straight through you.) It was a cool and funky place and I was in my element, surrounded by people with blonde hair and an accent. What more could I ask for? It was one of my fantasies.

Our first stop on our second trip to the Far East was Hong Kong, where we did a showcase of five songs for a group of English competition winners. The two Cornish fans made us laugh when they said 'idnit?' instead of 'innit?' It was a night to remember. We were so hyped up before we went on stage that we jumped around madly to the Gary Glitter song 'Do You Wanna Be In My Gang?' and hugged each other about a million times. I wrote in my diary:

Something beautiful happened last night. We did a performance at Planet Hollywood and we all came to the same high on stage at the same time. It was magnificent. The crowd were having a proper party. They all loved us and we loved them. We got that carried away, we even did an encore. It's so great to be putting the philosophy of the group into action. Trust, respect and honesty!

Obviously we were all very grateful to Simon, but even at that early stage I had slightly mixed feelings about his management methods. His power over us seemed enormous and I wasn't very comfortable with it.

What can I say about him? He's a wicked businessman and always gets what he wants with his determination. A great analyser, he can spot things you yourself haven't even noticed yet. He has a very subtle way of controlling other people's minds. He can make you high, low, scared, feel terrible or even just chilled. It's like he's studied people and knows what's going to happen next, but he doesn't know really. When he gets a wild card, it unnerves him. I can see through him a bit, but I'm not quite sure what to make of him.

Simon was a bit of a mystery to us. Normally when you meet people in this business it's not too hard to sum them up. You ask them about their family life and how long they've been working in the industry and you begin to build up a picture. But you wouldn't dare ask Simon about his relationships or if he planned to have a family. For a long time things were strictly professional between us, never intimate or personal. We didn't have the balls to discuss his private life, his family or his background, even amongst ourselves. We talked to him purely about business. We'd go to his house for dinner and after some beautiful food and wine we'd have a business meeting. We never crossed the boundary into his personal life, even when we were in his home.

Anyway, I was too busy with my own life to worry about Simon's. Things were changing. I was away from Richie for longer and longer periods and there came a point when there was always too much to tell him or I'd forget about stuff. We started to grow apart. There wasn't any bad feeling between us – we missed each other and we always kept in contact – but there was a distance growing because I was just so excited about my life. My career was taking over everything.

Then there were my family and friends. Because I didn't have time to think, I never considered that they would be as badly affected by my fame as they were. I knew that they were affected but they never mentioned it when I spoke to them because I usually phoned in a panic or crying or feeling homesick. I never phoned up completely happy. Luckily my mum knew my pattern of behaviour inside out. If I was calling regularly then something was not right. If I phoned now and again having a bit of a breakdown, she knew I was completely fine.

When I phoned up in tears my mum wasn't prepared to unload all her stuff on me. I didn't speak to my dad or Danielle much, it was my mum I spoke to, or Charlotte or Rebecca. They were fully aware of my sensitive emotional side, so rather than saying, 'Well what about me?' they just listened and tried to cheer me up. I can't count the amount of times I phoned Charlotte and said, 'I want to come home!'

'No Melanie, don't be stupid,' she'd say and then quickly change the subject so that it would be forgotten about. She knew that the last thing I really wanted to talk about was myself. Finding out all the Leeds gossip and having a good old chat with my best mate was far more grounding.

I later found out that my growing fame had a horrible impact on my close family and friends. My dad was photographed cycling to and from work and all his mates used to laugh at him when they saw pictures of me in the *Sun* and the *Mirror*. It would be *the* work gossip when something had happened to the band. 'Well is it true then? Come on!'

My dad would say, 'Well, I don't know. I don't talk to Melanie like that. I just ask her if she's eating her vegetables.'

My mum would get comments like, 'I don't know why you're still working here, with a millionaire daughter and all.' She ended up becoming quite introvert at work after that. It must have been strange for them all when I started talking about my life publicly. Sometimes my mum didn't fully approve of my comments:

Dear Melanie,

I hope you've caught up on your sleep and enjoyed your Sunday concert. Can you let us know what's happening in Sheffield, like the time and place? Will you please be able to come home even for an hour? It seems forever waiting to see you.

Last night you were the talk of the barbeque cos they couldn't believe you are the same person that taught at the Mandela Centre keep fit class. You ought to have done an interview with the Yorkshire Evening Post, *mainly because it's where you're from.*

Anyway I'm missing you all the time. Can't wait for Sunday.

See you soon love you

Loads of love,

Mum

PS Hope you like the G-strings that I'm sending with this letter.

Things were difficult for Danielle, although I hardly knew it at the time. Only last year she said, 'You don't know what it's been like for me.'

'Well tell me,' I said.

'I'm really proud of you and you mean the world to me but it has been hard for me,' she started saying.

'Why didn't you come to me before?' I asked, distraught.

'How could I? You were here, there and everywhere, flying off. You had all your own stuff to worry about, and then your marriage went wrong so I couldn't tell you then.'

I was nearly in tears as she told me how hard it was to get work, earn her own money and establish herself. The association with me was just too strong in everyone's minds. I remember offering help at the time but she always refused. 'No, I'm going to do it by myself,' she'd say. That's always been her mentality and still is.

Everyone stared at her when she went to auditions. 'What's *she* doing here? Surely her sister can get her a job?' You could hear a pin drop as she did her audition piece. It began to make her very self-conscious. She got beaten up a few times. 'You just wanna look like Mel B!'

'Well I can't help looking like her. She's my sister.'

'Yeah right!' Often no one believed her.

She got a lot of aggravation. 'Look at 'er trying to look like Melanie!'

There was a lot of press interest in what she was doing, which restricted her in ways I wasn't even aware of. For instance, while she was at music college, she went out busking with a keyboard player in one of the arcades in Leeds. Well, at the time it was felt that it would be totally inappropriate for my sister to be seen busking, so 19 put in a phone call and advised her not to do it again. There was (rightly or wrongly) so much paranoia about the power of the papers in shaping public opinion that she also dropped out of Miss Caribbean, because of the press it would have generated. She began to feel that she couldn't lead her own life. It must have been horrific for her.

Charlotte just used to have fights with people. Once she heard someone bitching about me in the toilets of a club and went for them. Of course, they didn't know Charlotte had any connection with me – why would they? Nevertheless she was always on major defence duty, as every best friend should be. She has sometimes stunned me in the way she's gone beyond the call of duty to support me.

I was also finding it quite hard to adjust to fame (although I was getting all the benefits too, which my friends and family obviously weren't). I used to go to 'top' parties but I hated them. I'd rather go down the pub. I was never big on clubbing on the London scene because it was all too much for me. I preferred to go back to Leeds where everyone was so much more relaxed. 'All right Mel!' or 'Hiya!' – that was it. Because I'd always been backwards and forwards to my hometown, people didn't think it was a big deal to see me out.

In London you are stared at from the moment you walk into a club. They shove you straight along to the front of the queue, you get given a bottle of champagne and as much as that's great and fantastic, people start thinking, Who the f*** does she think she is? even though it's not your fault that the manager is giving you these 'privileges'. Not long ago I was queuing up for a club and the bouncer tried to hustle me to the front.

'No.' I said. 'I wanna queue.'

That Christmas we were No.1 again with our third single, '2Become1'. The Christmas No.1 is one of the most important records of the year and so we really felt like we'd achieved something. We were overwhelmed. It felt like the whole world knew us now, which was a bit frightening.

'Say You'll Be There' had sold nearly a million singles in the UK. '2Become 1' topped the million mark (1.1m) and sold two and a half million copies worldwide. I remember pinching myself in disbelief. Every little girl dreams of being a ballet dancer, a pop star or an actress and somehow I was living that dream. You're told as a child that dreams come true, but come on, that kind rarely does. It took a while for it to sink in that this was fact, not fiction, soon to be enshrined in the Guinness Book of Records. The figures were astounding and I don't think anyone could quite believe them, including Simon. We'd boasted that we were going to do all these things and now they were actually happening. It was too incredible for words. All the industry people who hadn't even let us into their offices, who'd said, 'Girl groups will never work,' were eating humble pie.

The video for '2Become1' was shot against a green screen (the background was added later) and involved a lot of hanging around and not doing much, interspersed with loads of close-up camera angles. Oh, and there was a deer in the studio, because someone had had the bright idea of featuring one in the video. 'What the f*** is that deer doing here?' we whispered to each other. 'Oh dear!' we kept saying loudly. 'Oh dear, oh dear.'

I love video shoots and photo shoots because you get to chat to everyone, from the crew to the director, while you sit there having your hair and make-up done. It's very interesting when you reach the level we reached. We did so much and met so many different people that it was hard to remember names and faces. I have no trouble recalling faces, but I forget names. I'll notice instantly if someone's had their hair cut or changed their image or style and I often remember tiny details about their lives, but I never know what they're called.

There's a cable holder at *TOTP* who collects ants and I remember saying hi to him when we did our very first performance of 'Wannabe' on the programme. Six years later I saw him at the *TOTP* Awards and the first thing I said was, 'How are your ants?'

'Oh, they're breeding like crazy!' he laughed.

You do nothing for hours at a time on shoots, so you chill or sleep or go for a mingle. You get to find out who is the cocky one on the crew, who's bossing who around, who's having an affair with whom. All in all, shoots are great for people-watching, one of my favourite hobbies. Buses are excellent too, but I don't get to go on buses these days.

The big highlight of that December was turning on the Christmas lights in Oxford Street. It was unforgettable. We got ready in a hotel across the road. I was wearing what I call my sleeping bag – basically it's a long brown duvet coat, neck-to-ankle, with a white rope belt. It looks a bit like a home-made, keep warm outfit. (I've now given it to my security guard at home and he's so thankful because it's extremely cosy on cold nights.)

The crowds were held back by barriers, leaving a small circle around the control tower. As soon as we arrived, me and Geri got out of our car and ran madly around the edge of the circle, touching the hundreds of hands that reached across the barriers. It felt a bit like knocking dominoes down. The security guards shouted, 'Get back! Get back!' but we ignored them.

We climbed the tower and stood at the top feeling giddy. All those thousands and thousands of people looking up at us, necks craning, cheering, shouting, going mental! It was hard to take it in. The noise was staggering. Foxy (Capital DJ Dr Fox) did the countdown.

10, 9, 8, 7, 6, 5, 4, 3, 2 . . .

Everybody thinks that when you press that button, that's it, the lights turn on. Well they don't. For a laugh we started pressing it well before the countdown and instantly realised it was fake. It always is. People be aware! There's an electrical engineer out there somewhere, in his roadie black tracksuit, smelling bad because he's been up all night trying to make sure it all works – and he turns the lights on. Well it definitely wasn't us, anyway.

ONE!

The roars of the crowd were deafening as Oxford Street lit up. Row upon row of brightly coloured fairy lights illuminated the night. Foxy tried but failed to interview us. Almost drunk on the madness of the situation, we were shouting and screaming and falling about the control tower. Looking down on so many people looking up at you induced a weird kind of vertigo. The air was filled with chants and screams. It was an incredible, extraordinary buzz.

14

WALK LIKE A CHAMPION

Now I'm known for being in the Spice Girls – to this day I'm only beginning to make my name as a solo artist. So as much as I get screamed at and shouted at, I do realise that it's not actually me that's attracting all of that attention. I don't take it personally. It's not me who is famous, I'm a part of something famous – the Spice Girls and Girl Power and everything they stand for.

You get asked in interviews, 'When did you realise you were famous?' Well you don't really realise you're famous. You notice that people are taking an interest in you and looking up to you and that society is paying attention to you because you are a part of something special. There was never a moment that I could pinpoint and say, 'That's when I realised I was famous.' Going on tour was the biggest feedback of all and that came much later.

There was a moment when I realised I wasn't going to have to worry about money any more. At the 19 Management Christmas party in early December Simon called us into a wood-panelled room and gave us each a cheque for £200,000. We'd known it was coming, but not how much it would be, and the noughts merged before my eyes. I had no real concept of how much £200,000 really was, but I knew it was a f*** of a lot. Enough to start spending money without thinking too much about it, anyway.

I'd never owned a credit card until I got that cheque. I'd never had money in the bank apart from a couple of quid. I'd been overdrawn for years. To have ready cash that actually showed up on the screen when I called up my balance at the cash point (which I did quite a lot for a while) freaked me out a bit.

My first thoughts were, I can pay off my mum and dad's mortgage and get myself new wheels! It was Richie who suggested that I buy an Alpha Romeo convertible. He did loads of research into all the different models and when I bought the Alpha he said it was the best car ever. I used to drive him around London in it, with the roof down, late at night, really, really fast, even though he'd get incredibly angry with me and shout, 'Bloody hell, Melanie! Bloody hell!' I loved it. I'll never sell that car.

People ask how it's possible to spend a million in twenty-four hours. Well it's easy. You buy the car you've always wanted, you buy a car for your friend. You pay off your parents' debts, order the whole range by your favourite designer, buy an expensive diamond ring and that's it. Gone. I had no real concept of the value of money until the day I got divorced. That was the first time I began to add up what I'd actually spent on my house and gifts for other people.

I'd always had the ability to spend large. Even when I was broke, instead of frittering my money I usually saved up to buy something like a bed or a TV. I was conscious that some day I'd have my own house and I didn't want to get some designer to do it out for me. Nor, when the time came, was I going to go on a mad shopping spree for a week and buy everything new. I wanted to live with my furniture and enjoy it, build on it and create ideas.

Having money for the first time gave me a huge sense of freedom. It was amazing to be able to give people things that they'd always wanted or admired from afar. I'll never forget my dad's face the day he came down to see me on the train. There was a brand new Audi parked in my garage.

'Dad come here. Do you like this car?'

'Yeah, it's bloody lovely!'

'Here are the keys. It's yours.'

Some of my friends found it insulting that I wouldn't let anyone pay for anything, but I didn't care. The way I saw it, I was giving them a licence to be carefree. Having no money can be very restricting. When you're skint you can't relax. You constantly have to be aware of what you're spending. 'Right, I've got £15 for the night. I need my taxi or bus fare and I can buy a couple of drinks.' There isn't a lot of flexibility. When your money is gone, you rely on other people to buy you drinks or you drink water. I drank a lot of water when I was broke.

Now I could take my friends out for meals, to bars and parties. They'd come down to London and say, 'Oh my God! £2 for a pint of lager!' and I'd say, 'Don't worry about it. Money is not an issue.' It was great to be able to say that – and feel it. I didn't want to show off about it but I wanted to share it. I was very aware that I hadn't spent years and years working for my money. I hadn't, say, built up a vineyard from scratch or helped a community to become self-sufficient. Suddenly I was rich but it didn't mean a lot. The girls later teased me about my disregard for it. The money we earned became like Monopoly money to me.

It was great to be able to afford a proper holiday, though. Simon gave us three weeks off over Christmas and I flew to a posh resort in Antigua with Richie, my mum, dad and sister. It was meant to be a fairy-tale holiday, but it didn't quite work out that way. I'd booked a place where I was guaranteed fancy food, a fancy bedroom and a fancy pool, but it was bollocks really. You felt like you were on show the whole time. The other guests were generally a lot older, and Danielle and I were the only black girls in the whole place, apart from the people who worked there (who were the only people I made friends with).

Geri and her friend Janine were staying on a nearby island and one night they came to meet me in the hotel. I had an all-inclusive deal and they just buried their heads in the buffet. Nobody noticed. I was touched that Geri had come all that way. The next day she dragged me and Richie back to her resort, which was far more beautiful than ours. It had a private beach with hardly anybody on it and it was fine to go topless. At my resort sunbathing was all about lipstick and earrings.

On New Year's Eve we flew to Nevis to see Black Grandma and Grandad and Great Grandma. Like many of their contemporaries, Grandma and Grandad had gone back to spend their retirement there after forty years in England. Nevis was a huge contrast to the resort in Antigua. It's a tiny, very unspoilt island – thirty-six miles square and only seven miles across. Christopher Columbus 'discovered' it, but there were Arawaks and Caribs living there for more than a thousand years before he arrived.

When the Europeans colonised the Caribbean, the native population were wiped out through war and diseases brought from Europe. Then the English settled in Nevis in the seventeenth century and realised that there was money to be made from growing sugar. They built sugar plantations and imported slaves to work them, mainly from Africa. Before slavery was abolished, literally millions of slaves were brought to the Caribbean. They often worked in appalling conditions.

Only a tiny percentage of blacks and non-whites were free in Nevis. The atmosphere must have been very different back then. It was an island full of people who were treated worse than dogs. When they did something to annoy their white masters, they were often whipped, branded, tortured, lynched, mutilated or chained up. (Believe it or not, only a hundred years after the end of slavery, many Nevisians volunteered to fight for Britain in World War Two.)

The economy of Nevis is now mostly dependent on tourism, especially eco-tourism. It's got the most amazing lush rain forests and underwater reefs. Charlestown, the capital, is a beautiful colonial harbour town. And here's something you may not know. The education system in Nevis is brilliant. At 98%, the literacy rate is the highest in the western hemisphere. (I know all of this because I spent hours at a holiday trade show in Earls Court helping to promote the Nevis Tourist Board!)

Grandma and Grandad live in a virtually untouched village called Gingerland, the kind of place where everyone sits out on their porches saying hi to passers-by and the odd car or bicycle goes past with a toot or a beep. We went into the centre of the village late one night and there were kids everywhere and music playing. It's a lovely, lively place.

It was fantastic to see Grandma again. Her house was very light and airy, with a huge veranda. The furniture in the front room had plastic covers on. Typical! (I have to laugh when I get my car back from being valeted and I rip the plastic covers off the seats, knowing that Grandma would keep them on.) I'd brought her some Spice cups and other bits of merchandise, but she took one look and shoved it all to one side. 'That's nice Melanie, but how are you?' she asked.

I sat there trying to tell her all about it. Where do you start? 'I'm in this group and it's done really well and it's all about Girl Power . . .'

After a few sentences I noticed that she was looking at me in a slightly puzzled way. Then suddenly she saw my tongue stud and was horrified.

When I showed her my tattoos she screeched, 'You're piercing your soul! How can you do that?'

Not long after this outburst a load of people started arriving back from church. All the women seemed to have hats with false hair attached to them. My mum and I were in fits of laughter. 'What *is* that? Why has everyone got 'hat hair'? Do they go into a shop and ask for a hat with hair on it so that they can just plonk it on without any bother?'

I know I shouldn't laugh but we just couldn't help it at the time. I sneaked into my Grandma's bedroom and tried on her hat hair wig. It looked hysterical, but if she had caught me I would have been cussed to the floor. That night Grandma cooked us a fantastic soup. It's mad, she just lives off the land. She keeps pigs and grows all kinds of herbs and vegetables in the garden. 'What do you want in your salad?' she asks, before going out into the garden to pick it.

The next day we went to see Great Grandma, the woman who had brought my dad and his sister up when they were left behind in Nevis by their parents. I was very excited because I was meeting her for the first time. I was also fascinated to see where my dad grew up.

Unfortunately Dad hadn't told me that Great Grandma now had only one leg and one eye (the other eye was glass). When we arrived at her house my cousin went inside, chucked her over his shoulder and brought her to us. The whole thing would have taken hours otherwise, because she can only shuffle along. Instantly I thought of horror films and nightmares.

'Bend down and give Great Grandma a kiss,' said my dad, firmly.

'Dad, I can't. I just can't do that,' I pleaded in a whisper.

'But you've never met her. She looked after me and brought me up. Bend down and give her a kiss.'

So I did. And as I bent down, she looked up at me and said, 'Oh, you're beautiful!'

'And this is my boyfriend,' I said, motioning to Richie.

She flicked a glance at him and turned her back, dismissing him instantly because he was white. I wanted to have a go at her about it but Richie whispered that it didn't matter and went and stood at the back.

Someone shouted a hallelujah. We stayed for tea.

Later in the day I went for a walk with my dad and he pointed out a few of the remnants of slavery. In the main square there was a post with chains hanging off it, where slaves were tied up and whipped. In a way it was the first time that I became fully aware of the legacy of slavery. Until then everything I knew about black culture and history came from films and books – Maya Angelou, Alice Walker and Iyanla Vanzant in particular. It had never affected me directly but it was part of my West Indian culture and history and so I was always interested. Now here was the physical proof of it, a grizzly reminder of terrible suffering and injustice.

Three years later, while making a documentary for Channel 4 in Benin in Africa, I walked down the 'Route of Slaves' to the 'Gate of No Return', where slaves were brought to the ports from the slave markets inland. Benin was a major exit point for slaves being taken to the Caribbean and South America. It was a very poignant experience walking along the same path that so many captive people had trodden. It still haunts me. At the Gate of No Return I saw 'the tree of forgetting', which the departing slaves were led around while a corrupt priest did a spell to make them forget their identity and beliefs in voodoo. On the other side I saw 'the tree of remembering', where a good priest did a spell to make sure that their spirits and souls returned home, even if their bodies didn't. I think that they must have known they weren't coming back. It must have been heartbreaking.

I've never asked my dad if he'd go back to live in Nevis. I know that my grandad was a bit reluctant to return, but it's just what everybody did. Grandad has met up with a lot of the friends that he used to play dominoes with at the Mandela Centre, but it's a very different way of life and my dad worried about him re-adjusting. In Leeds Grandad was a bit of a one. It was Grandma who couldn't wait to get back to Nevis, not him.

In many ways it was great to see nothing but black faces everywhere in Nevis. It felt like home, a feeling I was to experience again on the Benin trip. There were never any black people at the meetings we went to as Spice Girls. Not one black face in all those high-up meetings with the heads of this company and that company and their marketing managers and financial directors. It really bothered me. Not that I constantly made a point of it, but I used to say to the others, 'God, there were no black people in that meeting.'

Vicky always used to say, 'I don't see you as a colour, I see you as Melanie.'

And I'd always reply, 'That's because you know me. If you were to see me in the street you would only see my colour.'

The other girls would say, 'We don't see you as black.'

'I'm not black.' I'd reply, 'I'm mixed race. You must see that.'

'Well no, we don't,' they'd say.

It was only when I took them to Chapeltown that they realised what it felt like to be in the minority. (Actually 'minority' is a very strange word and it irritates me because it doesn't have a very clear meaning. Women are called a minority group even though they are half the population; an Indian family living in a large Indian community like Peckham is referred to as part of a minority, even though Indians are the majority in that area. I think it's a word that can only be used very generally.)

Once I took Geri to a club and said, 'Look around. There are no white people. Do you know what it feels like now?'

'Yes,' she said. 'It does feel a bit strange now you've mentioned it.'

'Well that's how I feel, every single day.'

15

WELCOME TO THE HOUSE OF FUN

With things going so well in the UK, the second stage of our master plan began to unfold. Now it was time to conquer America. Refreshed from our holidays and riding high on our UK success, we were totally up for it as we boarded the plane for New York in January 1997. 'Here we go! Let's go get 'em!'

If we'd known what a tough market America is to crack then perhaps we wouldn't have been so confident. But to be honest, I don't think anything could have stood in our way right then. Someone probably told us that not one British act had made it big in the States for at least a decade, but that kind of comment was like water off a duck's back. We weren't like other bands. We could feel the world within our grasp, America included, and there was no way we were going to let it go.

'Wannabe' went into the Billboard Top 100 at No. 11 when it was released, the highest entry for a debut single ever (British or American). Easy! When I think now of all the brilliant UK bands who've slogged their way around the States without managing to make even the slightest dent on the American market, I realise how unbelievably lucky we were, but at the time it was just, 'Well, of course!'

Without doubt Simon played a huge part in our US success. He'd had the foresight to introduce us to Virgin America as soon as he'd signed us, which meant that the record company knew us and was already hyped up to promote us when the moment came. He was very forward thinking and I don't think I ever thanked him properly. So here it is Simon: thank you, you brainy git.

As the single climbed the Billboard charts, our days became ever more crammed with promotion. Everyone wanted to talk to us, from the biggest TV networks to the smallest magazines. Now the secret to cracking America is that you mustn't overlook anyone. You may not have heard of a particular radio station, or even the city or state it's located in, but you just cannot forget how vast the US is. So however insignificant a station sounds you can be sure it's got a massive audience if it's at all commercially viable. Piss off the DJ, plugger or programmer at that station and you instantly lose a huge potential record-buying market. A hundred thousand listeners may not sound much when you compare it to the population of America, but translate it into record sales and you start to think again.

So we worked our arses off during those weeks. We flew all over the place, meeting, greeting and mouthing off, being as nice as we could to absolutely everyone, from the presenters to the tea boys. (The tea boys were usually the cute ones, who in time would go on to engineer their own radio shows.)

Because America is quite a bit more conservative than Britain we tried to keep a lid on the more outrageous elements of our promo patter, but a lot of the time we just couldn't restrain ourselves. 'Tits! Bums! Ziga zig ah!' We'd kiss the head of the company on the cheek, or sit on his knee and make him blush. We'd pull people's ties off and embarrass them by making them dance with us. We were so enthusiastic about Spice Girls and the Girl Power message that we often got carried away. Still, no one seemed to mind. In fact they loved it.

When things were going really well I sometimes used to think, It can't all be like this! It can't all be this good. I need to feel a bit bad about something, surely? We can't be this famous. It's not fair really. You've got bands struggling all over the world that are far better than we are. I felt that I didn't deserve my success and I was convinced that something had to go wrong. But Spice Girls just got bigger and bigger. In the end the only way I could handle it was to tell myself that it wasn't about me. It was about the five of us. It was a group thing.

Often there wasn't time to think. We were so busy that all I could focus on was exactly what I was doing right at that moment. Car-interview-car-flight-car-performance-car-flight-car-interview-car-home. 'Where's my bag?' The staff at Heathrow told us that they'd never known anyone take so many flights. We were spending more time in the air than on the ground, literally and metaphorically.

Around this time things reached breaking point with Richie.

All he is bothered about is getting a good night's sleep. He just doesn't show me affection, which I need. He doesn't listen to Melanie Brown when she is in need of someone to talk to and understand. He just refuses to sympathise at all.

I think we both have everything and nothing to shout about. You'd think after not seeing each other for a couple of days we would hug and kiss, but no, we just say hi. And when I want a hug after work he doesn't quite give me one.

You can do things to show someone how much you love them but deep down you can't beat that long look in the eye and hearing the words I love you. I don't know, maybe I'm just a stupid romantic.

I'm always the first one to say, 'God I don't know what I'd do without him.' Maybe I shouldn't say that any more. He always upsets me so much. It's like he cannot handle me when I cry or get passionate about things; but it's all right when I'm happy and talkative, he can handle that. Perhaps we both need to get away from each other for a while.

I blamed Richie, but it wasn't his fault. It was my insecurity talking and Richie bore the brunt of it all. I started to criticise him and our relationship rather than looking at my environment and my work situation and what I was actually going through.

I'd come in at 3 a.m. after working all day, in a bad mood, feeling knackered and being demanding. He'd been working all day and the dinner he'd cooked hours earlier was probably waiting to be reheated in the microwave. Right then I wanted *this*, *this*, *this* and *this*, but he was exhausted and had to get up in four hours. Our lifestyles no longer met in the middle, which they have to do to a certain extent when you're a couple. So much was happening that it was hard to keep a real sense of who I was or what I was developing into. Scary Spice, Mel B, Melanie, Melanie Brown, home bird, council estate girl, pop star. It was confusing. I wrote:

Fame.
   You enter a whole new world. No one knows it or understands it. 'Hey, hey, hey!' they shout at you. You're not a human, you're not a person. You're trapped in a net and you don't know when that net is going to set you free. Free, as in you'll just sink back to the bottom and be forgotten about. Back to that normality that you've lost and want so much to be a part of again.

In the Spice Girls I was taught that you could never be in a bad mood. I had to function on a false-happy level a lot of the time. But I find that when you have to suppress your feelings and can't let them out, they grow. It's like watering a plant. As time went on I started taking my bad moods home with me and dumping them on Richie, which really wasn't fair. One day I got home to find him in a really angry mood. Two prostitutes had turned up at his work and tried to lure him into a 'honey trap'. Sent along to trick him by one of the Sunday tabloids, the deal was that they'd get him into bed and then sell their story. Nasty.

'What's going on, Melanie?' Richie asked, bewildered.

I was really upset. The more time we spent apart the more we seemed to argue, and in the end Richie moved out. We didn't split up on bad terms and we're still friends to this day but the pressures at the time proved too much for either of us to cope with.

I was fully prepared to be single for a while, but of course life got in the way. Or should I say Fjöl got in the way. We'd been writing to each other and occasionally phoning ever since Blackpool. Then a couple of weeks after me and Richie split, Fjöl phoned to say he was on his way to London. Oh my God! It was an amazing coincidence and I was really excited about seeing him again.

The day he arrived I had wall-to-wall interviews until 9 p.m. As soon as I could get away, I ran to my car and called him. 'Where are you?'

'Oxford Street.'

'Where on Oxford Street?'

'I have no idea. You know what I look like. Come and find me.'

On Oxford Street? Was he mad? (It's only one of the longest and most crowded streets in the whole of London. Plus, private cars are banned from going along it *and* it was dark.) Still, it was a challenge and I love a challenge. I knew I'd find him, I had to. Roof down, music blaring, I crawled along until I spotted him standing on the corner of Wardour Street, gorgeous as ever, all muscles and blonde hair. He got into the car, we took one look at each other, and that was it. Ding!

I took him to my favourite Thai restaurant. 'You're going to love the food!' I told him. But when we got there it was closed. No way! The lights were on and I could see people inside so I rattled the door and knocked. 'We're shut,' mouthed the waiter when I caught his attention.

'Please? For me?'

It was a wonderful, romantic dinner. We talked and talked and talked. Fjöl was even nicer and funnier and sexier than I remembered. It was fantastic to see him again.

The next afternoon he came over to my flat. I sat on the sofa, he sat next to me and within a minute we were in each other's arms. My Viking had returned! I was in love again. This time it didn't matter that we lived in different countries. I wasn't in England very much anyway, so often it didn't make much difference whether I flew home or to Iceland. Plus, I had enough money to fly Fjöl out to wherever I was and he could usually arrange his work around me. (He has done so many different jobs that it's hard to keep up. At one point he had his own radio programme. He's a snooker and skiing champion. He flies planes. Right now he owns six horses and spends a lot of time painting. He's an all-rounder, good at almost everything.) Fjöl and I were very well matched. He was incredibly relaxed and very loving, which was the perfect combination for me.

A couple of days after we got back from America, the group went into rehearsals for our performance at the Brits, where we were opening the show with 'Who Do You Think You Are?' the flip side of our AA-side fourth single 'Mama'. Now The Brits weren't really going to be seen outside the UK or make an impact on big markets like America, but in our minds there was no underestimating the importance of this performance on home territory. It was the (next) big one and we were all incredibly nervous about it.

Our choreographer was Priscilla Samuels, who had worked with Cathy

Dennis and came highly recommended through Simon. I loved Priscilla as soon as I met her. Wow, she is so cool, I thought. Priscilla is tall and lean, with muscles to die for, and she's always really beautifully turned out. I instantly liked her attitude towards things and she had a positive, clear-thinking way of doing her job. She was a fantastic dancer in her own right – and someone you just wouldn't want to get on the wrong side of.

Working with Priscilla was great, but as ever, when it came to doing the Brits dress and technical rehearsals we did what we always did and mucked about instead of concentrating. The director would shout exasperatedly, 'Come on now, let's do it properly!' and maybe two of us would do it properly while the others messed around.

We enjoyed the mayhem we caused. Whenever we were together we were like a massive electricity pylon, beaming out highly charged signals left, right and centre, zapping everyone and everything around us. People felt intimidated when they walked into a room to find the five of us in there. They didn't know what to expect because they'd heard we were like this and like that and nutty as fruitcakes. We definitely played on it. We were on a natural high together and egged each other on.

Still, despite our casual attitude in rehearsals (apart from Mel), there was no way we weren't going to give everything to the Brits performance. As we stood there in our silhouetted positions before the curtains went up and the music started, we all felt an enormous buzz. It was strange in a way, because we weren't holding hands like we usually did at the beginning of a set. We couldn't turn round and look at each other as we so often did. We had to stand stock still like statues. For once we were experiencing our own thing, in our own worlds, together but apart. Little did we know as we waited for the music to start that we were creating an iconic image of Girl Power. Even if we had, the excitement levels couldn't have been higher.

It was funny because although we'd always whip ourselves up into a frenzy when we got a No. 1, none of us ever said to each other, 'Jesus Christ! I've come from that to this!' or 'Can you believe that this has happened to us, to me?' I think we were scared of tapping into each other's vulnerability, of stirring up doubts like, 'Oh my God, I can't believe this is happening, I don't deserve this, I'm unworthy. Why is this happening to me? Is it real?' So we said nothing except, 'We can handle it. Together we'll be fine.' Protected by the other four, you didn't feel so exposed.

People who were at the Brits that year always tell me that we brought the house down with our performance and I do remember the audience going wild afterwards, but the whole night was a bit of a haze. Ben Elton introduced us. 'Yes we all want to be their lover, we are all more than happy to be their friend. Then get with them, friends. They are, of course, Ginger, Sporty, Scary, Baby and Posh. The all-conquering Spice Girls!' We won Best Video and Best Single. We were mobbed all day – outside the venue, inside the venue, and particularly in the press room. We gave interview after interview and posed for pictures with people like Diana Ross and Elton John. Oh my God! It was a mad night but we felt in control. Even though we'd never been in this position before, it all felt very natural at the time.

A couple of weeks earlier Geri had said to us, 'I've got this amazing outfit!' and when I first saw her Union Jack dress I thought, Go for it. It was clever of her to tap into the whole 'Cool Britannia' vibe. That was the first time I realised how brilliant Geri was. Because she'd studied so many different artists over the years – people like Madonna – she had a real sense of what would catch on with the press. She knew her weaknesses and her strengths, what would work and what wouldn't, but she never really shared her cleverness with the rest of us unless it was in relation to group events like concerts and launch parties. Still, she had some fantastic ideas for costumes, themes, songs and shows and she's still having them today in her solo career.

The evening of the Brits was incredible – all hype-hype-hype-crazy-crazy – and then suddenly it was time to go home. But as I went to grab my coat it struck me that I didn't want to go home at all. After all that buzz it would feel lonely and strange to make a cup of tea, take my make-up off and get into bed alone and in silence. Forty minutes later I was standing on my mate Southan's doorstep, all dressed up, with my Brit award in my hand, crying my eyes out. The madness and chaos of the night had finally caught up with me.

Southan didn't look surprised to see me as he opened his front door. We'd known each other for about a year (we met at the Four Seasons when he was filming a programme about Pamela Anderson). He's a great listener, well educated and very open minded, so I was definitely in the right place.

'Look what I've got and I can't believe it and what do I do now?' I sobbed, holding up my Brit award to show him. It was all too much for me.

'Why don't I make you a cup of tea and we'll sit down and watch some TV together,' he suggested. Thanks Southan. It was exactly what I needed.

In a way I guess it was ironic that, as we were fighting our own way through the prejudices of the music industry ('Girl bands don't last' 'Just do what the men in suits tell you to do' 'Don't bother your pretty little heads with the details') we were becoming more and more reliant on a man for guidance and reassurance. Simon was obviously a huge factor in our success – at least that's how we saw it at the time. As Spice fever grew and our lives became more frantic and public, we increasingly looked to him to keep us on course, advise and protect us.

I really do respect him for what he did. There are no ifs or buts about it. What he does for his living – his ideas, his creativity, his long term vision – is unbelievable. He used to tell us stories about how he made his money selling records at school; it was obviously in his blood and his destiny was undoubtedly to do what he's doing now. But I don't think he necessarily knew what he was playing at when it came to handling people's emotions, especially ours.

To give him his due, I suppose you can only cope with five very different women for so long before you think, Right, I'm going to sort them out now. And that's what he started to do. He chose Divide and Rule as his management method. It was probably the only way that he felt that he could control us, but it was harsh and draining.

If you're already false when you come into this industry, that's fine, you're not going to get hurt. But we were all open, honest, vulnerable girls. The last thing we needed was to be made to feel paranoid. Yet after a while it seemed that we couldn't do anything or go anywhere or even speak to our friends without checking with Simon first. He always asked us to check with him before we went out.

'Yeah, f***ing yeah,' was my reply. Then I'd go out without telling him. It was my time, why should I tell anyone where I was going? I wasn't prepared to be controlled, but on the other hand I felt intimidated by his fear of the press. We all did.

Admittedly Simon treated me a little differently to the others. He never stopped me having a boyfriend and rarely made a fuss about me going out, whereas I know that the others were more restricted. I was really lucky in that way. I think it's because my mother explained that if I wasn't settled with a boyfriend, then I'd definitely be out going wild, which would put me in the predicament of making headlines. Every tiny thing any of us did made the papers.

Looking back I think that Simon should have passed down some of the emotional responsibility of looking after us to a woman. He was excellent at motivating and getting us fired up, but when we were sitting there saying, 'I'm really homesick!' or 'I miss my boyfriend,' or 'I've got horrible period pains' he didn't know what to say. He wasn't that kind of person. How is an unmarried man in his late thirties who hasn't grown up with sisters going to know how to deal with five young women on a daily basis? You know, when you get that particular kind of moodiness and you don't know why you've got it and he's there talking about your next five thousand interviews. You can't be arsed to listen so you instantly get branded unenthusiastic and for the rest of the day he's got it in for you.

He was right, we just had to get on with it, but a little bit of sympathy would definitely have helped soften things. Emma seemed to get it more than the rest, but we all comforted Emma in one way or another.

If Simon had got somebody else involved right from the beginning, things might have been different. I think he was aware of the problem and that's why he assigned us Catri Drummond, who oversaw Camilla and our second PA Rachel Penfold.

Once we were doing some filming on a double-decker bus going through London and I said to the others, 'Let's just get off this thing and run away!' So off we got and off we ran, somewhere near Westminster Bridge. Honest to God, Camilla was screaming her head off, nearly crying, not because of what was going to happen to us (I guess) but because of what was going to happen to her when Simon found out what we'd done. I got a huge bollocking for it afterwards too, although it didn't change anything. (Whenever I get told off, it doesn't matter what it's about, I always get giggles. It's like being back at school in the 'naughty corner' and I have to look down while my shoulders heave with suppressed laughter.)

If you were to note down how Simon operated with us, it was very, very clever, very precise and very planned. The emotional waves the band went through were very much down to him. If, say, Geri had gone a bit far in one interview, she wouldn't get a bollocking for it. Instead there would be a slow-burning reaction. Maybe Simon would set me on Geri for some other reason, or he'd get Melanie to get the arse with her. You'd be talking about something completely unrelated and somehow he'd turn the conversation around and plant a thought in your head about one of the others. He did it in such a subtle way that it wasn't guaranteed that you'd walk out of the room, go and find her and have a go at her, yet somehow it was inevitable. Just like a mother, he knew which buttons to press.

He was very good at sizing people up. He worked on us all like a brilliant psychoanalyst. You could never point the finger at him and say, 'He did that!' He was far too intelligent for that.

I remember him saying to me, 'You can go and see your boyfriend this weekend.'

'I was gonna anyway!' I replied, a bit surprised.

'Yes, but who are you going to book your flight with?' he asked.

'I don't have to go through our agency to book my flight. I can go to any old travel agents,' I snapped.

'Really? Can you?' he questioned. That was all he needed to say. Of course I couldn't. 'Any old travel agents' would most likely be on the phone to the press with my travel details within seconds.

It was getting to us all. Once, when we were on holiday, the others ganged up on me by writing me a letter listing everything that they felt was wrong with me. It was so specific that it even said something like this, 'You always ask someone to go to the toilet with you but then as soon as you've finished, you're off, without waiting for the person who came with you.' Classic playground stuff.

'Oh really, is that what you all think of me?' I said. I was deeply upset but I didn't show it. Part of me knew that it was my turn to feel like this. I'd seen it happen before.

About an hour later Simon came into my room and asked if I was feeling all right, as though he didn't know what had happened. And in his eyes he didn't know. No one had told him what they were going to do. He'd just planted the seeds and created the climate for something like that to happen, as we later realised when we finally talked over what had been going on to make us all so distant from one another. Something similar had happened to each and every one of us.

I kept the letter to show Fjöl. 'Look what they've written about me,' I sobbed.

'F*** that, Melanie!' he said.

Still, it has to be said that it must have been very hard to keep a lid on the Spice Girls and at times we could be extremely demanding.

Geri always said to me, 'You should open up your own sex shop or have your own sex channel or invent your own sex toys,' and I actually sat down with Simon and said, 'That's what I think I should do.'

'Yes, well in the future we can talk about that,' he said. He took everything I said so seriously (or maybe he was just pretending to do so).

One day I told him, 'I want a harem of men!'

'Yes well I'm sure we can sort that out,' he replied.

'And a Lamborghini!'

'Okay.' (Anything to shut you up!)

Eventually he'd plead, 'Melanie, please keep out of the way of the other girls and stop putting ideas in their heads!'

That's because I went round like some activist saying, 'Do you know what? We decide what we wanna do and we RULE!'

At first the others would say, 'Really?' Then after an hour of me banging on they'd be shouting, 'Yeah! We RULE!'

The last person Simon wanted as an enemy was me, because I had the biggest mouth. He didn't need me on his side, but it was much better for him if I wasn't pissed off. To keep me quiet at weekends he used to let me fly off to see Fjöl in Iceland.

It took us ages to work out what was going on because for a long time we were moving far too fast to notice.

16

A WOMAN'S WORK

After the Brits life became even faster. 'Mama'/'Who Do You Think You Are?' became our fourth UK No. 1 in a row. Our album was well on the way to selling twenty million copies worldwide. We were in demand in every territory and our schedules were packed out. Life was work; work was life. We were always tired. There was no let-up. The 'next big thing' seemed to happen on a weekly basis and every appearance we made was apparently more important than the last. On 12 April we did our first-ever live performance, on the American comedy show *Saturday Night Live*. After a week of intense rehearsals with the show's in-house band, we sounded pretty good. It was proof that we could sing, the British papers grudgingly admitted.

Then it was off to Taiwan for three weeks of promotion in the Far East, including Bali, where we had a few days off. Those Eastern trips were always completely mad and we seemed to spend most of our time juggling or wrestling on weird Japanese-style game shows. One time Emma and Melanie were fastened to either end of a long elastic rope and had to run at each other and bash heads while the audience cheered. I sat there thinking, 'What the f*** is this game about?' There were lots of 'Meet a Fan' slots, where we were introduced to a fan who usually screamed and then fell completely silent, and there were live Q&A sessions with a TV audience. Not only did the translations coming through our ear pieces have a two-second delay on them, creating an awkward silence between questions and answers, but if you didn't quite understand what the translator said you couldn't ask her to repeat it. I don't think I gave many logical replies on those programmes.

Getting home was a huge relief. On 13 May we performed 'Wannabe' and 'Mama' at the Prince's Trust concert at Manchester Opera House. The next day we made headlines throughout the world for throwing protocol out of the window and covering the heir to the throne in lipstick. Now I'd never had ambitions to meet royalty. I just wasn't brought up in that way. I admired singers and musicians mainly. Neneh Cherry was Queen of England as far as I was concerned (even though she's Swedish!) So I was surprised at how much of a buzz I got out of meeting Prince Charles for the first time. I just wasn't expecting it at all. That night I wrote:

He asked me whether it hurt when I had my tongue pierced. I said that the first stab was bad but it was all right after that. Then he asked to see my nails. I said, 'I've got them painted like a tiger,' and he said, 'Very fetching!' He's very nice and he took time out for everyone. He's got a great voice and he's very pleasant. No matter who you were, he'd speak to you like a lady. I like him.

My mum and dad were very impressed when we were invited to Buckingham Palace to meet William and Harry about six months later. We arrived in a helicopter and landed in the garden, which was quite a funny experience. We chilled out with the boys and messed around a bit, although it was all quite polite. They showed us round their bedrooms and then I ordered peanut butter and jam sandwiches from the kitchens.

Four days after the Prince's Trust concert we flew to Cannes to promote *Spiceworld: The Movie*. It was another mad couple of days. Everywhere we went the traffic was gridlocked by parked cars and massive crowds of people. We were mega-mobbed, that's the only way to describe it. It was insane and we spent most of our time in speedboats trying to get away from potentially dangerous situations. The publicity generated during that trip was huge. You would have had to be living in a bunker not to know that the Spice Girls were making a movie.

Simon had taken our film ambitions seriously from the very beginning. Not long after we signed with him he introduced us to his brother Kim, a comedy writer who had written for TV programmes like *Not The Nine O'Clock News*, *Three of a Kind* and various projects with Lenny Henry. Our idea for the film had always been to base it on our real experiences, so we often went round to Kim's house in Notting Hill to tell him about what had been happening to us. There were so many mad stories.

Kim was a really good listener and he went on to include a lot of stuff that had actually happened to us in the script, like the scene when we all jumped off the bus and ran away. We were pleased with the way he adapted our stories and consulted us over our lines. Even though Simon probably had ultimate control over what was going on, Kim made us feel as though it was our film. We spent endless evenings telling him stories over dinner. Lucky guy, hey?

None of us even thought to have acting lessons before the shoot. We just went on set and did it. So it wasn't a surprise when our first scene didn't make it into the final edit. It was shot in a big haunted-looking house and we were at this long dining table having dinner with Richard E Grant, who played our manager. There was supposed to be all this witty banter going on between us but it was horrific. I don't think any of us were into it. We were like wooden sticks, forgetting our lines and stumbling over words.

Next we filmed the bedroom scene when we're all asleep together and the baddie is hiding under the bed. In the middle of the night we wake up. *Wearing full make-up.* Our make-up is so over the top in that scene!

I fully remember saying, 'Well I'm not taking part in a scene where I wake up with no make-up on!'

'And I've got to have bright red lipstick because I've got a red negligee on,' Geri insisted.

Our make-up artist Karin had a nightmare. By the time she'd finished we were all done up with mascara, lipstick, the lot. We were adamant that we wanted to look how we wanted to look, and didn't think about the context. 'No make-up? No way!'

I had about twenty different hairstyles during the course of the action and I loved it. Picking out the clothes in the wardrobe department every day was just brilliant. 'How many times am I going to have to wear that? How many scenes have I got in that?' I didn't always plan ahead and for one scene I stupidly chose a purple see-though catsuit that I'd bought in New York (Geri and Victoria bought one each too). I wore it with leopard skin knickers and a leopard skin bra, not realising I'd also have to wear the same outfit, for continuity, in some far less frivolous scenes in a hospital. 'Why didn't somebody tell me? This outfit is totally wrong for a hospital scene!'

Once we got into the swing of things, our performances quickly improved, mainly because we were very supportive of each other. Within about a week the scenes felt much tighter and our acting was a lot more natural and free flowing. We made things up as we went along and changed the dialogue every day, which drove the director Bob Spiers, completely mad. I loved Bob, who was most famous for directing *Fawlty Towers* and *Absolutely Fabulous*. The moment I met him I felt like I'd known him for ages. He had a funny little laugh and was always saying, 'Oh, whatever!' He was a lovely guy and always kept his sense of humour. He had a lot on his plate, but so did we.

Between takes and at the end of each filming day we'd disappear into a mobile studio at the side of the set to go on recording the second Spice album with Matt and Biff and Absolute. 'Spice Up Your Life' was written with Matt and Biff in the same kind of mad frenzy as 'Wannabe'. It was mayhem. Instead of taking turns to go into the vocal booths we sang the chorus all together because we were on such a brilliant vibe. That's why the final mix sounds so spontaneous and full of energy. However, doing two full-time jobs at the same time took its toll and within a couple of weeks, exhaustion set in.

In the film our manager says, 'You don't have lives, you have a schedule.' It was true. Individual choices and feelings just didn't come into it. One of the knock-on effects for me of working so hard was that I became obsessed with dates and exact timings. For some reason it felt comforting to write in my diary, *6.43 p.m. and I'm in the hotel room in Frankfurt or, 9.27 p.m. I'm on the plane to Italy*. Time was a way of pinning down my up-in-the-air life, keeping track of what was happening and staying grounded.

When I saw the final edit of the film I thought it was really funny. I liked Alan Cummings in it – that's what people were really like around us. In fact the whole thing was true to life in many ways. It's amazing that it's shown so much on TV. It's always on at Christmas, on some channel or another. I think it's brilliant and we all look great in it.

Recently I saw Michael Barrymore at a meeting with LWT and the film came up in conversation. 'I thoroughly enjoyed it,' he said. 'As I remember, you didn't shut your face.' He always had me in hysterical giggles on set and I found it hard to concentrate. I'd only have to look at him to crease up. He's like a kid, with a very childish sense of humour that everyone taps into.

After the film it was off to New York where we filmed the 'Spice Up Your Life' video. It was the first video we'd made with a credible director and strangely we weren't consulted about how it should look, as we normally were. We'd discussed it among ourselves and definitely saw it as one long carnival party scene, but that's not what we got. We didn't have the time (or energy) to argue, though. I guess the end result linked into the theme of world domination, but it wasn't right. I don't think any of us liked it much, even though we enjoyed making it. I still can't understand what's going on in it half the time.

I remember being really bored in the wardrobe room and saying, 'Oh for God's sake, just put a piece of fishnet around me.' So they did. Over my leopard skin bra I wore a pair of fishnet tights with the crotch cut open to fit my head through.

By now I was well known for wearing animal prints and I was perfectly happy with that. I've always loved them. Ask my mum! So I was genuinely outraged when people accused me of wearing leopard skin, zebra and Dalmatian 'because you're black.'

They didn't just come up and say it out of the blue. I'd be having an in-depth conversation with someone who had approached me in a newsagent's or somewhere similar, talking about an interview I did for *Black Britain*, and then the subject would come up. 'Why do you always wear animal prints?'

'Well I really like them.'

'Do you know that wearing clothes like that creates a bad image of black people, because of all the associations with the jungle and being foreign?'

Whoa! I don't even go that far in my thinking. It's like saying that if you're a boy who likes the colour pink then you're gay and if you're a girl it means you'll want pedicures every week because you're so feminine. That just isn't the way my mind works. I don't want to offend anyone but I genuinely like leopard skin. If you look back to old magazines – from the

1920s to the 1980s – you'll see it everywhere, whether on the fashion pages or in the interior design section. Animal prints are classic and constant. Designers like Dolce & Gabbana use them every season.

Back in England, I packed up everything I thought I could possibly need over the next year. Based on the advice of our accountants we'd made a group decision to take a tax year out. It meant that, if we restricted the number of days we spent in England over the next twelve months, we'd pay a lot less income tax and make a lot more money. It seemed like a good idea at the time because we were going to be on tour for most of the year, but it really pissed me off. I hated having to ring a lawyer or accountant every time I wanted to come home. 'How many days am I allowed in the country this month?'

Most of the time when we had a break we had to go on holiday. I know it sounds ridiculous – we were *forced* to go on holiday – but sometimes you didn't want to go on holiday. You just wanted to go home to your flat, make sure that there weren't any cobwebs and check that the TV and the front door key still worked. When you've got a month of hard work, then five days off followed by three more months of hard work, you *live* for those five days off. You just want to come home and see your mum and have a bacon sarnie and watch English MTV.

One time I went to Fiji because I wasn't allowed back to England. 'Book me a holiday anywhere Simon,' I said sullenly. Fiji was great but I just didn't want to be there. I wanted to go to my mum's for Sunday dinner. I wanted to see my friends and answer my own home phone and watch *Neighbours* and *Blind Date*. If I was going to have a holiday I wanted it to be my choice. Otherwise it just felt wrong.

Believe it or not, by the end of our tax year out the law had changed and we weren't entitled to any tax breaks after all. Why did we even bother?

In early September we flew to the South of France. It was Simon's idea to rent a chateau for a few weeks, where we were set to rehearse for our first live gigs in Istanbul in October. Situated near a village called Biot, just outside Nice, it became known as 'Spice Camp' (or sometimes 'Alcatraz').

Every day at Spice Camp we did band rehearsals, dance rehearsals, singing lessons, aerobics and gym workouts. Then food, then bed. It was full-on, all day every day. There was a lot of excitement, pressure and frayed nerves.

Wednesday 10 September

This house is unbelievable! Got up at 8 a.m. and we all had breakfast in the open air. Vicky cried, all unhappy. We are all knackered. Met Sandy (aerobics), Greg (gym) and Dave (singing) and went through what we'd be doing each day. It's a twelve hour schedule – pretty hard and gruelling, but fun. Tomorrow is when it all starts. I'll have to get early nights and healthy eating kicked into my system. The group vibe is great. I love it. Later we see Priscilla and meet the band. After that an aerobics class possibly. This is it, what I've been waiting for. It's going to be excellent and I'm going to enjoy every minute of it.

Well the first day went great. We listened to the band play fourteen of our songs and it sounded amazing. We then had a bit of a run through 'If U Can't Dance' and 'Who Do You Think You Are?' Came back, had some food, sorted out styles for costumes, had a bath and chilled out.

The group as a whole gets on so well at the moment – I'm quite touched and surprised, but I still keep a bit back and tell myself just to concentrate on the tour and learning things and keep out of all that 'he says she says'. I feel very tired and jet lagged at the moment. I hope the feeling goes because I wanna be on top form tomorrow.

Thursday 11 September

Woke up at 8 a.m., had breakfast then chilled out until 9.30 a.m., ready for aerobics class. Thinking about what we have to do today knackers me out already.

I jogged around a golf course twice, then we did a thighs, tum and bum workout. Then learned If U Can't Dance routine with P, which opens the show. It is a slamming routine. That lasted about an hour, then I did ten lengths in the pool, came back, had a shower and then lunch. I feel very alive. I'm actually liking it here, thank God. This afternoon we have singing, band rehearsals and more dance.

Got back at 6.30 p.m. for tea and then I went straight to bed. I slept for an hour then lay there feeling PMT and moody. I can hear Vicky and Emma doing aerobics downstairs. Simon arrives on Thursday. I know it is horrible to think this but it's a lot better when he's not around.

Found out today that one of the protocols for working with us is that if you're male you have to be gay, married or f***ing ugly. That is just sad.

Last night I started reading The Prophet *by Kahlil Gibran. I had Tracy*

Chapman on in the background and it was overall very relaxing and interesting. The book has some great poetic philosophy about love and passion.

Living in the house were the five of us, plus Simon, Camilla, our cook Cressida, Simon's chief security guy Alan and two more security guards, Vern and JP. Alan was very quietly spoken and it was hard to believe he was in security because he looked and seemed so normal. When you think of a security guard, you think, Action! Muscular men with darting eyes, constantly checking their surroundings, on their walkie-talkies, ready to defend you at all times. Alan wasn't like that and neither were Vern and JP, but when we got mobbed, they were there to protect us. They knew their job, but they were very chilled out.

Vern was a bit fatherly with us and he was always saying, 'Come on girls, you'll be all right.' Whenever he sensed that something was wrong with one of us he'd say, 'It will work itself out. Don't worry about it, whatever it is.' It was always nice to have him around.

Within ten days of being at Spice Camp I was totally drained and exhausted again:

I have just seen the schedule up until December and I don't think I'm going to be able to handle it. It wouldn't be so bad if it was just performances – the promotion and socialising are the parts I can't cope with. But I have no choice, do I? God give me strength. Come on Mel, you can do it, you're strong, tough and focused. I'm just thankful I have real friends who care about me and don't bullshit. And I know I am lucky and probably have one of the best jobs in the world.

With Simon around again the divisions between us reappeared. By now it was glaringly obvious that we all got on a lot better when he was away.

Monday 22 September
This group is f***ed up. It could be so good. We have all been through so much together that we should all, in theory, be best mates. But we are not at all, Simon has made sure of that. I want to be able to be comfortable within this group and I'm not. It's all like one big nightmare test but he has no chance with me. I have sussed him, mate. I'm just playing the game and

will carry on doing so until I can finally speak up and let rip. But then again is there any point in doing that? I believe in karma. I wish myself good luck, strength and happiness. Everyone gets what they deserve in the end!

17

AIN'T THAT FUNNY

The next month was a big one for us so I think it's time to hand over to my fake leopard skin diary. Here's what happened, day by day:

Wednesday 1 October, Spice Camp, France
Well it's 1 a.m. and I had to start writing in this book. I wonder what I'm going to be feeling and what mad stories I'm going to be a part of before I get to the end of it? All I am bothered about right now is that I stay strong, focused, real, honest and in love throughout this journey over the next eleven months. Back to rehearsals in the morning. I just can't wait to be on stage; that's where I belong. I love it.

It certainly doesn't seem like I've been home and to Paris and done TVs since I was here. Plus my cousin Andrew's girlfriend just gave birth to a baby girl ten minutes ago. Life goes quick and I am gonna try my best to appreciate everything that comes my way – enjoy myself and have a good old laugh.

Thursday 2 October, France
Woke up at 9 a.m., had breakfast, spoke to Fjöl, got dressed and here we go, let's start the day. We went through some steps then had a band rehearsal.

Now we're back at the house and it's time to go down to the pool for a meeting with Simon.

We actually had quite a good chat with Simon. I have a feeling that this year from my point of view will be the pants. Simon said that we have to accept that we are superstars and in one way or another take a bit of responsibility and act like superstars. Not by being rude or snobby, just being more aware that some people will make their name by associating themselves with us. I do understand what he's saying, but then again I refuse to act like or be a temperamental artist.

Mind you, fame is a very weird thing to have happened to someone. Talking to Simon like this has eased the pressure for me a little, but that is what he's there for. I already feel a new sense of togetherness with this group, even though we sometimes don't like each other. In a way, we have no choice but to need each other at the moment. Simon says he'll never let us down. All I can say is that he's put himself up there and if he drops, in my eyes he will never get back up.

I think my attitude to work and fame is getting better every day. Writing this helps and makes me even more aware of things. 'Simon says!' that in one way we are not normal, but I know what being normal is for me. Everyone's level of normality is different though. He should know that, seeing as he calls himself a wise guy!

Friday 3 October, France
Well I woke up at 8 a.m. and yes I am tired. Yesterday Vicki and I said we wouldn't mind doing the Playstation filming first thing. Why I said that I don't know! I'm lying in bed waiting for Cressida to bring me up some toast. I am knackered. I'm sure I don't need to be up this early – they're not going to be filming for two hours, are they? Anyway, there is no getting out of it so up I get.

It's 6 p.m. now and today went okay. Vicki and I did the Playstation game interview and the game sounds brilliant. Rehearsed with the band. Geri is all of a sudden on top form. Her mother is coming to stay so that'll be good for her.

I'm bored, I can't be bothered to do aerobics. C pissed me off today, saying that if I had that bacon and egg sandwich I'd regret it. 'Before you eat it Mel, just take a look at your body.' F*** her, old bag. I'm not so overweight that I have to watch everything that goes into my mouth. I *hate being made to feel paranoid.*

I've just had a bath and I was thinking that if we ever split and do our own things, will we still act the same with one another when we see each other again? I imagine Mel will come out of herself and be a really open this-is-what-I-want girl. I can already see it. She doesn't need anyone. She's going away this weekend by herself. She's a proper smart strong focused girl, but she's put herself in a situation where she can't say boo to a goose. That's the Mel that everyone's used to but I know she's a lot more than that. If only people around her could just let her be who she wants instead of keeping her down.

I don't know what to do with myself. I get like this every so often. I'm bored and it's frustrating. Well, the day after tomorrow I'm seeing Fjöl so that'll be great. There are perks to this job. I'm taking a private helicopter to a hotel in France at the weekend and it's my first experience in one. Even though it's costing an arm and a leg to get there, apparently this place is amazing. So that's something to look forward to. Vicky's going to a Versace fashion show with her friend Maria Louise. They're being put up in a castle, lucky girls.

Saturday 4 October, France
Today is the day I leave the house and head for love, sanity and freedom. First we start rehearsals at 11 a.m., have one run through then come back to camp to pack and speed off as quickly as possible.

6.15 p.m. and I've been in this helicopter for over two hours. What a buzz. What you can see from this height is amazing. Everything is so green and rich. I'm sure the pilot is lost, though. My baby's here, I love him. At the airport I just missed Roger Moore. I wanted to say hello because we never got a chance to speak on the film set.

Well I am here in Chateau de Bagnals. It has so much spirituality about it. It's a bit freaky, as though it's caught in a thirteenth-century time warp. How good it is to spend time here with my babe. I spoke to my mum, she's fine and so is my dad. I do miss home but then again I'm here making the most of what I have in a fantastic place with excellent company. What more could a girl ask for? This place is very, very posh though. So posh that all you can hear when you're eating is a low mumbling. No music! Just quiet voices, that's it. I've never experienced that before.

Sunday 5 October, France

2 p.m. and I'm still in bed, I just love it. I am completely relaxed. We've just had a lovely lavender bath together.

4 p.m. After room service and wicked sex, we decided to go horse riding. We trotted and galloped and it was excellent. The view was unbelievable. I now stink of horses. I love Fjöl, we are just made for each other. I am so lucky to be experiencing all of this.

Monday 6 October, France and Spain

5.30 a.m. woke up, had breakfast and got ready for our helicopter ride. Boy is it early.

Got to the airport and waited for Vicky to arrive. She and Maria Louise had a great time at Versace's house, mingling with the stars – Demi, Kate and Naomi. I'm glad. I did too, I think it was one of the best times I've had with Fjöl.

Got back to the house and me, Emma and Vicky had a trying-on-clothes session. I need to have a bath and pack because we are setting off to Spain at 12 p.m. for our album launch. We're having hair and make-up done there, so it shouldn't be too much of a rushed panic.

Got to Spain. Mad or what? Did a press conference and our album launch, then I went to my room. Virgin put on a fantastic fireworks display. The fireworks spelt out Spice Girls in the sky.

Tuesday 7 October, Spain and France

Was woken up by next door's TV. F***! After hair and make-up we left the hotel and went to do our thing in the town centre. Well I've never seen anything like it in my whole life. F*** are we famous. There were more than 12,000 people there. Talk about getting mobbed! We stood on the balcony and waved and sang 'Spice Up Your Life'. It was excellent. We met the mayor and he gave us a piece of metal on a chain. It was funny because we thought we were getting the keys to the city for a moment there.

We rushed back to our jet, which was too small and crap, and came back to Spice Camp. Spoke to my dad and cried my eyes out. He doesn't ever say he loves me. It's all about giving Danielle support. I got drunk.

Wednesday 8 October, France

Woke up at 10.30 a.m. with my stress lumps on my face again. Every time

I talk deeply it comes up. Oh well, that's life I suppose. Today is going to bring me happiness and a hell of a lot of joy. We're doing separate voiceovers for the film. This thing on my face is killing me.

I feel like shite and drained after all my conversations yesterday, especially with my dad. I'm tired and exhausted. Simon wants us all to go out tonight but no way, not me. I'm going straight to bed.

I was sick this morning and decided that I wasn't going to drink tonight, so I didn't. Did group voiceovers and solo voiceover dubs. It went well and I was pleased with myself for being spot on. Came back to the house with Simon in his car. We didn't really talk, just listened to the new album. His driver calls him Sir Fuller. How can Simon allow it?

Me and Priscilla had dinner and talked. She's great. Then we watched the Spice film together. It's a lot better than before, thank God. Three more days to go before the Istanbul show and I can't wait.

Thursday 9 October, France
Woke up at 10 a.m. and had one hour to pack my life away. I'm looking forward to Turkey. I'll get to see my mum and dad and, best of all, I'll be strutting my stuff on stage.

It's mad to think that I belong to a group of people who are looked upon so strangely by the so-called normal people of the world. They think that if you've been on TV then you're a bit of an alien and can't relate to them properly. Plus, they presume that because you're famous you'll have a snobby attitude towards them. Everything you do or say gets talked about for weeks and it's like, 'You'll never guess who I saw today! That girl from Spice Girls!'

Friday 10 October, France and Turkey
Woke up at 10 a.m. Packed the last of my stuff and off we went on the private plane to Turkey. The plane was quite cool. Arrived at the hotel feeling stressed. Fjöl got here just as I was having a serious talk with Geri about the group. Approved some photos and read an interview Geri did for i-D. It's so sad the things she says about loneliness. We all had dinner together, which was great.

Saturday 11 October, Turkey
Had a press conference. I can't decide if I'm nervous or what. All I know is

that I'm gonna rock. Fjöl bathed me and pampered me non-stop.

Sunday 12 October, Turkey
Well it's showtime. We had make-up and hair and we all looked the bollocks. On the way to the venue I realised I'd forgotten my armband, the one my mum gave me for my twenty-first. I wear it every day and it's a lucky charm so I sent a police escort to go and get it because I was not doing the show without it. No siree. Luckily they managed to get it to me in time.

The show was wicked. I felt at home on stage and ripped it up big time. I love performing. You just can't beat the high it gives you. I'm not just good, I'm shit hot. I give it large on stage, it's like it's my throne.

We met up with our families afterwards, then went to the Pepsi party which was a nightmare with all kinds of press hassling us. We just wanted to get the f*** out. Fjöl was pushed into our dressing room and I went mad, even though it wasn't his fault. I just don't really like him being around the girls, it's not fair on him or me. Still, it was a mind-blowing night. Fjöl has run me a bath so I'm going to chill and get a good night's sleep.

Monday 13 October, Turkey
Woke up at 10.30 a.m. with a bad throat. Went back to sleep for an hour but couldn't stay in bed any longer because we've got a shoot at 12 p.m. Geri came into my room for a nosy but it didn't really bother me because I know what she's like. I just laughed. We did a commercial for the Mirror *with Andy Peters. He is so good – he stayed up until 4 a.m. editing our stuff for TVs.*

Went to the venue and the traffic was unbelievable because of bad flooding. Our families didn't actually get to see the gig because they were stuck in traffic for hours, but Fjöl and Beckham made it just in time. The show was good, but knackering. Came off stage and read the Express *review of last night's show. Me and Mel got a big up and Simon said that all the papers were positive.* Fab 5 Turk 'Em By Storm! Live At Last, Spices Delight Turkey. *The* Sun *said: 'From the moment the lights went down and the spotlight revealed those five famous figures, the crowd became total prisoners of Girl Power for ninety glorious minutes.' Went back to the hotel and had a bit of a do with our families. We all got a bit tipsy and Fjöl said I was pissed. Oh well, all in a good day's work!*

Tuesday 14 October, Turkey and Singapore
Left the hotel, went to the airport and now we're on our way to Singapore. See ya Turkey!

I *know my life is bloody mad and hectic but I feel that I'm meant to be doing this, even though it's mentally draining. All the goings on and what-not are a real tester. I think I've done well up to now, considering what goes on. I suppose you have to laugh. I'm sat here on a plane, eleven hours to go, and Geri is cuddling a black leopard teddy, Vicky's all starry-eyed in love with Beckham, also cuddling a toy. Mel C is getting drunk, which is a very rare occurrence, Emma is asleep and I'm sat here listening to Maxwell and chilling and writing. We are all in our own worlds.*

When we eventually land the local time will be 7.30 a.m. and we will have lost a day. We are staying in the Four Seasons and we have to throw ourselves into work as soon as we arrive, doing interviews and promotion until the evening. It won't be too bad. As I sit here clinging to the white teddy that Fjöl bought me I realise that I am very lucky. I wish myself good guidance, honesty, pleasure and love to get through the next fifteen days.

Wednesday 15 October, Singapore
After a day of promotion, I got back to my room at 9 p.m., had a massage, a bath, ordered some food and phoned Rebecca. God I love her. I spoke to Emma and she said she has a few things to sort out in her head. I said I'd be there for her if she needs to talk.

Thursday 16 October, Singapore
10.30 a.m. The day starts in fifteen minutes. We've got people coming from all over the place to interview us for TV, radio and print – until about 8.30 p.m.

After all those interviews No Doubt came to see us, then me, Simon and Emma went out to dinner and had a good talk about life and the group's future.

Saturday 18 October, Singapore and India
I have two interviews and then off to Delhi we go. It's a bit of a nightmare flight but you gotta do what you gotta do.

We all packed and headed to the airport. Well, what a palaver. When we got there we were mobbed. Local security helped out a bit, but then things got worse when one of the security guards started singing '2Become1'. I told him to f*** off. We finally got on the plane. I sat next to Vicky. Simon is not with us – he's meeting us in Japan. I've been having a real laugh with Mel C, Vicky and Geri. I love being with them sometimes.

We are just about to land in India. I've never been here before. I wonder what it has in store. We've been told that when we arrive it's going to be a nightmare with the press etc. Oh dear. The weather looks a bit crap.

Well here we are. I was surprised at first because it is so lovely. Very poverty stricken but nice, triple bloody nice, people. When we arrived at the hotel we were given an amazing welcome. The whole of reception was packed with people and there were girls throwing flower petals at us and everyone was cheering. It was mad.

The hotel is quite bad but only because we've come from the Four Seasons – a big contrast. Me, Emma and Camilla stayed up for a while in the bar watching MTV. I had a chicken korma and it was shite. How can they get chicken korma wrong in India? I'm so glad I've got my fluffy white teddy with me. It's like being a kid again with your own comfort blanket.

Sunday 19 October, India, Hong Kong and Japan

9 a.m. wake up call. I am knackered. I just want to sleep. But there is no chance of that, not at all, not until we get to Japan, that is. We did our rehearsals but we are exhausted big time. Simon has changed the Japan schedules so that we get a day off. Wow. Went back to the hotel and had a good moan, then went sari shopping. We're going to wear them tonight – bindis and bangles galore.

The two women from the sari shop helped us get dressed, which was sweet of them.

Now we are off to the Channel V music awards. We are on first, singing 'Spice Up' and 'Wannabe' and we all arrive on stage in different coloured tuc-tucs with our names on them. We are going to be on the front cover of the Sun and the Mirror in our saris because we're No.1 again.

We got to the stadium at 7 p.m., did three twenty-minute interviews, then chilled in our dressing room. Jon Bon Jovi, No Doubt and Peter Andre came in to say hi. Seeing Peter reminded me of the first time I met him at the Smash Hits Awards. He'd been my fantasy boy for ages and suddenly he was there in the flesh. I was caught frantically trying to blow-dry my hair and look half-decent, but it was too late. He'd already walked through the *door and was saying hi to everyone. Knowing that I was embarrassed, the girls said, 'Oooh, look who's here Melanie!' I was shaking and spluttering, plus I was sweating because of the hairdryer. For the first two seconds it was fan-meets-fantasy-lover but since that day he's become a good friend.*

India is quite weird but magical too. You want to stay but the conditions are so bad that it puts you off the whole idea. I would have liked to go to a temple to soak up the real India, but instead, as usual, it's quick in and out, work, work, busy, busy, busy, on to Japan we go. Yes I'm tired and feel a bit homesick but I can't help thinking how lucky I am to be seeing the world and experiencing and learning so much all at once. We are all going to have a celebration drink to congratulate ourselves on another No.1. It doesn't even sink in these days – isn't that sick? It just goes to show how busy we are.

Well we are now on another plane. It's six hours to Hong Kong, stop off, then another three hours to Japan. What a palaver checking in was. Well, we do have twenty-six pieces of luggage. Yes, I know, but did we need all those security checks? The nosy bleeders! Anyway we are now safely on the flight.

I'm in Hong Kong airport now. I didn't sleep on the flight at all, but I had a good chat with Geri about work and Simon etc. I phoned Fjöl. I don't know if it's just me being moody but it's not as good as it was. I feel as though I just can't communicate on the phone with him. It does annoy me. As much as I want to cuddle him I want to punch him. I tried to call him back and apologise but my phone wouldn't connect. I do feel a bit bad now.

We got a limo to the Tokyo Four Seasons hotel and went straight up to Simon's room to tell him how tired we are. 'And please Mr Manager, can we have at least one day off a week, not including travelling?'

Well he said the usual, plus, 'Come on girls you are all jet lagged.' But if I don't stop and take proper time out soon I will be completely mentally and physically exhausted. Vicky and Mel C didn't say a thing so from Simon's point of view it probably doesn't seem that bad.

3.05 a.m. I've just spoken to my dad. He is so sweet. I miss my family like crazy. I wouldn't be able to handle this lifestyle if it wasn't for my family and friends.

My wake up call is 10.30 a.m. We have three interviews and a TV show to do. In these next few days I am determined to stay happy, strong, honest to my feelings and on the ball and focused. I know who I am. (I know I keep saying that but it clarifies it for me when I write it down.)

I love my life to bits but I also hate it. I know there is no point hating anything in life but it is hard not to sometimes, with all the mental bollocks we go through. Well, I'm gonna try and get some sleep so that I wake up on top of the world, feeling and looking alive and good. Life is there and I'm going to grab it by the throat and make the best of it. I do need a break though. A few days in Iceland would do me the world of good.

Monday 20 October, Japan
11.10 a.m. Up and ready to go. Unfortunately we don't finish until 7 p.m. but we are doing the show with boyzIImen and Vanessa Williams. Oh big deal.

The show was good. boyzIImen are great guys. Simon's back is playing up again, so we went out to dinner without him. Karma is playing a big part in this, I think.

Tuesday 21 October, Japan
Day off, stayed in bed watching films.

1 p.m. I had a good long chat with Geri about everything.

Mel's nan died today so I went in to see her. She is just so lovely. I hope one day she can open up and talk to me more.

Well, life goes on, as Mel said. I do hope it all works itself out because at the moment I feel like a headless chicken. I need to stay strong and focused. That 'I know who I am' feeling is slipping away but I refuse to let go of it. Up working again tomorrow – a very busy day indeed. Today has been such a lazy day, it's just what the doctor ordered.

Wednesday 22 October, Japan
8.40 a.m. Get today over with and it's home sweet home!

Well what a day. All in all we had a laugh. We did a live TV – very Japanese and bizarre – and three photo shoots, two twenty-minute interviews, one ten-minute interview and another one for forty minutes. None of us could give a sh** today. We even had to do a photo shoot with pretend snow. I mean, for f***'s sake, what's going on? Geri and Emma were drawing all over each other's legs in one interview.

The theme of the day was colour. One shoot all in white, next shoot all in red, another shoot all black. That's Japan for you. As we were driving around in the limo, me and Emma took a quick ten minutes and went off to buy six pairs of shoes each. We also bought some for Rachel.

Went back to the hotel and packed. Now, instead of seven pieces of luggage, I only have three silver trunks and a red bag. It's time to go downstairs for a drink with our Japanese record company. How exciting. I'm sure we will make the most of it and have a laugh. Mingling is the word for the next few hours.

Went down to see the people, had a drink. Got back to my room and phoned Richie. It was so good to be able to chat to him. He is a diamond of a man, I love him to bits, yes I still do. I know in my heart that I could never be with him again, but just to have him there as a friend is enough. I can talk to him. After all, I spent three years of my life with him and at one point he was my everything. Bless him and may he always live a happy and fulfilled life.

I think that my interview on Black Britain *is being shown tonight. I hope people understand where I'm coming from because it would be a gutter if they didn't. I know I was confident in what I was saying so I hope other people do understand. F*** it if they don't anyway. I've achieved something inside by doing it. It's now 2 a.m. I wake up at 7 a.m.*

Thursday 23 October, Japan and England

Woke up at 7.30 a.m. ready to go. My Black Britain *thing was excellent, so my mum said. Oh dear, Geri had a bit of a crisis in the car. She is making herself sick again. Making yourself sick is just the symptom. The problem is with yourself, your self-respect, self-esteem, self-motivation etc. Geri is crying out for help but it has to start from within. She needs to look at how to take care of herself, ask herself who she is and who she wants to be. But it's just so painful for her, isn't it? It's such a shame. Maybe one day she'll understand herself. I hope so.*

Well I'm on the flight home. Today we gain a day so when I arrive back in England it will still be Thursday. My throat is sore.

The time in England is 3.05 p.m. and we will be landing in the next half an hour or so. I've quite enjoyed this flight. We all had a nice chat and I bought a Gucci wallet for Fjöl and Emma got one for her brother.

Simon is in hospital with his back problem.

Fifteen minutes to land and I can't wait. This group's heart is full of adventure, love and passion but sometimes that gets spoiled on an individual level. I wish we could all clear our personal baggage, have a laugh together and live each day to the max, because I know we are never going to be this famous again. Why can't we just live it for what it is and what we are? But as a group we are funny. We're all sitting here shouting, 'Come on, Come on!' overly excited, on a yes-we-are-landing vibe.

5.28 p.m. I'm in the car on the way home. Me and Fjöl are going out to dinner at 8 p.m. at the Aubergine. I've left my mum's presents with Emma because she's going out with Pauline on Saturday. I miss my mum, I really do. Spoke to Rebecca. She has a new boyfriend and is working hard filming. I class myself as being very fortunate to have these genuine people outside this industry. Yes I'm famous and yes I'm still Melanie. I haven't got lost in the mix yet, it ain't gonna get me, no siree.

Friday 24 October, England
Woke up at 6 a.m. My body is out of sync completely. We went shopping and I bought my mum a wicked outfit from Prada: shoes, bag, coat, trousers, top and another bag. She'll get it tomorrow.

It's 6 p.m. and I'm just chillin. I got a lot of compliments at Harvey Nichols about my Black Britain *interview. I was proud of myself when I watched it. Me and Fjöl watched the Spice film. It's great.*

Saturday 25 October, England and France
It's 2.30 p.m. Bob [Spiers] came round and I did my three lines of voiceover for the film. I'm now in the car with Plastic Paddy my fave driver. (He is actually called Dave!) We are going to Germany to pick up an award and then I jet off to Paris to meet my baby. Geri seems better today.

We flew in a private jet to the Bambi Awards in Germany where we won the Shooting Star award. Everyone seemed in a good mood and we saw Harrison Ford. He is a very sexy man. Now we are back on the plane and on our way to Paris. I spoke to my mum. She's all dressed up in the outfit I bought her from Prada. I wish I'd been there to see her face when she opened her presents. She's having a great night tonight, out with Pauline at the theatre.

Well, what a great night. We went for a meal and Fjöl beat a guy in an arm wrestling contest. My room has a gym in it – amazing! I had a bottle of Crystal waiting for me when I got in. Fjöl's pissed, I'm pissed, it's great! Luckily I have the day off tomorrow.

Sunday 26 October, France
We both woke up with terrible hangovers. We made passionate love then went down to the pool and had a sauna. Fjöl is picking the dead skin off my toes. He's even biting it off!

We took a cab to the Eiffel Tower. It was so lovely. We walked and talked and cuddled, then went to a brasserie where we had chips and chicken. Fjöl ordered oysters, not realising that he hates them, which made me laugh. Got a cab back to the Hotel Bristol.

Me and Fjöl both feel a little ill. I think it was the steak we had last night. The restaurant was tacky and dirty – ee yuk. Not to mention we had about six bottles of champagne. The time is 6.40 p.m. and we're going to order a film and chill.

Monday 27 October, France
Woke up at 7a.m., packed a few things up and left. I've had such a lovely time here, it's just not bloody long enough. I'm not going to see Fjöl for about two weeks. We have interviews all day at the Hotel de Crillon.

Well I arrived at the hotel early. Alan the security guard does my head in. He allowed one hour to get here and it took three minutes. Make-up starts at 9.30 a.m. and I always do my own, so I could have stayed with my baby for longer.

Well, I suppose it meant I had time to unpack my stuff and have breakfast. I do not feel like working today at all. First we each have a fifteen-minute radio to do, then lots and lots of irritating TV all day. Break from 1–2 p.m. and 4-4.30 p.m. and finish at 7 p.m., very tired and bored. Well I'd better put my make-up on and start the day, hey.

Mel has her nan's funeral tomorrow. I do hope she is handling everything okay.

Tuesday 28 October, France
Well Mel has gone off to the funeral in Leeds. She'll be back later on today. We have about six TV interviews today but there is a break of one and a half hours to go shopping.

Work was quite a laugh. We did about ten TVs in total. Some lasted an hour and some only ten minutes. Mel got back from the funeral late afternoon and seemed okay. Before she got back, me, Vicky and Emma went shopping to Plein Sud and Joseph. We were supposed to be back for

Filming the 'Say You'll Be There' video. That night Geri and I took off into the desert with the director when we should have been in bed getting our beauty sleep.

Backstage at the Brits having just won an award. We're all dressed up ready to hit the town. What do you think of my Kelis impersonation?

I take my beauty regime very seriously…

On the set of *Spiceworld: The Movie* with my mum, Emma's mum, Richard E. Grant and Alan Cummings. Check out the over-the-top make up!

On tour singing 'Mama'.
What has Geri got on?

Naked? Sorry, lads, we were actually wearing flesh-coloured body stockings!

Taking time out together on safari in South Africa. We all became much closer on this trip – and began to think seriously about the future of the group.

A highlight of the safari was cuddling this gorgeous lion cub. We both wanted to take him home with us.

Meeting Nelson Mandela and Prince Charles at Nelson's house in South Africa. How did we manage to walk in those shoes?

On tour in a velvet catsuit. Great!

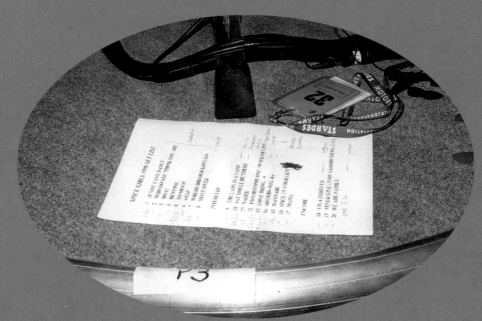

Our set list. Not once did we ever miss a song or an encore.

Doing our vocal warm-up, which I hated. Melanie was the only one who took it seriously – the rest of us thought we could get away with having a hot lemon and ginger drink just before we went on stage.

Hyping ourselves up to go on stage.

With my ex-husband to be, having a laugh on stage. He was always a lot more touchy-feely on stage than off it.

'There was a little girl who had a little curl, right in the middle of her forehead.' In the dressing room at Wembley with my dog Lord.
I was pregnant at the time.

5 p.m. but we were an hour late. Alan was furious.

I bumped into the president of Zimbabwe at the hotel. He had a police escort and when I walked up to him I was nearly pounced on by the police. Well I didn't know who the f*** he was, did I? Camilla got me the Nelson Mandela book. I just can't wait to meet him. We are actually going to his house, along with Billy Ocean. Wow, two idols of mine.

We also did MTV today. We are up for four awards along with people like U2, Oasis, Prodigy and Radiohead. F*** me, they're having a laugh aren't they? It's so mad to be voted for, but alongside these kinds of people it's unbelievable. I mean, this is only Melanie Brown from Leeds for God's sake.

I do hope Mel is okay. We never really talk, I mean talk properly, and I rarely get to see the real Mel C. I know her, but sometimes I think I know nothing about how she feels and thinks and what makes her happy, excited, depressed or sad.

Wednesday 29 October, France and England
Took the private plane to London, arrived at 10.30 a.m. and went straight to the Met Bar for hair and make-up. We all have to wear black for the poppy day appeal.

Later in the day I had a very annoying, personal interview with Andy Coulson from the Sun, then went shopping and bought myself a Rolex watch. We are now off to a Polaroid do, then back on the plane to Paris. I miss England. Emma and Vicky went to see Simon. He's a bit bored but physically okay. Went through An Audience With The Spice Girls, with Andy Peters. It's going to be fun and exciting and we're going to be in London for four nights.

I can't believe the watch I bought today, I really can't. This is just Mel B – and she's had the chance to buy a Rolex watch! It's covered in diamonds. It's the bollocks.

I do love doing what I do. Yes it's tiring but who'd have thought we could accomplish so much in just a few months? I spoke to Fuller today about ideas for the 'Too Much' video. It's going to be set in the sixties, which sounds good. It's all exciting stuff.

Thursday 30 October, England
9 a.m. Time to get ready for the Vogue shoot. They are styling us and I just hope they know what kinds of clothes we wear.

Well we did the shoot and we all looked different but still the same, if you know what I mean. Vicky was particularly tired. We seem to take it in turns. The photographer was Mario Testino. His friend Patrick told me all about the Andy Warhol parties he used to go to. They sound mad. I wish I could have been there – I probably was there in spirit! At the end of the day the hairdresser made me laugh when he tried to brush my hair dry. I sat there politely saying, 'No, don't do that. It'll go frizzy.' Meanwhile camp Mario and Geri are singing Abba songs badly out of tune.

So I'm trying to tell this French guy what to do with my hair and I end up shouting, 'You're shite! I'll do it myself!' Off I go upstairs. Patrick follows me, helps me to stick my head in the sink and it all turns out okay.

It's Mario's birthday so at the end of the shoot out comes the champagne and the vibe turns hysterical. By the way, this is all being filmed like it's In Bed With Madonna or something. Spice Girls serenade Mario with 'Happy Birthday' and then he starts doing this catwalk thing for us, taking off all the super models. We didn't have a clue who he was imitating, but we laughed anyway.

Four of us (bar Mel C) realise we could get a jet home as long as we don't land in England before midnight. So we do. And not only that, we ask for a week off. Well Si's on the blower to us all doing his spiel. But we are going home sweet home even if it is costing the Spice account seven and a half grand.

Before we got on the plane, I asked all four of us the question: Are we really friends? No one answered for a while then Geri said, 'Maybe underneath it all we are.' Who knows? It was interesting what Vicky had to say. 'I wonder who will keep in contact with who after all this is finished?' Me and Vicky both agreed that Simon has done a lot to spoil everything we all had together.

Got in about 1.30 a.m., my heating is working. Yes.

Friday 31 October, England
Woke up at 5 a.m. then 9 a.m. then 12. Lounged in bed all day and made a few phone calls. I've been lazy all day, it's been great. The flat's all warm and outside it's real Christmassy cold. It's good to be back in England.

The office phoned saying that the Mirror have a copy of the film, so we need to do a front cover for them. Very weird if you ask me. Anyway it means I'm being picked up at 7.15 p.m.

Well, we are now off on another trip – to South Africa. Our mums are going be there too. Then we are back in England on Thursday for a couple of hours before the MTV Awards.

6.20 p.m. Simon sent over a hi 8 of Turkey so we can watch it on our little screens on the flight! I'm going to meet Southan for a drink at the Dome. Then we have the Mirror front cover to do, yippee! I have an adventure ahead of me.

I've got myself just where I like it in the group. I'm there if anyone needs me. I rely on myself. I speak the truth but don't force it on anyone. I feel confident in myself, I have respect for myself and others, I don't bitch to anyone. I keep my private life private. If one of them wants truth, honesty and a deep chat then I know they know where to come. I'm not gonna lose my focus or zest for life for anyone or anything.

Went to meet Southan for half an hour and there were loads of people staring and asking for autographs. I signed kids' hands and T shirts – they were all out trick or treating.

We did the shoot for the Mirror with them handing over the tape! Then got on the plane. Had a chat with Vicky and Geri. I just hope we can stay sane through all of this. We read the letter Simon sent to us. He even sent a schedule so we know what we are doing, how kind! We approved the cover for 'Too Much'. It's from the Elle shoot.

I'm quite pleased with myself because I'm still taking all my vitamins. South Africa is 10 hrs, 15 mins away, with a two-hour difference. We land at 10 a.m. and go straight to Nelson's house. I can't wait to meet him.

I've just watched the Istanbul show on my little screen. It's not bad. I am a bit gutted because it doesn't show much of the dancing. Personally I could have done better overall. It's a real insight into how it all went though and I'm proud of this group.

Saturday 1 November, South Africa
What a bumper. Woke up nearly every hour. Ready for Nelson. We have about an hour to get changed and have make-up and hair in the airport VIP. I got such a big compliment yesterday. 'You look absolutely stunning tonight.' Well thank you Southan.

Well we met Nelson and Prince Charles and it was f***ing great. It was all very relaxed. Omar and Billy Ocean were there. The house was nice. I got Geri and Emma in the loo and we nicked some bog roll and pebbles from the plant pot. I told Nelson what I'd done and he just laughed. Bless him, he's not got all his hearing.

We went outside to the press and there was a red carpet. I stood between the prince and Nelson. I can't believe it. What a feeling! Charles was making me laugh when we had the pictures done. He is a lovely man. We also met all of Nelson's grandkids. Nelson said to me, 'I hope you're not married yet.' I think he might have been trying to set me up with one of his relatives. At the venue we met William again privately then had more pictures with Charles. This is the best trip ever.

Billy Ocean was on stage before us and we all had a singalong. We want him for our Audience With . . . We did our performance in front of about forty-five thousand people then got straight into our helicopter. You should have seen the send-off we got. People even left the stadium to come round the corner to wave us off. There were thousands of people waving. Then we flew off into the night to our palace of a hotel. I think I may have found my country!

Sunday 2 November, South Africa
Woke up and had hair and make-up, then did a press conference. I am absolutely exhausted. We met the competition winners and had lunch. Then we had a two-hour break so we all went horse riding. Me and Geri went ahead – we had the nutter horses. The others went on a slow walkabout. The view was amazing. But I am physically drained. I can't stand it any more. And no one gives a shit. No one.

We are now going to see the cubs and lions. All the wildlife is so exciting. Then we have dinner and a tribal dancing show in the bush with the competition winners.

Outwardly today has been one of the best days ever, but inside me it's been one of the saddest. I have lost my get-up-and-go. I do hope it comes back. I feel as though I can't talk to anyone about anything. I'm feeling a little bit sad and lonely, I guess. The weird thing is that what I have seen and experienced today has been amazing, it really has, and yet I feel so sad. Yet again I want to cry. Maybe it will do me some good.

Our mums have arrived and they are staying in the jungle tonight. They are having a ball. I'm so glad I can do this for my mum. Well, I'm gonna take a bath and chill. Alan is trying to find the mole (leak). Someone close is relaying info to the press.

Monday 3 November, South Africa
Woke up at 5 a.m. after a weird dream. I got kicked out of the group, then Bono asked me to sing with him. None of the other girls gave a shit, so I left the group and went solo. What does it all mean?

I'm now on a little jet on the way to meet our mums. I can't wait to see my mum. We only have about ten minutes left on this rickety little thing, thank God. Geri and Vicky are sat gossiping as usual. I'm next to Emma. Geri is going to start an explosion with Simon, I'm sure. And boy will it be hell, but in a way I can't wait.

Our mothers were there to greet us when we arrived. I cried my eyes out when I saw my mum. I was so glad to see her. We had a drink and something to eat, then went back to the hotel Sun City. We're off on a night safari at 3.30 a.m.

This country is still behind with the black and white thing. Earlier I went to buy some stuff in the shop and there was a woman in the queue in front of me. The next minute her husband dragged her out by her arm. Weird. Later I asked one of the waiters, 'Has that man been causing trouble?' 'Yes, he won't let any of the black waiters serve him.' Then it twigged. He'd dragged his wife out of the shop because she was standing next to me. So later, when I spotted him downstairs in the restaurant from five floors up, I shouted, 'Oi! You c***!' and gave him what for. It nearly got me chucked out of the hotel.

Well, what an experience the safari was. The lions were so close it was frightening. I was taking photos and my mum pinched me to make me stop. She was scared shitless and started trying to get underneath my legs to hide, which sent me into hysterical laughter. I wasn't scared, just a bit worried that she would scream and get us all eaten. But I felt at one with the surroundings and the vibe. It was fantastic. I am the luckiest girl in the world.

We all had dinner round a campfire, which was lovely. C did my head in a bit by saying I'm moody in the mornings! Shut up! But it's just lovely being with my mum.

Tuesday 4 November, South Africa
Was woken up at 5.30 a.m. for the safari but couldn't be bothered to get up. My mum and I lounged by the pool and had a good chat. But she told me that White Grandma has been taken into hospital with an enlarged heart

and is sicking up blood. I do hope she'll be okay.

Me, mum, Geri and her sister Natalie went on an excellent afternoon safari. We saw cheetahs eating a hog up close. Then we got on the private plane to Johannesburg. Mum and everyone else waved us off. I've got closer to my mum on this trip and it was just in the nick of time because I was starting to lose my faith and enthusiasm for the Spice Girls thing. I just hope the five of us can stick together through all of this. I think we've got a couple of interesting months ahead.

Wednesday 5 November, England and Holland
6.50 a.m. and just about to land in London. Me and Geri have decided to go on a mission and find out some things. She is going to do it her way and I'm going to do it my way. She's meeting with lawyers to find out where we stand legally with Simon and I'm going to visit Sue the spiritualist to see what she thinks.

It's bonfire night tonight. I wonder how Geri's meetings have been going. Fingers crossed. I went to Karen Millen and bought Danielle two outfits.

2.20 p.m. Everything I thought has been confirmed! We are gonna ditch Simon Fuller and break free. This group is ours, not his. Geri is waiting for me to arrive at her house. This is where Geri and I kick ass, motherf***ers!

5.40 p.m. In the car on my way back to pack. Spoke to the lawyer at Geri's house and we have planned the day that Simon hears about this. We fly to Spain on Tuesday and then he'll be told. Me, Geri and Vicky are meeting up on Friday morning to discuss it all. The lawyer is talking to the publicist tomorrow. He's the most important person because when this is out all hell will break loose. But hey man it's Girl Power. It is quite weird how Geri saw the lawyers and I saw the spiritualist and we both came to the same conclusion. This group will be just fine. Our schedule is already booked. We don't need him at all.

What is so mad is that it's BONFIRE night tonight. We couldn't have made this decision on a better night. Here we go, this is when real Girl Power kicks into action.

6.30 p.m. I'm now packed and on my way to Luton airport for the flight to Amsterdam. This is when the game begins mate and boy am I ready for it. I know who I am and what I want and no f***er is going to stand in my way, that's for sure.

Simon knows something is going on, but can he stop it? And can we convince Emma and Mel C that this is the right decision?

3.20 a.m. Here is the story so far. I went down to Vicky's room and Geri was already in there talking to her about leaving Simon. Then we decided to call Mel C in to discuss it further. To my surprise she agrees with her hand on her heart that this is the right choice. Then Emma comes in and we talk for a few hours. I don't think she's in the right frame of mind to make any decision just yet. While we're talking we find out all the things he has said to us individually. For me this is final – he is out.

I've kicked Alan the minder off my floor and he's now on Vicky's floor, so anyone who goes to her room has to sneak past his door. We all at some point got hysterical giggles and finally agreed to do something about Simon. We are going to confront him with lawyers there. Geri is on the phone to our lawyer Andrew Thompson telling him to set up the meeting in his office on Friday.

Oh the sh** is going to hit the fan big time. There is no way he is getting out of this one alive, no way. This group deserves to enjoy life. The only thing we owe him is to tell him what we think of him. 54321 Simon, your time is up! We need to get rid of him if it's the last thing this group does.

5.30 a.m. I've just got back from Geri's room. Boy was that funny. She rang us all up and said, 'Come to my room quickly I have the lawyer on the phone!' So off the four of us went again. We're on different floors so we were all creeping up and down the stairs trying not to be heard or seen by anyone. It was like a Carry On film. Anyway we all spoke to Andy Thompson and basically Simon is going to be told by Andy over the phone that we have sacked him. We then release a press statement saying roughly the same and Simon has a forty-eight-hour deadline to decide what to do. We have a meeting with Andy at 9.30 a.m. on Friday before rehearsals start for An Audience With . . .

Little did Simon know that we planned to sack him and little did any of us know that we've all been thinking the same thing for a long time. That's strange, my pen has run out. Oh well. Good night. Well done, Melanie. This time is my time.

18

I CAN SEE CLEARLY NOW

Well bonfire night certainly went out with a bang.

The next morning I tried to call my mum, but she was still on the flight back from South Africa. So then it was business as usual, starting off with rehearsals for the MTV Europe Awards where we were performing 'Spice Up Your Life'.

All day we had people left, right and centre telling us that sacking Simon was the wrong thing to do. They were doing our heads in. I must admit that it was very sad to have to say goodbye to Camilla and Rachel and the rest of the team (especially for me, Camilla). We'd been working closely for so long that I couldn't really believe this was it. But it was. As soon as Simon got the call from our lawyers, everyone from 19 was instructed to leave at once. It was as cut and dried as that.

There were lots of tears that day, but laughter too. In one way we were completely alone, with nothing but Geri's bag for back up. She had everything in that bag – my diary, her address book and everyone's phones and numbers, including Camilla's – and we didn't let it out of our sight. We were in trouble if anyone whipped it because it had all the names and numbers we needed to organise our lives.

In another way it seemed as though the whole world was on our side because just before we went on to perform 'Spice Up Your Life', we were told that we'd won the MTV Award for Best Group, over Oasis, Radiohead, U2 and Prodigy. It was incredible timing – just the lift we needed. At the end of the day I wrote in my diary,

I thank the Lord for giving us this day. Girl Power rules big time!

The next few days were so busy that there was hardly time to register everything that had happened. We had lawyers meetings to go to, schedules to sort out, press statements to make and just three days to rehearse for *An Audience With The Spice Girls* for LWT, with hardly any help from anyone. Luckily for me Fjöl had flown over and was being his usual caring self, which was a lifesaver, and everyone on the set of *An Audience With* . . . was incredibly helpful, especially Andy Peters, the director. Our days were hectic, though. The news of our split with Simon made headlines around the world, but we couldn't stop to read all the articles predicting the end of Spice Girls – and why should we, anyway? This wasn't the end of the group. It was a new beginning.

At first it looked like nobody we'd been working with was going to stick with us. In many ways we didn't mind, but on the other hand it was tough doing everything for ourselves. We had no security guards, no drivers, no PAs, no one, but we were still being chased and mobbed and hassled and obviously we had to work as hard as ever.

Then we had some good news. Vern and JP turned up at the studio. They were with us. Jennie Roberts and Karin Darnell (hair and make-up) were free agents and wanted to go on working with us. Rebecca Cripps, who edited our fan magazine, also stayed with us and agreed to take on extra responsibilities like photo approval and merchandise. And Victoria Williamson, who'd been our PA briefly before she left 19 Management, was also free to come and work for us. Victoria – or Tor as she was known – was quite proper, well-to-do and, crucially, efficient.

Slowly our new team was coming together, even though there were people from the old team coming to say goodbye for days afterwards. Every one of them (including grown men) cried as they said their piece. But my eyes stayed dry throughout. The night before *An Audience With* . . . I wrote:

In a way I am numb to it all. I seem to have this untouchable part of me

that's not insensitive but just won't let me cry. It's as if I don't need to cry. I'm not upset about leaving Simon, I'm relieved and totally back to the old Melanie 100%.

I got home from rehearsals and Fjöl had cooked dinner, bought me flowers and run me a bath. I couldn't ask for a more special person to love than him.

The next day it felt like the whole world would be watching to see if we could make it on our own. It was stressful, but the show went brilliantly and the line up of people in the audience was fantastic. Next we had the shoot for the 'Too Much' video (I didn't finish filming until 5a.m.) and after that we had meetings with Virgin before getting straight on a flight to Spain to do promotion.

Meanwhile the press continued to speculate about our future. No one, it seemed, could believe that we'd be able to go it alone, including our record company. Some of the people at Virgin were very nervous about this new development in Spiceworld. You could see it in their eyes even though they were trying their best to hide it. Who do these mad girls think they are? I wasn't bothered by what they thought, but we still felt the need to prove ourselves, and quickly. Unfortunately the trip to Spain didn't go very smoothly. In fact, if you believed what you read in the newspapers, you'd think it was a complete disaster. Here's what I wrote about it:

Thursday 13 November
The awards show was a nightmare. It was an industry audience with about fifty photographers and when we walked on stage everyone started booing, all because we told the photographers, 'Sign the forms or no pictures'.

It was standard practice to get photographers to sign release forms, but we probably didn't handle it very well. Well, we'd never done that part of the job before! It was the perfect excuse for the British press to have a field day. Is It All Over? Spice Girls Booed Off Stage! were just some of the headlines.

Friday 14 November
As expected the English press caught on and there were debates going on everywhere about us – is it the end or the beginning? Chill out everyone.

All we've done is sack our manager. He's not that important, he's not singing or writing the songs or doing the endless interviews, the Spice Girls are.

As far as I'm concerned, any press is good press and I couldn't really give a shit what the media think. At the end of the day the fans are still right behind us and that is what matters. Everyone around us needs to stop panicking and start enjoying themselves. I keep thinking to myself, yes we are free to do what we want! We are five sensible girls on a mission, not by ourselves but with each other.

We have found our friendship with each other again and nothing and no one is ever going to spoil it. We are gonna have our ups and downs but to be honest, I like it like that because otherwise it would be boring and I would have left by now. Everyone has grown up a lot and now we're gonna enjoy our fame in the way we were meant to. Between the five of us we have so much going for us that we just can't afford to let people or the media get to us in a negative way. Onward, forward till the end.

I'm now on the plane to Italy where we are doing a few TVs and radios, then the night begins. Me, Emma and Geri are out on the town big time tonight, even if we are knackered. We've got the whole of tomorrow off to sleep and relax. F*** it, we have Girl Power. I have never seen us so happy and normal, it's great, it really is.

'Sensible', 'grown up', 'normal'? If you'd met us that night you definitely wouldn't have thought so, because me, Geri and Emma went a bit mad. Oh yes. We let off steam in a big way on the night of 14 November and it was about time. In a month and a half we'd been halfway round the world, performed our first-ever live concerts, met Nelson Mandela and Prince Charles, won major music awards, filmed a video and our own live TV show, been mobbed, been booed and sacked our manager. I think we deserved to let our hair down for once.

And boy did we. It was a top night. We got dressed up together, messing around and giggling like teenage girls on their way to a youth club disco. Then we made our way to a gay club with Vern, followed by a massive entourage of paparazzi. After getting totally mobbed, we moved on to a psychedelic style restaurant/club where there were live rappers performing.

Earlier in the day we'd each been given a tiny but extremely powerful torch and we still had them with us. Why, I don't know, but they certainly came in handy.

'Mmmm! He's nice. Shine a light on him!'

'What about him in the red top?'

'He looks tasty too. Get him over!'

We used our torches to spotlight the men we liked the look of and then summoned them up to the VIP area. It was hilarious watching all these gorgeous hunks queuing up to meet us. If they weren't up to scratch, we threw them out again. It was a real role reversal. 'Who are the bimbos now?' The lucky ones got Bellinis – champagne and peach schnapps – the others were sent back into the crowd. It was crazy. Even Vern got into the spirit of things and climbed up on stage with the band to do a rap about freedom, cheered on by us and our hand-picked group of admirers. As Geri wrote in my diary later, that night we felt *fully famous, tough and bulletproof.*

We left the club in the same style as we'd arrived, sneaking out the back way to try and avoid the paps. Then there was a bit of a cat-and-mouse chase to a coffee shop where we wolfed down ham and cheese toasties, before we finally made it back to the hotel and Mel C's bedroom. Here's what she wrote in my diary after we'd knocked her up at 4 a.m.:

These three lairy birds have gatecrashed my room. It's so nice to see them truly happy and excited, but that's how we all feel now. Our life has been reborn and we've got each other and no one can take that away from us.

Now piss off and let me get my beauty sleep! Love you all, you slappers. Melanie xxxxx

The next morning I woke up to the sound of screaming fans outside the hotel, after a weirdly sexual dream about Prince Charles. A couple of hours later, me, Geri and Emma went to Gucci to do some shopping. There were two thousand people waiting outside the shop and we were mobbed again, so the people at Gucci locked us in and plied us with champagne while the fans outside banged on the windows and chanted. After a while we started feeling really hungry so off we sneaked to a small, old-fashioned restaurant where we had to put table cloths up at the windows to block off the rows of flashing cameras. *What an enjoyable fun famous weekend we've had*, I wrote.

It was now pretty obvious to us that the fans didn't care who our manager was, but we still had to get the press on our side, so we hired a new press agent, recommended by Virgin. We instantly trusted Alan Edwards when we heard about the scrapes he'd got other groups out of. Very intelligent and articulate, with beautiful blue eyes and hidden depths, Alan was straight and sober but very open at the same time. After a while I saw him not just as a press agent but as someone I would phone up and ask how his kids were, somebody I could relate to on a very normal level. At the end of every conversation he always said to me, 'Thank you for calling me up today Melanie. You've made my day better.'

We also realised that Tor couldn't cope alone with the deluge of work that was generated by the biggest band in the world. Now when I say that, it's not that I just thought it, it was a fact. We *were* the biggest band in the world. Tor didn't even have an office, let alone any back-up staff, and even though she was just about managing to keep the lid on things it was obviously a struggle. There were so many things that we'd taken for granted when we had Camilla and Rachel and 19 Management behind us. Now we were booking our own flights and hotels, organising meetings and schedules and planning strategy on top of fulfilling our mad, frantic day-to-day commitments.

Talk about hands-on. In a way it was just like the early days when we did everything for ourselves. So my old theory still stands. *A job isn't done well unless you do it yourself* – and we were, but it was bloody hard. Every day we had conference calls with lawyers and accountants, contracts to read, amend and sign, offers to consider and itineraries to juggle. It was exhausting and distracting and we realised that things just couldn't continue like that for very long. One of the reasons we'd left Simon was to give ourselves a chance to take things a bit easier, but in fact we'd quadrupled our workload. We needed help, and soon.

Tor suggested that we meet up with Nancy Phillips, an ex-colleague of hers who had more than twenty years experience in the music industry. Nancy had been a partner in Crax 90, a management company that looked after the Undertones and Thomas Dolby, among other acts, and she'd also worked at Brilliant, our TV pluggers, as well as the record company V2. She had contacts throughout the industry and a thorough understanding of all aspects of the business. If there was anyone who could help us manage ourselves, it was Nancy.

We met Nancy at the Hotel Bristol in Paris and liked her immediately. In her late thirties, she was quite mumsy in her attitude towards us, very calm and centred. Within five minutes of being introduced she'd gently told one of us off for using a glass instead of an ashtray. What a bunch of slobs! she was probably thinking. But she seemed confident about what she could do for us and inspired our trust, so we gave her the go ahead to start setting up Spice HQ back in London. It was as quick and as simple as that.

It was good timing. We only had a few months to go before the start of our world tour and there was a hell of a lot of organising to do. Thankfully we had Richard Jones, who'd been deputy to the original tour manager, Greg Lynne. With his dark hair and glasses, Richard seemed like a bit of a square, but a cool square, with a cheeky look about him. He worked incredibly hard to sort everything out in time and I still find it hard to believe that he did it. We were going on the road with a crew of 100 people, taking 300 tonnes of equipment, 800 suitcases and 2,500 flightcases in ten articulated lorries. It was a massive operation. How Richard got his brain around all the details, I have no idea, but he was brilliant.

Another key person who stayed with us was our choreographer Priscilla, who had some fantastic ideas for the show. I couldn't wait to start working with her again. But before we could get on with the tour, we had *Spiceworld: The Movie* to promote. There were premieres to attend in major cities around Europe, America and Australia. I sat next to Prince Charles at the London premiere. That was a real buzz – watching myself on film while the heir to the throne chuckled beside me.

All the premieres were amazing, especially the one in Hollywood, when we arrived in our white suits on a double-decker London bus and walked along a huge red carpet. It was the biggest turnout of fans at a premiere that LA had ever seen and it was incredible to see all those people behind the barriers. I used to think, 'Why are they behind barriers?' There was such a distance between them and us and I just wanted to go up and talk to them all. I was never scared by the crowds. I didn't get into much trouble in that way. I was touched a lot but I wasn't grabbed and no one pulled my hair or ripped my clothes.

It was different for some of the others though. Once in Spain Geri had her G-string pulled up her arse by a fan. She must have been in a lot of pain as she tried to walk away, while the fan hung on to her knickers for dear life. I was in absolute fits, even though I shouldn't have been.

Vern told us that when you touch fans, you have to touch them with your hand facing outwards so that they can't grab hold of you. It never registered with any of us and we all got grabbed. I loved it. We were also told, 'If they're screaming, never give them a cuddle.' Of course Geri, Melanie and me would be guaranteed to give screaming fans a cuddle. They often clung on for ages and we'd be pulling away shouting, 'That's it now!'

Just before Christmas I went to Iceland to see Fjöl. I love Reykjavik even though it's very small. It's like a dense village full of beautiful people who love drinking and all know each other. It was the time of year when there are only four hours of daylight and everyone cosies up at home, which was perfect for Fjöl and me. I spent a lot of time in bed. During the short days we zoomed around on snow bikes and sat in massive open-air jacuzzis surrounded by miles of snowy landscape, which was a great way to wind down from a mad year in Spiceworld. Finally I had time to recharge my batteries and prepare for the incredible journey to come, the next stage in our master plan, the world tour.

19

PRINCE CHARMING

Rehearsals for the world tour began in January at the K Club in Ireland, a fantastic country house hotel in County Kildare. We weren't staying in the main part of the hotel, but had apartments set in their own secluded part of the grounds. They were like a line of old granny flats all in a row. Each had a suite of rooms with antique furniture and fussy wallpaper – a bit Laura Ashley. Not my style, but certainly nothing to complain about. We had our own kitchens and every morning someone brought in fresh milk and bread so that we could make toast and cups of tea. After months of having to order up hotel room service for every little thing it was nice to be a bit DIY. In the mornings before rehearsals we went into each other's flats and made tea and toast for each other – very grannys' coffee morning – and at the end of the day we'd chill out round the TV together in a girly frenzy. It was like living on our own little council estate because there was no one else around.

We took over a large part of the big sports centre in the grounds right near our flats. The main gym area was partitioned off with a huge black cloth, just like in drama class at Intake High, except that we had a weights room and sun beds installed in the corner. It was much nicer and more relaxed than Spice Camp. This time we were our own bosses.

On the first day of rehearsals Priscilla our choreographer announced that the 'Spice Boys' were due to join us in a week. It had been her idea to throw men into the mix. We all liked the idea of having male versions of the five of us, to boss about on stage and partner in some of the routines. While we were doing quick-changes they could be on stage filling in, and they added to the humour factor too. For instance, when we sang 'Naked', we sat on reversed high-backed chairs wearing see-through body suits that made it look as though we had no clothes on (Christine Keeler-style). Priscilla suggested that when the song ended and lights went down, we'd disappear off stage and the boys would take our places on the chairs, also 'naked', just as a quirky little joke. As it turned out, it worked really well in performance and always made the audience roar.

Each dancer had to have a similar look to the girl he was partnered with and I was dying to know more about mine.

'What does he look like?' I asked Priscilla.

'He's very cool, with loads of tattoos, a bald head and a really good body,' she told me. 'His name's Jimmy and he's from Amsterdam.'

'And what's he like?'

'He's quite a mysterious kind of guy – you're definitely going to like him,' she said. 'Why don't you call him?' So I did. Dance rehearsals stopped. A couple of minutes later I was through to Jimmy Gulzar on his mobile.

'Halloo . . .' came the deep, foreign-sounding voice down the line.

'Hi! It's Melanie B here. You're my dancer, aren't you?'

'Actually I'm not *yours*, but yes, I'm your partner, as in dancing.'

I thought that was a bit of a strange reply. 'Have you got tattoos? How many tattoos have you got?' I asked, trying to be friendly.

'I've got enough,' he said frostily.

'Oh . . . well I can't wait to meet you . . .'

Talk about a cold call. He was very calm and direct, not intimidated at all, a bit offish even, which surprised me. I was used to people being taken aback by the whole Spice thing and I often played on it. To be honest, it was a bit of a power vibe. Usually you couldn't get a word in edgeways with me, but he didn't sound fazed, so I wasn't as full-on as I could be. I thought that maybe he'd heard things about Scary Spice and was trying to sound unimpressed. I was intrigued.

At the end of that week we flew off to do what seemed like a month's worth of promo in just two days. Meanwhile the dancers flew in to start rehearsals. When we got back, the girls immediately suggested going to meet them. I tried to put it off until the next day because I was looking like shite. My hair was matted and wild, I had no make-up on and I was still in my stinking travelling clothes, with a big yellow Tommy Hilfiger puffa jacket over the top. Still, the others insisted – 'No! We have to meet them *now.*' So I buried my head into the collar of my jacket and off we went.

Our flats were a five-second walk from the gym. Before going in we peeked around the door for a quick look. Instantly I spotted my dancer. Then my vision blurred over. Suddenly time stopped still. There was a heavy thudding in my chest. Oh my God! My dancer was the spitting image of Stephen, my first true love. It was weird, more than weird, it was freaky. He had the same shaved head, the same smooth dark skin, the same lean body. The only difference was his height – this guy was shorter. I knew it couldn't be, but all I could see was Stephen Mulrain in front of me. Even when I properly registered that it wasn't Stephen, I still felt a strong, strong sense of recognition.

I watched as Jim stood there talking to one of the other dancers. He was beautifully turned out, with a smooth silky oval face and a great body. He had a look of Yul Brynner as well. Everything about him was calm and confident. He moved gracefully and oozed self-assurance. I was rapt. I made a beeline for him. It felt as if he was pulling me towards him with a rope.

'Hi, you're my dancer, aren't you?' (I said it again!)

His eyes were light hazel and had a jabbing, piercing, hypnotic stare to them. They seemed to look further into me than anyone else's ever had.

Again he said, 'No, I'm not yours.' Then he smiled.

It was instant. Bzzzzzz! I couldn't take my eyes off him.

Me and the other girls didn't actually hang around for long – just said hello, goodbye and left – but it seemed like ages. On our way back to the flats I suddenly blurted out, 'God, I really fancy my dancer, can you believe it?' I was shocked to hear myself say it. What I was thinking and feeling hadn't quite registered in my brain yet.

Emma thought her dancer – Eszteca (pronounced Est-ay-ka) Noya – was possibly a bit too short; Vicky liked hers – gorgeous and proud Carmine Canuso. I remember Geri saying, 'Mine's quite fanciable as well.' But her partner, Christian Storm, had a bit of a reputation, so we'd been warned.

'No! Don't you go anywhere near him! He used to go out with one of the girls from Eternal. He's known for that,' we said immediately. (He's now settled down with Shaznay from All Saints.)

'Oh, okay.' She didn't seem too disappointed.

When I got back to my flat, I found Fjöl unpacking his case. He'd flown in for a week to stay with me. I flopped myself on the sofa and we gave each other a lovely welcoming hug.

'Have you seen your dancers?' he asked.

'Yes. Mine's got a bald head and lots of tattoos.'

'Oh right. What are we going to eat tonight?' said Fjöl and that was that. I didn't let anything slip about being attracted to Jim but unfortunately my unconscious side wasn't so discreet. That night I turned to Fjöl in my sleep and said, 'Come on! Let me see your tattoos!' Ooops. Fjöl knew there and then that my dancer had got inside my head.

I didn't know what it was – there was just something about Jim. I'd never been out with a dancer before and dancers are often very sensuous, so maybe that's what attracted me. Also, it's definitely a turn on to see someone doing what they're best at and I was seeing Jim dance every day, so you can imagine the impact that had on me. There was something in his uncanny resemblance to Stephen as well. I'd never really got over my first love. I wasn't still pining for him, but the relationship didn't end badly so I think there was always that feeling in the back of my head that it was unfinished business. I really don't know. Perhaps I just liked Jim because he was from Amsterdam and I was into that foreign vibe at the time.

Rehearsals were fine, really relaxed. There was a lot of messing around which made things more fun. I never put my all into rehearsing. As soon as I'd picked up the steps I just faffed about. Priscilla used to get so annoyed with me. I can hear her right now saying, 'Do it properly!' A lot of people would say it's an unprofessional way of doing things, but I've always been that way. I'll hum along to a song instead of singing it and move through a routine without really dancing it. I prefer the buzz and the excitement of doing something properly for the first time on stage. Putting myself under so much pressure allows me to enter into my own world.

Practising 'Say You'll Be There' was a laugh. We were using canes as part of the routine and when we got bored we'd get into kung fu stick fights. Priscilla would do her nut. She tried to take control of the situation by making us do the routines one-by-one instead of as a group, with all the dancers and other girls sitting around watching. It was cringe making, but enjoyable in an intense way.

I sensed a little bit of a buzz going on between me and Jim, but I must admit that most of the buzzing was coming from my side (in fact, all of it was!). It wasn't long before I was *on a mission*, even though he wasn't having any of it. Priscilla threw us all in at the deep end with our partners and made us rehearse 'Do It' first, a routine where you're literally all over each other. Great, I thought. But feeling so attracted to Jim, I couldn't even look him in the eye. As for him, he wasn't shy with me at all. 'Come on then, show me what you're made of!' he laughed. I just giggled meekly. When he said things like that to me my dancing went completely crap. Self-consciousness is an understatement.

It was obvious to me that I really fancied him, but he didn't seem to fancy me at all. He made me feel very nervy and I was like a ten-year-old when he was around. It was strange because I felt I had to earn the right to get to know him. It was like fancying your teacher, knowing you're not supposed to, knowing you can't. I was desperate to find out what was underneath that calm veneer. It wasn't an obsession, it was just, Ooh, it's a bit naughty to be thinking this, but hey, I like it.

I later found out that Jim didn't actually audition for the tour. Priscilla spotted him dancing in a club, got hold of his showreel, liked what she saw and phoned him. 'Would you like to perform with the Spice Girls?' Tell me a man who would turn down an offer like that! When he told his friends about his new job, they all jumped to the same conclusion. 'We bet you end up going out with Mel B!' They wouldn't shut up about it. So I guess he already had the seed of an idea in his head that he was going to get together with me. At least, that's what he told me months later. He'd also made his mind up that he wasn't going to be bossed around by me, he said. He treated me coolly and gave the impression that he wasn't particularly interested.

Well, he did have a girlfriend in Amsterdam. He was very open about his relationship and even showed me pictures of her. She was an absolutely beautiful blonde. He was always on the phone to her. Looking back, it's obvious to see that he was playing the 'I-know-I'm-going-to-get-you-but-I'm-going-to-make-you-want-me-really-badly' game. It's just that he was playing it very slowly, biding his time, reeling me in.

Over the next few weeks I made it obvious how I felt, but Jim just didn't respond. I was so desperate for signs that he liked me that I started imagining them. I began to interpret the tiniest things as significant, proof that something was going to happen. Our knees would touch when we were sitting watching TV, or we'd giggle at the same thing or glance at each other at the same time. Every gesture had hidden meaning for me, every little thing had a profound impact.

One day in rehearsals I said to him, 'You're going to have to get your tongue pierced if you're going to be my partner.'

'Well I wanted to get it done anyway,' he replied.

My jaw dropped. I was shocked at how cool and calm he was as he said it. Wow, I thought, that's my man! Now this tongue pierce thing was very significant for me. It meant we shared a bond, had something in common. When he actually went and had it done I genuinely thought, Oh my God, he's had his tongue pierced for me! Of course he hadn't. He just wanted a pierced tongue. Still, I convinced myself that it was an act of devotion. I thought, He's giving me a sign that he likes me! even though he wasn't really showing any sign whatsoever. It was crazy. What was I thinking?

Half the time, Jim didn't say anything, which made me curious about what was going on in his head. I was fascinated by his lifestyle and his past, being brought up in Surinam then moving to Amsterdam, surrounded by all the prostitutes and the multicultural in-yer-face lifestyle. I asked him about it all the time. The few times he did open up he told me stories about the parties he went to and the clubs with loads of different themed rooms where people had sex openly. He described how everyone would hang out on roller blades and party together throughout the summer. It sounded like paradise.

He said that he used to lead two separate lives, working very hard in a bar and then out with his mates, hardcore partying. He never mixed those worlds and had two groups of completely separate friends. I thought it was a bit funny when he told me he'd been in a boy band. He said he'd been kicked out, but didn't say why. Later on, thanks to the press, I found out that he'd also worked in a gay bar, dancing half-naked. Same thing really. (Well maybe not!)

His manager at that time also managed Jocelyn Brown, the soul singer and writer. I made friends with Jocelyn when we worked with Beverley Knight on 'Music of the Millennium' in September 1999, performing the Aretha Franklin classic, 'Respect'. I'm good friends with Beverley but I didn't know Jocelyn at the time. I was pooing my pants at the thought of singing with two such fantastic divas, but they were very encouraging. They're such nice people that I didn't feel too uncomfortable, although deep down I knew my voice wasn't half as good as theirs.

I got to the studio a bit late, changed and rushed on set. The music started. Out comes Beverley Knight. Fine. Out comes Jocelyn Brown. Thud! Smack, bang, wallop! Starfish on the floor. I was walking out on the same side of the stage as her and I didn't know where to look. It was hysterical. We had to start again. During the performance I just smiled and giggled along in the middle of Beverley and Jocelyn, wearing my outrageously bright Julian MacDonald outfit.

Some time after that I was round at Jocelyn's house with my then boyfriend Max and Phoenix. It turned out that Max and Jocelyn go way back to the old Jazz Café days. She's such an open, warm and motherly type and an incredible singer. I've got so much admiration for her and I felt privileged to be sitting in her house. There were people coming and going, music booming upstairs and someone playing the keyboards in the next room. It was a really buzzy home.

The subject of Jim came up.

'Honey, I've been wanting to talk to you about him for ages,' Jocelyn said. 'I know so much about Jim.'

By this point I was divorced. 'Why didn't you try and get hold of me before?'

'Well, honey child, I didn't know you then,' she replied.

And to be honest, I probably wouldn't have listened. Back then I lived partly in a fantasy and the world according to Mel was always beautiful and loving. I believed that, whatever happened, I'd be fine.

Valentine's Day came, Valentine's Day went. Fjöl flew over for a week and swept me off my feet, wining me, dining me and showering me with roses and presents. He was always very romantic, a brilliant boyfriend. He gave me back massages and foot massages and pampered me all the time. Lucky me, because he was a very unselfish lover with a really sexy, muscular body.

Fjöl was never moody. He had a fantastic sense of humour and was always supportive and loving. There was definitely something very Viking-like about him and he was protective without being controlling. I knew he'd be there if anything went wrong. In many ways he was the perfect boyfriend and the most spiritual man I've ever been out with. In my moments of anger and frustration, Fjöl would say, 'If anything happens to you or you don't want to carry on, you can forget about this life and make a home back in Iceland with me. I will look after you.' So why on earth did I fancy someone else? I've asked myself that question so many times.

A couple of days after Valentine's Day it was Jim's birthday. I thought, Right I'm going to give my dancer a present. So off I went shopping in Dublin and bought him a tight dark see-through Jean Paul Gaultier stretchy top. As soon as I laid eyes on it I knew I had to buy it for him. It was quite effeminate actually – the kind of thing I used to wear. I couldn't wait to give it to him.

Back at the K Club that evening I told Fjöl I was going out clubbing. 'It's a girls' night out tonight. No boys allowed,' I lied, although I did I tell him which club I was going to. Off I went to the dancers' hotel with Emma. The moment I saw Jim I gave him his present, which I'd wrapped up in flimsy beige tissue paper. He smiled, said thank you, tore open the paper and put on his new top right there and then, revealing his naked torso. Yet again my eyes went 'dong!' as I imagined what it would be like to touch his skin properly. The top looked great on him and he seemed pleased, so I was happy. Step one: get taste in clothing correct. Result: succeeded. We all had a drink in the bar and then headed into Dublin – me, Emma and the dancers.

Going out in Dublin is always great because the Irish are so friendly. Everyone's very happy-go-lucky and I love their sing-song accent. Back then Ireland had a real sense of escapism for us because the people seemed really relaxed, what with U2 living there and Bono owning a hotel/restaurant. Emma also had quite a lot of family over there, which made it even more of a home from home. We never felt like aliens, which we sometimes did in London.

That night we went raving to a club called The Pod. It was a really good night, a gay night with lots of transvestites and crazy people doing their thing. Me and Emma headed straight for the middle of the dance floor. She was dancing with her partner Eszteca and I was dancing with Jim, really getting into it, clocking a bit of a salsa vibe. Then the other dancers joined in and we really started messing around, being loud, doing silly moves and totally hogging the dance floor. We even formed a circle and made people dance in the middle – completely uncool stuff.

Little did I know that a bit later on Fjöl would turn up at the club, thinking it would be nice to surprise me. In fact it was Fjöl who got the surprise as he walked in and saw me in the middle of a bump and grind 'train' with all the dancers. The moment he realised I'd been lying about my girls' night out, he turned around and walked straight out of the club. The next day the Irish papers said that he'd seen me slow-dancing with Jim and had a fit, shouting and screaming the place down, which was rubbish. He wasn't a jealous boyfriend at all. Instead of marching up to me and dragging me off, he simply left. I had no idea that he'd even been there until later, by which point I was too drunk to be bothered about it anyway.

After the club, me and Emma went back to the dancers' hotel, which was a big country mansion, a bit like Cliveden or Babington House. We spent a couple of hours running in and out of everyone's rooms, being stupid and ordering drinks and sandwiches, then off we went back to our old biddy flats. Fjöl was waiting up for me, really annoyed. He punched his fist through a wardrobe door and shouted 'How dare you? You and Geri, you're just the same!' A couple of days before he'd heard Geri make a throwaway comment about how most boyfriends were good for sex, but not much else. Now he was assuming that I felt the same. How could he?

We soon made it up. When Fjöl shouted at me it never made much of an impact because he wasn't a naturally argumentative person. He was so loving and caring that he didn't like being confrontational. Plus, I had the upper hand in that I always beat him in any argument because his English wasn't as good as mine. In fact his English was crap. He used to rant and rave in Icelandic sometimes, but it always sounded really passionate and sexy and foreign to me, never threatening or aggressive. It just made me think, 'cor!' – the opposite effect to the one intended. All the same, he went back to Iceland the next day in a foul mood. He knew what was coming, or so he tells me now.

It wasn't that I wanted to have sex with Jim. It wasn't about that, because I had a fantastic sex life with Fjöl – and a brilliant relationship all round. There was just something about this mysterious guy from

Amsterdam. He really aroused my curiosity. He was the first man I'd met who made it impossible for me to get to him, and who didn't get shocked by anything I said, didn't get intimidated or offended. His personality was a blank and he showed me nothing. That made me want to find out more about him, get under his skin. I *had* to.

Me and Emma spent a lot of time with two of the dancers, Carmine Canuso and Louie Spence. Carmine is Italian and looks like a model or an actor. He's really intelligent and open, quite fatherly and caring, looks after you and is just a scream to be with. He gets on with women brilliantly, he's a bit flirty, he pouts, he's a stunning dancer and looks very masculine. On top of all that he's really into clothes and always has designer gear on, so he was well suited to be Vicky's partner.

Louie was one of the two reserve dancers. The only words for him are entertainment, entertainment, entertainment. Very camp, everything's a show. He was always dancing and had an energy that bordered on hyperactivity. I mean this guy is *full* of energy. You could really have nice chats with Louie, but you just couldn't help laughing too, because he comes out with some crackers and always sees a different side to things. He could bend his body in half, literally. He was very acrobatic on and off stage and often he'd be chatting away to you with one leg up behind his ear. But a part of Louie is very straight and sober and structured – he rarely drank, and stuck to his beauty routine without fail, morning and night. He was generally really positive and lovely to be around and he and Emma are still good friends to this day.

We often went out shopping and partying with Louie and Carmine and sometimes Jim would come along. Jim was always in control and very correct in his behaviour towards others, generous, open and giving. He had everyone entranced. The effect he had on people was quite miraculous actually. I missed him when he wasn't around, especially when he had a couple of days off to have his tongue pierced and went back to Amsterdam to see his girlfriend. The day he got back I asked, 'Did you kiss her? Did you have sex with her? Did you go down on her with your tongue pierce?'

'Well, yes,' he said. 'She's my girlfriend.'

That crushed me, even though it was perfectly reasonable and normal and natural. Wasn't he at all interested in me then?

He really fascinated me with his philosophies about life and his theories about spiritualism. Now when I look back and think about what he was saying, I'm not convinced. But you know what it's like when you're lit up by someone. You believe anything they say, you're under their spell. I was definitely hooked.

Those weeks in Ireland were incredibly exciting. We'd all been looking forward to the tour from the very earliest days of Spice and after the buzz of Istanbul, we just wanted to get up on stage and feel that high again. I suppose it was a bit daunting to think that we had over a hundred shows ahead of us, but that didn't really hit home until we were well into the European part of the tour. I just couldn't wait for it all to start.

In the lead up to our first night I had lots of dreams about being on stage, probably because I always practised my routines just before I went to bed. I find that if you can't remember a routine, it's good to go over it before you go to sleep, even if only in your head. I was so excited that every night I'd get out of the shower and go through every single step of every routine. The feeling of anticipation was intense and I loved it.

The very first show of our world tour was at the Point in good old Dublin on 24 February. Wow, what a day. It went brilliantly, from the first bars of 'If U Can't Dance' to the last lines of our final encore song, 'We Are Family'. In my diary I wrote:

There is a side of me that is very rarely tapped into, apart from when I perform. It's like it's kept under wraps until I let it out and then it takes me over completely. When I get out there on stage it helps me peak, gives me the right to go for it. It cushions me and puts me on a level where no one can reach me. Boy is it a buzz. It's more than just adrenaline or excitement or even the biggest multiple orgasm. In fact, times all those by a hundred, drop in the rush of a bungee jump, stick them in a pot with a cocktail of spirits, drink it, hold your breath for thirty seconds, scream as loudly as you can from the pit of your stomach, go under a spotlight – that's what I feel like when I perform.

After the show we were all on a complete high. Geri got drunk on sherry and danced on the table in the bar, which was unusual for her as the most she usually had was a sip. Vicky was happy because David was there, Emma was with her mum and brother, Melanie slipped off to bed quite soon after the show and I didn't notice what anyone else was up to because I was too busy keeping an eye out for Jim.

There was definitely a sense of, 'Look we did it again!' in the air. Fingers up to the people who were always criticising us, the ones that constantly chipped away, saying, 'You can't sing live, you can't do this or that. You're not going to last.' We showed them, but most importantly we showed ourselves. We'd used some recorded backing vocals in Turkey to help with the harmonies, but tonight had been more or less bareback. We still had some basic bvs, but not half as many as in Istanbul. It was a real live show and, for us, it was about effing time.

It was great to see my mum and dad and Danielle and Charlotte. They really liked the show, but I couldn't concentrate on what they were saying because Jim and I kept clocking each other across the room. I told Charlotte, 'Your job for the night is to keep an eye on Jim for me. Look out for where he goes and who he's talking to.' Strange, I know, but I'd done it for her a million times, so I didn't feel bad about asking.

Meanwhile Fjöl was at the bar having a great time being chatted up by Louie and Carmine, who were getting quite fruity with him, flashing their nipples and generally teasing him. Suddenly he turned serious and announced, 'If another man tries go near Melanie, I kill him.' He'd never said anything like that before. 'Jesus Christ!' said Carmine as he told me about it afterwards. 'He sounded like he really meant it too.'

My mum met Jim for the first time that night. As I pointed him out I said, 'Mum, I think I fancy my dancer.'

She looked over to where he was talking to Priscilla. 'Oh yes, he's good-looking,' she agreed. Then she looked at him again. 'No, Melanie. Noooo,' she said. Which, of course, made me want him even more.

20

RACING SO HARD,
YOU KNOW IT WON'T LAST

Our first show after Ireland was Zurich on 3 March and from then on it was a mad rush around Europe. Frankfurt, Bologna, Rome, Milan, Marseille, Barcelona, Madrid, Lyon, Lausanne, Paris, Munich, Arnhem and Antwerp – and that was just March!

I took three massive metal trunks with me. One for shoes, one for daytime clothes and one for going-out clothes. I lived out of them but they were so big that I could have actually lived in them. I also had a meditation chair that I took everywhere. It had to be strapped into its own seat on the private plane, which was very funny. I had the piss taken out of me several times because I was the one with the most luggage, plus the frigging chair. When we had the break between Europe and America I was told to send it home because it was taking up far too much space. I was quite sad to see it go because I was very attached to that chair. I'd sit and chill out in it every day. It always seemed to calm me down.

Every show day we had the same routine. Wake up early afternoon, go to the venue, sound check, rehearse a bit, do loads of press and radio interviews (and I mean loads) and have dinner with the crew in the catering hall. After a few weeks you were friends with everyone, so that the walk from the canteen to the dressing room could take you a good hour of saying 'Hi!' and catching up on gossip along the way.

Our dressing rooms always had a familiar vibe because we had certain things that went everywhere with us. Whichever part of the world we were in, we still had the same Indian wooden table and lamps and candles and throws around us. It was all just stuff from Camden Market but it helped us feel at home. After dinner you'd be able to fart about for a bit, get your costumes ready, have a chat, call home. Then it was time for make-up and hair and the inevitable tussle over who had theirs done first. 'Who's going next?' 'I'm not going!' 'Yes you are!' 'No I'm not' 'Yes you are!' 'No I'm not' 'All right then, I'll go.'

Karin, our make-up artist, had to draw up a nightly rota. She was a very steady and stable presence. No matter what was happening, either personally or within the group, you knew that Karin would be totally unbiased. You could say whatever you wanted while she was doing your make-up, you knew it wouldn't go any further. Karin was a straight-down-the-line professional, but also a really good listener and friend. She had quite a stunning look. Tall and athletic with long legs, she was a bit Annie Lennox facially, but with long blonde hair. She was clean cut and always looked fresh and immaculate, even in jeans and a black top. And why is it that make-up artists never wear make-up? For some reason they just don't.

Karin worked quickly because she knew our faces down to a T. Being the perfectionist that she is, she was always experimenting with new ways to get our make-up to stay on for longer. Because I held the mic too close to my mouth my lipstick was usually gone within half a song, so she went on a search for something more permanent. She came up with an artist's pigment that actually stained your lips, so much so that you'd be there at the end of the show desperately rubbing away to get the stuff off.

Our show was a full-on, high-energy sweatbox, which meant that our make-up mixed in with our perspiration, causing an all-over merging effect. As for our hair, well that just drooped, which was much too much for Vicky to handle. She was smart and employed her own wig. It looked great, but I'll never forget walking into the dressing room and seeing Ben Mohapi, our hairdresser, hacking away at her wig to transform it from a bob into a crop after she changed hairstyle. It was quite an eerie sight.

We each had our own blusher compact in our dressing rooms because we were all big on blusher. A lot of the time I couldn't be arsed with all that faffing about and I often did my own hair instead of hanging around while Ben spent ages gently teasing it into a nutbush. It used to flop down and I'd say to him, 'Just give me a brush!' then I'd back-comb it really violently. He'd stand there gawping at the state I was making of it. Ben looked like something out of a 1970s jukebox. Light skinned, little afro, beauty spots on his face. He wore big flares and danced like a funky seventies dude, a bit *Starsky and Hutch*/Jamiroquai.

Kenny Ho was our clothes and shoes man. Kenny was a strange-looking fella, of Chinese origin, and he was almost like a timid cat. He wasn't very experienced at this game, but he was fantastic. He'd been employed as an assistant stylist on *Spiceworld: the Movie* and was so enthusiastic that we'd decided to take him under our wing. Kenny's a very talented guy and his portfolio was a masterpiece. We offered him the chance to design our tour costumes and we loved all of his ideas. He really did his research on our individual styles and worked closely with us to create some fantastic outfits.

Backstage, Melanie would be the first one to get dressed, then Vicky, then Geri. Me and Emma were always the last. 'We'd better get ready then!' (Countdown to show: two minutes.) It wasn't that we couldn't be arsed. We were just so relaxed. Meanwhile Melanie would be off in a quiet room warbling away, warming up her voice with singing exercises that drove Vicky crazy. She was incredibly disciplined and really nurtured her vocal chords, but the rest of us didn't bother that much. The most we'd do was have a honey and ginger drink, thinking that a hot coating of that would be enough.

Sometimes we'd still be on the phone with seconds to go before we went on stage. Juliette, our freckly assistant tour manager, who was short and pretty but with a real voice on her, used to go completely mad at us. She'd be standing there with our mic packs shouting, 'Come on NOW! The intro's started!' and there would be a mad rush to attach the packs and run down endless corridors to the side of the stage in time. One of Juliette's aims was to get us on stage before the intro started, just once, but she never did. I loved leaving it to the very last minute – I always have. Often I'll be sitting at home, knowing that I've got to be somewhere by 2 p.m. That means I've got to set off at 1.30 p.m. So at 1.20 p.m. I'll start getting ready. It's like a test. Will I make it? I always do. Well just about. That is the way I live my life.

There was always something going on backstage, especially with Carmine and Louie around. They were just mad. They'd do things like shout, 'You silly cow!' from the side of the stage while we were trying to sing '2Become1' really seriously. Me and Emma got them back though. Stupid things, like using orange peel to spell out YOU TWATS on the floor of the boys' dressing room, or hiding their Y-fronts before they went on for the end of 'Naked'. We were like school kids, but worse.

In our slightly less manic moods, we'd all play 'Would you rather . . .?' where we asked each other to make ridiculous choices like, 'Would you rather . . . go to bed with one of the roadies or eat a pube sandwich?' While you were trying to decide, the others would be screeching, 'What are you going to do? What are you going to do?' It was incredibly childish but hilarious at the time. We played it endlessly.

There were quite a few quick changes during the show when we'd rush underneath the stage in between songs to throw off one outfit and struggle into the next. We had separate dressing cubicles and they were each customised. Vicky had David splattered all over hers, Melanie's room was a shrine to Liverpool FC and mine was bare except for a polaroid of Carmine and Louie wearing my costumes and 'Spice Up' head horns. We had dressers to help us along, but it was always chaotic. 'Where's my G-string?' 'Is my mic pack on?' 'Hurry-hurry-hurry!'

More often than not, the curtain would be pulled back before you were ready and there you'd be, nearly naked, for everyone to see – including Jim. In the end I used to have my curtain permanently pulled back so that I could chat away to Louis and Carmine while I was getting changed.

There were all kinds of things going on with the dressers. Sometimes they'd get on with each other, sometimes they wouldn't. There was quite a lot of competitive tension between them over who was quickest. If one of them managed to get, say, Mel C dressed first, then that dresser would be in a great mood for the rest of that half of the show. Whoever was the slowest would be in a really bad mood. It was very funny to watch.

There came a point, a couple of weeks into the tour, when I began to feel like a robot doing the same routines night after night. (It was like Blackpool all over again, but on a much bigger scale!) So I started picking people out in the audience and having conversations with them. That became my buzz. During the quick changes, me, Emma and Geri would shout to each other, 'Have you seen the guy five rows back?'

'Yes I have. Isn't he gorgeous?'

'Eurgh, no! He's horrible!'

'Well let's just tease him anyway.'

'Find your own! I'm teasing him during the next bit.'

Meanwhile Vicky and Melanie would be focused on getting dressed and getting everything right.

I played a game – and I think Emma did too – where you pick one person out of the crowd and sing an entire song just to them. It made their skin crawl, you could tell. At first they'd turn their head a few times to see if you were looking at someone behind them. So you'd point at them. 'Yes, you!' When they realised that it really was them you were looking at, they got incredibly embarrassed and you'd see them turn to their friend and say, 'She's looking at me!' After that what did they have left to do apart from watch? They were often staring at the floor by the end of the song, unable to look you in the eye a moment longer. It was a wicked mind game to play and I've noticed a lot of other performers doing something similar. R Kelly, for instance, concentrates on one person for a bit and then moves on to somebody else (I know this because he did it to my sister while she was standing right next to me), whereas I'd stay fixed on one person for ages, until it became really unbearable for them!

I've always had two ambitions on stage. One is to grab people up from the audience. The other is to do a stage dive. I thought '2Become1' was a perfect song for fulfilling my first ambition, but not all of us agreed that it would be suitable for the tour. In the end we did pull people up on stage during our Christmas '99 shows in Manchester and London, but I know that Melanie and Vicky didn't feel comfortable with it before that. As for the stage dive, I accepted that I could never do one because I'd crush all the five- and six-year-olds. Pity.

I talked all the time on stage – to the girls, the dancers, just anyone who'd listen. The last thing I wanted was for the show to become humdrum and boring, so I often went off on one, especially at the start of 'Sisters'. Emma, Vicky and Geri would come on stage and say, 'We've lost the two Mels – does anyone know where they are?' while Mel and I were doing a quick-change into our rock outfits. Then they'd go front stage to 'look' for us, while Mel and I had a proper banter backstage. We'd be panting from the last set, changing as quickly as possible and speaking into the mic at the same time.

'Where are you?'

'I'm up here!'

The audience could hear us, but they didn't have a clue where we were. Melanie would pretend she was up in the balcony and shout, 'Get off me, you idiot! No I won't sign an autograph!' and I'd yell, 'Come on you wazzaks! or 'Time to ho-down!' and other things that just didn't make any sense whatever.

I got a big buzz from being able to open my mouth and let any old rubbish come out. I thought I was absolutely hilarious in those moments and I'd get pains in my belly from laughing at myself. I really didn't care what I said. No one ever understood what we were on about but we'd have the band in absolute fits by the time we got on stage. They'd be giggling so much that they kept making mistakes. After a few weeks Simon Ellis, our musical director, said to me, 'The show would be really boring by now if it wasn't for your spiel before "Sisters". Nobody knows what you're going to say next.'

I found it so comfortable up there. I'd turn round and mouth 'F*** off!' to the band or tell someone a story. Other times I would prod Vicky while she was singing. That really put her on edge. 'Stop it!' she'd hiss. I'd suddenly announce, 'Vicky's got a surprise!' or 'Emma's got something really important to tell everyone!' and they'd have to make something up on the spot. Me and Emma pulled faces and tried to make each other laugh all the time. It was like being back at school when you're told to keep quiet during a library session.

At the start of the show, before the audience saw us properly, our silhouettes appeared behind a big screen. We had to stand totally still so that you couldn't tell if we were real or just cardboard cut-outs. If you lost your balance and moved, you'd ruin the whole effect, so me and Emma were always trying to push each other over before the screen came back. We even did it on the very last night of the tour. Melanie and Vicky didn't seem to notice. They were too busy concentrating.

'Naked' was the worst song for getting the giggles. Every third beat we looked directly right or left to the person sitting next to us. I sat next to Emma and every time we came face to face we'd burst out laughing. We tried to avoid looking at each other, but it never seemed to work. I'd think, Right, on the third beat I'm going to look to the right while Emma looks the other way. She'd think, Right, on the third beat Melanie won't be looking my way, so I'll look left. Bang! We'd end up giggling our socks off. You had to grit your teeth so you didn't smile because it was such a serious song. Even worse, the big screens showed close-ups of our faces throughout the whole song, so you really couldn't blow it.

We all got on well with the band, they were a real bunch of characters. Simon Ellis, the musical director, was a funny guy, very Austin Powers with his comments and smiles. 'Yeah baby, yeah, I like it a lot.' He was straightforward and down to earth, very loud and bubbly and a real family man. He never minced his words and often had us in fits with his observations about life.

When I introduced the band, I'd lob them all in it. I was sure that Michael Martin, the keyboard player, also known as Mr Luvva Luvva, had a girl in every town. He was a bald-headed smoothie, dripping in gold, and a really genuine person with a good heart. 'Here's Mr Luvva Luvva! I think one of his girlfriends is in tonight!' That would make him shake his head and laugh as he did his solo.

'This is Andy. He's a bit of a freak but we love him!' Andy Gangadeen, the drummer, was a bit of an eccentric. He had a funny way of walking, he almost hopped as he walked, and his dress sense was unusual, to say the least. He had long black hair and often wore a sarong and big workers' boots. Andy was very intelligent and talked about anything and every-thing – computers, music, the state of the world. He was very opinionated about things like Napster and we had a big debate about the future of record companies. Andy thought their days were numbered and the industry would be run on the internet. I don't think he ever got his due respect for his contribution to the programming for the show. He was very technically advanced and some would say he was more like a musical director. Because of my drums training at school, I was fascinated by the way he'd set up his drum kit and all his equipment.

'And Steve Lewinson on bass really fancies our make-up artist!' Steve was calm and collected as well as being a wicked guitarist. I loved the way he played, shaking his head so that his locks bounced around. I heard some quite sexy stories about him, so maybe he was a bit of a closet naughty boy, although he didn't look it. He had a lovely sister and seemed like a really homely, down-to-earth kind of guy.

'This is Paul. He's hard core and he knows the score!' Paul Gendler, on lead guitar, was the ultimate rock and roll musician. You wouldn't have thought he'd have much stamina because he was quite small-framed, but he could last all night and still walk in a straight line back to his room. He smoked hardcore Marlboro Reds like a child eats sweets. He didn't seem like a family man until you saw him with his lovely family. He was a real been-there-seen-it-done-it person, toured for years, knows the game, a really cool guy, quite shy, but always friendly. He walked with his legs wide apart as though he was carrying a lot of precious things down below.

'And this is Fergus, who fancies one of the cooks – Michelle!' He'd do his bit with gritted teeth. 'I can't believe you, Melanie!' Fergus Gerrand was our brilliant percussionist. He always appeared to be dancing when he played percussion and we thought he looked really sexy when he was performing (but not when he wasn't). He was quite thin and muscular, athletic-looking and very smiley. Unfortunately for him I got wind that he fancied Michelle in catering and never let him hear the end of it. Apparently he's still with her to this day, so he can't have minded that much.

Like all tours, ours had its share of on-the-road romances. One of the camera guys got together with Melanie's dresser and they've since had a baby. I bumped into him when I presented the UK Garage Awards in 2001 and he said, 'Isn't it mad? We met on tour and we're still together!'

'Lucky for some!' I joked, and we laughed.

The tour was a kind of cocoon, a Spice bubble. We were in our own world, on our own girl power world domination mission. It wasn't all fun and games. Because we didn't have a manager, we divided up the management roles between us. Melanie's was discipline, rehearsals and sound check. Vicky's was sorting things out with Charles Bradbrook at Deloitte's and our lawyer Andrew Thompson, dealing with all the financial and legal matters. Mine was TOUR CONTROL and I took it very seriously. I had weekly meetings with tour manager Richard Jones. We discussed what was coming up next and any problems that needed ironing out. And believe me, we had our fair share of problems.

I really got on with Richard because as well as being a nice person, he had all the information at his fingertips. He was incredibly organised and reliable and always made sure everything was in place. You knew that if anything went wrong he'd be able to pick up the pieces. He handled the Spice Girls great, whereas I think a lot of men would probably feel intimidated dealing with five females who were constantly questioning what he was doing. Richard had a really good way of dealing respectfully with all of us. I don't think many men would be able to handle us without thinking, I'm a man, I know what I'm doing. You don't. I'm going to question *you* now.

Because I was Tour Control I knew what everybody was up to, from the lighting men to the band. Every night I'd listen carefully to the music on stage and I'd go mad if anything went wrong. I used to tell the band off afterwards and they'd shit themselves, so they made out, although they probably didn't give a f*** in actual fact. Simon the musical director would get so carried away that he often missed out 'stabs', so we'd find ourselves doing moves to music that wasn't there. I'd write down all the mistakes then go looking for the band. 'Hey, you were out of tune on that bit. And you missed this and that.' Not that I knew much about instruments, but I instantly picked up when something wasn't following the right pattern. The band's concentration probably wasn't helped by the fact that they were necking over £100 a night on booze – and only half the band really drank. We had bottles of champagne put in our dressing room fridge every night but we rarely opened them, so they went to the band and the caterers. As soon as the encore finished and the stage lights went down, their mission was bottle-shaped.

One day in Europe I called the photo projector guys into a room and went mad at them. During one of the songs they'd swapped pictures of us for polaroids of themselves and projected them on the back screen. The photos showed one of these guys with my horns on, another in one of our costumes and someone else pulling a moonie. There was also a photo of a bunch of them half-naked in a steam room, with some girls. It's quite funny to think of it now, but at the time I felt angry and annoyed.

'This just can't happen. There are kids in the audience. People have paid money to see this show and they don't want to watch you up on the screens. We've calculated this photo montage down to the finest detail so that the pictures fit with the lyrics, and your bums just don't do it!'

I went berserk at the lighting guys a few times. It's only natural to get a bit lazy when you've been doing the same thing for a few weeks, but that's no excuse for doing your job badly. On the other hand I could really tell when they were on form because the spotlight would actually follow you around the stage. In that case I'd say, 'Oh my God, have you got a new lighting guy in because the lights were amazing tonight!' I thought it was important to give out compliments as well.

The group didn't let things slip so why should anyone else? We never missed our encore even though we were sometimes tempted to. It was a really long show and some nights one of us would say, 'Oh can't we just cut the encore?' The answer was always no. Another night someone else would give it a try. 'I just can't be arsed!' But not once did we cut that show down or, worse, cancel. We all had a really good attitude. If one person felt weak the others made sure they stayed strong.

We never had any problems with the caterers. They were all really nice. They set up camp in every new venue by putting up plastic tables and unpacking massive tins of baked beans, tomato ketchup, Marmite and all the other things we couldn't do without. They went to a lot of trouble to make delicious meals and the buffet was always huge. In America they often set up outdoors, which was wicked.

Me and Emma went out at night a lot in the first couple of months of the tour. It became our mission. As soon as we landed somewhere we asked Vern, (now our head of security), to find out where the best clubs were. It was almost more important to us than what the next venue was like or whether we'd have to adjust any of the routines to the size of the stage. There are some really cool clubs in Europe and we'd all pile in, a big gang of us, and take over. Me and Emma loved embarrassing the dancers on the dance floor. We'd do 'running man' and other naff moves to take the piss. I think Eszteca cringed the most. He's really quite cool, from a very talented musical family, and into his hip-hop and chatting and rapping, so he wasn't amused. Jim didn't always come along. It was usually just Louie, Carmine, Eszteca, Emma and me, the party crew.

There were always hundreds – sometimes thousands – of fans outside our hotels but we didn't let that stop us doing what we wanted to do. We went shopping and sightseeing whenever we wanted. One day in Italy we had about fifty people on scooters all zooming alongside our black people carrier, trying to tap on the windows. Later on me and Emma got trapped in Gucci because it was crammed with fans. We had to stay there until Vern worked out how to get us out the back way. It wasn't a problem. 'Oh well, let's just do a bit more shopping then!'

The fan stuff didn't affect me, except in the early days. After a while you go into a different mode that you don't know exists until you've been there and done it. There's always going to be, 'Wow, isn't this great. What's happening to us?' but I never dwelt on it. There really wasn't time. Things would stick in my head, like when someone cried because I smiled at them or signed an autograph, but I never allowed myself to get too analytical about it, just in case it all disappeared in a puff of smoke. It felt more comfortable to get on with it, live it and enjoy it for what it was.

I think I'd know what it feels like to be a real fan if I ever got to have a proper conversation with Neneh Cherry or Tracy Chapman. I've admired them both for so many years that I think I'd just come out with a load of shit. Even worse I'd know what they were thinking as I was talking: Oh yes, that's really lovely. Can't you just talk normally to me please?

Nicole, my friend who does amazing make-up, knows Neneh Cherry really well. If she even mentions her name I go white.

'Shall I send your love to her?'

'Noooo!'

We also train with the same boxing trainer and I gaze at a polaroid of her when I'm working out, thinking, 'She actually trains here!' She walked past me in the airport once and I cacked my pants. Another time she was on the same Lottery Show as I was, doing a song with her brother Eagle Eye Cherry. She came up to say hi and I couldn't even look at her. I was so embarrassed that I don't think I even said hello.

It's always an awkward situation. Not long ago I was in the newsagents on a day when the kids just happened to have a half-day off school. About ten girls, all teenagers, came in. One girl pointed to her friend and said, 'She's your biggest fan!' What do you say to that? Thanks? They're looking at you expecting something more than that. This time I tried to open up the conversation. Unfortunately I wasn't very successful.

'You've got the rest of the day off school have you?'

'Yeah!'

'Is school nice then?'

'It's okay.'

'Right, I'm off then. Bye!'

It's sometimes difficult when someone asks, 'Will you speak to my sister on the phone?' Usually I say, 'Please don't make me. It always goes wrong.'

You say, 'Hiya!'

'Hiya,' they reply, in a high pitched whisper. And then they say nothing. It's like talking to thin air.

'Hello, is anyone there?'

You pass the phone back and hear a little voice screaming through the receiver, 'Oh my God! Oh my God!'

We had one fan that followed us to every single show in Europe. He was an older guy with a big white and grey beard who often wore a hat. He seemed really lovely, never caused any trouble and was always by himself in the front row with a banner saying I Love Spice Girls. He knew every single word to every song.

'I wonder whose side he's going to be on tonight?'

'Look, he's on Melanie's side!'

It's a good job we changed our banter in between songs so that he saw a different show every time. We followed a vague script for the first couple of concerts, just in case we all started talking at the same time, but by the third date it was just a case of whoever wanted to speak.

There were two women – lesbians – that followed us around everywhere. I could have sworn they were Mel C's fans until one of them threw a ring at me on stage. I've still got it to this day. It's a silver ring with two dolphins on it and I assumed this was some kind of lesbian symbol. Oh my God, I thought as I picked up the ring, saw the dolphins and put it on my finger. I managed to keep smiling. 'Thank you,' I said while a voice in the back of my head whispered, Get it off your finger now! It's funny that I've kept it. It probably wasn't even meant for me.

Sometimes me and Emma would travel to the next show on the dancers' bus instead of flying. It was better in many ways because it meant you didn't have to rush off at top speed immediately after the show to get to the airport. On a plane you're up in the air for an hour at the most. You've got all that dehydration – and in mine and Vicky's cases the possibility of earning yourself a few more spots – then you have to get off the plane, get to the hotel, find your luggage, sleep, get up and repack. It was far more chilled being on the bus. We'd hang around for a while after the show finished, watch the set being dismantled, have a sandwich and a drink, then set off.

On the bus you could eat and sleep, there was music playing and we had Sky TV. It was always spick and span because Louie and Carmine were very hygiene-conscious with their carpet sweeper and their cloths to clean the surfaces of the little kitchen. There was a small lounge area at the back where everyone would sit and watch a film, tell stories or play cards and talk. It was cosy, like being around a camp fire. At the end of the night Louie and Carmine would often be the only ones still up, doing mad shows for me and Emma in their underpants. Then they'd start dragging people out of their bunks to join in their performances. It was fantastic, a really good vibe.

We went on the band's tour bus once, but it was full-on rock and roll. Lads burping and farting and drinking whisky and endless 'Yeah, I've had her' stories. It was a funny experience, but not to be repeated, which was probably the intention. I had the feeling they were deliberately overdoing it to put us off joining them again.

Generally we hung out with the dancers more than the band. We'd all started off as dancers, except Geri, so we had a lot in common and it often felt like we were a big family. On days off we'd meet up and go shopping or sunbathing or on a trip somewhere. That's when Carmine's talent for speaking languages came in very handy. He's fluent in about six languages. We spent a lot of time in each other's bedrooms watching TV and ordering room service. The room service waiters were often the focus of our jokes. 'Hello boys!' Because we were in foreign places most of the time we could talk in slang and they wouldn't know what we were saying. They'd be stood there for ages with their trays, looking confused, while we were running around in fits of laughter acting out a whole big palaver.

To my delight, Jim and I were getting closer by the day. We spent a lot of time talking and by now he knew how much I fancied him. Nothing happened between us, but there was definitely a vibe there. We began to behave like really good mates, messing around and having a laugh. I remember Louie and Carmine shouting, 'Oi you two, will you just pack it in?' as Jim tickled me and I rolled around on the floor in hysterical fits. We had good times together, but we were a bit like a couple of kids playing silly little games, like that slap-slap game with your hands. It was all very childish, innocent and naïve, although through it all I felt an underlying sexual tension. Only he didn't seem to. And that really got to me.

Previously I'd always been the one in control of relationships and sex, the one who made a man suddenly feel shy or intimidated. I've always been quite forceful and powerful with men, pushing things to the limit.

This time the roles were completely reversed. I felt nervous when I saw him, self-conscious about what I said and was always trying to impress him. He, on the other hand, just seemed totally at ease with himself and laid-back.

Off stage he seemed uninterested in me, apart from as a friend. On stage it was a different story though. He did little things to tease me, things that made me think he had to like me really. At one point during 'Do It', when we clasped hands and leant away from each other, he'd stroke my palm with his middle finger and give me a look. As time went on, he did things like that all the time. He caressed me, tickled me or even licked my cheek or arm as we moved towards each other. It was quite overtly sexual, but I couldn't react because I was singing. I was just like, 'Gasp!' In shock. Then when we came off stage, he'd revert to being matey, as if nothing had happened.

One night he hurt his back during a show. He had a recurring back injury and one false move could set it off again. I said to the girls, 'Jim has to come with us. He can't go on that bus.' On the plane I put my head in his lap and he stroked my face, but there was nothing sexual about it. Dancers are very touchy-feely and we were just being dancers.

Then slowly his attitude began to change and we began to talk about the possibility of being together. I rang Rebecca to see what she thought about it.

'Go with your heart!' she advised – ever the romantic Gemini (just like me).

So the next time Fjöl came to visit me I just came out with it and told him I didn't want to be with him any more. He didn't seem surprised. 'You want to be with your dancer, don't you?' he asked. He'd sussed me.

'Well, I haven't done anything with him yet, but yes I want to be with him,' I said. I was pretty much telling the truth. Nothing much had happened but it was about to kick off and I didn't want to do anything behind Fjöl's back. I owed him that at least. I know he was upset about splitting up, but we left on honest terms. Fjöl is a really, really good friend of mine to this day and I hope he always will be.

Strange things started happening with Jim. I'd be looking for him and he'd be looking for me and we'd walk round a corner and bump into each other.

'Are you looking for me?'

'Yes!'

Then one day during a break we went for a walk outside the venue, for a dose of green leaves and grass and trees. We both looked up at the same time and saw the trail of an aeroplane in the sky. As we watched, it began to form a heart shape.

'We are meant to be together, aren't we?' I said.

And he said, 'Well, maybe we are.'

Everything changed one night in March, just before I split up with Fjöl. Jim and I were in my hotel suite and Jim had just finished speaking to his girlfriend on the phone.

'I want to kiss you.' I said as he hung up.

Jim looked at me with a steady gaze. 'I can't. I'm with someone,' he said.

'Well I'm with someone too,' I said, staring back.

We kissed.

Jim had big soft lips and they felt amazing as they touched mine. We kissed once, very gently. It was over in a minute but I was on a high for days afterwards – really giggly and happy. I didn't care that he seemed quite awkward as he kissed me, didn't notice that he held my hips really stiffly, like an eight-year-old would, with rigid arms and hands. The only thing that mattered at the time was that something was finally happening between us. If only I'd known what I was letting myself in for.

21

YOU ARE EVERYTHING

I started panicking about what to wear as I was getting ready to go out on Friday 13 March. Not because I felt in the least bit superstitious, but because I had a sense that something was going to happen with Jim that night. We were in Barcelona, a fantastic vibey city, and the plan was to go out drinking and clubbing. I must have tried on practically everything in my going-out trunk before I decided on a pair of camouflagey, mustard and black meshed hipsters and a matching bandeau top with thin silver chain straps. Tonight's the night, I kept thinking.

As it turned out, it was and it wasn't. After a full-on night of tequila shot drinking a load of us went back to my suite at the Hotel Arts, which was kitted out with Bang & Olufsen systems and had an incredible view of the city through its floor-to-ceiling glass walls. There on the sofa was a massive bunch of flowers from Fjöl – thirty-two roses in all – with a note saying 'I'm really sorry we're not together any more.' They had just been delivered, about an hour before we got back, and I hadn't bothered to put them in a vase yet.

As the night wore on, people left in dribs and drabs until the only ones left were Jim and me. Alone at last, I thought, as we played music and talked and watched the sun come up over the city from the fifteenth floor.

It truly was a beautiful sight. Light streamed into the room and we found ourselves lying beside one another on the bed. But guess what? We both fell asleep.

I woke up feeling a bit gutted. Nothing had happened! Once again I began to question whether Jim actually fancied me. On the other hand, I was quite relieved. I hadn't spoken to any of the girls about him and felt I had to ask their permission before anything happened. It may seem stupid, but that's the way it was with us girls. By now Geri was well in with Christian Storm, her dancer, even though there had been quite a lot of resistance from the rest of us. Their relationship had set a bad precedent, so the Jim-and-me situation had to be kept pretty quiet until I was sure I wanted to go there.

As a group we had always insisted on total professionalism. We'd drilled it into each other that we had to set clear boundaries in our relationships with the people we worked with, especially the people who were in 'our gang' (like the hair and make-up artists) but not actually in the Spice Gang, which consisted of just us five. So you can imagine what going out with your dancer would do to the dynamic of the Spice Force Five. Obviously it caused tension and disrupted the unity of the group, which was far worse for me than for Jim. Then again, that woman's need kept rising up in me and I couldn't wait to have sex with him.

The next morning Emma popped into my room. I was in the bath and Jim was in the bathroom talking to me.

'Oh my God, what a great night! Great music, nice people . . .'

Jim froze at the sound of Emma's voice.

'I'm just in the bath!' I shouted, dying of laughter. I could see Emma through the crack of the bathroom door, sitting on my bed and chatting away as if to thin air.

Little did she know that Jim was edging his way behind the door, trying to remain inconspicuous. I'd told him that I didn't want the other four to know anything about us and he seemed petrified of being caught. Even though nothing had happened between us, it was obviously going to look a bit strange that, one: he'd stayed the night in my room and two: there I am naked in the bath in front of him. Panic-stricken he launched himself into the water with me, fully clothed, and hid himself behind the shower curtain. 'What the hell do I do?' he mouthed. I felt like I was back at school, trying to hold back the giggles. I just about held it together and yelled, 'Do you know what, Emma? I think I might just go back to bed for a bit. I'll come down to your room in half an hour.'

'Okay,' she replied, and got up to leave. As soon as we heard the door click, Jim stood up, his clothes sopping wet and dripping all over the place. The next minute we were rolling around laughing. Of course, I was delighted that he was going to have to take off his clothes to get them dried, revealing his gorgeous body.

A couple of days later, I asked the girls how they would feel if me and Jim got together.

'Well if you like him, you like him,' said Melanie.

'If you want to be with him, be with him,' Vicky said. 'Just as long as it doesn't interfere with work.'

Once we made it official a week or so later, it did change things. There was a definite distance between the dancers and Jim and between me and the girls. In Jim's case it seemed to the others that he played on it and behaved in a very self-important way. I think it made the other dancers a bit wary of him and when he sensed that, apparently he told them, 'Just because I'm f***ing one of the talent doesn't mean you have to shut me out.' If he'd been a bit cleverer he would have been much subtler – and if I'd been a bit cleverer I guess I should have *got out then*. Instead, the more ostracised he became, the more protective I felt about him. It was Them against Us.

Our first proper date was in Paris towards the end of March. I was really excited as I left my room at Le Bristol and got into the glass lift taking me down to where Jim was waiting in the lobby. I was wearing a little black skirt of Vicky's, my Dolce & Gabbana leopard skin basque, Dolce & Gabbana boots and I had my hair (and a false hair piece) tied into a ponytail plait. I looked fantastic. As the lift slowed before it reached the ground floor, I watched Jim staring up at me, with an awe-struck look on his face. It was like a scene out of a film.

He took me to the Buddha Bar, a beautiful restaurant in the centre of Paris with low lighting and candles everywhere, mosaic tables, Indian music and a massive statue of Buddha in the centre of the room. We had a great dinner and afterwards we went back to my suite and stayed up talking. I was dying for him to make a move on me, but once again he didn't. Normally I always make the first move but for some reason I was waiting for him (I don't know why!).

We didn't have sex together for a long time and, to be honest, I can't remember where or when the first time was. The only full-on sex I can remember us having while on tour was somewhere in America, round the back, behind the stage, where the tour buses were parked. Oh, and also in one of the bottom bunks on the tour bus one night. I don't remember it very well because, to be honest, it was unmemorable.

I couldn't understand why I liked Jim so much because sex was always very important to me in a relationship – and still is to a certain extent. In my previous relationships it was always a case of, 'Unless you give me orgasm after orgasm, then forget it!' Sex hadn't been a problem and was never lacking. I'd been out with people whose reaction to me was usually, 'Oh my God, I can't believe you fancy me!' I'd tended to choose the oddballs who were really grateful that I even looked at them. And in return I'd be grateful and happy to learn from them and experiment. It wasn't a power trip, it was more a voyage of discovery.

Jim was totally different, the opposite of everything I'd known. We'd have sex and that was it. Just sex. Even though it wasn't what I was used to, for some reason I was impressed. Wow, I thought, for the first time I'm with someone who could take it or leave it. It just didn't seem to matter to him whether he had sex or not. I couldn't understand it but I was intrigued – and determined to win him over.

If I analyse why I was so mad about him, I think it may have had something to do with the fact that he reminded me of my dad in some ways (my first love and my dad – what a combination!). Like my dad, Jim had his rules, a set way of thinking and he was very serious and authoritative. There were things he wanted me to change about myself, but at the time I felt he was genuinely trying to help me become a better person and I was open to it. At first he said things in a nice way. 'Don't be so loud, Melanie. Listen to what people are saying. Be calm.' Since he was around thirty – not a giddy young dancer at all – I assumed he was really wise.

There was so much about this relationship that felt new. Obviously he wasn't the first person to tell me to calm down but it was the first time I'd ever really listened. It was also the first time I'd given in to love and tried to share it fifty-fifty. I was usually the dominant one in relationships and I'd never let anyone come close to dominating me before, or even into that little bit of yourself that you call your own. (My essence? My core?

Whatever you call it, I'd never let anyone in there before). Most importantly, he was the first man I'd ever wanted to marry and have a baby with. I was so desperate for it to work that I was prepared to make allowances – in fact whatever it took. That was the start of the downward journey towards losing my identity.

I was passionate about him, but in my diary I wrote, *Please God, please help him to try and have sex with me.* It bugged me and bugged me until finally I sat him down one day and said, 'What is wrong with you?'

'I can't have sex in these circumstances,' he replied, looking pained. 'I feel under so much pressure that I just can't relax.'

'What do you mean, under pressure?' I asked, confused.

'You, know, going out with "Mel B", getting a hard time from all the dancers . . .'

He seemed genuinely upset so I believed what he was saying. I tried to put myself in his shoes and imagine what it would be like to be going out with a Spice Girl. To some extent I understood how hard it was to be put under the spotlight so suddenly. I hadn't forgotten the early days of Spice fame. But it was still difficult to accept it as an excuse for not having sex. I mean, come on, everyone's not in the bed with us when we're getting down and grindy. But what else could I do? I was in love so I dealt with it.

In early April, we arrived back in England for the UK leg of the tour. It was great to be home, performing to the home crowd. We played Glasgow, Manchester and Birmingham and did an amazing eight shows at Wembley, every single one packed out. It was a relief to have some time to catch up with family and friends and, in my case, go house hunting. It was high time for me to find myself a permanent base.

The lease had run out on my flat and I had to find somewhere quickly. Otherwise all my furniture was going to have to go into storage, which would be an expensive hassle. I looked at loads of houses, even a repossession around the corner from my flat, a ten-bedroom house with a tiny garden. I found an agent and he showed me round a few run down houses in Bishops Avenue ('Millionaire's Row') for £3 million. Most of them were dilapidated and needed to be gutted, in other words, no good at all. There was one house with a really psychedelic interior that I liked, but there was so much to do to it that I decided against it.

I called upon agent/designer Linda Paige to help in the search. By this point I knew that I didn't want to live in London. It's too stressful! I looked around Michael Caine's house and a few other country houses that were amazing, but just not me. Often the downstairs area was great and you'd envisage what you could do with it, but then the upstairs would be like back home in Kirkstall. Tiny bedrooms next door to each other and one communal bathroom. I thought, If I'm going to pay this much money, I want my family and friends to be able to set up camp in their bedrooms and not be disturbed when they come and stay with me.

One house I saw had two stuffed lions at either side of the door, which was a sign of authority within the owner's religious group, apparently. I walked in, screamed the house down and ran out again. The lions looked so alive that it was freaky. I had to be coaxed back inside. A woman in a sari showed me round. The whole house had been 'prepared' for someone to view it and it seemed unlived in and bare. I might have bought it, but it just wasn't homely enough. There was one beautiful Hansel and Gretel-type house that I loved, but I instantly saw danger. I had visions of a two-year-old tumbling down the creepy old stairs and getting its head stuck in the banister.

A couple of days before we went off touring again, I went to see a manor house on the Thames near Marlow. It was the sixth and last house that we viewed that day. As we drove through the gate Linda told me that Fergie already had her eye on it. Originally built in the sixteenth century, it's a beautiful house with an amazing history and wonderful grounds. Well I knew I wanted it before I'd even seen what it was like inside. I walked right round the whole outside of the house, then said, 'I'm having it. I really want it.' The housekeeper showed us inside. It was all green walls and Picassos – just hideous – but I took in the oak beams and overall structure and decided, This is where I'm going to live. My offer was accepted the next day.

Meanwhile Nancy, manager of Spice HQ, had found some fantastic premises in Marylebone for the Spice Office as we ended up calling it, and employed four people to work with her. First there was Jo Allen, our feminine, well turned-out accountant, who always had time for you (well, she did for me). I loved our conversations, which were mainly about men! Nancy's PA Julie Cooke had that fresh wash-and-go hair look. Julie was cool even in the middle of a disaster and her exciting social life intrigued me. Calm and consistent Julia Curnock was a lovely fair-skinned redhead who seemed totally professional. You could dump a load of stuff on her table and it wouldn't faze her. She was precise about everything, even her lunch – a sandwich, a packet of crisps and half a can of Coca Cola. Needless to say her files were in perfect order and her desk was perfectly arranged. Julia ended up working on my diary and organising my day-to-day life.

Finally, there was Jamie Vickery, the only man in the office. His personality goes without saying, because coping with intense, demanding, sometimes stressed-out female colleagues takes a certain kind of man. I loved Jamie from the first time I met him. He really understood women and was never judgmental. A hard worker, he enjoyed learning and set himself a different new task each day. What topped it off was his sense of humour. It definitely got him through! When I asked his opinion about what I was wearing, he looked at me as a friend would, not in a pervy way. (Great husband material, or the ultimate big brother.) I used to leave stupid notes on his desk, saying 'I love you' and when I talked to him I sometimes had the feeling that I could possibly get done for harassment at work! Rebecca Cripps, editor of *Spice Magazine*, was also allotted a section of the office and I often popped in for a chat with her when I was passing. She was great to talk to. Her desk was piled high with fan mail, photographs, contact sheets, newspapers, magazines, books and Spice merchandise.

We had a five-day break after the final Birmingham gig so I arranged a short holiday for me and Jim in the South of France. I found a little two-bedroom flat way up in the mountains above Saint Tropez and hired a scooter for us to get around on. It was an odd little apartment, all done out in marble, with furniture and art that just didn't go together. Still, we had a very chilled time there, eating and sleeping and riding the scooter to the beach.

One day we were lying on the sand hiding behind some slightly unsafe DIY windbreakers that we'd constructed when I heard a familiar voice shouting, 'Melanie! Melanie!' It was Charlotte's sister Lisa, my idol from dancing class, who now lives in France. It was lovely to see her with her family and have the chance to catch up on an adult basis. That evening we met up with her and her husband Steph and went to a fantastic club. As the night went on the wine started flowing and I got on one of my mad ones. I hit the dance floor. The music was great. What *is* this song? I thought to myself. Then it clicked. 'Oh my God! How funny.' It was a remix of 'Who Do You Think You Are?' and there I was, dancing to it.

I took three pregnancy tests with me on that trip because I was really hoping I'd be pregnant, although the odds were probably against it. Every other day I got up and rushed to the loo to see if I could make that blue line appear in the tiny window of the tester stick, but it didn't. I was going to have to persuade Jim to have sex more often if it was the last thing I did.

Our first show back in Europe was in Paris on 12 May. The next day I decided to surprise Jim, who had recently had his eyebrow pierced.

'Come on Emma,' I said. 'I'm going to have my eyebrow pierced and I need you there to hold my hand.'

'Oh Melanie, you're mad,' she laughed.

Jim had his own surprise planned that day. We'd arranged to go out to dinner after the show, but instead of seeing my boyfriend in the lobby when I came down in the lift, I found Vern waiting there instead.

'Come with me,' he said with a conspiratorial grin. I couldn't understand why Jim wasn't there, but Vern was so smiley-smiley that I just went along with it. I had to walk along in high heels with bare legs in the freezing cold and I wasn't happy but I sensed that, whatever was going on, I was going to like it.

Vern dropped me off at the Buddha Bar. A waiter took me to a table and sat me down opposite a huge bunch of flowers. What's this about? I wondered. I reached over and took out the note that was wedged among the stems. Inside a small envelope was a card with the lyrics of 'You're The Only One' by Luther Vandross written on it. My heart missed a beat.

Jim came over to the table. By now I could tell that something funny was going on. I didn't say anything but inside I was totally churned up. What's happening? We had a lovely dinner. Jim had pre-ordered the exact same meal that we'd eaten at the exact same table on our first date. Then he poured a glass of champagne, got down on one knee and said shyly, 'Will you . . .'

Before he had a chance to finish I said, 'Yes!' I sat there entranced as he took a little box out of his pocket and placed it in my hands. Inside was a thumb ring engraved with the words 'To Be Or Not To Be', the same phrase he has tattooed on his back. I guess there was a pun there but I didn't notice it at the time. I was too busy brimming with happiness. I put the ring onto my left thumb and gazed at it speechless.

For a few moments we were fixed on each other, lost in our own world. Then with huge grins on our faces, we went up to the bar for a drink. Grace Jones was there with some famous artist friend of hers. She summoned us over with a wave of her hand so we sat down and started chatting. She's quite an intimidating woman. Her sunglasses were lying on the bar top and as I reached over to try them on she roared, 'Who told you that you could put those on?' Then she let out a huge laugh. 'Hey Melanie, we're going to loads of clubs tonight. Come with us!' she offered.

This time I laughed. 'No, I've just got engaged. I'm off home.' We air-kissed and left the Buddha Bar.

Back at the hotel, I ran straight to Emma's room and screamed, 'Guess what? I've just got engaged!'

'Oh really!' was Emma's response.

I took her by the hand and dragged her into my room. 'Noooo, Mel, I'm not supposed to go in there!' she protested. I opened the door and gasped. There were white lilies all over the room, on the bed, on the tables, hanging from the light switches, in the wardrobe, everywhere.

'Did you know about this, Emma?' I demanded. She just smiled and looked sheepish.

'Right, I'm going to leave you two to have a romantic night,' she said.

But I didn't want her to go anywhere. I was incredibly excited and wanted to share my excitement with her. Weird, huh? I was more bothered about spending the rest of the evening with Emma than with Jim. He and I had a very strange relationship. Needless to say, although he slept in my bed that night, we didn't . . .

I put off ringing my mum to tell her the news because I knew her reaction wouldn't be positive. I was right. When I finally phoned her a couple of days later, she said, 'Oh Melanie,' in a tone of voice that spoke volumes.

'It's fine, Mum, it's fine,' I said. 'We're meant to be together.'

I had convinced myself that me and Jim were destined for each other because we had so much in common, especially when it came to our backgrounds. It seemed as though we'd been through so many of the same things at the same time in life. Experiences like being struggling dancers, no one understanding you when you were younger – the usual kind of stuff that in fact a lot of people go through. Also, Jim never knew his dad and I'd hated mine for my teenage years. A lot of our past experiences were similar, as I saw it. Everything seemed to link up (and if it didn't, I found a way to make it link up).

Jim proposed on 13 May and after that I began to see the numbers one and three everywhere. You know how that happens when you've got something in your head? Like when you get pregnant and you suddenly see babies everywhere. It's synchronicity. I was seeing number 13 buses go past, staying in room number 13 and finding myself in dressing room 13 all the time, so I decided it was my lucky number. I know, I'll get married on a thirteenth, I thought. I should have remembered back to that Friday the thirteenth when a wayward electronic barrier shattered my windscreen on the way back from picking Melanie up at the David Lloyd gym in Watford. It wasn't my lucky number at all.

Next we decided to tell Jim's family. I organised a massive do in a hired room at the Grand Hotel in Amsterdam (and paid for it). I really made an effort with my appearance that day and wore a tight red Plein Sud cat-suit. Apparently they all thought we were going to announce that I was having a baby, which made me want to get pregnant even more. It was a bit of a weird day because I hardly saw Jim, but I was happy all the same. I'd found the person I wanted to be with forever, so I thought, and I wanted to tell everyone.

Jim held a lot back, which kept me wanting more. I thought I had a lifetime of discovery ahead. He was going to teach me about spirituality and how to be calm. Obviously it didn't work out that way.

But nothing could shake my faith in him at the time. That evening the usual gang went out to a club – me, Emma, Eszteca, Carmine, Louie and another of the dancers, Robert. Jim went off to get drinks for everyone. In the meantime this beautiful blonde came swanning across the dance floor, heading straight for me with a look of concern on her face. I didn't know her, although she looked vaguely familiar. She seemed to know me.

'Be careful,' she whispered. 'Just . . . be careful, that's all.'

Suddenly I remembered where I'd seen her face – in a photograph in Jim's Filofax. She was *that* ex-girlfriend. I was taken aback but managed to splutter, 'Don't be so stupid,' before I turned my back on her. I never told Jim about it.

During those weeks I was so wrapped up in what was happening with Jim that I hardly noticed what was going on with the group. To be honest, as our lives became ever more manic we'd begun to lose touch with what was going on in each other's heads. There wasn't the time or space to dig as deep as we had in the past. When one of us was in a bad mood, we often couldn't stop to discuss it because we had twenty interviews ahead of us. 'Let's talk about it tonight,' we'd agree, but by the evening we'd be knackered or on another plane going somewhere else. We became a bit too busy to actually care as much for each other as we had done.

Of course I'd registered that Geri was becoming increasingly distant from the rest of us, but I didn't think much of it. I assumed that it was because she wanted to spend her time with Christian. But as the European tour went on, it was impossible not to notice how secretive she was becoming – and her weight was going up and down like a yo-yo. She seemed to be off in her own world and the more she ostracised herself, the more the rest of us closed ranks.

Earlier on in the tour we'd had a bit of a disagreement about her role in 'Denying', one of the songs in the first part of the show. It was set in a café and Geri had decided to play the part of a roller skating waitress. She did this whole acting thing as though she was in a major Broadway show and her name was Dizzy Dora The Roller Skater With Her Very Own Spotlight. You've got to hand it to her, she had big balls, because she couldn't really skate and was uncoordinated.

Well, there I'd be singing away, and suddenly Geri would be in front of me, gliding precariously back and forth and blocking the audience's view. What the f*** is she doing? I'd think. In the end she was told by the group that she could only skate in one particular area. Possibly feeling a bit guilty, she bought us each a pair of roller boots, which was nice. We all spent our time whizzing around between sound checks after that. It was great.

From the very beginning we'd had a pact that we'd tell each other if any of us wanted to leave the group – and it would be our own little secret between the five of us. So although I started to feel that something was wrong I didn't have a clue that Geri was planning to go her own way.

On 26 May we flew back to London from Helsinki. It was one of those mad flights we sometimes had, with loads of shouting and laughter and messing around. Geri seemed fine – we all did – but the next day she left the group. In the morning Andrew Thompson called to let us all know she wasn't coming back. I don't think any of us really believed it at first. Then

Mel, Vicky, Emma and me turned up at Television Centre for the *Lottery Show*, and Geri didn't. It was as simple as that. She was gone. It was a huge shock. I was devastated. 'God, she calls me a friend and never even told me!' To cover our tracks until we sorted things out we pretended she was ill.

What's happened? Where is she? Is she all right? Why has she decided to leave? Is there anything we could have done to stop her? The questions went round and round my head. But there wasn't really time to think. We were taking the evening flight to Oslo where we had a show the next day and if Geri wasn't coming with us we had a lot of rearranging to do. It was mad. We didn't have a spare moment to absorb what had happened. We just had to get on with things. Still, I couldn't stop the thoughts whirring inside my head. What was she playing at? Geri's the kind of person who thinks ahead, so it must have been planned.

Finally I realised that I had to stop torturing myself. What was the point in asking questions when Geri wasn't around to answer them? I couldn't get depressed. I had a job to do. The four of us had less than twenty-four hours to sort out new vocals to all our songs and rearrange all the choreography. On top of that, the next day was my dad's birthday and he was flying out to Oslo for a party I was supposed to be organising. The day after that was my birthday. Talk about brain overload.

There was a part of me that found it all really exciting, though. In a sick kind of way I'm at my most productive in a crisis. No longer could I get through the show on auto drive, because half the time I wasn't sure if I was supposed to be singing one of Geri's lines or not. We'd all look at each other on stage as if to say, 'Is it me now?' because we had to rearrange the vocals on every song. It was more strange than difficult, especially doing the opening lines of 'Wannabe' with Melanie. Her voice is a lot higher than Geri's and in the beginning she'd sing the words, whereas they were meant to be shouted. Melanie was really nervous about doing that bit. 'Are people going to enjoy it as much?' she'd say. Then she got into it and we started having a laugh with it.

As soon as Geri left, I asked Victoria Williamson about her plans. By now Tor and I didn't see eye-to-eye on many things. Being from totally different backgrounds we had different ways of approaching and doing things. I'm direct and up front; she's more subtle, which makes me a bit wary.

She'd always got on best with Geri but obviously the rest of us needed her with us. It was hard enough having only one PA for the whole group anyway. I'll never forget the conversation we had, in a wood-panelled hotel room full of black leather upholstered furniture.

'We need to know now what you want to do,' I told her. 'If you leave and go to work for Geri, you will have betrayed everyone's trust in you.'

'I would never, *ever* do that to you lot! I just wouldn't,' she exclaimed.

Somehow I didn't believe her. 'Look, I know what you're up to. Just be honest and say it. Give me that, if nothing else.' She kept on insisting that she was staying with us but within a week she was gone. Where? To work with Geri of course. And where's she working now? Not with Geri.

My dad flew out to Oslo for his forty-fourth birthday on 28 May. It was great to have him there.

'Dad, I've got you a surprise,' I said, about half an hour before I went on stage.

I'd arranged for some piercing to take place in my dressing room. Everybody gathered round in anticipation. I walked my dad into the room, sat him down and said, 'Happy Birthday Dad. You're gonna get pierced.'

'Oh great. You must be joking!' he laughed.

In walked this gorgeous Singaporean girl with long flowing hair, wearing a really tight outfit. Her piercing tool was a dagger. My poor dad went into shock when he saw it and I was in fits of laughter on the floor. I'd bought him two diamond earrings from Tiffany's.

'This is what's going in your ear!' I told him.

'All right,' he whispered.

As the dagger went in he let out a high pitched squeal and I took Polaroids of his grimacing face. It was hysterical. He couldn't really let go and show the pain because there was a roomful of people watching him. Everyone got caught up with it and Jade, Emma's boyfriend, ended up having his eyebrow done. It was a great way to start the night.

Later in the evening I held a 'Ho-down party' in my suite to celebrate our birthdays. The dress code was jeans and a white T-shirt and when each guest arrived they were given a cowboy hat, a bandanna or a sheriff's badge to wear. It was a brilliant night. And what did the girls get me? A strippergram!

The next night was our last show in Europe and then we had a break. It was time for a proper holiday at last. Nancy Berry, international president of Virgin, had offered us the use of her villa in Tuscany, so me, Danielle, Emma and our mums headed straight off to Italy at the end of May. It was a fantastic ten days, sunbathing, swimming, snoozing, watching videos and eating great Italian food. Danielle's boyfriend Cory flew out as a surprise for her eighteenth birthday – along with Emma's boyfriend Jade and Jim. Me and Emma met them at the door and brought them upstairs to where the others were. Danielle went into shock when she saw Cory because she had no idea he was coming. We had a fantastic slap-up meal that night. It was a lovely, quiet, family vibe.

For me – and I think for Emma too – it was also a difficult time. Geri's departure from the group hadn't really hit me until then and as the reality sank in, I experienced some moments of deep sadness. I started questioning what had happened all over again and continually asked myself what I could have done to make things different. When I look back now I don't think it was anyone's fault, even though the press tried to point the finger a few times. It was just something that Geri had to do for herself. I wish she'd done it differently and given us all a chance to say goodbye, but I accepted her decision to go. It was hard, though. I really, really missed her.

It didn't help that as the holiday wore on I could tell that my mum didn't think much of Jim. She was nice enough to him, but I could see that she wasn't keen. One morning, when we were all lying by the pool, we heard an ear-piercing scream coming from inside the house. Everybody rushed in to see what had happened and found Jim in the shower, yelling his head off. He'd cut his foot and there was quite a bit of blood, but it turned out that it was only a surface wound. My mum got pretty impatient with him. Her opinion of him was near to zilch.

The next day me and Jim travelled across Italy to stay with his best friend Ozzie in a town near the Italian lakes. Small, skinny and lanky, Ozzie was a very nice guy and obviously a good mate to Jim. He was still living in the same flat that Jim had fled to several years before, when things went wrong for him in Amsterdam. The flat was very basic, but it was nice to see where Jim had lived all those years ago. Downstairs there was a funky little bar where he and Ozzie used to practise their dance routines. We'd go down there at night for a drink and spent hours messing around doing Amsterdam jazz dancing together.

I'd had a beautiful engagement ring made by Boodle & Dunthorne a few weeks before and took it to Italy with me. I'd designed it myself and was really pleased with the result. It was quite chunky, but there was something delicate about it too – two joined circles and a diamond-studded cross linking them. A friend of Jim and Ozzie's was a photographer and offered to take some pictures of us at the beach. The day before the shoot, I took him to one side and told him that I planned to propose to Jim and give him the engagement ring while he was taking the photos. 'So when you see me speaking, take a photo!'

At night me and Jim slept on a scuzzy mattress on Ozzie's floor. The bedding was horrible and the mattress brought me up in a rash on my face. I am pretty sure that it was around this time that I became pregnant. Me and Jim had sex so rarely that it couldn't really have happened at any other time.

Back then I was so in love with Jim that I just didn't see the warning signs, even when something quite disturbing happened towards the end of the week and Jim told me that he needed to borrow some money.

'I've got to meet this girl. I owe her some money,' he said.

'What do you mean, you owe her money?' I asked.

Jim explained that he'd borrowed a whole load of cash from one of his ex-girlfriends a couple of years before. Stupidly I gave him the money to pay her back. I didn't like it, but went along with it anyway. Neither of us mentioned it again. It was just swept under the carpet with everything else.

22

STUTTER, STUTTER

Touring in America was a very different experience to Europe. A lot of the venues were open air and people made a huge amount of effort. It wasn't only the kids who dressed up as Spice Girls, the mums and grannies had a proper go at it too. So you'd see fifty- and sixty-year-olds in bunches and babydolls or leopard skin basques, with full-on hair and make-up and Buffalo boots. It was great. The crowds seemed to scream louder than they did in Europe. 'I love you! I love you! I love you!'

Our first two shows were in Miami on 13 and 14 June and boy, was it hot! On stage the sweat was pouring off me and backstage the costume changes were easy because everything just slipped off. The spotlight on us was intense in more ways than one. Would America still love us without Ginger Spice? It seemed that they would. We put signs outside each venue stating that Geri would not be performing and that refunds were available. Out of everyone who had bought tickets, only around seven people asked for their money back.

The tour cycle began again, endlessly rolling across the plains and through the cities of the fabulous US of A. During those three months, three quarters of a million people came to see us in concert. Our Madison Square Garden shows in New York sold out within twelve minutes of going on sale – at a rate of 1,200 a minute. The Los Angeles show sold out in eight minutes. The Spice Girls were in demand in America.

We were constantly on the go, rushing around in cars and planes and meeting all kinds of different people. But even though it was manic, it felt quite normal and safe because we were always with the same crew, who'd become our extended family in a way. Quite a few times we organised trips to places like Niagara Falls and Disneyland for the entire crew. We were like a cross between a travelling circus and a school. Every couple of weeks the kids were let out to play.

In all we travelled 14,337 miles to do forty shows in thirty-two cities. Vicky always knew exactly how many more dates we had left to go. Even in Europe she was saying, 'We've got sixty-four performances left, girls!' By America we'd all joined in the countdown. There were times when I absolutely hated being on tour. Times when I just wanted a bit of peace and quiet for a couple of days and knew I couldn't have it. There was always the next show to get to, the next hotel, venue, dressing room, sound check and performance. I still gave a hundred per cent to every show, I never thought of giving less, even though it was tiring and sometimes I felt like I was in prison ticking off the days.

We had promotion to do before each show and a few of the American journalists just didn't get it. 'Does Girl Power mean you hate boys?' 'Why do you wear sexy clothes if you don't want to attract boys?' and the dreaded 'How did you guys get together?' Some of them obviously hadn't ever heard of the word 'research'. Half the time we answered tongue-in-cheek or one of us would go off on a tangent. Not once were any of our interviews completely straight and serious. That was impossible for us.

There were lots of questions about Geri but what could we say? We were still completely in the dark ourselves. I tried ringing her to see how she was. The one time she answered she was at George Michael's house.

'How are you?' I asked.

'I'm fine.'

It was a bit of a nothing conversation and she changed her number soon after that.

TV and radio idents came after the interviews. 'Hi we're the Spice Girls and you're watching *Music Tonight!*' Then a last-minute meet-and-greet with local VIPs and their kids. I used to dread these because I could never think of anything to say to a roomful of complete strangers. 'All right! Hi! How are you? Looking forward to the show?' It was all a bit forced and half the time the people we were meeting were speechless.

Sometimes there were people there to see us after the show. We met Steve Tyler from Aerosmith, with his wife and kids, as well as Bruce Willis and Demi Moore and their kids, Missy Elliot, Steve Baldwin, Andy Garcia, Gary Oldman, Vanessa Williams and Lionel Richie. We invited Madonna to our Madison Square Garden show and she brought her daughter to see us at the interval. Lourdes was so gorgeous that we spent the whole time fussing over her and hardly spoke to Madonna.

Prince invited me to his album launch in New York and I took my mum and her friend Bernie. It was held at an Italian club a couple of doors down from the SoHo Grand Hotel, where we were staying, and it was a brilliant, funky party. I met some of my favourite R&B artists there, including Joe and Zhane, as well as Stevie Wonder. My mum and Bernie looked like French and Saunders as they stood on either side of Stevie, cuddling him and giggling.

Prince had the same four women round him all night. 'What do they do?' I asked.

'They do anything I want them to,' he replied.

Oh, right.

In LA we went to Courtney Love's party and met Drew Barrymore, who seemed really nice. Everywhere you looked you saw faces you recognised – Cameron Diaz, Danny DeVito, Lisa Marie Presley, Seal, Meatloaf, Marilyn Manson, Patricia Arquette. It seems funny when you can reel off celebrity names like that because the more of them that you meet, the more you come to terms with the fact that they're all just normal people.

The celebrity stuff mostly went on in New York and LA. The rest of the time it was just the crew, the dancers, the band, the tour manager and the group, day in, day out. The journey from the airport to the hotel or venue was always quite interesting. Often we'd ask the driver to turn the music up really loud so that he couldn't overhear us chatting about what we'd been doing the night before. We'd be in somewhere like Oklahoma where there was nothing on the radio but country music and one of us would ask, 'Er, can you change the channel please?' The driver would flick through all the different stations but the choice would be country, country or country. In some places there wasn't any R&B at all, just really strange folk tunes. And nine times out of ten the driver would make the mistake of turning around and saying, 'Can I have your autographs for my niece?'

Me and Emma were still travelling on the bus quite a lot. During the break we'd bought everyone on the bus a pair of BHS light and dark blue striped pyjamas. They were comfortable, easy to wash and made us look like tubes of Aquafresh toothpaste. Carmine customised his by cutting little bits off here and there while Eszteca removed one whole leg, which looked quite strange.

One night we pulled into a service station and decided to put on a bit of an act. We trooped into the shop wearing our stripy pyjamas like we were something out of *One Flew Over The Cuckoo's Nest*. We all got into character. Louie was doing back flips around the sweet stands, someone else was standing at the front of an aisle, rocking silently and staring into space. Then two Spice Girls went up to the counter and bought a basketful of sweets. The staff were in a state of shock when we left. It was brilliant. It's times like that that you never, ever forget.

Me and Jim always had a great time when we were with the others, but things didn't go so well when we were alone. I remember one of the dancers saying to me, 'If the sex isn't happening, Melanie, that must tell you something.'

'What are you talking about?' I asked.

'There must be a problem,' he went on. 'Do you not see that? Look beyond loving him and wanting to be with him. Look to what your future is going to be like together.'

'Oh stop being stupid.'

Of course, he was right. At one point he pleaded with me, 'Please don't be with him. He's not right for you.'

I started feeling really bad, desperate. Why aren't we having sex? Why doesn't he fancy me? I vividly remember having crying breakdowns to Louie and Emma. They just didn't know what to say apart from, 'Well, it needs sorting out, doesn't it?'

Louie got right into it and started setting me tasks. 'Ask him what his other relationships were like,' 'If you don't have sex within a week, report back to me and we'll review the situation.' I felt like a little girl. It got to the point where I'd done the underwear thing and I'd done the sitting down and talking and feeling compassionate towards him for being under pressure and not being able to feel aroused. One of the funnier things I did was to get drunk and shout 'F*** me! F*** me!' I didn't know what else to try.

I began to think there was something wrong with me, but then I'd be in my knickers and bra in the dressing room and Louie would pin me down and say, 'How could anybody not find you sexual? Look at you! Can't you understand, it's not you!'

I started to treat him and buy him presents, Gucci tops and things. I remember Melanie C saying, 'Please stop buying him presents. Stop it!' She really had a go at me. But I am very generous and I like giving presents. It's not that I think I'm buying you, I just like buying gifts.

It was great to be able to pay for my mum and Bernie to come over and meet me in New York. It was my mum's forty-second birthday and I wanted it to be a celebration to remember, but there was trouble almost from the moment she arrived. She just didn't like what she saw in Jim. The afternoon of her birthday she took him upstairs to her room and had a really heavy chat with him, accusing him of all kinds of things. Bernie was there too. My mum can be very direct at times.

'Why are you marrying my daughter?' she asked. 'Are you marrying her for money?'

Soon Jim was in tears. 'How can you say something like that?'

'The only way I will be convinced that you're marrying my daughter because you love her is if you sign a pre-nuptial, because I don't believe you do love her.'

'No I won't,' he said at first. Later he said, 'All right then, I will if you want me to.'

This episode created a distance between me and my mum. I was torn. I loved her dearly and I did partly listen to what she was saying, but I was also madly in love with Jim and I wanted to get married and settle down and have a family with him.

That evening I held a party for my mum's birthday in a little Indian restaurant in SoHo and organised a strippergram. Obviously Jim was not invited. The restaurant was a fantastic place, with multi-coloured silk partitions, belly dancers and hookah pipes, but I was hardly speaking to Mum because of what had happened earlier with Jim. I couldn't believe she'd been so rude to him. We had a good heart to heart before she left New York, though. She didn't mince her words. I didn't know what to think. Heartbroken, I went off to find Jim.

'I love you. I love you. I want to be with you!' he implored when I told him what I had to say.

'Well I don't think I can,' I replied weakly.

We got into a huge discussion about it. I kept saying, 'I want to be with you but . . .' The problem was that I wasn't splitting up with him because I wanted to. I split up with him after hearing what my mum and other people had said. For a while it made me think, Well maybe I am better off without him. I don't know how it happened, but the next day it was front page news in England. Scary Spice Splits! It was official and I had to live with it, but I wasn't happy about it. Although it seemed like the right thing to do, I felt miserable.

A couple of days after that, Vicky came bursting into my room and announced, 'I did a pregnancy test last night. I'm pregnant.'

She was grinning from ear to ear, obviously ecstatic about the idea of being a mum. 'That's fantastic news Vicky!' I screamed, hugging her tightly. 'Get me one of those tests!' I exclaimed on impulse.

'Come up to my room then,' she replied, and off we rushed.

I did the test in her bathroom. For some reason I thought you had to shake the tester stick for this particular brand so I was flicking wee all over the place. Then I checked the test window. A faint blue line began to appear. 'No I'm *not!*' I shouted. It couldn't be true. Not now. I went straight to the same doctor Vicky had been to earlier in the day and there it was, a tiny little dot on the scan. Oh my God! I was about three or four weeks pregnant. I had to tell Jim.

The pregnancy made everything all right again. I couldn't get back together with Jim fast enough. Suddenly everything had slotted into place. I wanted to be with him, I'd always wanted to have a baby and now I was pregnant with a miracle child. There was no escaping my destiny now, even though I knew in my heart that the relationship just wasn't right.

23

MY PREROGATIVE

Life is like a bus stop. You sit there for ages while nothing happens, then suddenly three buses come along at once. I'll take the analogy a little bit further. I was already living in a busy bus terminal and suddenly it became a train station and an airport all in one.

I thought it was a joke when Ashley Newton (now working for Virgin America) phoned to say that Missy Elliot's record company had got in contact. They wanted to know if I'd be interested in recording a song with her. Well I'd been a huge Missy 'Misdemeanour' fan for a very long time and couldn't believe that she wanted to work with me. I didn't know it at the time, but the track was for a movie about Fifties doo wop singer Frankie Lyman called *Why Do Fools Fall In Love?* Missy was collaborating with a whole array of established black producers and performers on the soundtrack, including Usher, Mace, Destiny's Child, Timbaland and Next.

When Ashley called me about it, I said I'd have to think about it. This was partly because I was in shock and also because I wanted to consult with the other girls. It was the first time that one of us would be working away from the group and although it wasn't going to disrupt our schedule, it was a new direction and I needed to discuss it with them. I was relieved that they were more than happy for me to do it if I wanted to. They were very, very supportive.

Happy days are here again for Mum and Dad.

Me, Mum and Berni at Prince's party in New York. Guess who we bumped into – the legendary Stevie Wonder. Mum and Bernie nearly wet themselves with excitement, as you can see from their expressions.

On the set of the 'I Want You Back' video shoot, the song that I recorded with Missy Elliott. It was a long day, with six different costume changes and hairstyles.

Live and heavily pregnant on *SM:TV*, wearing the armband that my mum gave me for my twenty-first birthday. I was very superstitious about that armband and had to wear it for every performance we did.

I love this photo. Originally shot for the cover of the *Sunday Times Magazine*, it became the main image of the Blackliners 'HIV Positive Attitudes' campaign and later appeared on posters in clinics throughout the UK.

Phoenix had a personality of her own from day one. She's a real independent spirit – and very strong-willed.

Phoenix became the most important person in my life the moment she was born.

One of my favourite covers. I was very proud to be asked to do it.

Which one is the waxwork?

Listening to Dr Fox's chart countdown about to go onstage. I'd just heard I'd got to number one with the single I recorded with Missy Elliot.

Dropping some moves on a night out with my choreographer and dancers on my solo European promotional tour.

Two days later Missy called me on my mobile as I stepped off the tour bus on my way to do some promotion. I completely pooed my pants. I thought it was a wind-up at first. 'Are you sure you've got the right person?' I asked nervously.

'Yes!' she replied.

'Are you sure you want to do this with *me*?' I asked anxiously.

'Of course baby!' She sounded really lovely and just as excited as I was, which shocked me. She gave me her mobile phone number. Wow! I had Missy Elliot's phone number keyed into my mobile phone.

I recorded 'I Want You Back' on one of our days off in New York. The day before I was due into the studio I dropped by to say hello and introduce myself. I'd been on the phone to Missy all week but I wanted to meet her in person before the big day. When I got there, Destiny's Child were hard at work recording a track. Their reaction to me was really mad – 'Wow! It's Melanie from the Spice Girls!' – and I was just as impressed to meet them, if not more. It was funny, because we all stood there a bit awkwardly, not knowing what to say.

I coyly introduced myself to Missy, totally in awe, like a fish out of water in her environment. I was really hoping that this was the right move to make at that point in my career, while at the same time I knew that it was a unique opportunity and I had to grasp it. Missy struck me as a friendly faced girl's girl, open, relaxed and calm, decked out in urban street style, cool as can be. She had that grungey but perfect 'just got out of bed' look – even her baggy pants were well ironed. 'Yeah Melanie, I want you in at 12 p.m. tomorrow,' she said. I replied that I was busy in the morning and couldn't make it until 1 p.m. 'Okay,' she said with one eyebrow raised. I got the feeling that when Missy makes an arrangement, you really shouldn't question it.

That night, in my penthouse suite at the SoHo Grand, I went over and over the song. I wanted to do it proud, I wanted Missy to be pleased with my interpretation and, most importantly, I wanted to feel that it fitted my skin. Usually when I get on the mic in the studio my knee-jerk reaction is, 'I can't do it. I can't do it!' I couldn't be like that with Missy. I knew that I would be disappointed with myself if I got into the vocal booth and freaked out because it didn't feel right. It was a challenge – I had to face my fears and be instantly confident, rather than expect her to give me confidence.

Originally the track was supposed to start with a rap that said things like, *I'm so emotional, my hair is falling out, I'm drinking liquor and smoking and going crazy in my head*. There was also some swearing. I didn't like the fact that this woman (the song's narrator) was a complete wreck and out of control without a man and that the only way she could express herself was by swearing. She sounded a bit dim to me. On a professional level, I thought that the swearing might offend some of our fans. So I suggested that we make some changes. It was a really difficult subject to broach because it was Missy's song and you have to respect people's work, but she was all right about it, thank God.

When I arrived at 1.30 p.m. she wasn't around, which was slightly worrying because my schedule was so full that I only had one afternoon to put down the track. There were two really nice producers on the mixing desks and after I'd explained my predicament we got stuck in to some recording. Then Missy walked in and the atmosphere changed. Obviously the desks were her domain. She was a powerful woman and her presence was enough, not to frighten people, but to exert ultimate authority. The producers left us alone and we got down to work. I felt a little embarrassed singing in front of Missy but I soon got over it.

After I'd recorded the backing vocals and harmonies, Missy asked me to step outside. Why? What's going on? Nerves, fear, anxiousness, sweating came upon me. Oh my God, am I crap? Am I good? What does she think? She shut the studio door with a bang and I wondered whether I was going to be allowed back in there or not. Nobody explained that she needed some time alone to rewrite the beginning of the song. Her people were so loyal and in awe that they didn't say a word. Missy's got ultimate respect because she's a woman of integrity who has worked and struggled for what she believes in without let up. To have come so far and achieved so much is incredible, and in doing so she's breaking down the barriers for other people. So if Missy shuts the studio door and doesn't want anybody in there, you don't question it, except in your own head.

I was with Karin, our make-up artist, Vern and Dean Freeman, a photographer who was working closely with the Spice Girls to produce a book documenting our world tour. Jane from Virgin America was also there. I liked Jane a lot because she was down to earth, easygoing, and knew her stuff. We found our way into the chill out room, which was full of dudes and underground 'ghetto' rap artists watching MTV and eating mounds and mounds of M&Ms. No one spoke to us, I couldn't believe it. Overcompensating, I started to make conversation. 'That bowl is full of M&Ms, isn't it? It looks like everyone's picked out all of the green ones!' No one responded. Maybe they didn't catch what I was saying because of my accent. Then they started talking to each other in New York street slang and we couldn't understand a word they were saying. I looked at Karin and got the giggles. I had to get out of that room. I needed a bit of normality.

Me and Karin went off to the toilet for a giggle attack and when we came back Missy had rewritten the first part of the song, thank God. A big sigh of relief, I can relax now! But no. Back in the studio, she said, 'I want you to do your own thing at the end of the song.'

'What do you mean, "my own thing"?'

'Just rap, just chat.'

'What do you mean, "chat"? In my Leeds accent? Will anybody understand it? Oh dear.'

I got on the microphone and said, 'Actually I've been thinking about it. I don't want you back at all. Bye! See ya!' I was taking the piss as usual, but she kept it on the track anyway. She loved it – and, funnily enough, was fascinated by my accent.

I flew to New York from Nashville on a day off to shoot the video with Missy. Jim also featured in it, although the director, Hype Williams, didn't know he was my fiancé. I'd just sent off a picture with a note saying, *I want this guy in the video.* Hype Williams had had no objections. 'Yeah. He's good-looking and cool. Okay.'

My make-up on the video was amazing, applied by Missy's personal make-up artists. The Americans treat make-up as an art. They sculpted my face with light and dark contouring and made me look almost too perfect. But I took it all on board and went with it. My eyebrows were trimmed down and dyed light blonde and I had six different hairstyles during the shoot, from braids to extensions. In the last scene my body was covered with luminous green make-up. It took so long to apply that Hype Williams joined in and painted the black cat stripes on my legs that completed the 'tiger' look. He enjoyed it more than I did, but at 3 a.m. who gives a sh**? And all that body painting and messing about with my hair was worth it because the final cut of the video was wicked.

Back in Nashville me and the other girls recorded 'Goodbye', which turned out to be the first single from our third album. We wrote and recorded it with Matt and Biff, in the studio where Elvis did a lot of his recording. It was really nice to see Matt and Biff after so long on the road and the session had a real family vibe to it, a home away from home. Deep down 'Goodbye' was a tribute to Geri and it went on to sell more than two and a half million copies worldwide.

Strangely I didn't actually feel pregnant for those months on tour, whereas Vicky was throwing up all the time, especially whenever she smelt strong odours. You couldn't spray perfume anywhere near her. It was the same with her second pregnancy. She felt sick non-stop. (I immediately guessed that she was pregnant again. I texted her saying, 'Are you pregnant?' a week before she made it official. When I didn't get a reply, I knew my instinct was true!)

I didn't have any of the usual pregnancy symptoms and I went about everything as normal. The only change was in my weight. I kept saying to the wardrobe ladies, 'God I must stop eating so much in catering!' Like most pregnant women, I didn't want to make an announcement until three months were up. (About one in six pregnancies end in a miscarriage during the first three months.)

My hormones had their moments and so did Vicky's. We had a ridiculous fight in the dressing room toilets in somewhere like Phoenix or Fort Lauderdale towards the end of the tour. It was nothing major, just a silly gripe, but it blew out of all proportion because our hormones were racing and roaring. Somehow we ended up screaming at each other unnecessarily, faces almost touching, practically spitting at each other.

She wanted to beat shit out of me and I wanted to beat shit out of her. Then, in the middle of all that slanging, a toilet flushed and Melanie walked out of one of the cubicles. Me and Vicky instantly took deep breaths, looked each other in the eye and stopped squabbling. Realising how completely high-pitched and hysterical we must have been sounding, we burst out laughing. Whatever it was that we'd been arguing about was forgotten in a second. That's pregnancy for you.

I definitely went slightly mad. At the beginning of August I wrote a wish list. Wish number 17 was, 'To become MP of Marlow'. Well you never know, do you? I loved Marlow from the moment I moved there. When we got back to England, Jim and me lived in a cottage in Bourne End while we were waiting for work on the Manor House to be completed.

Our last four concerts of the tour were back in front of the home crowd – at Don Valley Stadium in Sheffield on 11 and 12 September and at Wembley Stadium on 15 and 16. These were our biggest ever UK concerts, playing to something like 70,000 people each night. So of course it had to be at this point that the girls got me back for all the stupidity and tricks I'd played on them during the previous 99 shows. Oh yes, it was payback time for me in a big way, in front of our largest audiences.

The day before I got married, they summoned Jim onto the Don Valley Stadium stage and made him get down on one knee and say, 'Will you marry me?' in front of that enormous crowd. It was a complete nightmare because they made such a palaver out of it, plus the show was being shot for video. As Jim knelt, smiling at me expectantly, I was supposed to play along. 'Oh my God. Yes I'll marry you,' I mumbled, then impatiently added, 'Can we get on with the rest of the show now?' I gave the others jokey dagger looks. Okay you got me back. Fair enough.

'I Want You Back' was released in the UK on Monday 14 September and the next Sunday, the very last day of our world tour, we listened to the chart rundown in our dressing room at Wembley. I sat there thinking, Is it? Isn't it? Is it? Isn't it? It was all a bit much, because the girls were being overwhelmingly supportive and I couldn't really take it in. 'There's a brand new No. 1 this week! It's Melanie B and Missy Elliot,' announced the DJ. The dressing room shook with whoops and screams and jumping girls and dancers. I sat there feeling embarrassed, but obviously I was totally over the moon. I couldn't believe it. A wedding and a No. 1, both in the same week, and I was about to be a mother! I was part of an incredibly successful group, I'd finally got my home sorted out and I had lots of time off ahead of me. I had every reason to be ecstatic and thankful.

A few months beforehand, when Richard Jones had told us about the final UK dates, I'd had a silent fit. One of the Sheffield dates was scheduled for 13 September. Oh my God! That was the day I planned to marry Jim if we were still together, although I hadn't told anyone. It was a secret. Luckily I convinced Richard to change the dates to the 11 and 12 without saying why.

Vern organised my wedding day and he did a fantastic job. Forget wedding organisers – I couldn't have chosen anyone better to do it. 'I want a big white wedding and lots of dancing!' I told him and just let him get on with it. What else could I do? I was thousands of miles from home at the centre of a touring tornado. There just wasn't enough time in my day to start ringing around to find the perfect portaloo or tent flooring. I trusted Vern with everything, from the salsa band to the ice sculptures. Knowing me and Jim so well, he added his own touches, including a fantastic statue of Buddha placed right behind our table. Thanks Vern. It can't have been simple but you made it look easy.

4 September 1998

Well I have just tried on my wedding dress and it's beautiful, it really is. But for some reason me and Jim are not right with each other. We still haven't had sex and that is a big worry. Is it because I'm pregnant? Doesn't he like me? Or maybe we will never have sex again. All these kinds of questions are in my mind, day in day out.

I had a blast with my mum today, so many tears, unbelievable. I am not feeling so good right now but all I can say is, I hope things get better. All I know is that me and Phoenix need some sex badly, we really do. Please God, help him out. I want him not to miss out on this.

Having been brought up with a sense of tradition, I obviously spent the night before the wedding without Jim. He went to a friend's and I stayed in the cottage in Bourne End. I was very nervous the next morning, far more than I'd expected to be. This was supposed to be a girl's ultimate day, a fantasy come true, the day that was never expected but always longed for, the day your life changed forever. I was driven to the Manor House grounds where a dressing room had been set up. Although the house was still not finished, the reception was being held in the garden. Rebecca and my mum helped me get ready; Charlotte and Danielle kept popping in to check that I was okay. These were the people I loved most in the world so it was really nice to have them by my side on such an important day. They gave me unconditional support – even though I was aware that some of them weren't sure about Jim – and that's what got me through the day.

Before I put on my dress I took Danielle into the garage. There in front of us was a brand new yellow Punto convertible with a leather interior and a number plate saying DAN 800. I was very proud of myself for choosing that particular car because I knew it would suit her.

'Happy Birthday!' I said in an over-the-top, big-sisterly way.

'Thanks,' she said in a subdued voice, obviously a little bit overwhelmed.

'Do you like it? Tell me, tell me!' I insisted. I wanted a reaction there and then, but she was dumbfounded and couldn't think of anything to say.

My wedding dress was designed by Dean and Dan, the lovely Italian twins behind the label D squared. It was a long silk slip dress with a corset underneath and a diamanté-and-feathers tunic. The matching headdress was amazing. My mum gave me a pair of antique earrings to wear with it, Melanie gave me a brooch, Vicky lent me her friendship ring and Emma gave me a white and blue lace garter. Old, new, borrowed and blue.

The service was in the little church next to my house. I chose the hymns randomly – numbers 13 and 113. I'm afraid that I didn't even look at the words to see whether they were appropriate. I was just obsessed by the number 13. It was a bit unfortunate, because they were quite obscure, had no recognisable melody and didn't fit the occasion at all! I don't think some people even bothered to sing and I don't blame them. Luckily the choir was amazing. Vern had hired The London Gospel Community Choir and I was moved to tears as they sang during the signing of the register and when we walked out of the church at the end of the ceremony. Their voices were beautiful.

My father gave me away, looking fantastic in his beautifully tailored white suit, with his hair tied neatly back. I was proud to have him beside me. We made our way across the gravel to the church together and at the door I changed out of my trainers into my strappy shoes. Then, just before we walked down the aisle, I looked at him and said, 'Dad, it's traditional for the father to turn to the bride and say, "You don't have to go through with it if you don't want to." Aren't you going to say it?'

'I'm not going to ask you that now!' he replied. 'There's no point. You've made up your mind.'

'Okay, let's just go then,' I snapped.

Rebecca made a vow that day never to get married until somebody looked at her in the same way that Jim was looking at me. She described it as a look of pure, true love. He cried at the altar when I cried, looked lovingly into my eyes when I looked into his eyes and clasped my hand affectionately whenever I reached out my arm towards him. It all looked so perfect.

There were 250 people at the reception. All the guests wore white.

I was amazed at my dad's speech. One: he didn't stutter once; two: what he said was very touching and real. Of course he also told everybody what a difficult, hyperactive child I'd been, but my eyes were filled with tears by the time he'd finished. Rebecca also gave a great speech and Charlotte got up to say a few lovely words.

Then some of Jim's relatives put on a comic play about his life, which is the Dutch tradition at weddings, apparently. It was basically a few key scenes from Jim's life strung together: Jim in a nappy, Jim going shopping with his mum and Jim imitating Michael Jackson's moonwalk. The shopping scene was particularly telling. Jim's 'mum' is trying to persuade him to buy a cheap pair of trousers, but he insists on getting a pair six times the price. The implication was that from childhood he'd insisted on looking good and having the best shoes and clothes, even when he didn't have two pennies to rub together. He was the type that liked to present himself as chic, rich-looking and stylish. (He was a very, very stylish man.) Everyone roared with laughter. In hindsight, let's face it, he was lucky to be marrying a woman who was happy to pay for both our outfits and wedding rings, along with his family's flights and hotels. The list goes on and on. However this wasn't the time for those kinds of thoughts and nothing negative went through my mind that day. I gave myself up to the romance of the occasion and loved every minute of it.

There was only one hiccup. I wanted our first song to be 'You Are Everything' by Mary J Blige, but the salsa band launched into that good old pissed-up Benidorm standard 'Hot Hot Hot' and called us up to dance. So instead of being swept into Jim's arms and held tightly while Mary J serenaded us, we ended up jigging around doing the salsa. Jim kept me at arm's length throughout the song. I don't know if he was worried about one of my stilettos digging into his foot, or whether he was just embarrassed.

I should have known from that moment that the marriage wouldn't last. The first song that you dance together as man and wife is so important – and ours went totally wrong. I wonder if anyone noticed that we didn't snog once during the entire day? Certainly no one said anything, but it's not the kind of thing you say to a bride, is it?

Still my wedding day, I have to say, was everything a girl could want, from the emotion of the church service to the incredible fireworks display in the grounds of the Manor House at the end of the night. The fireworks were synchronised with the most wonderful opera music I've ever heard. It was like a Hollywood film. As we went out into the garden, I imagined me and Jim and Phoenix living in the house, a very happy family.

It was magical, a fairy tale. All the things I'd ever dreamed of happening happened. We even had our mate Claudio there to tattoo our fingers with permanent wedding rings – the letters M, P and J intertwined in a delicate pattern. During the night Claudio was bombarded by my aunties. 'Tattoo this!' 'Tattoo that!' They were all a bit drunk. As I was getting my tattoo, my cousin Christian held on to my shoulder asking repeatedly, 'Does it hurt?' (It did, but not as much as when I had it lasered off in LA!) At the time, the permanency of the tattoo was a symbol of my marriage. This is it, this is for life, I thought. No going back, this is the way forward. Everything's going to be perfect from now on. I felt unbelievably happy, completely head over heels in love, blinded by my feelings.

An old-fashioned Rolls Royce with curtains on the windows – very *Chitty Chitty Bang Bang* – took us from Marlow to the Hempel, a smart hotel in the centre of London. I'd done an interview at the Hempel a couple of weeks before and fallen in love with it. It's very relaxing and the rooms are all feng shui'd. I was really hoping that by the time I arrived there with my husband I'd feel completely different about life. Many times I'd swept aside my anxieties with the thought, It will be all right once we get married!

I thought I'd arranged the night to perfection. I even phoned the concierge and told him that it was my wedding night. I imagined that there would be flowers and champagne and soft music awaiting us, but our 'bridal suite' was plain and cold and minimalist, as impersonal as a business suite. Sadly, no romance had been added to the setting, not one flower. We just didn't feel comfortable there. So we called a black cab and, believe it or not, rode home in it to Bourne End. The journey passed in complete silence. I was gutted. We undressed and got into bed. Then Jim kissed me on the forehead and said, 'Goodnight wife,' before turning his back to me and falling asleep. Maybe it's normal, I thought. Maybe this is what married life is supposed to be like. I didn't sob myself to sleep that night but I wasn't far from it.

The next day I bought a dog, a beautiful little golden Labrador puppy.

He was the fattest, thickest and clumsiest in the pack and I had to have him. I named him Lord. I don't know whether I got him because I wanted to feel needed – after all, having a dog is a big responsibility – but I wonder how many women wake up on the day after their wedding with a burning desire to buy a dog? It's a ridiculous thought.

Sad to say, Lord became my main source and outlet of love and happiness until Phoenix was born. As the pregnancy went on, sex with Jim became a complete no-no, due to the pressure he was under, he said. He has also since said that he finds pregnant women a real turn-off. Sex became not just a physical thing, as it had been for me in past experience, but in this relationship it became a way of knowing that Jim loved me. I swung between depression and exhilaration, one minute having doubts about him and then the next minute writing things like this in my diary: *I'm gonna really work at this relationship because I believe in it so much and so does Jim and everyone else can just f*** off with their opinions.*

In the beginning his criticisms were constructive and I tried to please him by taking them on board. I embraced them and felt that he was teaching me. I definitely polished up my personality while I was with him. I became calmer, more approachable and a lot stronger. Then as time went on I began to feel more sensitive about his comments – there seemed no end to them. I didn't know how to cope with what seemed like constant disapproval. It hadn't bothered me when boyfriends criticised me in the past. I just said, 'Oh God, so what?' It was so different with Jim.

To be honest, I'd never experienced a man dumping me. I hadn't been deeply hurt in a relationship unless I'd brought it on myself and I'd never, ever had my heart broken. I hadn't even really cried over a boyfriend. Until then I'd experienced a really good run of relationships – or maybe I saw it that way because I'd always been the one in control. Now, for the first time, I'd totally put my trust in someone else. Also, I'd been brought up to be very loyal and morally correct, to stick things out. I *had* to try and make my marriage work but I was failing faster than I could begin to come to terms with.

Jim would often complain about the amount of pressure he had to deal with. 'It's very hard being labelled Jimmy "Goldcard", or just "the husband of Mel B" in the press,' he would say.

When he said something like that my heart would ache with guilt. I felt so protective over him. I didn't pay much attention to what the press said, but I was very sympathetic and tried hard to help him get over it. Although I knew that he'd eventually come through it and not be bothered any more, I felt responsible. It was my fault that the press were calling him that. I began to feel bad about what I'd achieved and wish I were just a normal girl. Then I started to need Jim's opinion and approval on everything I did in my career. I stopped writing in my diary. If I wrote about what was really going on in our relationship, I knew I'd have to take action and I wasn't ready for that.

I was in denial that our relationship wasn't working, so much so that I took on board his insecurities. Pressure, being married to somebody famous, not having a job – these were the reasons why we never seemed to make love, so he told me. I also wondered whether it was something to do with being pregnant. Maybe he felt as though sex would injure the baby. In due course, I had to resort to masturbation, which I'd mastered by that point anyway. And I ended up getting a real insight on what I did and didn't like. I got in touch with my fantasies and played around with my sexual desires and emotions because there was no one else to do it for me. I do thank Jim for that because I really discovered what makes me tick sexually.

I knew that Jim was a very talented, expressive, imaginative guy and I wanted him to realise it too. I tried to help him by employing him to direct the video to my single 'Word Up'. I also offered to support him through film school or any other course or training that interested him. I wanted him to have a part of his life that was nothing to do with me – a career or at the very least a passionate interest in something. I was like Mr Motivator. I tried so hard to help him that it probably seemed patronising. 'Come on! You can do this or that! I'll find a course book and look it up.' I was obsessed with finding something that would make him feel good, because I knew it would subsequently improve our relationship. At the very least we'd have something to talk about, apart from my career. He got excited about the 'Word Up' video for a while but when it was finished he slumped back into inertia.

So then I began to rebel. And I rebelled in front of people, because I wanted to see how they would react. Had they ever felt the same or had a similar experience? I wanted to shock people into discussing my relationship with me. Unfortunately I shocked them so much that they didn't react at all, just sat there and said nothing. At dinner parties at my house I'd shout something outrageous like, 'Does anybody know what sex is, cos I don't! I haven't f***ing had it in ages.' How could I have expected anybody to respond to that kind of outburst?

Carmine was the only one at that time who knew what I was really going through. I used to ring him three or four times a week, crying my eyes out. He came and stayed with me when I was feeling down and was a supportive ear, always there to listen, even though I repeated myself a lot. He never told me what to do or how to do it. He just said, 'Listen to yourself. You're saying the same thing over and over again.' He was a really good friend who didn't want anything from our relationship apart from friendship.

Jim borrowed my gold card all the time. In actual fact, I was adamant that he use it. I wanted him to be equal. I was desperate to share everything I had with him, partly because at least that way I knew that it wasn't my money that was emasculating him. I didn't think he was going to take it as far as he did, but perhaps it was my fault for not setting clearer boundaries. The first people to notice it were Charlotte and Danielle, who saw him hiding bags of designer clothes in the utility room after a full day's shopping. He more or less came downstairs in a new head-to-toe outfit every day. Or that's how it seemed. I'd say, 'I don't remember buying you that!' I was aware deep down that it was getting a bit out of control, but I ignored it. It was a minor issue compared with our other problems.

It was far more worrying that we were arguing much more frequently. After one particularly nasty row, I decided that I had to get out of the house. Quickly. I sneaked downstairs in the dark, not wanting to attract Jim's attention by turning on lights. I crept around, looking for my car keys. 'Where are my keys? Where are my keys? Oh my God, where are my keys?' I kept repeating to myself. Little did I know that Jim was standing silently in the shadows at the other end of the room.

Suddenly he shouted, 'Bye Melanie!'

I jumped. His disembodied voice was creepy beyond belief. My imagination started spinning out of control and I began to feel like I was playing a starring role in *Scream*. He's there. What's he going to do? I have to get out of here. Jesus Christ!

'Fuuuuuck!' I screamed and ran.

I rushed out to the car, still wearing my fluffy cream pyjamas. Jim followed me at a slow steady pace, then stood at the side of the car staring in. My Range Rover had always been my safe haven but suddenly it felt vulnerable. I was shaking. Jim's face was emotionless. Reverse! was the only word in my brain. You see it in movies, but until you actually experience it you cannot imagine the fear and the panic of that kind of situation. It's surreal. Adrenaline rushes through you and you think incredibly quickly but life goes into slow motion and the engine doesn't start as fast as you want it to and the car doesn't move as soon you want it to. I skidded backwards, sparks flew everywhere and the car pulled away. I flicked a look in the mirror as I drove through the gate. Jim was still standing there, a silhouetted statue in the darkness.

I drove like a maniac to Charlotte and Danielle's flat in High Barnet. They didn't have to ask what had happened. They could tell by the way I was acting that I was seriously upset. They calmly made me a cup of tea and sat there as I let it all spill out. I was in shock and still slightly hysterical. I just wanted someone to put their arms around me and tell me that everything would be all right.

I actually thought I was going certifiably mad for a while. I was distraught, highly strung, whimsical and making a big deal about tiny things. I even got freaked out by the way shopkeepers looked at or spoke to me. Our arguments were all documented in the press and I constantly had the feeling that people were watching us. At home we'd go to bed in silence and sleep with our backs facing, miles apart in my enormous bed, me muffling my sobs, asking myself over and over again, Is this how marriage is supposed to be? I was embarrassed to ask anyone – and probably fearful that they'd reply by saying, 'No. It's just not normal.'

Someone suggested therapy. I needed to sort out why I'd got myself into such a state so I gave it a go. My first therapist helped me out initially, but didn't seem to want to work through the different layers to get to the root of what was wrong. If I turned up to a session looking happy, he wrongly assumed that I was happy and didn't bother to look beyond the surface. I wasn't trying to fool him. I just expected him to know more than I did, whereas in actual fact I knew more about myself than he could ever know. Still, at least he started me down the road to understanding what on earth had gone wrong in my life, and why. It was about time.

24

BROWN GIRL IN THE RING

Work can be a great way to escape from personal problems. Being in my position, it was also a way that I could help promote different causes that I believed in. So I jumped at the chance of co-presenting the *Music of Black Origin Awards*, also known as the *MOBOs*, the first year that they were televised in October 1998. Set up to celebrate British black music, they'd been running for a couple of years but hadn't achieved a very high profile. I wanted to get involved – and I think my involvement helped clinch the TV deal. I was a bit nervous when the *MOBOs* committee asked me to perform 'I Want You Back' live for the first time, but I was definitely up for it, even though I'd be performing without Missy.

I was presenting the show so I had to wait until the end of the rehearsals to go through my song, even though I was singing it quite early on in the set. Puff Daddy was that year's big celebrity performer and he was the final act. Of course he turned up with about twenty security guards and friends and family and there was a huge hoo-ha around him. I was presenting *and* performing, so I couldn't see what the big deal was. Yeah, get on with your song. You're not in America now; you're on our turf.

Puffy was the last to rehearse and he just wouldn't get off the stage. The doors were opening about 7 p.m. and by 6.30 p.m. I was getting worried. When would I have a chance to rehearse? I was nervous because I was singing my song live for the first time, with dancers. I was about five months pregnant and I was a bit hormonal, but keeping it under control.

I started feeling like he was taking the piss so I decided that I was going to go up to him and say something. As I walked towards him he turned his head and said, 'I want to run through my song again.' It was now 6.45 p.m. I'd watched him rehearse four times already. Why did he need to do it again?

'No. You can't do it again,' I said bluntly. 'I need to rehearse my song. I'm presenting the show and I haven't had time to rehearse because of your rehearsals. Now I need to go over my bit at least once or twice.'

He had a live mic in his hands. Very confidently he stared out into the auditorium, raised the mic to his mouth and said, 'Get this b**** off the stage.'

Silence. I can't believe he's just said that! I thought. How dare he? I plucked up the courage to speak. I prodded his shoulder sharply. 'Oh no. Absolutely not. Get *what* off the stage? Listen you, I'm here. If you're going to say anything, say it to my face.'

He was arrogant and angry. I thought, F*** that, who does he think he is?

To my surprise, what happened next actually made me piss myself. Along came Jim, looking somewhat intimidated. 'Don't you talk to my woman like that!' he blustered. Puffy looked at him and laughed. I couldn't help myself, I started smirking as well. But I stuck to my guns, turned back round to Puffy, clocked the ten bouncers behind him and said, right up close to his face, 'Listen. I'm introducing you tonight, so I'd be nice if I were you. The doors are opening in ten minutes. I need to rehearse. Can you get off the f***ing stage?' I walked off. I was fuming.

Well, I managed to get my rehearsals in and my performance went great. When it came to introducing the man himself I paused and thought about it. Payback time. 'I'm very happy to introduce, Mr Puff . . . . . Daddy!' thinking, You arsehole. You can't talk to people like that. You can't even begin to treat people like that.

Then I thought, Hold on a minute. This is supposed to be a celebration of British music and you've got Puff Daddy ordering Crystal champagne in the biggest dressing room while UK stars like Beverley Knight just aren't being looked after in the same way. I guess that's the hype that Americans get when they come over to this country. Everyone's in awe that they've come all this way. Little do they realise that they're just like any other artists, plugging their song, doing their promotion work.

Apparently Puffy had already cancelled about three or four times. 'I'm not coming over unless I can bring so-and-so with me.' I started to feel righteous indignation. What is this frigging organisation? It's a British-based event to promote British acts that don't often get a chance to be heard. It's the first year it's being televised and yet we have someone like Puff Daddy on it. Why? Surely people aren't really that bothered about seeing him? It annoyed me so much. Even the organisers told me not to make a fuss about my rehearsals. 'Let's just give Puffy as much time as he wants.' No! Why should we?

A bit later on, Puffy's bouncers came up to me and apologised for his rudeness. It was incredible – his own people feeling that they had to make amends for his behaviour. I think they were really embarrassed about what had happened. 'It's all right you saying sorry, but you're not the ones I need an apology from,' I said sternly. At the end of the night Mr Diddy, as he now calls himself, sent a jacket round to my dressing room. A peace offering with his name splattered all over it, a cagoule that would have come in handy on a camping trip, but that's about it. Then in a radio interview a few days later he made a public apology. Apparently he said something like, 'I'm sorry about how I behaved towards Melanie and I hope she forgives me.' Oh, how nice of you, I thought.

Two days before Christmas Day me and Jim moved into our new home.

23 December 1998

Well I'm here in the Manor House, in the music room, listening to Toni Toni Tone track 6. I feel great. It's my very first night in the house. It truly is amazing. Everything about it is a vibe. I feel so lucky as I look around me right now. Lord the dog is happy and so is Jim. I'm nearly seven months pregnant and boy do I feel big, like a house in fact.

I like being married but it does have its ups and down and I never thought that it would have, to be honest. So many things have happened to me in this last year. Let's just say I'm glad I'm still sane. At this point in my life I feel I know myself better than ever, but at the same time my family and some of my friends think I've lost it and turned into a different person. I would say that I'm more aware these days, calmer inside and outside. It's such a nice feeling for me, but for other people it's confusing and unsettling.

I got married because I believed in fairy tales. I just thought that people fell in love, got married and lived happily ever after. Cinderella never experienced the seven-year itch, did she? And how did Snow White and her prince cope when their 'honeymoon period' was over? I had no idea that phrases, or concepts, like 'honeymoon period' even existed. When I first heard it used I thought, What do you mean? I went on honeymoon for two weeks a few months ago so of course it's over!

I used to think that you shouldn't have to try in a relationship. It should just work of its own accord. Of course when you're younger that's the way it is. You see a boy on the school bus and it just happens. If you like him, it goes on happening. If not, not. Now I think the complete opposite. You really have to try – otherwise it's f***ed. Oh, isn't it great becoming an adult?

The dining room table was delivered on Christmas Eve and Jim's family arrived for dinner that evening. I was heavily pregnant, but I managed to cook Christmas dinner without any major disasters, apart from dropping the turkey on the floor when I got it out of the fridge. Oh well, I thought, they've never had a traditional English Christmas dinner so they won't notice a bit of muck, will they? Jim's family spoke mostly Dutch and I found myself in the weird position of not being able to understand what anyone was saying in my own house, but it was nice to see them all again, especially Jim's mother Ilse.

28 December 1998

1.30 p.m. Boxing Day, what a laugh. We had a big party and I was Miss Entertainer to Carmine and Chris. This house is fantastic. I love it. All Jim's family and friends are STILL here. I don't mind them – the house is big enough, but I do want to spend some time here by myself. I even want Jim to go away for a couple of days, just so that he can sort his head out, and I can too. We both need to remember why we got together in the first place. Yes, our marriage is very difficult at the moment, but I've given up fighting, so whatever happens, happens. Most importantly, I know who I am.

11 January 1999

4.30 a.m. I've just woken from a nightmare, dripping in sweat. It was all about Jim and this other woman. It was horrible. I caught him in bed with her and everything!!!

I called him and he was asleep in a hotel in Amsterdam. Very weird it was, but I'm okay now, I think.

Mum came to see me today. I cooked dinner and we took down the Christmas trees. I had a really nice couple of hours with her, light-hearted chat. Yes, it felt good. I have Lord in bed with me. These three days alone in the house have been good for me, but lonely at night. I don't think Jim knows yet how I tick inside, my needs and wants. I know his – leave him alone in nearly every way – whereas I need extra attention at the moment. I can't stop worrying and yes, I look like shite. My belly is even bigger! I get myself so worried about things these days. I know I've got to stop it. Enough of my negativity now. I watched Geri on Parkinson on Friday night. She was good and came across well. Good night.

It wasn't long before Jim wasn't really a part of my life, even though he was living in my house. He spent his days watching films in the TV room saying, 'Yeah man, this film's wicked.' His friends would be round all the time, before, during and after my pregnancy. I put up with all of them and insisted on only one rule. No filling the house with thick pungent smoke.

Phoenix was born unexpectedly, a month early, in February. She just couldn't wait to experience the world so out she came prematurely. I'm not exaggerating when I say that the day she was born was the most important, wonderful day of my life so far. I cannot thank God enough for bringing me Phoenix.

Emma and her mum Pauline were convinced it would be a girl. I thought it would be a boy. But either way, Jim and I had already decided on the name early on, whether it was a girl or a boy: Phoenix, after the firebird, and Chi, after my first tattoo, which means 'Spirit, Heart and Mind'.

Now you won't find any details about Phoenix in this book because I believe absolutely in a child's right to grow up in a private environment. I chose my own path and encountered fame and stardom as an adult with a passion, whereas Phoenix isn't at an age when she can make life choices like that. Until she is, I owe it to her to protect her.

But one thing I will share with you is my experience of labour. Here's what I wrote in my diary the day after she was born.

20 February 1999

Well, I was sat here in the music room at about 4 a.m. in pain, not knowing my labour had started. Lord was with me all the time, being so sweet. Jim was asleep, saying I had food poisoning. Typical! He had brought me some spicy rice chicken and peas earlier and I puked it up and diarrhoeaed, so I too thought I had food poisoning. I was lying on the leather sofa squeezing Lord's ears with every contraction, praying for the pain to stop, asking God to make it all go away. I was knackered, falling in and out of sleep in between each contraction. I gave in to six hours of mind-blowing torture.

I eventually decided to call Dr Gillard. He said, 'Call back in an hour and if the pain is still bad, come in.' I called him back at about 8 a.m. This time the contractions were coming every two minutes. We rushed to the Portland. Dave the driver got us there safely – he made it to my house in about two seconds and we arrived at the Portland in about ten. I had my head hanging out of the window to numb the pain. It didn't work.

I got to the hospital and there was a wheelchair waiting for me. I sat in it and thought, 'What am I doing? I can walk!' so I stood up and said, 'I'm not sitting in that!' Then my contractions started, the pain kicked in and I instantly sat down in the wheelchair again.

Luckily I'd packed my two bags that week, so I was prepared, although I still hadn't gone to any antenatal classes. I was wearing Jim's blue tracksuit, had no make-up on and looked a mess. I got the last labour room, number 7. It was a cosy room with its own toilet. I undressed and set up camp, first putting on the hospital gown until I looked at myself and thought, Not! So I opted for my La Senza tight blue low cut top. I called the office and told them all, 'I'm in labour.' I couldn't get hold of Mum or Dad for ages. Finally I did. Mum was at work. They both rushed down. It only took them two hours to get there.

Within half an hour my hospital room was full. First to arrive were Vicky and Jackie, then Rebecca with her mum, then Ozzie. Following them were Emma, Mel C and her mum Joan, my mum and dad and Emma's mum Pauline. I'd had a mobile epidural by then so I couldn't feel the pain so much.

My midwife Sarah was really nice, talking me through things. The strange thing was that Vicky and me had an appointment that day at 3 p.m. with Dr Gillard to talk about labour. Well it was a bit f***ing late for that, wasn't it? Four weeks early, I was. I'd had three days of period-type pains as a warning, but not really noticed them. So there I was, already three and a half to four centimetres dilated, numb all around the waist, surrounded by friends and family chit-chatting away. Jim couldn't stay in the labour room longer than five minutes at a time. I think he didn't want to admit that his wife was going to give birth to a beautiful daughter just yet.

So then I'm all strapped up, the baby's heart is on the monitor and everything is fine. Jim and Jackie went out to the shops and came back with a Moses basket, which was really sweet. Outside, the press had cottoned on to me being in labour and the chaos had started. My room was clean and tidy and full of friends and family. My mobile epidural was working a treat but I could still feel the baby banging to come out. Me and Jim still didn't know that she was a girl.

At 6.30 p.m. the doctor checked me and yes, I was 10cm dilated. So I kicked everyone out and the real journey of motherhood started. I was going into unknown territory, the area that no one tells you about, the area of fear, panic, love and insecurity.

He broke my waters. It wasn't how I expected it to be. I'd thought there would be a flood of water but there wasn't. It was just like pissing with a bit of blood added. There I was with both legs up, one foot on the doctor's hip and the other foot on Sarah the midwife's. Jim was behind me, by my neck. The bed had been raised so it was like I was squatting. Hmm, very nice.

Ooops! The midwife left and there I was with my leg now up on Jim's hip. He could see everything. I felt sick. It was hurting now, really hurting. Emma, my mum and a few others, I'm told, were listening outside the door. I started grunting, 'Get it out, just get it out!' and they said they felt sick and my mum's knees went weak. As for me, I was waging World War Two with my own punani.

Finally, after twenty minutes pushing, she came out – by the second push her head was nearly out. They fiddled around with her then put her straight into my arms and I put her straight onto my boob. She just looked at me with calm, curious eyes. I felt numb. I couldn't cry or anything. No, hold on a minute, before they put her in my arms I had to deliver the placenta. Yes, that's right, because the pain hadn't stopped. Oh no, not yet. I started panicking. Have I pooed? and Are you going to cut me? were the only questions I had, because I didn't want to poo and I certainly didn't want stitches, even though stitches prove that you haven't got a bucket crutch.

Mel C had bought me a radio so that I could remember the song that Phoenix was born to. Lo and behold it was her song! P came out to the sound of Mel and Bryan Adams singing, 'When You're Gone'. I remember because Dr Gillard said, 'Push,' and the radio was saying, 'And Mel G's in labour as we speak,' which was freaking me out. It sent my voice into a high-pitched state. 'I can't believe it! They're saying I'm in labour and I am!'

Dr Gillard just said, 'Shut up and push.' Oh yes, it was all kicking off big time. No, I didn't poo, yes I did have stitches. As I held her in my arms I realised that the pain had gone and she had appeared, weighing a little over 5lbs. She was so tiny and neat, but in the meantime Dr Gillard was in between my legs stitching me up. All dignity had gone out the window. Jim rushed out to the press shouting, 'It's a girl! It's a girl!' and Danielle phoned from her holiday to hear the news.

Everyone rushed into the room, the champagne was opened and we all celebrated. How mad was that? In the morning she was in my stomach, banging to get out and by the evening this little girl had entered out into the world of people and noise. But most importantly she met her mum and dad face to face on Friday 19 February.

As soon as Phoenix was born, Jim went straight into the next room and announced to everyone that it was a girl. Then he came back into the delivery room. 'I'm going out partying,' he told me, 'but first I'm going downstairs to tell the press.'

So off he went outside to be interviewed and when he came back he just sat there drinking champagne with his friend in the next room. All I wanted was a cuddle but it felt like he just wasn't there. Then he said. 'Right, I'm off out now.'

'No, don't,' I said.

'But it's a tradition in Amsterdam. We go out and celebrate the birth, "wet the baby's head" as they say in English.'

My mum was furious but didn't show it. Feeling vulnerable, I asked her if she'd stay in the hospital with me but in the end Jim stayed and slept on a little bed on the floor. The next day we went home, taking our beautiful baby daughter with us. I was adamant about going home as soon as possible. I wanted to leave as soon as I'd given birth but it's routine to stay over in case there are any complications with the baby. As I arrived home I noticed a pair of swans on my back lawn. The image of those two beautiful birds stayed with me a long time.

Two days later I had a group meeting at my house. Vicky was heavily pregnant at the time and – at least for me and Vicky – it seemed sensible to agree to take six months out from Spice Girls. Melanie was disappointed at first, but soon realised what a great opportunity it was to get on and make her first solo album. She's always been completely driven and it didn't surprise me that she wanted to carry on working, even though we'd all been on the go non-stop for at least four years. I love her first album *Northern Star*. The demos I've heard from her second album also sound wicked. Melanie is very talented.

Meanwhile my priorities had changed overnight. Forget work, I just wanted to be a good mother.

The day after my daughter was born my mum said, 'I'm going to give you one piece of advice. Never ever let yourself go. Forget about make-up, but make sure your hair is washed, your nails are done and your clothes are always clean.

'I never ever want to see you looking like shit with that baby, Melanie. You must take care of yourself. Always make sure you're dressed before she is. Don't slouch because then you'll get depressed and think you're fat and not worthy. So make sure you're up and ready before that baby is and you won't get into bad patterns.'

It was such a 'mum' thing to say. It's true, a lot of people go down the route of just looking after their baby and forgetting about themselves. You see some young mums looking totally hideous and their excuse is, 'Well, I've got a baby.'

Actually I've found that it's quite possible to look after your baby and yourself. My mum was always very loving and focused on her kids and I'm exactly the same way.

I made the mistake of telling her once that I was considering cutting the feet off some babygrows to make them last longer. Now my mum's never had any money but she always made sure that our clothes fitted. As soon as they didn't fit, they were packed in a bag and saved or passed down to cousins or relatives. It was a hard and fast rule. You don't try and make clothes fit, you just don't wear them again.

So there I was, sitting in my big mansion, saying, 'Well I thought it would be easier to cut the toes off.'

'Don't you ever dress your family in cut-off clothes!' she said furiously.

I really took it to heart. When you've just given birth you want to get it all right and you're a bit vulnerable. Later my mum admitted that I seemed to know a lot more about looking after a baby than she had when I was born. I had everything written down. I breast fed from my left breast for exactly twenty minutes. Then it was on to the right breast for exactly twenty minutes.

'I just used to flop you in the bed and that was it,' my mum told me. 'I didn't know when to change your nappy or feed you.'

I took my mum's advice and made a real effort with my own appearance too, but it didn't get me very far with my husband.

I'd been totally distraught about the state of my marriage for a long time. I thought I was to blame, that it was all my fault. I was a bad person. I was crazy and irrational and stupid most of the time. Or that's how Jim saw it. I'd always loved arguing with my previous boyfriends – it was a great way of sorting things out – but it was different when me and Jim argued because it was like getting a telling off from my dad. I'd usually kick off the argument, then I'd sit there in silence and maybe blurt something out at the end.

There were some tragic moments in my marriage. After an argument I'd end up crying in the corner and he'd look at me like I was pathetic. I'd cry even more because I couldn't believe that I was actually the person sobbing in the corner being treated in this way.

I held out hope for far longer than I probably should have done. In April we went to Lanzarotte in the Canaries for a week's holiday. We stayed in a private mini-villa within a large hotel complex. All I wanted was a relaxing time with my family, plus lots of sun, sea and sand (and sex? If only!). The first day was fine – it was wonderful to be able to switch off from work and the restaurants in the hotel were great.

Then, on the second day, *everything* began to go wrong. First of all, a local photographer climbed the wall of our villa to try and sneak some pap shots. Jim went mad when he saw him. 'Don't react!' I begged him. 'Let's complain to the hotel and leave them to sort it out.'

Before the words were even out of my mouth Jim was over the wall and sprinting down the beach after the guy. 'Don't!' I shrieked. 'Come back!' Things were fast moving from bad to worse. I watched helplessly as Jim grabbed the photographer's camera and removed the offending film, amid shouting and bad language in Spanish, English and, I think, Dutch. There was a bit of a tussle and the photographer ran away, shaking his fist and yelling. Suddenly Jim looked panicked. He dropped to his knees and began searching for something in the sand. 'What is it?' I shouted over the wall. 'What have you lost?'

'My engagement ring!' he screamed. 'My engagement ring's gone!'

The next two hours were spent combing the sand in search of the Boodle and Dunthorne diamond ring that I'd given him in Italy. We never found it. Jim was gutted. I saw it as a sign. The symbol of my love for him had disappeared, along with my actual love.

It didn't stop there. The next day the photographer pressed charges against Jim for violent robbery. Apparently his camera had been broken in the fracas. 'I told you not to go after him!' I couldn't help saying. The last thing I wanted right then was an explosion of publicity, which was, of course, inevitable, even though I tried my best to stay out of it all. Although I believe to this day that the photographer didn't have a case against Jim, I deeply regretted the way Jim had reacted. When a summons to court arrived for him later in the day, I broke down and wept. Our holiday was being ruined because of this ridiculous incident.

The next few days were spent endlessly trying to sort things out with lawyers and hotel personnel. Jim made an appearance in court and swore and made obscene gestures at the local press. The story hit the news wires and swept its way around the world. Our quiet break from the world had turned into a media circus. I couldn't wait to get home.

The year we were married felt like ten years. I got so low, I couldn't get any lower. It's almost like I was with Jim for the purpose of self-torture, because he highlighted every negative aspect of my personality. Among a million other things, he pointed out that I change my mind all the time, that I'm fickle, that I can be happy one minute and sad another. They weren't major defects, frankly, but as a result I ended up questioning absolutely everything about myself. But I came back stronger than ever – not changed, but stronger. I came back fighting. 'What you're saying is wrong, absolutely wrong!' In the end the only person that could pick me up was me. I began to love and respect myself, which got me thinking, What the hell am I doing with him?

For months I'd been saying that I wanted a divorce but it wasn't until the Minneapolis/LA trip in the summer of 1999 that I realised I meant it. The divorce papers had arrived some time before and I think Jim had seen them, but I'd never had the balls to hand them to him. After every argument that ended with the words 'I want a divorce!' he'd come and find me and say, 'Are we going to get back together? Is everything all right?'

Usually I'd say yes although deep down I knew that I didn't want to be with him. I was never quite sure when would be the right time to say it to him.

Obviously everything I say about my ex-husband in this book is told from my point of view. It's what I've gone through. I don't know his viewpoint because I don't know who he is. All I can write about is what I've gone through and my journey with him. And it's my belief that Jim had a plan. I've lived with it and I've seen it and I've had to put up with him and the aftermath of not being with him.

There was a story going round – I don't know whether I believe it or not – that Jimmy was overheard talking to a friend in the men's toilets at our wedding, two hours after the ceremony.

'That's it. I've done it. I'm a millionaire now!' laughed my new husband.

25

GET ON THE GOOD FOOT

I didn't actually leave Jim for more than six months after I came back from that disastrous trip to America. It was partly because I really wanted the family to stay together. Plus, somewhere deep inside I was still in love with the idea of being in love and married. I didn't want to see everything I'd created just crumble. It would make me feel like a failure. I'd been brought up in a very traditional way – and had even felt a bit guilty about getting pregnant before I got married – so divorce was obviously something I wanted to avoid at all costs. But it was no longer possible.

20 August 1999
Phoenix's first tooth (on the bottom in the middle) came on 7 August 1999 when she was nearly six months old. She hasn't been too bad during the teething phase and she's also an expert at doing rollovers. Her second tooth was 16 August, poking through at the bottom as well. I just wish things between me and Jim weren't so bad.

We were arguing on a daily basis, and I felt drained. I knew in my heart that I had to go.

It was just a question of timing. I spent the last half of 1999 concentrating on those closest to me and work. Jim didn't really come into it. We were virtually ignoring each other and when we did talk, we argued. Every day I thanked God for Phoenix. Without her life just wouldn't have been worth living. I could write a whole book on how wonderful she is, how much she means to me and all the ways she cheered me up when she was a baby, but those memories are very special to me and I want them to stay private. Children need to have space to grow up without having every aspect of their life in the public eye.

In the late summer, the BBC got in touch with the Spice Office to ask whether I'd be interested in presenting a music programme on BBC2. *Pure Naughty* was my first attempt at presenting and I really enjoyed it. Based mainly on R&B, it gave me the chance to meet and interview people like Usher, Mr Vegas and Method Man, all of whom I admired in a big way – and still do.

Pure Naughty was shown at 12.30 p.m. on Sundays. When I asked Angela Ferreira, the director and co-producer, why it was scheduled at such a strange time, she took me into her office and pulled out a sheet of statistics. 'Most white people switch off their TV or turn it over when they see a black face on the screen,' she told me. 'Here are the viewing figures to prove it.' I was stunned. Could what she was saying be true? I looked at the figures. She was right. Most channels only have a black person fronting a programme late at night, unless the programme is specifically aimed at satellite viewers. Right then and there the seed of an idea began to form in my mind. No black faces on mainstream TV? We'll see about that!

Meanwhile music was keeping me busy enough. Melanie, Vicky, Emma and me began work on the third Spice Girls album in August. We spent a week with Matt and Biff in the Abbey Road Studios in North London followed by a couple of weeks at Whitfield Studios, N1 with Jam and Lewis. Then Rodney Jerkins, a hot young American producer whose work we also admired, flew over with his team. Rodney is a very cool guy, religious, open, honest and approachable. He's in his early twenties but looks a bit older, possibly because he's quite a large guy. He's a McDonald's foodie. The McDonald's bill for Rodney and his gang was over a hundred pounds a day! They got a lot of teasing for that.

Rodney came over with his older brother Fred, a bit of a giggler. You can see that Fred's got a twinkle in his eyes for the ladies. The other key member of the team is LaShawn Daniels. LaShawn is a very quiet family man, devoted to his wife and kids. He obviously missed them dearly. He's a very talented producer but it seemed as though he didn't really get to express his talent fully. It wasn't that he was under the thumb, but they all worked together in a certain way and Rodney was definitely the boss.

On our first day in the studio they started talking over the kind of songs we would write. It was all, 'Love, love, love' and 'I love you' at first. We reacted strongly against their ideas. 'Yeucchh, I don't think so! F*** the f***ing men!' we laughed. Rodney and Fred, being real Christian types, cringed visibly. They don't swear at all, ever.

Rodney and his team were easy to work with and made recording a very enjoyable experience. They were funny, too. They say that Americans don't have much of a sense of humour, but this lot did. We four tend to bring out the louder person in everyone because we're so full-on when we get together, so it wasn't long before they were making up stupid dances and involving themselves in our games, calling each other silly nicknames and stuff. They also played practical jokes. You'd be in the vocal booth singing your heart out and when you'd finished one of them would say, 'Oh my God, Melanie. That was terrible!'

'Was it?' you'd reply, feeling crushed.

'Ha ha ha, got ya!' In fact it would be the vocal they used on the final edit.

At the end of each day they played each track full blast on all the speakers round the studio. It was so loud that you'd instantly disappear into your own world while you listened. You couldn't talk over the noise because you wouldn't be able to hear a word. I loved it.

One night me and Emma took them to China White – a West End club – for a boogie. They've all got the rhythm in them. Believe it or not, the bigger you are, the more you can move – or the more of you that moves, anyway! You may only take a tiny step but your whole body sways and ripples. It's quite amazing to watch.

I co-presented the MOBOS with Wyclef Jean on 6 October and this time Beverley Knight won Best Album, which made us all cheer. (Vicky and Emma were also there.) Beverley has been a good friend for ages. She's very loving, very instant, very opinionated and very supportive. A few days later I flew back to America to work on some more tracks for my album with Dru Hill and Cisquo, among others. I was flattered and amazed at the people who said yes to working with me. I really didn't expect them to. It was all really good experience. Instead of working with a group of people and inevitably having to compromise your ideas, it was all down to me for once.

In November I recorded a track with Max Beesley. Now I'd known Max for a while, having first met him in New York two years earlier, quite by chance. Or was it chance?

In late 1997, Max was in New York with his mate Jason Orange (ex of Take That) studying acting with his drama coach Sheila Gray. On their third afternoon, they were walking through New York to get a juice before an acting session when they saw a load of mounted police outside Planet Hollywood. Max looked over to see a sign saying, SPICE GIRLS BOOK SIGNING in the window. 'That band again!' he said to Jason. They'd been talking about us only a couple of days before, especially about how Max had fancied me ever since the release of 'Wannabe'.

Well, Max being Max, he decided that he wanted to meet us right there and then. 'We'll never get through the security,' argued Jason, who obviously knew more about these things than Max did. 'Don't worry, brother,' Max assured him, 'I'll sort it.' He marched into the shop and found his way to the front of the queue of fans waiting to get their books signed. A big burly security guard was standing in front of the barriers. Max instantly went into acting mode.

'I need to speak to one of the representatives of the Spice Girls,' he said confidently. 'It's Max Beesley, their PR consultant.' He took out his mobile phone and pretended to take a call from his office.

'They're busy at the moment,' said the guard.

'That's fine. I need to see them in about an hour,' said Max looking totally unperturbed. 'They know all about it but it is very urgent that you get this message to Melanie Brown or one of the others.' He handed over the phone number of his hotel and briskly walked away.

'I've got a vibe about this, brother!' he said to Jason. 'She's going to call. I know it!'

He and Jason were staying in a bit of a dive because they were paying their own expenses and New York isn't cheap. That night Jason tried to persuade him to go out, but he was so sure that I was going to call that he insisted on staying in. Meanwhile I was back at the Four Seasons with the others, waving Max's number around in my hand.

'So shall I call him?'

'What, Max Beesley? Who the f*** is he?'

'I don't know!' (None of us had a clue who he was, even though New York was full of billboards with his face on, advertising his TV series *Tom Jones*. He was definitely the new hot young actor in town.)

I phoned the number and was put through to Max's room.

'Hiya, it's me! Who are you?' I asked.

'It's Max.'

'Oh yes, and what do you do?'

'I'm an actor.'

'What have I seen you in then?'

'Nothing probably darling, because you live in a cocoon,' he replied rather patronisingly.

So what if I thought Tom Jones was a singer. He is, isn't he? Now if Max had told me that he was also a musician who'd worked on the Incognito albums, as well as with the Brand New Heavies, JK, Earth Wind & Fire, Paul Weller and Miça Paris, I would instantly have known who he was. I've got all their CDs.

I shouted over to the girls, 'He's here with Jason Orange. Shall we meet them or what?'

'Get 'em over!'

Back to Max, 'Yeah, we'll meet ya. How about in an hour?'

'Well, we're doing an acting course here and we've got a class now,' he explained. 'Can't we meet a bit later on?'

Back to the girls, 'He can't meet us now girls! What shall we do?'

'Oh well, f*** it then.'

Back to Max, 'Look –'

'We're finishing at 8.30 p.m.,' he interrupted. 'We'll come to your hotel at 9 p.m.'

Back to the girls, '9 p.m. – what do you think girls?'

Back to Max, 'Yeah we'll meet you then. How will we know you?'

'We'll wear yellow daffodils in our button holes,' he said.

At 9 p.m. I was downstairs in the bar having a drink with Emma, Geri and Vicky (Melanie had flu and was in bed). Vern was there too, as usual. In walked these two boys. Max walked straight up to us and said with a big smile, 'How are you doing girls?'

There's something about this guy, I thought immediately. 'Ooh, come and sit here!' I said, tapping the seat beside me.

Now he read that as, I really like you. Come and sit next to me. I think there could be a bit of a vibe here. But honestly, I wasn't thinking that at all. I just thought he seemed nice and funny.

'Bad body language!' I said after he had settled into the seat next to me. 'Your knees are facing away from me! Come on, open yourself up to me a bit more.'

As the night went on first Geri went to bed, then Vicky, leaving me and Emma and the boys. 'Let's go out and party!' I suggested.

Max wasn't having it. 'Why don't we just stay here?' he said.

'Well what do you suggest we do here?' I asked.

'I suggest we go up to your room and have a couple of drinks,' he said cheekily.

'You're a bit forward aren't you?' I said. Suddenly I felt shy. I thought about it for a few minutes and then said, 'Okay then. We'll go up first. You come up in ten minutes.'

Fifteen minutes later we were sitting together in my room. Me and Emma were giggling away, getting a bit fruity with them, but nothing major.

'Can I get a beer then?' asked Max

'No! The drinks are coming!' we shouted in unison. Being wankers, we had ordered two bottles of Dom Perignon, strawberries and cream. It came on a silver tray.

Jason started feeding strawberries and cream to Emma in a very jokey way. Every time I looked at him I thought, Oh my God, we've watched you on video so many times! I wanted to say, 'You'll never guess what we used to do over you!' But you can't say that sort of thing. He was no longer in the group and maybe he didn't want to talk about it. Max and me started dancing, then Emma came up to join us in a bit of a 'sandwich' vibe. I caught Emma's eye. Time for a wind-up! We turned round to Max and said, 'Well, do you want both of us or what?'

Max thought we were serious! 'No, I don't think I could do that,' he said. Later he told me that he turned us down then because he didn't want to spoil his long-term chances with me. He'd already been waiting more than a year for me, without even knowing me. I started to feel a vibe between us. There was definitely something very attractive about him. Then the phone rang. It was Fjöl. Instantly I forgot about Max. The atmosphere changed.

'I think that's it now,' said Max when I'd hung up. 'I think me and Jason will go home,' He was being cool, so he thought. 'We've had a great night! See you in LA,' he said.

'What do you mean?' I asked.

'You're going to be there in three days and so are we,' he replied with a grin. 'Call us!' The door clicked behind them as they left.

Apparently when they got in the lift, out of earshot, Max punched the air and screamed, 'Yes!' Even funnier, he still believes to this day that me and Emma would have had a threesome with him.

I said I'd call him but I didn't. He was so disappointed. The next time I heard from him was when he sent me a really slushy track that he'd written for me. It had lyrics like, *Baby if you think you were meant to be with someone else you didn't see.* Of course I didn't register that the words were directed at me. 'Yeah, it's a great track,' I said when I phoned him. 'Can't talk now. I'm on the way to Ireland to rehearse for the tour.'

'Great, let me come and see you there!' he suggested. 'I've got loads of friends and family I can hook up with in Ireland.'

'Okay, I'll give you a call in a few days.' Click.

The call never came. Unfortunately for him (and me!) I'd met Jim.

Three months later I called Max again. 'Hiya.'

'This is getting ridiculous!' he said sounding more than slightly irritated. 'You say you'll call in three days and it takes three months.'

'Well where are you?' I asked.

'In Manchester,' he answered.

'I knew it! We're in Manchester too, doing our shows. Are you going to come down?'

'Yes, all right, we'll pop down.'

'There's good news and bad news,' I said. 'The good news is that I'm not with Fjöl any more.'

'Great,' laughed Max, sounding genuinely happy about that.

'The bad news is that I'm seeing one of my dancers.'

Pause. 'Well what am I coming for then?' he asked.

'Because I wanna see ya!' I replied with a giggle.

He sighed.

I wasn't feeling great that night. Jim's back was really bad and it was touch-and-go whether he was going to have to pull out of the tour. What would I do then? Still, in the middle of the concert I remembered to announce, 'And we want to say hello to Max and Jason, in the audience tonight!'

I bumped into Max backstage after the show. I was amazed how happy I was to see him again. I was genuinely thrilled. 'Am I glad to see you!' I shouted, jumping into his arms. 'Come and meet my family.' The next night I saw him at a hotel in Manchester. This time I was with Jim and some of the dancers and Max was having a drink with a friend. Well, Jim and Max got chatting and I leaned over to listen in to their conversation. Jim was telling Max that there are many different ways to climb onto an elephant, 'but at the end of the day, whichever way you get up there, you are on the elephant.' Somehow Max managed to look interested. He's a brilliant actor.

After the MOBOS later in the year, I happened to see Max at Brown's nightclub. 'Just because I'm married doesn't mean you can't phone me, you know!' I said. She wants me! he thought, although honestly, I was just being friendly. I didn't see or speak to him again for three months, when I saw him at the *Batman* premiere with his girlfriend Melanie Sykes. As we were walking out after the film, I turned back to Max and Melanie and for some reason I said, 'God, I'm so glad you two are together!' Where that came from I just don't know. Why did I say that? I wondered to myself. Of course, Max again thought, Ah! She likes me.

In autumn '99, the Spice Girls published our fourth book, *Forever Spice*, a collection of photographs by Dean Freeman, the photographer that trailed us while we were on tour. I invited Max to the book launch, at the Imagination Gallery in London WC1. 'I've written a track for you,' he said as soon as I saw him. 'Can I send it to you?' He sent the track to the Spice Office and waited.

A week later Nancy rang Max and told him that I liked 'Step Inside', as it was called. He immediately suggested some recording dates. We settled on 6 November. I rang him the night before, at the end of an exhausting Spice Girls shoot with Lorenzo Aggius. 'All set for tomorrow?' he asked. 'Yes, see you there!' I replied, excitedly.

Unfortunately that night I had a huge argument with Jim and I just wasn't in a fit state to record the next day. But two days later I made it into the studio in North London, right at the bottom of the road from the flat I'd shared with Richie. Max suggested that we have lunch before we started work so we went to the local Irish pub for a roast dinner. Back in the studio Max explained that he had a couple of adjustments to make to the backing track before we started. I later found out that he had deliberately left these adjustments until I arrived so that he could demonstrate how talented he was on the decks. So he twiddled around – and yes, I was impressed – and then we recorded the track. It was beautiful (and so, I was starting to think, was Max).

A week later, just over a year after our last live show, rehearsals started at Elstree Studios for a series of Spice Girls Christmas concerts in Manchester and London. I loved being up on stage again. It was strange to look back and remember how relieved I'd been when the tour ended. Performing had always been what I loved best about being in a group, but I guess that 103 shows was just a bit too much of a good thing. It's funny how, in the same way that I'd forgotten about the pain of giving birth, I'd forgotten about the trials of touring. Why did we ever stop? I wondered. 'Let's do another world tour!' I suggested. The others just looked at me as if I was mad. Babies, husbands, boyfriends and solo careers had made the prospect of touring again seem very remote. Maybe things would have been different if we hadn't been managing ourselves. I know things would have been different if we'd still been with Simon.

15 December 1999
Last night the concert was filmed for Sky and tonight was our last show. I felt a bit sad, because I love performing so much, but at least I've got a holiday to look forward to. We go away to Thailand on Boxing Day for three weeks – not sure if I'm going with Jim or my sister.

After all the drama and the ups and downs with Jim, the final moments of the relationship were a bit of an anti-climax. I asked him to leave but he didn't – or wouldn't – take me seriously, so I realised that I would have to be the one to go. I asked Melanie if I could borrow her flat while she was away on tour and thankfully she said yes. Then I bided my time, waiting for the right minute to say to Jim, 'Right, I'm off,' although it never seemed to come. Eventually I just went, a few days before Christmas.

The girls were very supportive, Emma particularly. I had a lovely Christmas – this time with my family rather than Jim's. Emma and her mum Pauline came over and we had a very happy time, then we all spent Millennium New Year's Eve on Emma's balcony at her lovely flat in

Hampstead, watching the fireworks and the stars. It was the perfect way to see in the New Year.

In early January I asked Danielle to come with us to Thailand, where I'd booked a villa and arranged to share it with some friends. The first week was a bit hazardous because we were followed everywhere by paparazzi. They were knocking on our windows at all times – early in the morning and late at night – and after a few days I began to feel that I didn't want to spoil everyone else's holiday by having to dodge the press. All I wanted was a good relaxing time with my sister and baby, so I decided to opt for something very, very flashy and spent a shit load of money on hiring a boat. Poncey? Yes, but hey, that's what pop stars do, don't they? It was the best treat I could have given us. For the next week we sailed along the coast in peace visiting different beaches and islands.

It was very relaxing. In the evenings Danielle and I lay on the deck, looking at the stars, being rocked to sleep like babies. One night there was the most incredible shower of shooting stars. I will never forget the sight of all those meteors trailing a blaze across the sky, lighting up the night like natural fireworks. We looked up in amazement, closing our eyes tightly like kids, making a wish with every shooting star.

Those weeks in Thailand gave me time to sort my head out. I spent hours and hours just gazing out to sea, thinking or not thinking, while the madness of the previous year and a half gently processed itself through my brain and finally found a place to rest. When I got back from the holiday I felt ready to take on the new millennium and the world, free at last from self-doubt and insecurity. I was back to feeling like myself again.

Black Grandad came to stay not long after I was back. Sitting at my dining room table with my dad and me he suddenly turned to me and said out of the blue, 'You've been married and now you're getting divorced. It's time to have some fun and experience another man's body. Get yourself a brandy, knock it back and off you go!' Well, I was shocked – and of course my dad was really embarrassed – but I appreciated his support.

'Where's the brandy then?'

26

ON MY OWN

There's no doubt about it, being a single parent is no joyride for anyone. People may think that it's easier for me, because I've got money and lots of support around me, but in more ways than not I'm just like any other single parent out there. Yes, I may have more money – but let me tell you, it doesn't take away from the emotional pressures.

In some ways it's more difficult for me because I'm in the public eye. On a lot of occasions I haven't even noticed that there are photographers around, and there I am enjoying a nice, peaceful family day out, doing normal things like feeding the ducks or going for a walk. There are endless press cuttings floating around, plus the stories that my ex-husband has sold and his infamos documentary, *Mel B's Ex*, of course – the constant reminders of a failed marriage.

I had many fears about the marriage break up, which is probably why I delayed it. I agonised about whether I would be able to cope alone, but the truth is that you do cope and you do get on with it, because you have to. There's also the added worry of starting a new relationship. For me, my child became the most important person in my life the moment she was born and anything or anyone else comes second. End of subject.

When I got back from Thailand me and Max started dating. Our relationship was different to any other I've had, mainly because I was a mum this time. When you're a mother you can't say to your man, 'I love you more than anyone else in the world' because it's not true. At least it isn't for me. You can't do things like play loud music and make outrageous uninhibited love or book a last-minute surprise trip without forward planning. You wouldn't want to anyway, unless your child was coming with you.

In April 2002 Max relocated to LA to pursue his career. He's so talented that I know he'll do well. He's already got work lined up without even having to try. I wish him all the luck in the world.

Four years after five giggly wannabes nearly wet themselves being introduced to Take That at the Brits, the Spice Girls were given a Brits lifetime achievement award. We performed three songs, 'Spice Up Your Life', 'Say You'll Be There' and 'Holler', the first single from our (as yet unnamed) third album. Darren Henson, who choreographed our Christmas shows, helped us with our set. We were singing live and dancing with partners, which we hadn't done since the world tour.

It was an eventful night, to say the least. A few hours before the show started, a very serious-looking Vicky called the rest of us into a room. 'I've got something to tell you,' she said anxiously. 'I've had death threats, but you mustn't get scared because they're directed at me, not at you.' We sat there in shock as we heard about plans to kidnap Brooklyn and the bullets and threatening letters that Vicky and David had been sent in the post. Poor Vicky, she was going through hell. We did our best to comfort and reassure her, but she was on edge for the whole evening, unsurprisingly. I was worried for her. Thank God it all came to nothing.

After that bombshell, I started to get ready for the show. Julien McDonald had designed our outfits and I was wearing a beautiful gold catsuit which had arrived that morning. As I tried it on I said to my sister, 'I'm just going to bend down and make sure that this material doesn't rip.' Well, as I touched my toes the catsuit split all the way up the back. Oh my God! What was I going to wear? Call it coincidence or luck, but I happened to have a gold snakeskin catsuit in my bag which had been sent to me the day before by a designer. Unbelievably, it matched the other girls' outfits.

About half an hour before we went on, I started to feel really nervous. What's going on? I thought. It was a very long time since I'd felt anything like this. I was shaking as we walked along the corridor to the wings. We started the set standing hidden in a giant egg above the side of the stage. I was absolutely shitting myself as we waited for the egg to open. I don't think I've ever been so nervous in my life. A familiar thought whirred around my brain. Council flat to lifetime achievement award! Is it really me? 'Oh my God, Oh my God!' I kept saying to Vicky. She was as white as a sheet, her mind preoccupied by guns and kidnappers. The egg opened, we walked down a series of silver mesh stairs in our high heels, with our partners, and went straight into 'Holler'. It was the best buzz ever for me, but I felt bad for Vicky. She was absolutely terrified throughout.

Robbie Williams was backstage that night. When I walked past his dressing room I noticed that he had his door open. There was a security guard just along the corridor. Now I didn't approve of something that Robbie had done to a friend of mine and he knew it. 'Get out here, you f***ing twat, I'm going to batter you!' I shouted into his room. And do you know what he did, instead of coming out and fronting me? (After all, I am a girl, not some masculine heavyweight champion!) He slammed his door and made sure that the security guard stood outside his room for the rest of the show. He was scared! Needless to say, he didn't turn up to our after-show party.

In March I went back to LA to record three more songs for my album with Rodney. The very last song we wrote together (Fred, LaShawn, Rodney and me) was the one I eventually chose as the first single off the album, 'Tell Me'. The track speaks for itself really.

What made you think I would be fooled
I now see through you
And you're the fool
Tell me
How do you feel when you see me
And I disregard you
There's someone new
And they're true
I can't believe I was so blind I didn't see
That you couldn't be the type of man to meet my needs
Strangest thing is that everyone tried to tell me
But I did what they told me not to
You nearly had my everything, by running game on me

You told me all I had to hear I thought love was finally here
But then one day the truth I'd see your game was incomplete
Cos when I realised the truth
I see your plan, you're not my man so get from under my roof –
I don't want you
It was the saddest thing I thought there was no help for me
Cos you made me think I wasn't worth anything
Now I see you didn't have no self esteem
And all you loved was Mel B's money

My mum and Rebecca both cried when they first heard it.

A month later I was back in America, this time in Miami with Vicky and Emma to write and record three final tracks for the third Spice album with Rodney and the gang. We stayed on Fisher Island, off Miami Beach, which could only be reached by boat or plane. The hotel was like a little housing estate. We had self-contained flats and drove round to see each other in golf buggies. Emma was there with her mum Pauline; I was with Danielle and my family; Vicky brought her child too, and her sister and her mum. Melanie recorded her bits a few days later.

On our first day, while we were laying down a track, Rodney wandered off to his own little suite.

'What do you think you're doing?' we shouted at him when we finally found him. 'Get in here now!'

He was putting down tracks for other people – apparently artists like Britney Spears were demanding his attention. So we took the piss out of Rodney all the time after that. As we listened to the beats he was putting down we'd say, 'That's shit. Definitely give that one to Britney!' When no one was listening we'd wonder aloud, 'Did we get the backing track that nobody else wanted?'

From Miami I flew to LA for my album shoot with Dean Freeman. The family came too.

Standing in front of a photographer's lens can be quite a frightening experience. Usually I set up a load of defences that the photographer has to break through. 'Don't tell me to do sexy. I can't do sexy!' I'll announce at the start of the shoot. But with Dean, there's no, 'Come on darling, show me what you've got.' None of that, he just takes pictures. Because he's so occupied with the lighting and the setting, you can feel relaxed and do your thing. He doesn't say, 'Great, wonderful, marvellous,' after every shot. He lets you feel that naturally. Occasionally he mutters, 'Mmm, good,' and that's enough, because I can't take compliments.

Dean is very passionate and focused about his work. He doesn't notice if your make-up is wrong or if you've got a hair out of place. He will adjust the light to you, rather than say, 'The make-up isn't right.' That's the sign of a confident, talented photographer. He is unique and I love him to bits. He's not precious and hasn't got any airs and graces. He works with what he's got and he makes you shine.

When I got back from LA, I got a call from Patrick-Spencer Salami, Blackliners marketing manager. I'd first got involved with Blackliners, who provide services to people of African, Asian and Caribbean origins living with or affected by HIV and AIDS, when they asked for permission to use a photograph of me in a poster campaign. The shot, which showed my naked pregnant belly with Jim's hands clasped over it, was taken by Nadav Kander for the cover of the *Sunday Times Magazine*. I helped launch the 'HIV Positive Attitudes' and made it clear that I was up for helping on an ongoing basis.

'So would you be prepared to host a fund-raising ball?' asked Patrick.

'Why not?' I replied. 'And let's have it at my house!' The date was set for 8 December.

For years there were so many charity requests sent to 19 Management and the Spice Office that we couldn't read more than a tenth of them. We donated all the proceeds from our single 'Who Do You Think You Are?' to *Comic Relief* and appeared on *Children In Need*, but we didn't have much time to do a lot more, apart from occasional hospital ward opening. We had always donated mountains of signed merchandise to various causes but when we came off tour we had more time to get more involved hands-on. Vicky supported a meningitis charity, Mel became patron of Disability Sport England and Emma became even more involved with Art Start, the local community arts programme that she'd supported for a couple of years. I decided that I wanted to focus on two charities, one with an ethnic orientation and the other directed at women. I wanted at least one of them to be Leeds-based as well.

Apart from Blackliners, the other charity that came to my attention was Leeds Women's Aid, which provides refuge for abused women and their children. Refuges like this are crucial in a society where a woman dies every three days as a victim of domestic violence. What's more, women's minister Barbara Roche recently told a conference that at least one in four women has been beaten up at home at some time. The statistics are crushing.

I was hoping to take a few weeks off in the summer of 2000, but it wasn't long before I started promoting my first single and the album, which I'd decided to call *Hot*. And then there were the Spice Girls photo and video shoots, in preparation for the launch of our third album, which we finally named *Forever*. We had two videos to shoot because the first single was a double A-side and to save time we shot 'Holler' and 'Let Love Lead The Way' back-to-back in a week. That was an exhausting five days. We arrived on set at 9 a.m. and stayed until well past midnight. On the final day, the Friday, the others were all desperate to go home and spend the weekend sleeping. Not me, though. At 1 a.m., when I was finally free to leave the set, Dave my driver drove me straight to Newcastle.

Why, you might ask, did I choose to drive all the way to Newcastle? Well, here was another one of my magical, mystical, unexpected ambitions: acting. That weekend I'd agreed to play a part in a short film called *Fish*, directed by Bruce Goodison. I knew Bruce as a documentary maker – he had made two documentaries about me – and I enjoyed working with him. I liked the script of *Fish* as soon as I read it. I was playing the part of a single mother with a twelve-year-old kid, torn between her new boyfriend and her child. I didn't have to say a lot, but I did have to act alongside some brilliant actors, which was nerve-racking.

I arrived in Newcastle at around 6 a.m. and had an hour's sleep before going on set, a council estate on the banks of the Tyne. The lack of sleep suited my part because I was meant to be a bit older than I am, and slightly ravaged. In the 'dressing room' – an empty bedroom in one of the flats – I picked out some truly revolting clothes and the make-up artist painted dark circles under my eyes to make me look older. I enjoyed getting ready. It wasn't hard to make myself look like a single mother living on a council estate and working down the fish market. Give or take a few years with the Spice Girls, that is easily how I could have ended up.

Making *Fish* was a lot of fun. It's only a fifteen-minute film, but a hell of a lot of work went into it. Although I wasn't very confident about my acting, I managed to get through without messing up too badly. I had a lot of trouble with one particular line, though. I was standing in a fish market, wearing an apron and wellies, hair tied back in a net, hosing down the floor, and I had to look wistfully into the middle distance and say (about my son), 'He's all I've got.'

'He's *all* I've got.'

'Can you try that line again, Melanie?' asked Bruce gently.

'*He's* all I've got.'

'One more time?

'He's all I've *got*.'

'And again!'

'He's all *I've* got.'

Needless to say, that bit didn't make it past the cutting room floor. I was quite pleased with my other scenes, though, thank God.

I went back south to begin a mad whirl of promo that continued for the whole of the next year. It kicked off with photo shoots and interviews for *Sky Magazine*, *Time Out*, *Esquire*, *Touch*, *Loaded* and the *Sunday Times Style Magazine*; I did radio chats from Birmingham to Bucharest; and there were road shows, interviews and TV performances all over the UK and Europe.

'Tell Me' came out on 25 September and went straight to No. 4. From what I recall, the papers classed me as a failure from that point on, because it didn't go straight to No. 1. The Spice Girls were used to being No. 1 but as a solo artist I didn't expect it. I'd chosen a track on my album that was very R&B because I wanted to show a different side of me. The fact that it even reached the top ten was a major success – and a shock – in my eyes. My album *Hot* came out on 2 October. 'Holler' was released on 10 November. *Forever* came out on 6 December. Hectic, yes; disorganised, possibly; but we had thought it all through. That autumn was a frenzy of activity and I worked incredibly hard promoting both albums and singles.

To be honest, I don't think my album was given much justice by the media when it was released, but obviously I would say that, wouldn't I? In hindsight I wish I'd been clear from the start exactly how I wanted the album as a whole to sound. Then, I think, the songs might have had more of a sense of continuity, instead of being a bit here, there and everywhere. There was no real thread to hold the tracks together. I did get the best out of every song, but when you listen to them one after the other it doesn't sound like somebody's album, it sounds like a hotch-potch compilation. I'll definitely do things differently when I come to write again. I'll have more concrete ideas and won't be swayed. Having said that, I don't regret making the album at all. I'm really glad I made it.

There is another factor as well. For some reason the Spice Girls haven't been taken seriously as solo artists. We've always been seen as part of a whole and each of us has constantly been plagued by questions to do with the group, which can be tedious and annoying. Why can't the media understand that we're still together but pursuing solo ambitions?

I've often questioned why *Forever* didn't do as well as the other two albums because to be honest it's my favourite Spice Girls album. It's a little bit more down with it than *Spice* and *Spiceworld*. Okay, we didn't do as much promotion as we could or should have done as a group and I think we could all have been more inventive about the campaign, but it's still a fantastic record.

However, the bottom line is that if you don't promote, you don't sell. Being in the public eye helps tremendously. I know underground music sells on the basis of word of mouth and credibility, but when you've got an international profile, you need to get the word out there as a group, not individually.

Not long after I got back from LA, where I made the video for my second single 'Feels So Good' in porn baron Larry Flynt's old house, I held my first Blackliners Ball at home in my garden. It was a fantastic night. I felt very proud to have my lawn exposed to so many people of character and cause, especially since the last time I'd had a tent there was when I got married! It was good to crush that memory beneath the feet of such a wonderful group of people. The fact that my charity was focused on AIDS and black people and ethnic culture made it seem all the more important to hold it there, in my garden, making an imprint on my lawn.

The invitations for 'Mel's Night In Rio' were designed to look like boarding passes. With a few steps into the massive marquee you entered a whole new world. The heat was tropical; there were huge palm trees, exotic plants and vibrant orchids everywhere. It was a wonderful contrast to the crisp December night outside.

The theme was Brazilian but it wasn't all salsa and samba, there was something for everyone. Sasha Baron Cohen did a hilarious fifteen-minute spot as Ali G and brought the house down with his outrageous (and unprintable) jokes about David and Vicky. Beverley Knight packed the dance floor for the whole of her incredible funky hour-long set and Jocelyn Brown's performance of 'Somebody Else's Guy' blew us away. My aunties cleaned up in the raffle and spent most of the evening queuing up for the tarot reader, asking questions like, 'When am I going to meet a handsome stranger?' For the auction, photographer Dean Freeman donated a professional portrait of the highest bidder, Ray Winstone gave a signed movie poster and David Beckham offered up a signed Man Utd shirt, among other things. Chris Eubank bid thousands of pounds for the dress I was wearing and Richard Desmond, owner of *OK!* and the *Express*, offered around the same amount for a dinner date with me and Emma. Everyone gave their services for free and I think we raised something like £60,000 for Blackliners. I was on such a high when I went to bed that night.

What happened next reminded me that life is full of ups and downs. Just before Christmas the group met up in the Spice office to discuss our plans. This wasn't just your everyday meeting, the chance to throw a few ideas around. It was major decision-making time. Where do we go from here? It was our moment to be totally honest with each other as to what we were and weren't prepared to do as a group. In a way it was nice to get everything out in the open, but there's no doubt that it was awful and depressing when it hit me that we weren't going to be doing stuff together for a while. Only Emma and I were up for doing anything as a group right then.

I guess I was slightly shocked but to be honest, deep down I'd known it was coming. For a long time it had been obvious that the hunger wasn't there any more, at least not in all of us. As friends and colleagues who have been through a lot together, we have total respect for each other's opinions and so there was no room for argument. Yet it was hard to accept, for all of us.

Feeling slightly detached and bewildered I drove home and put on a video of Spice Girls at Wembley to comfort myself. And it was then that it truly hit me how amazing our achievements were. When you're in it and you're working like a nutter, you don't actually realise what you've achieved, for yourself, for music, for your fans and for each other. That comes later. Still, I'm convinced that we will make music, perform together and entertain again as a group – at some point. It's just that that point is yet to be decided and enjoyed.

That Christmas was fairly quiet, spent with close family. It gave me much-needed time and space to reflect on the frantic year I'd had and think long and hard about the future. What next?

27

I WOULD DIE 4 U

It may be a myth, but I've heard that Sigmund Freud, the grandfather of psychiatry, died asking the question, 'What do women want?' Well I don't know about anybody else, but I think that women want what everyone wants – love, support, good sex and a fulfilling role in life, whether it be in the workplace, the family or both.

I was enjoying my life and work, but I knew that there would have to be changes when I'd finished promoting my album. I wasn't entirely sure that Virgin was the right label for me as a solo artist and as the year went on I came to the decision that it would be better if we parted ways.

But before I'd finally made up my mind, Julia rang from Spice Office to say that Granada had made an approach to find out whether I'd be interested in presenting a primetime talent show during the summer. My heart leaped at the idea. Was I interested? Of course I was! My first reaction was to feel totally over the moon. I'd already agreed to make a documentary in Benin in Africa in June and the idea of exploring TV further definitely appealed. But then I started to think seriously about it. Would it be the right move to make at this point in my career? It seemed a natural step, a big opportunity and a challenge, but what about my music? In America, it's totally acceptable for performers to cross over – Jennifer Lopez, Tupac Shakur and Bruce Willis are just a few of the artists who have had dual paths at some point in their careers – but in England, crossing over rarely goes unquestioned. Still, I believe that it is perfectly possible.

Unfortunately we had a difference of opinion at the Spice Office as to which direction I should go in, which made me doubt my career path and decisions for a little while. The other girls were always supportive, but some people seemed to think that I had to make a straight choice between music and TV because it would be almost impossible to juggle the two successfully, although deep down I knew that I could. All I needed was encouragement and a bit of help in making sense of my decisions. The way I look at it, there's no point doing something unless I can see where it's leading. I could never do something 'just for now', it has to be a positive choice. There has to be a reason for it and a goal, and it must fit the ongoing journey of my career.

Now, out of the blue, a brilliant opportunity had landed on my lap. My own primetime TV show, with live singing, a live band and a live audience of millions. What more could I want? This was it, I knew. It was different to anything else I'd done in the public eye, but the timing was perfect and, as a trained all round performer, I loved the whole idea of a talent show. I instantly wanted to say yes to *This Is My Moment*, my instinct told me to do it, but I still needed to feel as though I had a clear reason behind it. Where was it going to lead? How would I follow it up?

I gave myself exactly fourteen days to think over all the pros and cons. About a week later I was performing on *This Morning with Richard and Judy* when Nigel Hall, one of the bigwig Granada TV producers, came to see me in the studio in a total flurry.

'We'd love you to do this show,' he said earnestly. 'It's perfect for you. Why haven't you given us an answer?' I nearly told him that I'd already made up my mind, but I held back. I didn't want to seem too eager and part of me was waiting to see how much Granada actually wanted me. In some ways it was a risk for them because my only presenting experience to date had been the *MOBOs* and *Pure Naughty*.

I remembered back to the viewing figures that Angela Ferreira at *Pure Naughty* had shown me. Once again it struck me that there are hardly any black people on TV, especially mixed race. Then it occurred to me that *This Is My Moment* was more than a challenge. It was the opportunity to put myself into millions of people's front rooms on a Saturday night, to stand up for my mixed race society. It really was 'my moment'.

Having more time at home with the family was another good reason for doing the show. The music promo circuit is very gruelling and you often have to work for three months at a go with hardly a day off, which isn't ideal if you're a mother. The fact that *This Is My Moment* was being filmed in Manchester definitely tipped the scales in its favour. I would be near my family and with my mum's help I wouldn't have to disrupt our routine too much. The schedule was well structured, giving me most of my day free for my family.

Also, the idea of live TV really excited me. It's an instant buzz and I thrive off the nervous energy that it produces in me. It's similar to how I feel on stage. I just enter my own world. Plus, I've always been comfortable in front of strangers, which is basically what TV is. I love it.

Granada eagerly put their money where their mouth was so I had the encouragement and belief that I needed. I now had a clear vision of what taking this step meant and where it was leading.

Inevitably, I began to think that maybe it was time to break away from the Spice Office. This seemed a good moment for a fresh start, in addition to the fact that I didn't want to justify why I wanted to do certain things or go in a particular direction. I needed somebody to understand and believe in me without having to go through all of that. The other girls were totally cool about my decision. We all realised that as individuals we each had different needs to the needs of the group.

The more I thought about it, the more obvious it all seemed. Nancy Phillips, who we had employed while we were on tour, was very much focused on (not my kind of) music and I wanted to go down a different path for a while. What's more, her attention was inevitably divided between the four of us. At the time of the release of *Forever* I could see that she was being torn between everybody's different ideas about how they did or didn't want to promote the album. The girls ended up communicating through Nancy, just because it was easier that way. None of us was ever free at the same time, or so it seemed.

Nancy was under a lot of pressure during that time and her workload was huge. It must have been very difficult to cope with four girls with completely different needs. Making a group decision meant anything between four and forty phone calls for her. Ashley Newton would call from Virgin America and she wouldn't know whether he was phoning about Melanie, Emma, Victoria, me or the group, so it was a constant merging. She was obviously overworked and I started to notice that she was staying in the office until late into the night almost every night, overseeing our separate schedules and waiting for calls from LA. I began to feel sorry for her and tried to minimise the workload that I gave her. As a result, my work suffered a little bit. We didn't see eye to eye on long-term issues – Nancy was so busy that it was all instant-instant – and I felt I needed someone to look after me personally. It was time to leave.

I took Julia Curnock with me. She had been working on my diary for a long time and her five years at Andrew Thompson's offices before she joined Spice meant that she had a good grasp of the legal side of things. She was very organised, correct, professional and supportive. Just as importantly, we got on really well. Not long afterwards I met Sandie Shaw, who later became my creative consultant. In Sandie I found someone who was on my side and could see what I saw. And at last I began to build a team around me that contained people of colour, including Michelle Griffiths, my personal trainer, Thelma Mensah, who works with my press agent Sandra Casali, and Rene MacDonald, a very talented stylist.

As the final stage of my promotion campaign came to an end, I started to think about developing other TV projects. I scribbled ideas down all the time. The more I thought about it, the more excited I became about the idea of spending the next phase of my career in television. It made complete sense. Working in TV would be far less disruptive than doing the promo rounds, which involved flying here, there and everywhere, doing twenty interviews in a row with no time to eat, drink or fart.

Still, the bonus of my promotion work was visiting new places and meeting amazing people. Words can't explain how fantastic it was to see my daughter giving Nelson Mandela a kiss at the Celebrate South Africa concert in Trafalgar Square at the end of May. Mandela is a legend, admired and respected throughout the world, and somebody I've looked up to from the year dot. Phoenix obviously doesn't know who he is or what a huge impact he has made, but one day she will feel so proud. Nelson and me have a very warm relationship and I hope to see him again soon. There's recently been talk of working together, so we'll see what happens.

Phoenix was with me in Morocco when I filmed the video for my third single, 'Lullaby' the song I wrote for her (with Biff) when she was a baby. I found Marrakech quite a strange place, partly because absolutely everyone was dressed in the same way. It was like entering a completely different world. Phoenix loved it, of course. She made friends with a little Moroccan boy and played happily with him all day, even though they couldn't speak a word of each other's language.

Less than a month later I was back at the Albert Hall performing for Prince Philip's eightieth birthday. I hardly saw my extrovert daughter that day because she was so busy running in and out of people's dressing rooms. When I bumped into Lionel Ritchie in the corridor he laughed and said, 'I instantly knew exactly whose child she was as she rocketed past me along the corridor!'

We flew to Benin in Africa two weeks later to film a documentary about voodoo. Then, after a trip to Romania with Blackliners, at last I had some time off, thank God. It was just over a month before I started work on *This Is My Moment* and I was determined to spend precious mother-daughter time before it all kicked off. So the rest of June and most of July were made up of lazy days in the garden, feeding ducks in the park, trips to the Wacky Warehouse and days out to Legoland. Then in late July I flew to New York for my best friend Rebecca's wedding.

Recording of *This Is My Moment* began in late July and I loved every second of it. It felt special to be giving people who normally wouldn't have the opportunity the chance to perform in front of a huge national audience and win thousands of pounds. The format was great. Each week hundreds of people auditioned by phone. If they were chosen, they went through to the last fifty, who auditioned in Manchester. I was always at the auditions to provide moral support! Most of the contestants seemed to think that they could wheedle me into fixing them a place in the final, but in fact there was a panel of judges who chose the final six to appear on the Saturday show, where the winner was decided by a viewers' vote.

I was completely and utterly thrown in at the deep end. The Saturday show was live and every week I wondered to myself, Am I going to fall down the stairs tonight? Will I get my lines right? What should I do if any of the contestants freeze? I had all kinds of concerns, but nothing really went wrong, thank God.

There were a few embarrassing moments, of course. During one of the shows I was chatting to a guy about how much in love he was with his girlfriend. Suddenly he got down on one knee. 'You're not going to ask her to marry you on air, are you?' I guffawed. Well yes, he was.

'Did I ruin it for you?' I asked later.

'Actually yes, you did!' he replied cheekily.

Then at one of the Wednesday auditions I was asking a contestant how he felt after he'd performed his song when his friend interrupted us to say, 'You've met him before.'

'Have I met you before?' I asked curiously, turning back to the contestant.

'No!' he said and he seemed quite genuine about it.

But I could see his friend in the corner of my eye whispering, 'Yes you have!'

'Where have I met you before?' I asked.

'You haven't!' he insisted, signalling his friend to shut up. So I left it at that.

A bit later I took his friend to one side and said, 'Where have I met him before?'

'You've snogged him!' came the swift reply.

I flushed. 'Really? Have I?'

'Oh yes, you certainly have!'

I told the cameras to piss off and went up to the guy. 'Come on,' I said. 'Your friend just told me that I snogged you once.' He hesitated. 'Actually you did. You might not remember because I had long curly hair at the time.'

I took a closer look at him. It didn't help that he was practically a skinhead now. Suddenly it clicked. Backstage at the *Clothes Show Live*, 1996, just before the Spice Girls went on stage.

'What's that in your tongue?' he'd asked me.

'Oh, it's for extra sensuality. Why? Do you want a go?' I teased. A few seconds later I snogged him, thanked him and went on stage. I never saw him again until I met him at the *This Is My Moment* audition. Suddenly I was worried. 'Are you sure I didn't do anything else?' I asked anxiously.

'No, you just snogged me and that was it,' he laughed.

Six weeks later, Granada held an after-show party to celebrate the end of the series. All my aunties came along and we had a blast. Auntie June worked the room exuberantly, telling anyone who would listen that,

'She's the next Cilla, you know!' And do you know what? Maybe I'm speaking a bit out of turn, but perhaps she's not far wrong.

EPILOGUE: GO! ALWAYS BELIEVE IN YOUR SOUL

11.35 p.m., Thursday, 29 November 2001

Well, you'll never guess where I am. I'm here in bed with Phoenix in my old bedroom. Jesus, this is freaky – so many memories. I feel like a little girl again.

Let me start off by explaining how I came to be here. Dad came down last night to be with me because I had a bit of a breakdown on Saturday night over a legal meeting I had scheduled with Jim on Wednesday morning. Up at 7.30 a.m., in court by 10 a.m. It took us two frigging hours to get there. I'm there on time sitting in the meeting, but lo and behold, Jim isn't. He's stuck in traffic. He turns up one hour late.

It's all wrapped up at 12 p.m. It was strange to see him. My throat went tight and I got a stabbing pain in my belly. I entered a strange head space, full of emotions, doubt, impurities, anger, bitterness and disappointment.

My dad drove us up to Leeds this afternoon. It's strange to be in this house again – we're staying here because my mum's got the builders in. Since I bought my mum and dad their new house, this house has been rented out to students. It hasn't changed a bit. It's weird because the towels on the banister are exactly the same. The old stereo in the kitchen is the same stereo that my dad's played his music on for the last twenty years.

The graffiti in my bedroom is still there. The bedroom light switch has the same teddy dangling off it. It says 'World's Hottest Lover', a present from Stephen. The fridge is in exactly the same place with the same brown microwave on the top. It's the same kitchen table where I used to eat my dinner and was told off for not finishing my vegetables – the same table that I shagged Stephen on when my mum was in the front room. My mum's Artexing still looks fantastic, as if it's just been done.

It's the same shower. Now our showers and baths were a big thing in those days. You could only fill your bath up to X amount because of the cost and more often than not you shared the water with someone. My dad would time Danielle and me when we got in the shower. You were only allowed in there for three minutes. Tonight I was in there for ages, even though my dad was nearby, no doubt thinking, By now I would have shouted at her about five times, 'Get out! Get out of there now!'

I'd phoned my dad on the Saturday before the meeting and told him how afraid I was of going to it alone. The thought of not having someone supportive within the vicinity terrified me. I needed a cuddle or at least a reassuring pat on the back. I went through so much with Jim alone and it was time I had someone to comfort and support me through the painful aftermath of the marriage. Don't get me wrong, Jim probably felt just as awkward and stressed, but I was really dreading being in the same room as him again.

I hadn't thought about it much because I was so busy, but that Saturday night I suddenly realised what was ahead of me. So I called my dad up and had a complete breakdown. As much as my parents are there for me, they're so angry towards Jim that to a certain extent they forget that I was actually completely in love with this man once. All they can see is that their little girl got hurt, which was out of their control. Okay I made a mistake in marrying him – although it wasn't that much of a mistake because we've got a beautiful child together – but it's me who has to deal with the fallout. I have to see him because we still share a responsibility.

'I don't want to have to face him alone,' I sobbed to my dad. For once I was admitting that I couldn't do something by myself. I needed support and help. It's funny – throughout your teenage years you just want to get away from your parents, but then you get to a point where you actually want them there again.

Without pausing my dad said, 'Don't worry. I'll book the day off work and come with you.'

I sighed with relief. He understood how important this was for me. When the meeting was over Dad leant over me and reassured me again. 'You won't ever have to go through anything like this by yourself. I'll always be there for you. I'm your dad.'

My relationship with my dad has grown so much – and continues to grow – into something very special. My mum is still the fantastically supportive person she's always been. She is the best mum anyone could have and seems very content these days. Having struggled hard for so many years I think she can finally relax, happy to see that her children have turned out all right and aren't wasting their lives.

The evening of the meeting with Jim I was due to make a presentation at the first *Top of the Pops Awards*. My dad came with me. He looked sh** hot in a suit with a lime green shirt and a lime green tie. I was wearing a black dress.

'I'm not walking up the carpet with you!' he protested when we arrived at the Lowry Hotel in Manchester. He hates the attention of the press.

'Dad, you're gonna have to. You're my date,' I insisted. 'Although the way you're looking, they might think you're my new boyfriend!' I added.

He looked appalled. 'That's it! I'm not doing it!'

We got out of the car and there was only one way to go – up the red carpet. Press were lining one side and there were TV cameras down the other, but my dad jumped out and tried to sprint around them all, leaving me in front of the cameras.

'Dad! Just come and pose for pictures, please!'

Reluctantly he came over and stood next to me. As he went to put his arm around me, he accidentally put his hand inside the back of my dress.

'Dad! Your hand's in my dress!'

Well that was it. He was so embarrassed that he ran off again.

Still, for about three days afterwards he said, 'I had such a fantastic night!' We had a real laugh and even went to the after-show party together, dad and daughter. My dad found it all amazing. I'm often surrounded by famous people and sometimes I forget that my friends and family aren't used to it in the way that I am. I'll never forget how flabbergasted my mum was when we sat next to Sting on a plane once.

'Hi Melanie, are you all right?' said Sting casually as we were storing our luggage in the overhead compartments.

'Oh my God!' sighed my mum and sank into her seat. She couldn't eat for the whole flight.

There were a lot of top artists at the *TOTP Awards*, including Mariah Carey, Kylie and Jennifer Lopez. It was a great turn out considering that it was the first year the awards were being held. Lying in my old bedroom later that night I thought about how I've become accustomed to that kind of environment, but when I was growing up I could only dream of being somewhere like that.

It didn't even occur to me back then that I might find myself acting on the West End stage. Dancing, maybe, but not acting, even though I was trained in drama as well as dance and music at school. It's strange how it came about.

By chance I went to see *The Vagina Monologues* before Christmas 2001. At the end of the show, I felt an instant sense of liberation. A door had been opened inside me, a door that I was completely unaware of. This was a kind of theatre that was different to anything I'd ever been exposed to. It was theatre with a passion, with a reason.

Now I don't like to read fiction all that much – I prefer to read something that's true – so *The Vagina Monologues* appealed because it is based on people's true lives. It was written after the author interviewed two hundred women – 'older women, young women, married women, single women, lesbians, college professors, actors, corporate professionals, sex workers, African-American women, Hispanic women, Asian-American women, Native American women, Caucasian women, Jewish women.' Some of the monologues were based on one woman's story, others were based on several women's stories surrounding the same theme.

To sit there in the audience and watch three barefoot women on a red stage, dressed in black, lit up in white, telling stories about vaginas, was amazing. It gave me a real sense of Girl Power, a sense of women standing together, without completely excluding men. (By the way, did you know that Girl Power is now officially recognised in *Roget's Thesaurus?*)

The Vagina Monologues has a fantastic message, as well as being good entertainment. At times deadly serious, at other times hilariously funny, it deals with anything from rape, sexual abuse and female genital mutilation (which still goes on at a rate of two million young girls a year) to orgasm workshops and pubic hair.

Basically the play says, 'Look, it's all right if you don't like your bits, it's all right if you feel funny when your boyfriend comments on your vagina. It's all right to moan out loud during an orgasm.' Some women don't ever look at their vaginas, apparently. They haven't got time for it. Well *The Vagina Monologues* suggests that it's worth taking time out to look at yourself and like yourself and learn how to give yourself pleasure. Get to know yourself! The message came across so strongly that I was like, Wow! I found it very inspirational and enlightening.

'Don't believe him when he tells you it smells of rose petals. It's *supposed* to smell of pussy.'

After the show I went to the bar with Sandie, Julia and Mark, who works for Sandie. I was on a complete high because the play injects an incredible energy into the audience.

'Would you like to do this play?' Sandie asked, quite unexpectedly.

'Are you joking or what? 'Course I would!' I replied, without hesitating.

The thought that I could be a part of this empowering movement – as I've now come to see it – was unbelievable. It fitted in so well with what I'd already achieved in my career.

The cast of *The Vagina Monologues* changes every month and I was asked if I would appear in it in March 2002. I went on a family holiday to Malaysia and had a think about it. Once again I'd be taking a major new step. Decision time drew nearer. My main worry was whether I'd be good enough. Would I be mocked? It was pure insecurity. It didn't bother me that the English press would have a field day if I messed up. I just didn't want to make a fool of myself in my own eyes.

Somebody very close to me once said, 'Can't means won't' and they were damn right. I loved and believed in the play and I was prepared to work as hard as possible to make sure that I gave a good performance. I accepted the part with three weeks to go until my opening night and spent as much time as I could practising.

The first night was like being back in regional dance competitions. I was shaking with nerves. Yet the moment I got up on stage, I felt completely relaxed and at home. It felt very natural to be up there in front of an audience again. I had a lot of support too. My mum was there, and

Danielle, as well as (a very pregnant) Denise Lewis, my trainer Michelle and my friends Sinead and Joanne.

Thelma from my press agency watched several very frustrated reporters leaving the theatre at the end of the show. One was barking into a mobile phone, 'Well what can I say? She was good, damn her! I'd like to slag off her performance, but I can't.'

We all went to the Ivy for dinner, where Elton John kissed my hand and I had a nice chat with Joan Collins. 'I've just finished my first night!' I kept saying to anyone and everyone, 'I made it through!' I was so excited. Over the next month thousands of people came to see the show – all different ages, walks of life and backgrounds. Among them were a whole host of film, TV and theatre people. Subsequently I've had a lot of approaches about acting, performing and presenting work and I'm in a very good position to pick and choose what I do next.

One of the most significant things for me about doing the play was that I made very good friends with the other two actors, Rhona Cameron and Ingeborga Dapkunaite. Rhona is a fantastically witty Scottish stand-up comedian who oozes excitement and spontaneity. We got on like a house on fire and she reminded me in some ways of the early Geri. 'Oh f*** it, let's do it!' Ingeborga is a beautiful Russian film star. Very ladylike, yet outgoing and a little bit outrageous, she taught Rhona and me all about being classy. I think that the three of us got on because we were girls' girls. We had some great chats backstage and discussed everything from politics to our love lives.

So where next? Well, I spent years as a dancer, years doing whatever I could to get by and five intense years in a fantastic, phenomenal, world-famous group. I've chosen all these things and they've chosen me in a funny way. Now that I'm moving on to the next phase in my career, the same thing is happening all over again. Everything I choose to do just seems to feel right.

10 April 2001, Brazil
9 a.m. I'm sitting on the beach in Bahia, staring out to sea, wondering what to do with my day. There isn't a lot going on. It's off-season at the moment, which is why I'm here. Well, should I swim and sunbathe? Or walk along the hot sand to the lagoon I was told about yesterday? Maybe I'll get a boat to a deserted bay or explore the jungle. I could always read in my room –

or even walk up that enormous hill into town. So many choices suddenly.
Hey man, it's a metaphor for my life!

I've now realised that all those auditions and dancing competitions, the seasons in Blackpool, the Spice years and my solo projects have been my training ground for what is to come next. I've grown up and I'm a lot wiser. Girl Power has become Woman Power for me, particularly now I'm a single-parent mother. The principles are the same – believe in yourself, stand up for yourself – it's just that I'm not a girl any more (although I'm still in touch with my childish side, especially since I've become a mother).

I also understand what 'Man Power' is. A real man isn't threatened by a strong independent woman. He is proud of her and wants to see her shine.

All through writing this book I've been aware of the impact it may have on the people close to me, but the conclusion I've come to time and again is that you can either paint life as a pretty picture or you can tell it raw and real. There's nothing I wouldn't want to share with anyone, because I'm open. I believe that if you're not open you don't learn about yourself or other people. It's important to express yourself as well as listen.

I would never have thought that facing up to myself and what's happened to me would be such a cleansing process – it's been a kind of therapy, without having to pay for it. Reliving and analysing the past in detail has helped me understand how I've grown into the person I am today – not necessarily a better person but someone who has learnt a certain amount of lessons along the way. It has also made me realise again how lucky I am to have such fantastic, supportive friends and relations – and to have been given the chance to create my own safe home and family.

The world as I now know it is my oyster. Forget about questions like, Can I do it? Will I be successful? I'm far surer of myself than I've ever been. Oh yes, this is inner confidence with a vengeance. I believe that I've got so much ahead of me – and I fully intend to make the most of it. Without, I hope, seeming pretentious, I've got one last thing to say: Just you wait and see what I've got in store for you. Catch me if you can!

PICTURE CREDITS